PETER McGEE

foreword by **JOHN DOWD**

KAYAK ROUTES

OF THE PACIFIC NORTHWEST COAST

GREYSTONE BOOKS

Douglas & McIntyre Publishing Group

VANCOUVER/TORONTO/BERKELEY

04 05 06 07 08   5 4 3 2 1
Second edition 2004

Greystone Books
A division of Douglas & McIntyre Ltd.
2323 Quebec Street, Suite 201
Vancouver, British Columbia
Canada V5T 4S7
www.greystonebooks.com.

National Library of Canada Cataloguing in Publication Data
Kayak routes of the Pacific Northwest coast / (edited by) Peter McGee;
foreword by John Dowd. — 2nd ed.

Included index.
ISBN 1-55365-033-6

1. Sea kayaking — Northwest coast of North America — Guidebooks.
2. Northwest coast of North America — Guidebooks. I. McGee, Peter, 1970–
GV776.15.B7K39 2004   797.1′224′09795   C2003-907344-0

Library of Congress Cataloging-in-Publication Data
Kayak routes of the Pacific Northwest coast / (edited by) Peter McGee;
foreword by John Dowd. — Rev. and updated.
p. cm.
Includes bibliographical references.
ISBN 1-55365-033-6 (2nd ed.: pbk.: alk. paper)
1. Sea kayaking — Northwest Coast of North America — Guidebooks.
2. Northwest Coast of North America — Guidebooks. I. McGee, Peter.

GV776.5K39 2004
797.1′224′09795 — dc22   2003067534

Editing by Lucy Kenward and Naomi Pauls (second edition)
Cover design by Peter Cocking
Text design by Jessica Sullivan
Cover photograph: *Addenbroke Point, Central Coast,* Peter McGee
Maps by Darryl Jensen
Printed and bound in Canada by Friesens
Printed on acid-free paper
Distributed in the U.S. by Publishers Group West

We gratefully acknowledge the financial support of the Canada Council for the Arts,
the British Columbia Arts Council, and the Government of Canada through the Book Publishing
Industry Development Program (BPIDP) for our publishing activities.

To all those who care for the coast

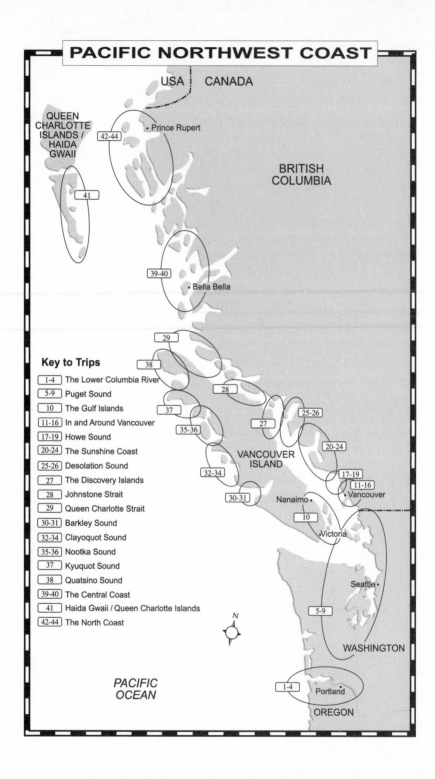

PACIFIC NORTHWEST COAST

USA | CANADA

QUEEN
CHARLOTTE
ISLANDS /
HAIDA
GWAII

42-44

• Prince Rupert

BRITISH
COLUMBIA

41

39-40

• Bella Bella

29

38

Key to Trips

28

| 1-4 | The Lower Columbia River
| 5-9 | Puget Sound
| 10 | The Gulf Islands
| 11-16 | In and Around Vancouver
| 17-19 | Howe Sound
| 20-24 | The Sunshine Coast
| 25-26 | Desolation Sound
| 27 | The Discovery Islands
| 28 | Johnstone Strait
| 29 | Queen Charlotte Strait
| 30-31 | Barkley Sound
| 32-34 | Clayoquot Sound
| 35-36 | Nootka Sound
| 37 | Kyuquot Sound
| 38 | Quatsino Sound
| 39-40 | The Central Coast
| 41 | Haida Gwaii / Queen Charlotte Islands
| 42-44 | The North Coast

37

35-36

27

25-26

VANCOUVER
ISLAND

32-34

20-24

17-19

11-16
Vancouver •

30-31

Nanaimo •

10

• Victoria

Seattle •

5-9

WASHINGTON

N

PACIFIC
OCEAN

1-4

Portland

OREGON

Contents

Foreword

For the past 15 years, pessimists have been predicting the "leveling off" of sea kayaking as the fastest-growing water sport in North America, yet the growth continues. In 2003 when a new kayak shop opened in Vancouver, 80 per cent of its customers were new to the sport.

Since the first edition of this guide six years ago, the number of kayakers on the sea has increased dramatically, particularly at such popular destinations as the San Juans, the Gulf Islands, the Broken Group Islands, Desolation Sound, Tofino and Johnstone Strait.

More and more kayakers are seeing the Pacific Northwest coast as a "wilderness" playground. We would do well to welcome these visitors. They leave little trace of their passing and will take back the word that this coast is a treasure under siege, one worth preserving for its own sake, not just for the resources extracted. In the long term their presence may help to preserve the wild nature of those special places. Happily this edition has been expanded to include more wilderness areas in the United States, the Oregon marine trails.

The best protection our coasts can have is for environmentally aware individuals to visit them often and participate in their maintenance. The B.C. Marine Trail Association (BCMTA) used the proceeds from the first edition of this book to build a solar-powered composting toilet at Blackberry Point, on Valdes Island in the Gulf Islands. Unfortunately, thieves took the solar panels and, incredible as it may seem (surely this could happen only in B.C. and Brazil), the island is now flagged for logging by Weyerhaeuser.

It is hard to maintain citizen initiative for a project such as a marine trail when people believe that an area is part of a park overseen by some level of government. This is frequently not the case. Great hallelujahs greeted the expansion of B.C.'s marine park system, which has to be considered a step forward, but kayakers must let their voices be heard. A deep-water harbour with docks, generators and all-night parties are not the features most kayakers go to the wilderness to enjoy. For financial planners and cash-strapped governments, the benefits of a pristine beach pale beside docking fees, liquor sales or the quick, one-time hit of pulping a forest. They need to be reminded.

In the USA, kayakers are concerned primarily about access. In Canada, wild spaces like forests and empty shoreline are often viewed as unlimited, particularly in the north and mid-coast. Marine trails will help to preserve access to these areas for future kayakers, but they will not endure and thrive without our active participation. The new parks are great, but they will not usually provide even the minimal services kayakers need unless the paddling community sees to it that they do. And don't assume your favourite spot is part of a park and therefore protected. Remember Blackberry Point.

According to Mercia Sixta, one of the original board members of the BCMTA, the next area to be threatened appears to be the mid-coast north of Port Hardy and south of Prince Rupert. This area includes some of the finest kayaking spots in the world. It is rich in wildlife and dramatic seascapes, yet with surprisingly few good campsites. Competing for the best protected areas are fish farms, log booming areas and, most recently, commercial tour operators lobbying for tenure over desirable campsites.

Recreational kayakers need a voice at the table when the future of such areas is being decided. The B.C. Marine Trail Association is the ideal forum for Canadian kayakers in these land management issues, focusing as it does upon informing and educating kayakers rather than on restricting and controlling access. Implicit is the recognition that the flip side of this emphasis on unrestricted access is a lofty combination of responsibility and vigilance. That ties in nicely with sea kayaking at its best. This guide reflects these values, and this new edition is a timely expansion of the West Coast paddler's library.

Thanks to Pete McGee and others for continuing to show confidence in the B.C. Marine Trail by donating their time and the proceeds from this book to the future of sea kayaking on this coast.

John Dowd

Preface
to the Second Edition

Welcome to the second edition of *Kayak Routes of the Pacific Northwest Coast*. Not only have the existing chapters been updated but it is with great excitement that we have expanded the guide to include Queen Charlotte Strait and Klemtu in British Columbia and the Lower Columbia River Water Trail in Oregon. As always, *Kayak Routes of the Pacific Northwest Coast* has a strong educational component regarding minimum impact camping and cultural impacts. All the contributors live or work in the areas they describe, and each went to great lengths to ensure that local and environmental concerns were addressed in the site-selection process. In addition, all royalties from this book will be used to help with a number of causes including site cleanups, outhouse construction and the continued lobbying of the B.C. Marine Trail Association for paddlers' rights along the coast.

The first edition raised close to $15,000 and it was great to see the community come together as a legitimate and concerned interest group, dedicated to protecting the environment that means so much to us all. Ultimately, however, responsibility for the coast rests with each of us and depends on our conduct as individuals.

Tread lightly when you visit the areas described in this guide, but always speak loudly for their preservation. Don't be afraid to express your love or concerns for an area. Remember, it is your actions both on and off the water that will help keep the spirit of our coast alive.

Thank you for choosing *Kayak Routes of the Pacific Northwest Coast* as your kayak guide to British Columbia, Washington and northern Oregon. Happy paddling.

Peter McGee

Acknowledgements

This book has been a collaborative effort from the very beginning so it is difficult to list everyone who has helped in its creation. To give the authors their appropriate due, small biographies are supplied at the back of the book. All these authors deserve enormous thanks for volunteering their time and local expertise to ensure this guide happened.

For their help with content and editing, thanks also to John Dowd, Louanne Ralston, Jocelyn Lymburner, Ross Tweedale, Chris Hathaway, Natalie Fournier, Mary Ann Snowden, Paul Chaplow, Rich Brame, Stuart Smith, Glen Harris, Michael Pardy, Chris Ladner, Cathie Findlay-Brook, Nicki Browne, Bob Austad, Wally Priedolins, Meredith Reeve, Dr. Helga Sickert, Pauline Scott, Rueben Weir, Joel Rogers, Jennifer Carpenter of the Heiltsuk Cultural Education Centre, John Bolton of the Heiltsuk Fisheries Co-Management Program, and the Gwaii Haanas Archipelago Management Board. We are also grateful to David Getchell, Mary Monfort, Sandie Rumble, Jamie Little, Catherine France and all others who have helped with the B.C. Marine Trail Association over the years.

A special thanks goes to Lucy Kenward, Naomi Pauls, Nancy Pollak, Rob Sanders, Nancy Flight, Terri Wershler and Leanne Denis for their incredible patience in dealing with a publishing rookie such as myself. Finally, thanks to my parents, who allowed the B.C. Marine Trail Association to evolve in their basement and, at various times, take over every other room in their home.

Introduction
Marine Trails of the Pacific Northwest Coast

A paddling trail that winds its way along the coast of the Pacific Northwest has, in essence, always existed. For thousands of years people have paddled these waters, travelling from camp to camp and village to village, as they worked their way north or south along the Inside Passage. Times are changing, however, and pressures from industry and private development, as well as from increased recreational use, are putting a strain on the number of suitable camping and resting areas available for the growing paddling community.

In light of this, the B.C. Marine Trail Association (BCMTA) and the Washington Water Trails Association (WWTA) were formed in the early 1990s to establish marine trails in their respective parts of the coast. When connected, these trails will form a marine trail system without political boundaries. The Cascadia Marine Trail, as it is known, will be the longest and most spectacular protected marine corridor in the world.

More recently, various groups in Oregon have banded together to form the Lower Columbia River Water Trail Committee (LCRWTC) and create an amazing 235-km (146-mi.) water trail that follows the Columbia River from the Bonneville Dam to the Pacific Ocean. Although their route is technically not part of the Cascadia Marine Trail system, the people behind the Lower Columbia River Water Trail have the same goals as those at the BCMTA and WWTA, and we are thrilled to have the Lower Columbia River Water Trail included in this edition of the guidebook.

All three trail organizations work incredibly hard to preserve areas that are important to paddlers and other small boaters, and all three organizations rely on the support of the paddling community. If you

∧ *Gnarled driftwood, Queen Charlotte Strait,* PETER MCGEE

have not already done so, don't wait until it's too late to protect the beauty of the coast. Join your local water trail association today!

British Columbia Marine Trail Association
c/o Ecomarine
1668 Duranleau St., Granville Island
Vancouver, B.C. v6H 3S4
Web site: www.bcmarinetrail.com

Washington Water Trails Association
#305–4649 Sunnyside Avenue North
Seattle, WA 98103–6900
Tel.: (206) 545-9161; fax: (206) 547-0350
Web site: www.wwta.org

Lower Columbia River Water Trail
c/o Lower Columbia River Estuary Partnership
811 SW Naito Parkway
Portland, OR 97204
Tel.: (503) 226-1565
Web site: www.columbiawatertrail.org

North American Water Trails Network
1428 Fenwick Lane
Silver Spring, MD 20910
Tel.: (301) 589-1886
Web site: www.watertrails.org

How to Use This Guide

The paddle routes described in this guide are divided by region, and the format for each chapter is roughly as follows:

Map, Background, Getting There, Weather and Hazards, Special Conditions, Trip Summaries, Trip Descriptions and Additional Routes.

Although each category is fairly self-explanatory, it is worth noting a few points. First, the maps are not for navigational use but merely to orient the reader to the information in the chapter. Always travel with the appropriate nautical charts. Second, the trip summaries are in point form and give a suggested trip length and skill level(s) which are based on the prevalent paddling conditions of an area. However, it is essential that you make your own assessment as to whether the conditions of a particular day and time of year are compatible with your paddling ability. Even a trip labelled "Beginner" can be extremely dangerous if weather conditions don't cooperate, and it is up to you to exercise good judgement in selecting your destination and determining your paddling route.

Finally, although this is the most complete guide to the Pacific Northwest available, as you adventure along the coast you are bound to discover places that aren't included here. There are a few reasons for this. First, we may not have known about them. Second, due to space limitations we included only the best, most practically located sites. Third, we never intended to put out a book that would take away your sense of discovery, and several sites were left out as little gifts for the more adventuresome paddler to stumble upon—a small reward for those willing to take the path less travelled. Finally, there are spots of local endearment that, in a sense, belong to the communities. You are free to find and use them, but it was simply not appropriate for us to point them out.

∧ *Louscoone Inlet, Haida Gwaii,* PETER MCGEE

1

Kayaking the Pacific Northwest Coast

SAFETY FIRST

Safe travel in the Pacific Northwest is entirely dependent on your skill, judgement and common sense. Although the routes listed in this book were selected with the limitation of ocean kayaks in mind, they still have inherent dangers.

You are on your own when paddling in the Pacific Northwest, so be prepared. If you get in a jam, there is not a lot of help out there. If you are injured, the nearest hospital may be many hours away. The following are suggestions to help you head off catastrophe. They are not the only issues a kayaker may face, but they are important bases to cover.

- Be prepared to solve your own problems. For example, pack the necessary supplies to make emergency boat repairs and have extra food in case your paddling schedule is delayed by poor weather.
- Whether paddling solo or in a group, have your techniques for self- and assisted rescues so well learned that you can do them under any conditions. The Eskimo roll is great for a quick recovery but should not be counted on. Practise alternative exit and re-entry techniques.

- Enhance your boating skills by taking courses or travelling with more experienced boaters who can share their knowledge.
- Do not paddle alone unless you are experienced and have your act well in hand regarding skill, physical condition and mental preparedness. If you are travelling solo, leave yourself a wide margin of safety.
- The greatest single danger to sea kayakers is hypothermia. Cold water kills. Dress appropriately and educate yourself about hypothermia.
- Get a marine weather forecast each day *before* you head out on the water.
- The Canadian and U.S. Coast Guards recommend that all boaters file a float plan with someone. That person should know where you are going and when you are due in port. If you make major changes to your plan during your trip, update your contact party.
- Always carry a compass when paddling and know how to use it. A deck-mounted compass will help you keep your bearings over long distances. Also, carry the appropriate marine charts, not facsimiles or topographic maps. A GPS can be extremely helpful but should not take the place of a compass and charts.
- Carrying a VHF (Very High Frequency) radio aboard is a good idea but will not eliminate the need for any of the above. Keep in mind: electronics do not fare well in small open boats and may fail when you need them most. Small hand-held VHF radios (including weather radios) have a very limited range and work on line of sight. Do not expect to pick up VHF channels (either sending or receiving) while on shore, because the land mass on which you are sitting may be blocking the signal. To reach a VHF channel, you may have to paddle 150–200 m (500–650 ft.) offshore. The same limitations apply when travelling up a steep-sided inlet; you may have to completely leave the inlet to use your VHF radio. A cellphone can also be quite helpful if there is coverage.
- Always tie up your boat when you go ashore, even when it has been pulled well above the high tide line. A sudden squall can toss a lightweight boat right back into the water. As for beaching your boat "for just a minute," you may not realize how fast the tide rises until you turn to see your pride and joy drifting off to sea.
- Always carry a first aid kit. Know exactly what it contains and how to use it. Make sure that others in your group know where to find it. A full equipment checklist can be found at the back of the book.

- Do not try to keep to a tight schedule, because doing so may tempt you to take unnecessary chances. Relax, and adjust your schedule to fit the weather and other circumstances. Better to hole up short of a goal than to risk your life and those of your companions.

Remember: Safe travel involves having not only the appropriate knowledge, but a healthy respect for the sea and an ability to expect the unexpected. These are gained through experience and by living according to the rules of the sea.

PRINCIPLES OF MINIMUM IMPACT CAMPING

The purpose of this guidebook is to help people discover the beauty of the Pacific Northwest and the joys of paddling. The authors agreed to voluntarily contribute to this project on condition that the guide also help teach the essentials of minimum impact camping. If we are to preserve the natural beauty of our islands in the face of increasing use, we must all take responsibility to educate ourselves and to become equipped with the skills and habits that enable us to minimize our impact on the environment. Minimum impact camping is the mark of a skillful camper, yet years of experience are not required to master the simple techniques that make the difference between a mess and a site that blends naturally into its surroundings. If you concentrate on the effort to leave little or no mark on the land, you will find that it works. It's that easy.

Much of the information in this section has been drawn, with permission, from the Maine Island Trail Association Guide and the National Outdoor Leadership School's "Leave No Trace" brochure on temperate coastal zones. The Leave No Trace Center for Outdoor Ethics is planning to publish a sea kayaking skills and ethics booklet in 2004 so please check out their Web site, www.lnt.org, for the latest information.

PLAN AHEAD AND BE PREPARED

Unnecessary impact in coastal areas can be avoided by carefully preparing for your trip. For example, if you fail to bring enough fuel and are forced to make fires in areas where wood is scarce, you further deplete an already diminished supply. Proper preparation includes knowing what to expect; having the proper equipment; researching the area you plan to visit; adequately planning and packaging food supplies; and having the proper skills to travel safely. Consider the mottos "Leave No Trace" or "Minimum Impact" as inspiration to develop the right attitude and plan appropriately to lessen your presence in the backcountry.

Carefully plan your rations to reduce waste from leftovers, and repackage your food to reduce the amount of potential trash. If possible, visit the backcountry during seasons or days of the week when use levels are low, and limit your group size. Try to avoid travel when the environment is particularly fragile, such as during critical waterfowl and marine mammal breeding or hatching periods.

Proper training or experience in paddling the coast is essential both to your safety and to minimizing your impact. Poor decision making, injury or illness can force you into a situation where outside help is needed, at which time minimum impact concerns go out the window. The basis of safe and sensitive paddling is sound judgement, technical competence and self-responsibility. This includes developing skills such as leadership and wilderness first aid.

SELECT APPROPRIATE CAMPSITES

Selecting an appropriate campsite is perhaps the most important aspect of low impact coastal travel. It requires the greatest use of judgement and often involves making trade-offs between ecological and social impacts. A decision about where to camp should be based on the level and type of use in the area, the fragility of vegetation and soil, the likelihood of wildlife disturbance, an assessment of previous impacts and your party's potential to cause or avoid impact.

Allow enough time and energy at the end of the day to select an appropriate site. Plan ahead to avoid being forced to use a poor or fragile campsite due to tiredness or foul weather. Avoid camping close to trails and fresh water sources: a distance of 90 m (300 ft.) is a good standard.

There are four basic principles to selecting a campsite.

Concentrate Impact on Established Sites It is best to camp on sites that are so highly used that further careful use will cause no additional impact. Ideally, all tents, traffic routes and kitchen areas should be confined to places that already show use to avoid enlarging the disturbed areas.

Minimize Site Alterations Good campsites are *found*, not made. Do not dig trenches for tents or construct lean-tos, tables, chairs or other rudimentary improvements. Allow others a sense of discovery by leaving the site in its natural state.

Avoid Places Where Impact Is Just Beginning Most campsites can withstand a certain level of use and still recover to a pristine state. However, a threshold is eventually reached where the regenerative power of the vegetation cannot keep pace with the amount of trampling. A general guideline is to avoid all sites that show slight signs of use. If these areas receive no further use, they can revegetate and revert to their natural appearance.

Spread Use and Impact in Pristine Areas On any pristine site, spread out and avoid creating traffic routes over vegetation. Ideally choose an area that is well suited for absorbing impact, such as the area of beach that is below the highest winter tide level but above the current high tides. If you must camp in a forest or meadow, try to find a non-vegetated area to avoid crushing plants and seedlings. Finally, when breaking camp, take some time to naturalize the site. This extra effort will help hide the fact that you camped there and make it less likely that others will follow.

USE FIRE RESPONSIBLY—AND INFREQUENTLY

Campfires in the backcountry were once necessary for cooking, and their use is steeped in history and tradition. The tradition is so entrenched in our minds that for some, the idea of going on a backcountry trip without having a fire is almost unthinkable. As a direct result of the past misuse of campfires, however, a new attitude is developing. Fires are no longer advisable or even permitted in many areas along the coast. Reasons include the increasing number of backcountry travellers, diminishing firewood supplies, alterations to the ecosystem when dead trees and branches are removed, and the chance of an escaped wildfire.

Camp stoves should always be used in areas where fires are prohibited, a fire hazard exists or there is little available dead wood. Keep in mind, however, that even in areas where fires are allowed, a stove is preferable because blackened circles of rocks and charred wood significantly diminish a wilderness experience.

If you must have a fire, use an existing fire ring or a site below the high tide line but above the sensitive intertidal zone. Build fires on rocky or sandy soil away from overhanging trees, dry vegetation or root systems. Use only dry and downed dead wood and collect only what you need, taking it from different locations. Do not break dead branches off live, standing trees as this leaves a discernible and long-lasting impact. Do not burn food scraps or plastic. Driftwood is an ideal source of firewood although you should avoid painted, laminated or creosote-treated wood products because they emit toxic fumes when burned. Small pieces of wood are best: they are much easier to burn thoroughly and will not leave half-burned logs that remain as obvious signs of your fire.

Leave your firewood in natural lengths until you are ready to burn it. If you have any unburned lengths left over when breaking camp, they can easily be scattered around the area and will blend in naturally. Burn wood down to a white ash before extinguishing the fire, then stir and pour water on the ashes until you feel no hot spots with your bare hand. Collect any remaining refuse, then scatter the ashes and blackened rocks below the tide line so that no sign of your fire is noticeable. Disperse any wood that is left before you leave camp and cover the fire site with a thin layer of sand or gravel.

If you are building a fire below the high tide line, scoop a shallow pit in the sand or gravel. If the beach is made up of larger stones that will scar, you can line the pit with an inch or two of sand or small gravel taken from another suitable location. If you are unable to take advantage of the beach, it is best to forgo a fire.

PACK IT IN, PACK IT OUT

Pick up and pack out all of your litter. Burying, dumping or leaving trash in the backcountry is unacceptable. On the way out—when your boat space has increased—try to pick up litter left by others.

Reduce litter at the source. When preparing for your trip, repackage food into reusable containers and remove any excess packaging.

This simple practice lessens the chance that you will inadvertently leave litter behind and will likely help free up some space in your boat. A few hints: use knots, not twist ties, to secure food bags, and put your garbage bag in a nylon stuff sack to ensure it doesn't tear when pulled in and out of the boat.

PROTECT WATER QUALITY

Many intestinal diseases are transmitted through water so it is important to be very careful not to contaminate water supplies in wilderness areas. Of particular concern in the Pacific Northwest is giardiasis. This internal infection is caused by the parasite *Giardia lamblia* and is transmitted through water contaminated by the feces of infected animals (including dogs) and people. In order to prevent its spread, you should never urinate or defecate directly into fresh water, either in camp or when travelling. As a general rule, washing and disposing of any waste should be done at least 90 m (300 ft.) from a fresh water source. If a toilet facility is provided, use it; if not, practise the disposal techniques listed in the following section.

To be completely safe when collecting drinking water, you should consider *all* water to be contaminated and in need of treatment before drinking. Three common methods are boiling water (minimum one minute at a full boil), or using water filters or chemicals for purifying water. Regardless of whether you treat water, it is best to collect from a clear and flowing source and away from the shore. The higher up the source of running water, the less likely it is to be contaminated.

PROPERLY DISPOSE OF HUMAN WASTE

Visitors to coastal areas create certain types of wastes that are hard to pack out. These include human waste and waste water from cooking and washing. Although often unpleasant to deal with in the absence of a toilet facility, human waste needs to be properly disposed of to maintain your health and the health of others.

Ocean Disposal The ocean is a vast and dynamic reservoir of bacteria—and the best location for feces decomposition in the absence of a toilet or outhouse. It should not be used, however, in areas of little water movement or areas where people commonly swim. In more populated areas such as Puget Sound, always make the effort to find an established sanitary facility or, at the very least, pack out your waste and dispose of it on the mainland at a pumpout station.

When disposing of human waste in the ocean, the best option is to use a "honey bucket" or bag and deposit the fecal matter by kayak well offshore. The container can then be rinsed and reused. If this is neither feasible nor attractive, the next best option is to dispose of your waste from the shore into the ocean. Take the time to assess the shoreline to determine if there is an accessible area with strong water movement such as tidal currents or wave action. Headlands or rocky points are usually good sites for disposal; calm protected bays are not. Take care to avoid tide pools, shellfish beds and other sensitive areas. Once you have chosen your site, do your business directly into the water (preferably at low tide). If this is awkward, you can try the infamous "shit-put." Find something such as a large, flat rock to serve as a platter to launch the feces into the water. Then do your business a comfortable distance from the water, take the rock to the water's edge and throw it as far as you can into the ocean. It may not be pretty but it works.

Cat Holes and Latrines Cat holes are a widely accepted method of waste disposal in certain situations but are less commonly used in coastal environments and should be viewed as a last resort. Beaches that make good campsites are often too wet or confining or receive too much use for the cat-hole method to be effective. There are appropriate places, however, to use cat holes, such as when you are camped in a calm bay with no water movement. Cat holes must be located 90 m (300 ft.) from fresh water, trails and camp. Select a site that is inconspicuous and where other people will be unlikely to walk or camp.

With a small garden trowel, dig a hole 10–15 cm (roughly 6 in.), removing the sod intact. Make sure the depth does not exceed the dark-coloured, biologically active layer of topsoil where decomposition will occur. Soil removed from the cat hole should be placed nearby in a pile; after each use, spread a light layer of soil back in the hole. After the final use, fill the cat hole with the remaining loose soil and tamp the sod lightly back into place.

One cat hole per group is suggested rather than one per person. When the hole is used for multiple uses, it is typically called a latrine. To make a latrine, dig a trench of similar depth and width as a cat hole but increase its length to accommodate all users. Since the higher concentration of feces will decompose very slowly, location is especially important.

Toilet Paper Use toilet paper sparingly and only the nonperfumed brands. Toilet paper must be disposed of properly: placed in plastic bags and packed out, or completely burned. One way of dealing with toilet paper used for urination is to keep it in a small plastic bag dedicated to this task until the end of the day, when a hot fire can be built to burn the used paper. Burning with matches or lighters has resulted in a number of forest fires, so this technique should only be used on fire-resistant beaches or rocky shores. If you do use matches or a lighter, be sure the paper burns completely. Keep it dry and "fluff it" before you light it or there will be incomplete burning. Burning the paper in a hot campfire is a much better alternative, assuming the site is suitable for a fire.

The low impact camper willing to go the extra mile might consider forgoing toilet paper altogether and using natural alternatives. When used correctly, natural toilet paper is as effective as regular toilet paper. Popular types of natural toilet paper include stones, vegetation and snow. Some experimentation is necessary to make this practice work for you but it is worth a try.

Used tampons and sanitary pads should also be bagged and packed out, or burned in a hot campfire. They should never be buried.

Urination Urination has little direct effect on vegetation or soil. However, urine may draw wildlife, which are attracted to human salts and may then defoliate plants and dig up soil. It is best to urinate directly into the ocean or below the high tide line where the ocean can absorb it; be sure you're at least 90 m (300 ft.) away from a fresh water source. Avoid urinating in dry areas close to campsites that are protected from the elements—they may hold odours.

Grey/Soapy Water Disposal The primary consideration when washing yourself or your clothes is to avoid contamination of fresh water or intertidal life. Without soap, you can bathe directly in the ocean. If you prefer to use fresh water, carry a supply in a pot or jug to a bathing site below the high tide line and well away from fresh water sources.

Bathing with soap is a luxury as opposed to a necessity. Soap is foreign to the coastal environment and can adversely affect local flora and fauna, so its use should be minimized. This includes biodegradable soap; although it breaks down more quickly than other soaps, it still harms local life forms in the short term if misused. If you choose to bathe with soap, get wet first and then lather up on shore, far from fresh water and any intertidal life. Rinse off by pouring water over yourself. Avoid lathering up directly in the salt water, as this will probably cause you to use more soap than is necessary. When brushing teeth, spit toothpaste below the high tide line or into the ocean.

Also, limit your use of soap to wash dishes. Try using sand or gravel instead. If you are unable to properly dispose of your grey/dishwater in the ocean, consider using a sumphole. To build a sumphole, dig 25–30 cm (10–12 in.) into the soil, a good 90 m (300 ft.) from any fresh water source, and pile the dirt to the side of the hole. Pour in your grey water and, after the final use, replace the soil.

CAMPING ETIQUETTE

When you are paddling the Pacific Northwest coast in the summer, be prepared to find other people on the site you have chosen for the night. Conversely, don't be surprised if another camping party lands on "your" island before sundown. On most sites, paddlers should have no trouble making room for other visitors. As for the smallest of islands and campsites, there are the traditions of the sea to consider. It is hardly courteous and may even be hazardous to others to tell them to camp elsewhere when there is no place nearby where they can safely or legally do so. Most paddlers will be compatible souls who will also treat the site and others with respect. Accommodate them if you can.

Finally, leave your pets at home—you will do yourself, others and the coast a big favour. On small islands, especially, wildlife is vulnerable to harassment by pets, and in a few spirited seconds a dog can wipe out a bird's progeny for an entire year.

RESPECTING WILDLIFE

One of the great attractions of the coastal environment is its large variety of wildlife. As visitors to these areas, you must be aware of how your presence affects the animals. Most animals react with alarm when approached by humans and specifically by paddlers: our approach tends to be silent and without warning. Such reactions are stressful and cause the animal to expend energy—to swim, run or fly away—in order to feel safe. Although a single disturbance may not affect an animal to a large degree, multiple or prolonged disturbances may add up to higher energy expenditures than the animal can afford. Repeated disturbance may cause wildlife to completely avoid an area, even one that offers the best food or nesting sites.

MARINE MAMMALS

Marine mammals are an essential concern to sea kayakers, especially when they are in their breeding or nursery areas, sites that they use year after year. Seals and sea lions that are "hauled out" on beaches, rocks or ledges are more vulnerable and therefore more easily frightened. Seals nurse their pups only on shore, so a pup can lose up to a day of valuable nursing time or become separated from its mother when they are frightened into the water by humans. Haul-outs and rookeries should not be approached—use binoculars to observe animals from a distance. Back off if seals or sea lions show signs of disturbance such as stretching their necks or moving towards the water.

Sometimes seals, sea lions and sea otters appear inquisitive and will watch or follow a kayak in the water, where they feel relatively safe. In these situations it is appropriate to observe the animal from whatever distance it chooses; however, you should not approach it. To leave the area, paddle on a course perpendicular to or away from the animal, not towards it.

Some marine mammals are discussed in greater detail in chapters 10 (orcas), 13 (gray whales) and 15 (sea otters).

Finally, don't feed animals. Human food does not provide proper nutrition for wild animals, and eating your food may lead to their eventual starvation or potentially dangerous habituation. (For information about bears, see Other Hazards later in this chapter.)

SEABIRDS

Seabirds are abundant on the coast. It is important not to disturb birds during their nesting season because you may endanger chicks or eggs by scaring away the parents. Give rookeries a wide berth and observe with binoculars. The biggest danger here is that predatory birds such as eagles will take advantage of the parents' absence to raid the nests. Along beaches, watch for signs such as a "broken wing" distraction display, which will alert you to the presence of nearby nests. When walking, be careful to avoid stepping on camouflaged nests; if you discover one, leave the area quickly and carefully.

INTERTIDAL LIFE

Marine intertidal areas are home to a host of fascinating animals, each adapted to a particular habitat. Because most of these creatures are so small, they are easily overlooked, and coastal campers must be especially careful to avoid causing them harm. All these animals are susceptible to pollutants in the water such as concentrations of soap, and many are crushed by human traffic and simple tidal exploration. Take advantage of low tides to view these animals in tide pools and along the beaches, but be aware of the harm you may cause.

CULTURAL IMPACTS

Traditional routes of canoe travel by native peoples cover the entire Pacific Northwest coast, and virtually every area that has appeal to paddlers today has a human history stretching back thousands of years. This puts paddlers in a unique and privileged position because the areas we visit are the traditional lands and waters of the First Nations. It is important that we recognize and respect the historical significance and ownership of these areas.

The First Nations have a long history of dealing with the many encroachments on their territories. They have been active, even proactive participants in some developments; the challenge today is to preserve the values that sustained their ancestors, resources and environment in the face of new developments and encroachments, and to ensure a healthy and meaningful lifestyle for future generations. Visitors are encouraged to learn about traditional territories, history and values from the First Nations themselves.

To help you in this regard, we have tried to include the names and numbers of the appropriate First Nations in the Useful Contacts section at the back of the book. Nonetheless, you may have to do some additional research to find the contacts for specific sites or villages you plan to visit. This can take time, and it is best not to leave it until the last minute. Keep in mind that areas marked as Indian Reserve (or

Reservation) on nautical charts represent only a portion of the hundreds of native sites along the coast that provide resting and camping opportunities for paddlers. These unofficial spots are important archeological sites that most likely have contemporary significance too, so please treat them with the same respect you do the legally recognized Indian Reserves and Reservations.

It is our hope that you will embrace the following guidelines and do your part to acknowledge the peoples who first paddled the islands and inlets of the Pacific Northwest coast.

Ask Permission Most Indian Reserves are marked with an IR on nautical charts and are private property. If you wish to visit First Nations sites on your paddling trip, call or preferably write the local tribal council well before your trip. Be sure to seek permission from the tribal council, not from individuals, and consider a lack of response from a tribal council to be a negative response. Avoid First Nations sites unless you have been granted permission. Once you have been granted permission, look, photograph and enjoy—but do not disturb.

Leave Artifacts Alone What may appear lost or forgotten to our eyes is often of great significance, and part of that significance is where the object lies. Artifacts, including whale and human bones, are often tied to a specific location and are deliberately left in their natural surroundings rather than removed to a museum or private collection. Once they are removed from context without proper study, they can no longer speak to the past history of the place. If you suspect the artifacts or sites you have found are unknown, then contact the local tribal council and the Archaeology Branch of the B.C. Ministry of Sustainable Resource Management. In Washington State, contact the Governor's Office of Indian Affairs. In Oregon State, contact the Bureau of Indian Affairs.

Note: It is strictly illegal to remove any object that has heritage value without the appropriate permit(s).

Respect Harvesting Areas Clam beds and other intertidal harvesting areas should be approached as areas of traditional food harvesting that may still be in contemporary use by First Nations and other local residents. Be sure to minimize your impact on these areas. Take no more than you need, eat what you take and avoid harvesting in popular areas. Check with the local tribal councils for advice on this matter.

Avoid Damaging Midden Sites Middens are basically refuse heaps: deposits built up over time from discarded material—usually kitchen garbage—associated with past human occupation. The term "shell midden" refers to the middens left by coastal aboriginal occupants, often dating back many hundreds to several thousands of years. These contain large amounts of shell fragments (left over from the consumption of clams) mixed in with rich, dark, greasy soil often containing broken pieces of fire-charred rock. They can be anything from a few centimetres to several metres in depth. The rates of accumulation vary greatly depending on the intensity and duration of resource use. They are as valuable to understanding human history as the pyramids of Egypt or the peat bogs of Northern Europe—but only if they are protected and investigated in an appropriate manner.

Shell middens are typically found on any reasonably level area above a shoreline with good access to sandy beaches, fresh water and suitable canoe landing places. These are the same types of places paddlers today find desirable to land, camp and picnic on. They are often evident from a distance by the presence of slightly greener, more deciduous vegetation, or even a lack of vegetation. In some cases, middens may be associated with burial or petroglyph sites.

Shell middens in B.C., like other types of archeological sites, are protected by law under provisions of B.C.'s Heritage Conservation Act. A person must not damage or alter them, dig in or remove objects from them. This means zero impact camping or visitation—and only after the appropriate permission has been secured.

CLIMATE, WEATHER AND HAZARDS

The Pacific Northwest is a region that intertwines land and sea in a setting that is as dramatic as it is beautiful. When we first planned the section on weather, we intended to keep it separate from the section on paddling hazards. It soon became apparent, however, that like the land and sea, the weather and hazards of this coast are intertwined. Quite simply, if you do not have a basic understanding of the climate and weather you will be paddling in, they will quickly become hazards. Although weather patterns are by no means easy to understand, let alone predict, the following section gives you a brief background to the climate, weather and hazards in the Pacific Northwest and will help get you on the water safely. We strongly recommend that you spend some time researching the topic thoroughly. Much of the information in this section has been drawn, with permission, from Environment Canada's *Marine Weather Hazards Manual*. For more information or your own copy, contact Environment Canada (see Useful Contacts).

The Pacific Weather Centre, a part of Environment Canada, issues marine forecasts for all of B.C.; the National Oceanic and Atmospheric Administration issues forecasts for Puget Sound and the Columbia River. Always have a weather radio or VHF with you and be sure to listen to the weather forecast before you plan your day. For more information on weather services, see Useful Contacts.

PRECIPITATION

Annual rainfall in the Pacific Northwest ranges from less than 1000 mm to over 5000 mm (40–196 in.). Much of the rain on the coast is called orographic precipitation: rain caused by warm moist air being forced up over mountains, cooling as it rises, condensing and falling. With this in mind, and the fact that most fronts approach from the west due to winds high in the atmosphere, it is relatively easy to predict the areas of heavy rainfall. Essentially, areas just west of a mountain range receive more rain than areas to the east or in the lee of the range. Barkley Sound, for instance, just west of the Vancouver Island Ranges, often receives as much as five times the amount of rain as the Gulf Islands even though they lie less than 80 km (50 mi.) to the east. The effect is so dramatic that much of the west coast of Vancouver Island is classified as temperate rain forest while the Gulf Islands, San Juan Islands and much of the Sunshine Coast are said to have a semi-arid, even Mediterranean, climate. Such variations can also be found near the mainland of B.C. and in Washington State as a result of the Coast Mountains. Yet, for all the talk and jokes about the rain in this part of the world (you don't tan in the Pacific Northwest, you rust...), summers are typically quite pleasant and precipitation is limited to about a quarter of the days during the prime paddling season.

TEMPERATURES

Summer temperatures typically range from 6 to 27°C (43 to 80°F) while the average daytime temperature hovers between 18 and 24°C (65 and 75°F). Although this is quite comfortable, visitors to the region are often surprised by the damp chill of foggy days and the brisk, clear nights, so be sure to bring warm clothing at any time of year.

Paddlers must also be aware of the cool ocean temperatures, ranging from 5 to 15°C (41 to 59°F). No matter how warm the air temperature, the northwest Pacific Ocean remains cool year round, and immersion can lead to numbness in as little as 5 minutes and to hypothermia in 20 minutes. Never head out without practising rescue techniques, and consider wearing a wet suit or dry suit if you are paddling exposed coastal waters, undertaking a major crossing or travelling in areas of unusually cold water.

WIND

As a paddler, winds are one of your most important concerns. Although the overall patterns of winds are quite well understood, it is their daily variation—where and how strongly they blow—that remains a problem. This becomes even more difficult as the rugged coastline of B.C. and Washington modifies wind-flow patterns in many different ways.

For the most part, summer winds are predominantly from the northwest or west and reach peak velocity during the afternoon. This is a general rule, however, and you should check the weather reports each morning *before leaving camp* to ensure you will not be caught by unusual conditions. In the 1990s alone there were two huge southeasterly blows in August on the west coast of Vancouver Island, so be prepared for dramatic weather changes at any time of year.

In the winter, winds are predominantly from the southeast, with the strongest winds accompanying intense lows and their associated fronts. Typically, as a low approaches the coast, winds back into the southeast and increase in speed, often reaching gale or storm force. With the passage of the front, winds usually shift to the northwest. Again, these are general patterns. There are also some specific types of winds that you should know about.

∧ *Cape Caution swells, Central Coast,* PETER MCGEE

Sea and Land Breezes Sea and land breezes are localized phenomena that occur commonly during the summer. Both kinds of wind are caused by the different rates of heating and cooling of the land and sea. Over the course of a sunny day, the land heats up faster than the water. As the heated air rises, the cooler ocean air flows onshore to replace it. This onshore breeze is known as a sea breeze. Its counterpart is the land breeze that develops at night, when the land cools faster than the ocean: it blows from land to sea.

Afternoon sea breezes can develop at any time of year when strong daytime heating occurs, so don't be caught off guard by this predictable phenomenon. For the most part, speeds don't exceed 25 knots, but localized funnelling can increase this to upwards of 40 knots, so it is important to be aware of the surrounding topography. In particular, during the spring and summer months, the Columbia River is exposed to extremely strong westerlies, as winds tend to blow off the cool Pacific Ocean towards the rising hot air of the inland deserts.

Anabatic and Katabatic Winds Although you may rarely hear the terms anabatic and katabatic winds, they technically describe the local prevailing conditions of most mainland inlets and behave in a very similar way to land and sea breezes. Anabatic and katabatic winds often contribute to land and sea breezes and result in increased wind speeds. To safely paddle many of the inlets in this guide, it is important to have a general understanding of the conditions that cause anabatic and katabatic winds.

During the day, the sides of coastal valleys become warmer than the valley bottoms because they are more exposed to the sun. As a result, the winds blow up the slopes. These daytime, upslope winds are called anabatic winds. At night, the air cools and "avalanches" down the slope and out to sea. These cool night winds are called drainage, or katabatic, winds and are often quite gusty and strong. This is a simple description of these winds and will help you plan around them; however, bear in mind that other local factors may either intensify or cancel these phenomena.

Outflow Winds Outflow winds differ from katabatic winds in that they are driven by temperature differences as well as by large-scale pressure differences. The most famous outflow wind, possibly in the entire world, is the Bute Wind that flows out of Bute Inlet during the winter. Bute Inlet snakes about 50 km (30 mi.) into the mainland and is surrounded by British Columbia's highest mountains, some reaching heights of 4000 m (13,100 ft.). These mountains are besieged by massive glaciers and huge ice fields. All this ice produces cold air that "falls" down the mountainsides and valleys out to the coast. During the winter, the winds are subzero in temperature, and as they travel over any body of water, they create a deadly, freezing spray. A classic outflow condition, where winds reach lethal proportions, occurs when intense high pressure ridges in the interior of the province are accompanied by intense low pressure systems offshore. In 1990, one such condition produced winds estimated at about 200 kph (120 mph), flattening hundreds of hectares of forest on the windward side of Stuart Island (Desolation Sound). Although this was an extreme case, winds exceeding 100 kph (60 mph) are common. A similar wind, although less dramatic, also occurs in Washington's Hood Canal—a fiordlike inlet at the base of the Olympic Mountains. Although it may not be as powerful as the Bute Inlet outflow wind, it can be as sudden, and it is not uncommon to see whitecaps before you actually feel the wind.

As a general rule when paddling in inlets, start paddling early and finish by lunchtime. Sometimes the wind effect is virtually nil or very mild tempered—but don't ever plan on it. The mountains of the inlets rise straight out of the ocean, and it is often necessary to paddle several kilometres to find a safe place to haul out. Of course, when it is overcast and rainy, the heating cycle is interrupted and you can usually rely on smooth, windless paddling conditions.

In closing, it is worth noting that the inlets of this coast are born of mountains, and any climber will tell you that mountains are unpredictable and extreme places to travel. So too are their inlets. Remember to paddle with humility, and keep your eyes and ears open.

Gap and Corner Winds When winds are forced to flow through a narrow opening or gap, such as through an inlet or between two islands, the wind speed will increase and may even double in strength. This effect, called funnelling, is similar to pinching a water hose to create a faster, denser spray. The coastal topography can also change the direction of the wind by forcing it to flow along the route of a pass or through a strait. This is referred to as channelling.

Winds that are modified by funnelling and channelling are called gap winds. The constricted channels not only increase wind speeds but also strengthen tidal currents. Care is necessary when the increased winds are directed against strong tidal currents. The result is steep, breaking waves and much rougher waters than in more open areas.

Paddlers should also be aware of corner winds that occur off the points of islands or around a headland. These can be up to 25 per cent stronger than the average wind speed due to a convergence of airstreams, so take note of the wind when passing by "corners" of land.

FOG

Fog is a common companion on the West Coast and can result in sudden and total disorientation. Two types of fog that you are likely to encounter are radiation fog and sea (or advection) fog.

Radiation fog forms when moisture from the ground evaporates into the lower layer of the atmosphere. It tends to develop over land during the early morning and is primarily a problem in harbours and estuaries, rarely spreading far out to sea. After the sun comes up, the fog usually dissipates over the land and then clears more slowly over the water. Radiation fog is quite rare in the summer but occurs more often from late autumn to early spring.

Sea (advection) fog, on the other hard, is most frequent during the summer and fall and is formed when warm, moist air moves over colder seawater. Unlike radiation fog, which requires calm or light wind conditions, sea fog may form when winds are moderate and may even persist as winds become strong. In fact, dense fog is often noted in Juan de Fuca Strait with westerly winds up to 30 knots.

The bottom line is that fog can be encountered at any time on the coast, so you need to prepare yourself. Always carry a compass when paddling—navigating by compass is not a hard skill to learn but must be practised when conditions are good. Avoid crossings in the fog. If that is not possible, make your crossings short or try to split a long crossing into two shorter crossings by altering your route. Do not aim for tiny islands and always allow a good margin of error. For example, do not aim for the tip of a peninsula; instead, shoot for the midsection and work your way along the shore until you have reached the point. In addition to the compass, you can gain some orientation from the sounds of beach surf, bells and fog horns as well as from steady wave and wind direction, so stay alert from the time you leave shore until the time you land. A deck-mounted compass will help you keep a bearing over a long distance, and a watch will help you calculate approximate distances travelled. A GPS (Global Positioning System) also helps but will not eliminate the need for any of the above.

If you feel uncomfortable about travelling in the fog or find yourself in an area of high boat traffic, sit it out. Unless you have modified your boat, radar will not pick you up and it is quite likely that ships will not see you until a collision is unavoidable. Finally, try not to rush when navigating in the fog. Fog and speed don't mix, and hurrying can get you lost that much more quickly and thoroughly.

SUPERSTORMS

Every now and then the Pacific Northwest coast gets nailed by what locals call superstorms. Similar in strength to hurricanes, these storms develop as low pressure systems far away in the tropics or subtropics and gain strength on their journey north. Although rare, they are frequent enough that it is worth knowing the tell-tale signs. Wind speeds increase dramatically, with gusts exceeding 100 knots, but your best bet is to keep an eye on the barometric pressure for an early warning. Whenever weather radio broadcasts warn of an approaching low that reads 975 millibars or less, pay close attention to all updates. If the barometer reading indicates a 3-hour pressure drop matching or exceeding 6 millibars, be prepared to seek immediate refuge and secure your boat carefully. The low pressure and increased wind speeds will also create what is known as a storm surge, or a rise in the normal tide level, so be sure to place your gear and campsite high on the shore or in the trees.

TIDES AND CURRENTS

The tide refers to the daily movement—the rise and fall—of the ocean that is produced by the gravitational forces of the sun and moon. Tides actually move as a long, shallow wave with a period (the time interval between the passage of two wave crests) of around 12 hours. The passing of the wave is gradual, and the result is two high and two low tides in a 24-hour period. Because the wave moves south to north, a flooding (rising) tide is therefore typically accompanied by a north-flowing current and an ebbing (faling) tide by a south-flowing current. There are a few exceptions to this trend, however, the most notable being the northeast coast of Vancouver Island, where the flooding tide actually wraps around Cape Scott and heads south.

To predict tides, paddlers should always carry a set of tide tables, which are available at most marine stores. Don't forget that the time indicated in the tide tables refers to Pacific Standard Time; you will need to add an hour during Pacific Daylight Saving Time (April to October).

On shore, tides are a concern to paddlers because they affect where a camp is located and how high boats must be pulled up for the night. The difference between the high and low tides can be up to 7.5 m (25 ft.) on some parts of the coast, so knowing how to use tide tables is critical to selecting a safe, dry camp. The highest and lowest tides occur near the time of a new or full moon and are called spring tides. Tides with the minimum range, known as neap tides, occur when the moon is in the first or third quarter.

On the water, tides are a concern to paddlers because of the tidal streams and currents they create. Although the strength of the flood and ebb tidal streams within the Strait of Georgia and other unrestricted channels and inlets seldom exceeds 2 knots, currents can frequently aggravate conditions caused by adverse weather, particularly when current and wind are opposing. In certain cases, currents can actually cause difficult eddy and wave conditions, even on utterly still days, from the sheer force of their flow. When currents exceed 5 knots, the result is what is commonly called a tidal rapid. Canadian Hydrographic Nautical Charts refer to this hazard as "heavy tidal overfall."

TIDAL RAPIDS

Essentially, a tidal rapid occurs when millions of tons of water are forced through relatively small openings in a fixed period of time. During times of extreme tidal activity, conditions within the boundaries of a rapid are highly turbulent and erratic. Because of the incredible volumes of water, extreme depths and constantly changing flow rates, it is difficult to predict what the water will do. Surface water speeds can exceed 13 knots, standing waves in excess of 2 m (6.5 ft.) are not unusual, and known whirlpools are capable of sucking under large vessels. Clearly, this is no place for a kayak.

Tidal rapids are linked to the movement of the tide and hence are cyclical in nature. Calm periods can be predicted by using the Canadian Tides and Current Tables, the National Oceanic and Atmospheric Administration's (NOAA) guides or other independently published current (not tide) tables. If you do plan on navigating a tidal rapid, read the relevant chart carefully to help identify danger points, use all available information to estimate slack or favourable currents, and time your passage or crossing for that period. As always, exercise caution when the current and wind direction oppose each other. Like paddling in surf, it is best to paddle in currents under controlled conditions to familiarize yourself with the effects on your boat before you head out on a trip. For some recent information on tidal rapids, check out www.discovery-islands-lodge.com/tidal_rapids.pdf.

SURF, SWELL AND THE OPEN COAST

Although the open coast is one of the most scenic areas to paddle, it is not a place for beginners. If you are planning a kayak trip along a stretch of exposed coastline, be sure you have both the necessary paddling skills (including surf skills) and mental preparation. When considering a run down the open coast, remember that ocean swells are generated far away by distant storms. Local winds have no connection to the swell size on a given day; calm winds locally do not generate calm seas. Rather, local winds generate local waves that add to the tops of existing ocean swells; this is what weather radio forecasters mean when they say "Sea states are combined wind wave and swell height."

Swells also pose a hazard when they break on offshore reefs or shallow rocks, often called boomers. Read your charts carefully and scan the horizon constantly. Be very alert and remember that swell size is random and can change. Do not be lulled into a false sense of security because "the swells are small today."

When landing in surf with a loaded boat, the goal is actually not to surf—the weight of the gear can damage you and your boat quite easily if you capsize. A surf-free landing often can be accomplished by tucking in behind islets or reefs, but if you are forced to land on a surf beach, wait for a window of opportunity and paddle to shore between breaking waves. This takes experience and should be practised with an empty boat and under the watchful eye of a qualified instructor.

OTHER HAZARDS

Aside from the hazards relating to weather and water conditions, there are a number of potential encounters or emergencies that paddlers should be aware of and prepared to deal with on the coast.

BEARS

Although it is unlikely that you will encounter bears when paddling in Washington State and/or Oregon, British Columbia has about a quarter of all the black bears in Canada and half the grizzly bears. Paddlers must respect the fact that the wilderness is home to bears, and as a visitor you must do your part to help conserve bears and their home.

The best way to avoid an encounter with bears is to keep a clean camp and never leave out food or garbage. When storing food, always use a bear cache if one has been provided. Otherwise make sure food is hung at least 5 m (16 ft.) high and 1.5 m (5 ft.) from the tree trunk. One system that seems to work quite well is stringing a single line between two trees and draping a second line over the middle; the second line holds the food and can be lowered and raised easily.

Do not sleep in the same clothes you cook in, never keep food in your tent and try to camp at least 50 m (164 ft.) from your "kitchen." Finally, do not cache food or garbage in your kayaks when on shore.

All bears can be dangerous, so try to anticipate and avoid encounters. Never approach or attempt to feed a bear. Respect their territory and avoid areas they frequent, such as the mouths of streams during spawning season. It is your responsibility to ensure that you do not force bears to leave their habitat, teach them to eat human foods or place them in situations where people or bears get hurt.

MOTOR VESSEL TRAFFIC

One of the most dangerous hazards paddlers must deal with is the presence of other boats and ships. Your best bet is to assume that no matter what the right of way, you will not be seen by other boaters and it is you who must move. As author and kayaker John Dowd writes, when a ship appears to be coming straight for you, you may find it difficult to decide which side to move to in order to get out of the way. It is worth a few seconds' pause to get it right. Resist the common reaction to scuttle across in front of her; instead, watch the line-up of the bow and mast (or another high point toward the stern of the boat) closely to see if she is likely to pass in front of you or astern. Then paddle away from her line of course, taking care to watch the vessel until she is past—just in case she alters course.

In fog, of course, the danger of a collision is heightened. The first question you should ask yourself is, should you be on the water in the first place? If you do take to the water and hear traffic, point your bow to the source of the noise so you can pinpoint the traffic's location and determine your relative position. If the noise becomes louder and remains off your bow, you will likely have to change course. If the source of the sound moves in relation to your bow and compass setting, you are probably safe. In either event, you should avoid getting into such situations if at all possible.

Stay together when travelling in a group across shipping lanes or busy channels. It is much easier for ships to avoid a tightly clustered group than a string of multicoloured speed bumps. Take your time before setting out on the crossing and make sure everyone involved understands the final destination and compass bearing. Keep in mind that ferries and other ships move extremely quickly and a small speck on the horizon can quickly become a hazard. Also remember that many vessels on the coast have booms or barges in tow—always stay alert for towlines or cables.

HYPOTHERMIA

The loss of body heat or lowering of the deep body core temperature known as hypothermia is a deadly serious matter. Once cooling begins, a person's body temperature drops very rapidly, and unconsciousness, cardiac arrest and death can result.

Immersion in cold water is the quickest way to get hypothermia—and any immersion in Pacific Northwest waters will be *cold*. You are also susceptible on shore and in your bed, especially on cool, wet and windy days. Anybody who is exhausted, cold and exposed is at risk. Be alert to your own condition and to that of others in your group.

Hypothermia can set in quite rapidly at any time of the year. Prevention is the best strategy. Always dress for cold water immersion, regardless of the air temperature, and keep extra warm, dry clothes readily available in a waterproof bag. Eat adequately to replenish your energy stores—aim for 4000 calories a day (regardless of gender). Drink adequately, too—up to 3 litres (3 qt.) of water a day. And take sufficient breaks to avoid getting exhausted.

PARALYTIC SHELLFISH POISONING

Paralytic shellfish poisoning (PSP) is caused by the contamination of bivalve shellfish by microorganisms called dinoflagellates. These microorganisms are always present in the water but when salinity, nutrient and temperature conditions are right, a population explosion or "bloom" occurs. Sometimes the bloom turns the water red, hence the name "red tide," but toxic conditions can exist without any trace of colour. You may hear of people "testing" for red tide by rubbing the shellfish on their lips to see if it causes a tingling sensation or by feeding it to an animal first, but these methods are not reliable. Unfortunately, there really isn't a reliable test for paddlers to use in the field, so skipping the mussel feast is a good idea—particularly in the warm months when a bloom is likely to occur.

If someone experiences symptoms of PSP, paralysis and respiratory failure may occur quickly. Seek medical help immediately.

2

The Lower Columbia River

Donna Matrazzo,
Cindy Scherrer and Steve Scherrer

The Great River of the West," the Columbia River, forms the state boundary between Washington and Oregon, and is renowned for its power and immensity, its mysterious beauty and its fascinating human history. By volume, it is the second-largest river in North America, its tributaries draining nearly 673 400 square km (260,000 sq. mi.). Its shores are lined with glacier-carved cliffs, golden sand beaches and views of magnificent volcanoes. Along this liquid highway have travelled finely crafted Native American canoes, the high-prowed bateaux of the French fur-trading voyageurs, the rough dugouts of Lewis and Clark's Corps of Discovery, steamboats transporting gold seekers and gamblers, and today's international cargo ships. A journey along the lower Columbia River is spectacular and fascinating, a rich melange of gorgeous landscapes, historical sites and working ports of call.

BACKGROUND

Once-abundant salmon were a major source of trade for the Chinook peoples, who used the Columbia River as an avenue of commerce.

< *Cape Horn in the Columbia Gorge*, NEIL SCHULMAN

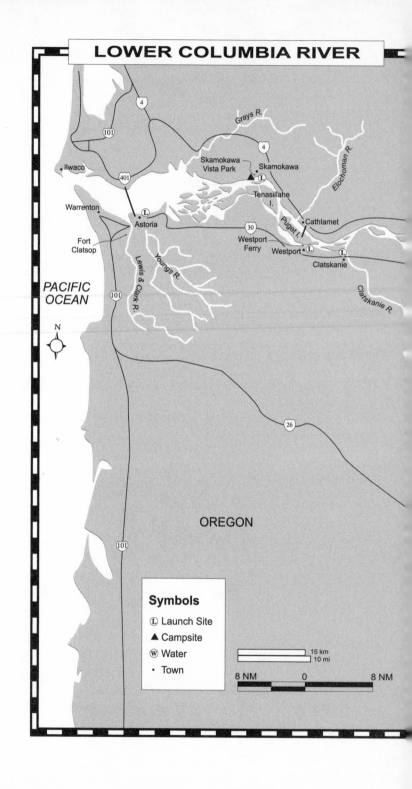

LOWER COLUMBIA RIVER

Grays R.

4

101

Ilwaco

401

Skamokawa
Vista Park

Skamokawa

Elochoman R.

Tenasillahe
I.

Warrenton

Astoria

Fort
Clatsop

30

Westport
Ferry

Puget I.

Cathlamet

Westport

Clatskanie

Lewis & Clark R.

Youngs R.

PACIFIC
OCEAN

101

Clatskanie R.

N

26

OREGON

101

Symbols

Ⓛ Launch Site

▲ Campsite

Ⓦ Water

• Town

15 km
10 mi

8 NM   0   8 NM

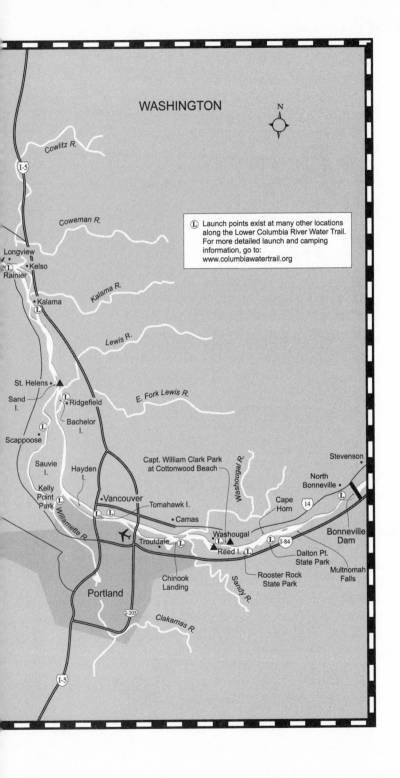

WASHINGTON

N

Cowlitz R.

I-5

Coweman R.

Ⓛ Launch points exist at many other locations
along the Lower Columbia River Water Trail.
For more detailed launch and camping
information, go to:
www.columbiawatertrail.org

Longview
Ⓛ •Kelso
Rainier

Kalama R.

•Kalama
Ⓛ

Lewis R.

St. Helens •
Sand
I.
Ⓛ •Ridgefield
E. Fork Lewis R.

Bachelor
I.
Ⓛ

Scappoose

Sauvie
I.

Hayden
I.

Capt. William Clark Park
at Cottonwood Beach

Washougal R.

Stevenson
•

North
Bonneville •

Kelly
Point
Park Ⓛ

•Vancouver

Tomahawk I.

Cape
Horn

14

Ⓛ

Willamette R.

Ⓛ Ⓛ

• Camas

Washougal

Bonneville
Dam

Troutdale

Ⓛ

Ⓛ

Ⓛ I-84

Reed I. Ⓛ

Dalton Pt.
State Park

Chinook
Landing

Sandy R.

Rooster Rock
State Park

Multnomah
Falls

Portland

I-205

Clakamas R.

I-5

They successfully traded shells from tribes of the coast for buffalo hides from Indians of the Interior. After Lewis and Clark's journey revealed the wealth of furs, trappers and traders exploited the populations of sea otters and beavers. By the late 1800s, salmon was king and Astoria became known as the "salmon canning capital of the world." Steamships plied the waters, carrying gamblers and gold seekers to booming towns upriver. Oregon Trail pioneers who wanted to detour Mount Hood risked their lives in the wild, churning whirlpools of the undammed river.

The mighty river is named after the *Columbia Rediviva*, the ship of Capt. Robert Gray, who explored the mouth of the Columbia in 1792, searching for the mythical Northwest Passage to the Missouri River that would connect the Pacific Ocean with the Atlantic. Today the river continues to be a busy water highway, albeit with plenty of stretches for solitude and for experiencing the beauty of the natural world.

The Lower Columbia River Water Trail (LCRWT) committee was formed in September 2001, to make the lower stretch of the river — the 235 free-flowing km (146 mi.) from the Bonneville Dam to the Pacific Ocean — more accessible to paddlers in small boats. The group, working under the auspices of the Lower Columbia River Estuary Partnership, is a bi-state coalition of individuals, organizations and agencies with diverse interests and connections to the river. The committee has divided the river into seven reaches of approximately 32 km (20 mi.) each. A Web site and reach maps are designed to introduce people to the boating and camping facilities, natural scenic wonders, and the cultural and educational attractions along the river's length, including historical and maritime museums, abandoned riverfront towns, Fort Clatsop, Fort Vancouver and former Native American village sites.

The trips in this guide offer but a taste of the river's many paddling options. To plan other routes — from day outings to multi-day journeys — check a map for information about the many launch and landing sites along the river. Outfitters offer guided explorations, from day trips to an eight-day adventure paddling the entire 235 km (146 mi.) of the water trail. The "Rediscovery of the Rivers" committee of the Lewis and Clark Bicentennial of Oregon has drawn up plans to commemorate and make accessible the 14 Lewis and Clark landing sites in the Portland-Vancouver metropolitan region.

No matter where you launch or pull your boat out of the water, the lower Columbia River offers its charms and challenges to paddlers of all abilities.

GETTING THERE

By land In Washington State, Highway 14 follows the lower Columbia from North Bonneville to Vancouver, then Highway 4 runs from Longview to the junction with Highway 101 to Ilwaco. Interstate 5 connects Longview and Vancouver. In Oregon, Interstate 84/Highway 30 goes from Cascade Locks to Portland, then Highway 30 continues to Astoria. There are many boat launch points along the way. See the LCRWT Web site for details on launch and landing sites, and facilities on shore.

By air If coming by air, you will most likely arrive at Portland International Airport. Rental cars and bus service are available at the airport terminal, including the Max (Portland's light-rail rapid transit system), which can take you downtown. See Useful Contacts for kayak rentals and tour operators.

WEATHER AND HAZARDS

Wind is a powerful force on the Columbia River, which is why the region is known as a windsurfer's paradise. During the summer months, the cool Pacific air is often sucked up the river to fill the void left by the rising, hot air of the inland deserts. These winds are often extremely powerful and, when set against the downstream current, can cause havoc on the water. Although this westerly wind is common during the warmer months, a change in the weather and a fall of barometric pressure can also quickly bring easterlies. Regardless of the wind direction, paddlers should take care: the water might be placid one minute, then transform quickly into breaking waves. Because the river is so wide, it is generally classified as "open water," where wind and waves can build with great ferocity. Winds often pick up in the afternoon, so many paddlers plan to be off the water by then. In addition to the NOAA's weather reports, you can also track the winds through the windsurfing site www.iwindsurf.com.

Shipping lanes pose a danger from the heavy traffic of commercial cargo ships and long barges that move quietly and deceptively fast.

Islands can appear and disappear with the changing of the tides, making navigation confusing. Strong currents and tidal influences can make paddling very difficult.

SPECIAL CONSIDERATIONS

Be sure to pull out in protected waters away from the wild and dangerous mouth of the Columbia. Although the mouth is technically between Clatsop Spit to the south and Cape Disappointment to the north, all paddling west of Astoria should be approached with extra caution. There the river is 8 km (5 mi.) wide, and exposed. The Columbia Bar, where the river empties into the Pacific Ocean, is one of the most dangerous river bars in the world and has been dubbed "Graveyard of the Pacific." Crossing the bar is a challenge to even huge ocean-going cargo ships.

The Columbia River is tidal all the way to the Bonneville Dam. The National Ocean Survey produces tide tables for the Pacific Beaches with adjustments for various locations as you move upriver. The actual reversal of current (as opposed to the height of the water) depends on the strength of the tide versus the amount of river flow. River flow varies from year to year, with hydropower releases both for power and for flushing salmon smolts to sea. The NOAA's weather service provides information on river levels, or you can check their Northwest River Forecast Center map at www.wrh.noaa.gov/Portland/public_hydro/lc_swwa.html. The best "dot" or link to indicate flushing is for the Columbia River below Bonneville Dam.

It is somewhat difficult, however, to forecast at what stage the tide will reverse the flow. Some of us just assume, especially on the upper river, that between February and June, the flow will be high enough to prevent a tidal reversal. Also, keep in mind that the effect of tides depends on where you are—the ebb current lasts longer and reverses much slower in the shipping channels than in the shallows.

Much of the shoreline along the Lower Columbia River Water Trail is owned by private landowners and public agencies that manage the land to benefit wildlife. It is important that small boaters along the trail respect private property rights and obey agency regulations. Stewardship of the river's environmental resources is a long-standing interest of many paddlers currently travelling the waterways of the lower Columbia River.

TRIP 1 The Columbia Gorge

SKILL: Intermediate to advanced
TIME: 1–2 days
HAZARDS: Shipping channel and winds
ACCESS: Dalton Point, Rooster Rock State Park
CHARTS: 18531 · Vancouver, WA to Bonneville Dam · 1:40,000
TIDE TABLES: Pacific Beaches with correction for Ellsworth, WA (estimate only)

Over millions of years, lava floods, glaciers and the river's timeless carving have created the spectacular Columbia Gorge. This paddle offers some of its best scenery, including steep basalt cliffs, a rock island, sandy beaches, stunning waterfalls, and Lewis and Clark encampments.

LAUNCHING
Launching from the Dalton Point boat ramp in Oregon is free. If you're travelling west on Portland Interstate 84, look for the sign about 3 km (2 mi.) west of Multnomah Falls, take the Dalton Point exit at milepost 29 and turn right down the boat ramp. There is a boat ramp sign. If you're heading east to Hood River, take the Multnomah Falls exit and backtrack to Dalton Point. Another option is to launch further west at Rooster Rock State Park, also off I-84, approximately 6 km (4 mi.) down the road, at exit 25. There are large parking lots and a state parks fee (tel.: 503-695-2261).

Chinook Landing boat ramp, about 13 km (8 mi.) west on I-84, is an alternative put-in site or a good take-out spot for a one-way trip. To get there, take the NE Marine Drive exit off I-84. Travel west on Marine Drive until you reach 223, turn right and follow the signs to Chinook Landing. The launching ramp and parking area are day-use only. The fee is $4 per car per day.

SITES
From Dalton Point, paddle across the river to the dramatic glacier-carved basalt cliffs of Cape Horn, reminiscent to early navigators of the stormy cape at the tip of South America. Along the way, you'll pass Phoca Rock. This basalt pillar in the centre of the river was named by Lewis and Clark for the many harbour seals, *Phoca vitulina*, they saw in the vicinity. Be careful in the shipping channel. Tugs pushing as

∧ *Puget Island sloughs, Columbia River,* joelrogers.com

many as five barges come swiftly and almost silently around the bend, unseen until they're dangerously near. As well, the winds can pick up at any time, turning the water into breaking waves.

The sheer walls at Cape Horn rise directly from the river, an impressive 152 m (500 ft.) of exposed rock layers laced with waterfalls and small caves. The beach below is a gnarly gravel of broken basalt. Although many parts of the Columbia have been developed, this point looks just the same today as it did in the 1880s, when artist Cleveland Rockwell painted a scene of a square-rigger sailing ship rounding the bend at Cape Horn.

On the return trip, stop at the sandy beach in Rooster Rock State Park, but don't be surprised if you encounter nude sunbathers. Rooster Rock itself is a basalt monolith formed by the same geologic forces as Phoca Rock. On November 2, 1805, on their way west, Lewis and Clark encamped under Rooster Rock, where they "saw great numbers of waterfowl of Different kinds, such as Swan, Geese, white and grey brants, ducks of various kinds..." Complete your paddle by returning to Dalton Point or, if you have left a second vehicle at Chinook Landing, continue the 14 km (8–9 mi.) downriver past the confluence with the Sandy River and more gorgeous gorge scenery.

Reed Island State Park and Capt. William Clark Park For an overnight trip, continue west from Rooster Rock and head back over to the Washington side of the river. Camp at Reed Island State Park (5 km/3 mi.) or Capt. William Clark Park at Cottonwood Beach (6 km/4 mi.), another Lewis and Clark landing site. The main party camped here from March 31 to April 5, 1806, on the return journey. Clark wrote, "We determined to remain at our present encampment a day or two for the several purposes of examining quicksand river [the Sandy River], making some Celestial observations, and procuring some meat." A trail connects the beach to inland parking areas, where there are currently no supporting facilities, although major site developments are in the works. Cottonwood Beach is located south of Highway 14 in Washougal, Washington, between Steamboat Landing at SE 15th Street and Steigerwald National Wildlife Refuge.

TRIP 2 The Ports

SKILL: Beginner to intermediate
TIME: Day trip
HAZARDS: Shipping channel and winds
ACCESS: McCuddy's Marina/Kelly Point Park/Vancouver Marine Park
CHARTS: 18525 · St. Helens to Vancouver · 1:40,000
18526 · Port of Portland · 1:20,000
TIDE TABLES: Pacific Beaches with correction for Vancouver, WA

The lower Columbia is a working river, and that's no more evident than in the waters around Hayden Island, which are lined with houseboats, dock facilities for the ports of Portland and Vancouver, shipping channel anchorage areas and ship turning basins.

LAUNCHING

A marina ramp that puts you into the mellow channel behind Tomahawk and Hayden Islands is the McCuddy's Marina ramp north of Portland, Oregon. To get there, take Interstate 5 to the Jantzen Beach exit, then drive east .8 km (.5 mi.) along NE Tomahawk Island Drive to the Alder Creek Kayak & Canoe store parking lot. Further west is Kelly Point Park. Take exit 307 off I-5 and follow signs for Marine Drive west. Go past Smith and Bybee Lakes and part of the Rivergate Industrial Area. Watch for a small sign indicating a right turn into Kelly Point Park. Turn left after entering the park. There is a small parking area and both a dirt and mud boat ramp on the Columbia Slough, which feeds into the Willamette and then the Columbia. You can also drive further into the park and, with a moderate carry and a good sense of balance, launch from the shore directly into the Columbia. The park is open from sunrise to sunset.

In Washington, launch from Vancouver Marine Park, located off Highway 14. Take exit 1, westbound or eastbound, to SE Columbia Way, turn south, pass beneath the railroad bridge and turn east at the light. At approximately 4 km (2.5 mi.), a sign on a brick pillar says "Marine Park" and another sign marks the boat ramp.

SITES

From any of the launch sites, it's easy to follow the shore and experience the intriguing wonders of the workaday lower Columbia. To the south of Hayden Island is Port of Portland's Terminal 6 and, to the north, the Port of Vancouver docks and facilities. Huge cargo ships from around the world dock for repairs, the evidence of their travels visible in the scrapes and worn paint of the weathered metal hulls. Ships with enormous rudders and propellers are anchored midriver. At docks and grain elevators, ships load and unload. Airplanes landing or taking off from Portland International Airport fly low overhead. Charming houseboats brightened with flowers line the channel. You can paddle up to a number of restaurants, including a floating cafe. On a clear day, Mount St. Helens, Mount Adams and Mount Hood jut from the horizon. At Kelly Point Park, the Willamette River flows into the Columbia, two major rivers merged, heading to the sea. Lewis and Clark camped just north of the centre of Hayden Island on their return trip on March 30, 1806. Lewis noted, "This valley... is about 70 miles wide on a direct line and its length I believe to be very extensive, this valley would be competent to the maintenance of 40 or 50 thousand souls if property cultivated."

TRIP 3   Bachelor Island

SKILL:	Beginner to intermediate
TIME:	1–2 days
HAZARDS:	Shipping channel and winds
ACCESS:	Ridgefield
CHARTS:	18525 · St. Helens to Vancouver · 1:40,000
TIDE TABLES:	Pacific Beaches with correction for St. Helens, OR

A favourite day paddle is the 16-km (10-mi.) circumnavigation of Bachelor Island in Washington State, part of Ridgefield National Wildlife Refuge. Other options entice from across the river, including a lighthouse and trails on Sauvie Island, camping on Sand Island just across from St. Helens Marina and brunch in the charming waterfront town of St. Helens.

LAUNCHING

The launch site is the public boat ramp in the town of Ridgefield, Washington. To get there, take Interstate 5 north from Vancouver to exit 14, then head west on Highway 501 for about 5 km (3 mi.). In town, turn right at the stoplight, then left in two blocks onto Mill Street, which leads to the public boat ramp. There is a fee for parking.

SITES

From the ramp, turn north and head downstream a short way on Lake River, then turn south at Bachelor Island Slough and paddle along the southeastern border of Bachelor Island. The narrow tree-lined waterway along the refuge offers fantastic bird-watching. Overhead you might see bald eagles, osprey, great flocks of ducks, sandhill cranes, snow geese and swans. Flying from tree to tree are great blue herons, kingfishers, red-winged blackbirds, flickers and many other species. River otters frequently swim in the channel.

This area was the site of the large Chinook village of Quathlahpootle (estimated population 900), and plans are underway by U.S. Fish and Wildlife to construct a longhouse and interpretive centre as part of the refuge.

At 5 km (3 mi.), the slough meets the Columbia in a dramatic transition from tiny waterway to immense river. At the confluence is a sandy beach, which makes a perfect lunch spot.

Beginning paddlers can return the way they came, up the slough to Ridgefield. To circumnavigate Bachelor Island, continue north on the Columbia until its confluence with Lake River. From there, paddle east to return to the boat ramp.

Sand Island For a longer paddle or an overnight option, cross to the west shore of the Columbia and the Sauvie Island Wildlife Reserve. Near the northern tip of the island is the remnant of historic Warrior Rock lighthouse, another perfect lunch spot. From there, a hiking trail leads south following the shoreline for 5 km (3 mi.). A shorter interpretive loop trail is being developed near the lighthouse site.

From the tip of Sauvie Island you can see Sand Island directly ahead
and the quaint town of St. Helens to the northwest. There's a dock at
St. Helens for easy take-out and access to the waterfront shops and restaurants. Water is available at the marina. Sand Island is an excellent
camping spot, with wooded campsites, docks and composting toilets.

TRIP 4 Skamokawa

SKILL:	Beginner to advanced
TIME:	1–3 days
HAZARDS:	Shipping channel and winds
ACCESS:	Skamokawa Vista Park/Skamokawa Paddle Center
CHARTS:	18523 · Harrington Point to Crims Island · 1:40,000
TIDE TABLES:	Pacific Beaches with correction for Skamokawa, WA

Skamokawa is a Chinook word that means "smoke on the water." The
smoke is the beautiful, mystical fog that frequently shrouds the land
and settles above the water, taking on the apricot, mauve and crimson
colours of sunset. With the historic town of Skamokawa, Washington,
as your home base, and the Lewis and Clark National Wildlife
Refuge just across the way, a delicious variety of paddling opportunities abound.

LAUNCHING

Ideal launch sites are the Skamokawa Vista Park boat ramp, the sandy
shores of the park's campground or the docks of Skamokawa Paddle
Center. To get there, take Interstate 5 north from Vancouver to Kelso
and drive west on Highway 4 to Skamokawa.

For a more charming approach or to get there from Oregon, take
the Westport ferry, one of the few remaining small river ferries in the
region. From Portland, head northwest on Highway 30 to Westport,
where for a small toll you can board the 12-car ferry to Puget Island.
Drive across the island on Highway 409 to the Cathlamet Bridge,
then head west on Highway 4 from there to Skamokawa.

SITES

The paddling options from Skamokawa are infinite. For beginners,
there are many delightful little winding sloughs—Brooks Slough,

Steamboat Slough and Elochoman Slough plus Skamokawa Creek—
which are lined with tidy houses, floating homes, boathouses and
long-unused pilings now sprouting plants and small trees. In between
Brooks and Steamboat Sloughs, and across the river on Tenasillahe Island, is the Julia Butler Hansen National Wildlife Refuge for the
Columbian White-Tailed Deer, a haven for this endangered species.

To do an intermediate trip, paddle from Skamokawa in either direction (downstream is more scenic) along the shore of the Columbia. You'll experience the big river, with open water, mountain views
all around and a steady stream of cargo ships. The shipping channel
is close to shore here. Small beaches are good resting or lunch spots,
and exploration can reveal remnants of long-ago life along the river.

More experienced paddlers can cross the Columbia and wind
through the maze of islands that constitute the Lewis and Clark National Wildlife Refuge. The islands change by the hour, with the ebb
and flow of the tide, and the shallows and flats, marshes, swamps and
uplands are revealed or hidden in an area virtually unchanged since
the Corps of Discovery journeyed past. Good navigation and paddling skills are required, since winds can pick up with great force and
there are only a few upland areas where you can be sure of getting out
of your boat.

Skamokawa Vista Park Skamokawa, once known as "Little Venice,"
is a historic river community that captures the essence of the lower
Columbia's history. The Skamokawa Paddle Center offers a b&b,
general store and cafe. Skamokowa Vista Park is an ideal site for pic-
nics or camping. Its sandy beach is at the confluence of the Columbia
River and Steamboat and Brooks Sloughs, and its riverview campsites
offer expansive vistas of the islands in the refuge. Cargo ships pass
close to shore like phantoms on foggy days and moonlit spectacles on
clear nights.

ADDITIONAL ROUTES
Heading east The U.S. Army Corps of Engineers is currently planning a Northwest Discovery Water Trail from the Bonneville Dam to
the Clearwater River in Idaho—adding another 570 km (355 mi.) of
water trail to the region.

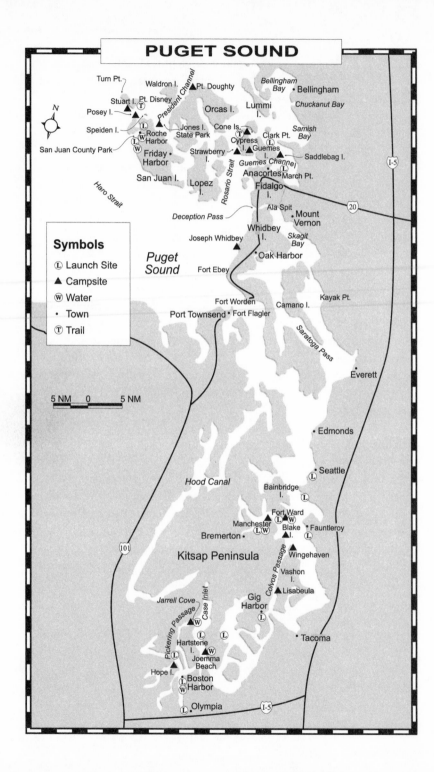

PUGET SOUND

Symbols

- Ⓛ Launch Site
- ▲ Campsite
- Ⓦ Water
- • Town
- Ⓣ Trail

Turn Pt.
Waldron I.
▲Pt. Doughty
Bellingham Bay
• Bellingham
Stuart I.
Pt. Disney
Ⓣ
Orcas I.
Lummi I.
Chuckanut Bay
Posey I.
▲
Speiden I.
Ⓛ
Jones I.
State Park
Cone Is.
Clark Pt.
Samish Bay
Ⓦ Roche
Harbor
Cypress I.
Ⓣ
Guemes I.
Ⓦ San Juan County Park
Ⓦ Friday
Harbor
Strawberry I.
Saddlebag I.
Guemes Channel
Anacortes
March Pt.
San Juan I.
Lopez I.
Rosario Strait
Fidalgo I.

Haro Strait

Ala Spit
Deception Pass
• Mount Vernon
Whidbey I.
Joseph Whidbey ▲
Skagit Bay
Puget Sound
• Oak Harbor
Fort Ebey
Kayak Pt.
Fort Worden
Camano I.
Port Townsend • Fort Flagler
Saratoga Pass

5 NM 0 5 NM

• Everett

• Edmonds

Hood Canal
Ⓛ Seattle
Bainbridge I.
Ⓛ
Fort Ward
Ⓛ Ⓦ
Manchester
▲ Blake I. • Fauntleroy
Ⓛ Ⓦ
Bremerton •
Colvos Passage
▲ Wingehaven

Kitsap Peninsula
Vashon I.
▲ Lisabeula
Jarrell Cove
Case Inlet
Gig Harbor
Ⓦ
Pickering Passage
Ⓛ
Hartstene I.
Ⓛ
Ⓛ Ⓦ
Joemma Beach
• Tacoma
Ⓛ
Hope I.
• Boston Harbor
Ⓦ
Ⓛ Olympia

3

Puget Sound

Allen Palmer and Reed Waite

Native Americans plied the waters of Puget Sound long before the arrival of white explorers. They knew the sound as *Whulge*, which loosely translates as "big salt water." Several tribes inhabited this coast, living on the abundant marine life and using the towering stands of forests to build villages and dugout canoes. Although boats of all kinds now travel these waters, paddling Puget Sound continues to be the best way to explore its beautiful shorelines. The slow, silent pace of a kayak will allow you to absorb the spectacular vistas of Mount Rainier, cabin-dotted islands and wildlife at play.

BACKGROUND

Puget Sound has always been a water highway for the Pacific Northwest. The region's rugged topography and dense old-growth forests made land travel an arduous if not impossible endeavour for early travellers. Although the region had many visits by Europeans between the 1500s and 1700s, Puget Sound remained relatively unexplored until 1792, when British Capt. George Vancouver sailed the sloop *Discovery* into Juan de Fuca Strait. Two officers from this voyage,

Lt. Peter Puget and Joseph Whidbey, a surveyor, explored much of southern Puget Sound. Originally, only the waters south of Tacoma Narrows were given the name of Puget Sound, but over time and with the aid of an unknown chartmaker, the range of Puget Sound was extended to include all of the area south of Admiralty Inlet.

The sound currently has a resident population approaching 4 million. Geographically, Puget Sound stretches approximately 242 km (150 mi.) north to south and 24–32 km (15–20 mi.) east to west, with the widest shore-to-shore distance averaging 6–10 km (4–6 mi.). Amazingly, with such a high population in such a small area, there are still many shorelines with stretches of uninterrupted beach and undeveloped coves and bays. This is largely because most of the population is clustered in the six major cities of Olympia, Tacoma, Bremerton, Seattle, Everett and Bellingham. As thousands of people move to the Puget Sound area each year, for its growing employment opportunities and quality of life, public access and water quality issues intensify. The once pristine wilderness is now being loved to death.

In hopes of reversing this trend, the Washington Water Trails Association (WWTA) was formed in 1990. Similar to the B.C. Marine Trail Association, its Canadian counterpart, the WWTA was established by a group of enthusiastic paddlers committed to the vision of a marine trail system designed for kayaks, canoes and other small beachable human- or wind-powered craft. The B.C. Marine Trail and the Washington Water Trail will eventually combine to form a Cascadia Marine Trail that covers the Inside Passage. Currently, the Washington State portion of the marine trail stretches more than 242 km (150 mi.), from the state capital in Olympia to the Canadian border, and includes over 44 camping sites throughout Puget Sound and the San Juan Islands. All the trips listed in this chapter use Cascadia Marine Trail sites.

GETTING THERE

By land People planning a trip to the Puget Sound area will find ready access by car, bus or train. Interstate 5 in conjunction with many state and local highways provides vehicle access to the entire Puget Sound basin. The I-5 is the major north-south freeway for the region, and various local roads will take you to the launch sites described below; most of these roads are paved, and others are of good quality gravel and suitable for almost all vehicles. Most Cascadia Marine Trail launch sites are within 160 km (100 mi.) of Seattle. Driving time to these access points will vary depending on road conditions, time of day and destination.

Please note: Be particularly cautious when parking on boat launching ramps or beaches. Ensure that your vehicle is capable of handling soft or slippery conditions, and set the parking brake or chock the tires. Also, don't tie up a boat launch (and annoy other boaters) while loading your kayak. Instead, deposit your boat and gear at the side of the ramp and then move your vehicle out of the way.

Commercial bus service and community transit systems are available throughout the Puget Sound region. Routes and schedules vary, so check with the individual carriers to see how your trip can best be organized.

By water The Washington State Ferries system provides transport across the sound at several points as well as into the San Juan Islands. By using these ferries, you can create shortcuts to points throughout Puget Sound. Ferries provide a welcome break from being behind the wheel, terrific views from the water and a valuable fallback plan if the weather turns rough. You can either drive your car onto the ferry, walk on or, if you have a kayak cart, roll on as you would with a bicycle. Check ferry schedules prior to setting out on your trip because conditions may change. The ferry system is very crowded during the summer months, especially in the San Juans on weekends; you should expect delays. Note: If you walk your kayak onto the ferry, be sure you can legally launch at the other side. Few ferry terminals have nearby public launch sites, so arrange for transport of your kayak, equipment and party to a launch area well beforehand and be prepared to seek out a place to load and unload well away from the terminal. Contact the WWTA for information on launch sites.

By air If coming by air, you will most likely arrive at Seattle-Tacoma International Airport. Rental cars and bus service are available at the airport terminal.

WEATHER AND HAZARDS
Weather in the Puget Sound area varies greatly depending on your location, the current weather pattern and the time of year. With many

different microclimates, it may be raining in one spot yet be sunny a few miles away. For most of the summer, the Pacific High brings fair weather westerlies and northwesterlies. These winds enter the Juan de Fuca Strait, often reaching 20–25 knots by early afternoon, and typically spread to the north and south as they approach the mainland. Southwesterlies are sent towards the San Juan Islands, and northwesterlies blow down across Port Townsend and into northern Puget Sound. The south sound typically experiences milder weather conditions during summer months. Still days and flat water prevail, providing the experience of paddling on a calm, glassy sea.

Precipitation is also varied within the sound. Moving northward, you begin to experience more of the effect of the Puget Sound Convergence Zone, where marine masses sweeping around the Olympic Mountains collide, producing localized rains. The San Juan Islands enjoy the benefits of being located in the rain shadow of Vancouver Island, which blocks or diverts many weather systems coming inland from the Pacific Ocean. When it is raining in Seattle, it is often sunny in the San Juans. Nonetheless, water conditions can become quite severe due to strong winds coming up the Juan de Fuca Strait, causing many of the channels between the islands to become hazardous for small boat travel.

The National Oceanic and Atmospheric Association's Olympia Station broadcasts on WX3 and their Seattle Station on WX1. Be sure to listen to local weather reports and ask advice from other mariners before setting out. Tides, currents and wind all present challenging water conditions in Puget Sound. The San Juan Islands are especially subject to fast tidal flows, which may create hazardous conditions even in calm weather. Special hazards exist at the north end of Orcas Island in the San Juans and at Deception Pass at the north end of Whidbey Island. Indeed, this region is one of the most hazardous sea kayaking areas in North America.

Water temperatures in Puget Sound range from approximately 9–12°C (48–54°F) year round, and hypothermia resulting from immersion is always a major consideration.

Shipping traffic and a large recreational boating community require the kayaker to always be alert for other watercraft and to yield the right of way when necessary. The speed of tankers and container

∧ *Seattle's Elliot Bay*, joelrogers.com

ships, as well as cross-sound ferries, is quite deceptive. When in doubt, cross behind all such vessels.

SPECIAL CONSIDERATIONS

The Washington State portion of the Cascadia Marine Trail is inter-twined with urban and rural areas. Sites on the trail are managed by many different landowning agencies, which have particular condi-tions under which their site(s) may be used. Please also keep in mind that this part of the coast has a long and rich Native American history. Although none of the sites listed in this chapter are currently recog-nized as Native American land, they undoubtedly have a history of Native American use. Please treat all the lands you visit with respect but be particularly careful not to disturb any archeological sites. For more information, contact the Governor's Office of Indian Affairs.

Many different agencies and landowners manage the water trail sites, and each has their own fees and policies (the trail no longer uses a permit system). The majority of Cascadia Marine Trail campsites are managed by Washington State Parks and Recreation, where the standard primitive campsite fee is $10 per group up to a total of 6 persons per night. Be sure to carry exact change and pay for each night's stay. Also, please be flexible: you will be encountering a trail system that is subject to ongoing changes.

Due to the close proximity of many trail sites to residential areas, fire danger is a very big concern. Most paddlers visit during the summer and early fall months, the driest time in Puget Sound, when fire danger is at its highest. Even where fire containers are provided in a camping area, fires are discouraged. Several sites in the trail were approved based on a "no fire" policy, and these sites will be lost to paddlers if fires are detected. The environmental impacts of fires are another concern in the Puget Sound region. Wood smoke is a serious air and visibility pollutant, and a smoky fire is a very unpleasant experience, especially when campers are located in a confined space.

Most campsites have no water, so carry your own supply.

Most of the beaches and shoreline in Puget Sound are privately owned. Be aware that you should not beach your watercraft wherever you like, but only at known public access areas. Please obey private property signs. Failure to do so may result in landowners becoming hostile to kayakers' use of the Cascadia Marine Trail.

Please follow the guidelines in chapters 1, 10, 13 and 15 regarding the minimum distance to be maintained while observing orcas and other marine mammals.

Finally, share the sites with other users. The WWTA works to preserve public access to Washington State waters, and it relies on kayakers to serve as ambassadors for the sport and to be exemplars of shoreline use.

PUGET SOUND TRIPS (5–9)

Washington State's Cascadia Marine Trail can be travelled in one go, with some very long days between isolated campsites, or explored in part easily on a day, weekend or weeklong venture. Indeed, most trail users are out for the day, with a destination in mind for lunch, and an aptitude and openness to drift with the jellyfish for a while or dip paddles quietly near shore as conditions allow.

As you travel from the more placid and rural southern portion of Puget Sound northward, you'll encounter increasing suburban and urban density on the land. Heavy vessel traffic picks up north of the Tacoma Narrows, as ships move cargo to and from the ports of Tacoma and Seattle and military centres at Bremerton, Everett and Bangor. The pace of life in mid-sound is faster, with ferries, fishing and recreational boats, and sailboats adding to the water ballet. Despite all this traffic, entirely natural inlets and islands still let you find peace only a few miles from the main population centres of the state. Northward to Admiralty Inlet, Whidbey and the San Juan Islands, natural forces again assert their power. Wind, currents, rocks and ships entering and exiting the Strait of Juan de Fuca to Vancouver and Anacortes make for challenging yet rewarding trips. In the summer the very popular San Juan Islands are filled with vacationing people and surrounded by all manner of boats. Try the shoulder seasons in spring and fall for a more rewarding visit, and enjoy the islands with the native and migrating fauna.

Although it is not possible to describe all of the paddling routes available in the sound, the ones listed in this chapter provide a good cross-section of the region and its delights. The trips can be paddled in part or in their entirety depending on the experience level of the paddlers, time available, and weather and water conditions. Tread lightly—and enjoy!

TRIP 5 South Sound

SKILL:	Intermediate to advanced
TIME:	1–3 days
HAZARDS:	Traffic and currents
ACCESS:	Boston Harbor/Olympia/Hammersley Inlet
CHARTS:	18440 · Puget Sound · 1:150,000
	18445 · Puget Sound—Possession Sound to Olympia · 1:80,000
TIDE TABLES:	Island Canoe Puget Sound

Southern Puget Sound offers outstanding paddling experiences year round. Long, placid inlets provide habitat for many varieties of birds; harbour seals and river otters are frequently sighted. Acres and acres of sand dollars can be seen in many places as you glide along the beaches, sending red rock crabs scurrying for cover amidst the kelp. Pickering Passage and Case Inlet offer a terrific circular trip for discovering the wonders of the south sound, with opportunities for further exploration in Budd, Eld, Totten and Hammersley Inlets or eastward through Dana Passage along the Cascadia Marine Trail.

LAUNCHING

Pickering Passage and Case Inlet form one of the most pristine waterways in southern Puget Sound. You can access this part of the sound via many of the state and county parks in the region. One approach is to launch at Boston Harbor, a small community north of the state capital of Olympia at the head of Budd Inlet. Take an exit on Interstate 5 for visiting the state capital (105 or 105B) and proceed north on East Bay Drive NE, which runs along the eastern shore of Budd Inlet and into Boston Harbor Road NE. After about 11 km (7 mi.), turn left into Boston Harbor, where you will find a marina and protected harbour. Parking is limited, so you may want to consider alternative launching points with overnight parking. To the west is the Arcadia boat ramp at the mouth of Hammersley Inlet or Latimer's Landing at the Hartstene Island Bridge; to the east, Zittel's Marina on Johnson Point. These alternative put-ins will obviously affect the distances for this paddle route. You can get maps and additional information on launch trailheads for the Cascadia Marine Trail from the WWTA.

SITES

Paddling the waters of Pickering Passage north to Jarrell Cove State Park, you travel a waterway once explored by Lt. Peter Puget. Along the way you may also want to stop at Hope Island State Park South — now a Cascadia Marine Trail site. The campsite is on the southwest point of the island, or individual tent pads are also available across the cove to the east. The entire island is park forestland with an orchard at the south end where, in autumn, you can pick apples. Deer may greet you here or walk through your camp. Do not feed them or the raccoons; they are living well on the natural vegetation along the

shore and upland. Hiking trails extend around the island; stretch your
legs if you're staying longer than a quick lunch break. If you camp on
Hope Island, take time to circumnavigate the island and admire the
views both underwater and skyward to Mount Rainier. Washington
State Parks has installed kayak racks at this site to minimize the clut-
ter of boats on the shore.

Jarrell Cove State Park To get to Jarrell Cove State Park, continue
north on the west side of Squaxin Island, which is entirely Indian
reservation property, and on up to Hartstene Island. As you cruise the
shoreline, keep an eye out for bald eagles, kingfishers and the many
great blue herons that inhabit the area. If you paddle this route during
the fall, watch for salmon doing acrobatic jumps as they prepare to
move upriver for spawning. After the 16-km (10-mi.) paddle from
Boston Harbor, set up camp at Jarrell Cove and enjoy the showers
available in the main camping area. The site is set back from the
beach. If you're lucky enough to be here during a period of biolumi-
nescence, look over the dock railing at the unrivalled light show
caused by barnacle cilia waving up and down the pilings.

Joemma Beach State Park The next day's travel heads around the top
end of Hartstene Island across Case Inlet and then south to Joemma
Beach State Park. Your route to Joemma Beach can include a stop at
McMicken Island State Park (on Hartstene Island), which makes a
good lunch break where you can get out of your boat, walk around
the island or enjoy the view while you eat. (For the paddler who wants
to explore more of Case Inlet, turn your boat north to Stretch Point
State Park or Vaughn Bay.)

After paddling about 13 km (8 mi.) south from Jarrell Cove, you
can pull your boat onto the smooth stones of Joemma Beach. The
water trail site is up the hill, just above and to the left of the group picnic shelter. Even though it is a bit of a hike to make camp, the sunset
views from your tent will be worth the effort. For years this park was
an undiscovered gem, but with many improvements and the construction of a boat dock, you will likely have to share the pleasures.

As your tour of the south sound winds down, the final leg of the
trip takes you through Dana Passage to Boston Harbor. Consult the
local tide tables and current guide to determine the best time to pad-

dle this narrow channel. If you are starting out from Joemma Beach on an ebb tide, stay well to the north before rounding the southern end of Hartstene Island, or you may be in for a long, hard paddle to get back to your car. Enjoy the scenic, isolated beaches on the southeast end of Hartstene Island, cruising past into Dana Passage. If you have timed it right, the current will whisk you back to Boston Harbor and your vehicle.

TRIP 6 Mid Sound

SKILL:	Intermediate to advanced
TIME:	1–3 days
HAZARDS:	Traffic and currents
ACCESS:	Kitsap Peninsula/Vashon or Bainbridge Island
CHARTS:	18440 · Puget Sound · 1:150,000
	18445 · Puget Sound—Possession Sound to Olympia · 1:80,000
	18449 · Puget Sound—Seattle to Bremerton · 1:25,000
TIDE TABLES:	Island Canoe Puget Sound

Located within sight of the towering buildings of Seattle, the mid-sound still offers the paddler a wilderness experience. Blake Island remains a jewel of central Puget Sound, an entire island park where deer and eagles can be seen with regularity—a great spot for your first night out. For paddlers looking for a few more days of adventure, nearby Vashon Island has some great campsites at Wingehaven and Lisabeula.

LAUNCHING

To include Blake Island in a tour of Puget Sound, there are numerous launch sites on the west side of the sound. If you are approaching the area from the Seattle side of Puget Sound, ferries from Fauntleroy, Seattle and Edmonds will take you to various launch sites. Blake Island is a short paddle from Southworth, the Manchester boat ramp or from the state parks on Rich Passage—Manchester and Fort Ward—which also have Cascadia Marine Trail sites. Please note that to camp at the following Cascadia Marine Trail sites, you must arrive by water (*not* vehicle).

SITES

Blake Island State Park The water trail site on Blake Island is on the northwest point of the island and offers excellent views northward and a spectacular nighttime view of the Space Needle and Seattle's skyline. If your schedule allows for a one-night stay at Blake, stop and enjoy the deer and other wildlife. Experience the Native American culture at Tillicum Village and treat yourself to the catered salmon buffet. Showers are available in the boat harbour and the main camping area. Enjoy a paddle around the island, hike its many trails or enjoy a swim from one of several sandy beaches. The island is a joy to visit at any time, but plan your trip during midweek for a bit more solitude.

Wingehaven and Lisabeula (Vashon Island) With a few more days of paddling available, travel south to Vashon Island and choose either the east or west side. Water trail sites are located at Wingehaven on

v *The west shore of San Juan Island with Mount Baker in the background,* joelrogers.com

the eastern shore and at Lisabeula on the western shore—neither will disappoint you. Go for a circumnavigation of Vashon and see both sites in one trip.

From Blake Island to Wingehaven it is about 8 km (5 mi.). Be sure to yield to any cross-sound ferry traffic as you paddle around the top of Vashon Island. It is about 16 km (10 mi.) down Colvos Passage to reach the camp at Lisabeula. The tide through Colvos Passage will make your trip either a workout or an easy cruise, so check the local tide tables and current guide. Current conditions through Colvos almost always run in a northerly direction, on either a flood or ebb tide. No open fires are allowed at either Wingehaven or Lisabeula.

For paddlers charting a course around Vashon Island, expect at least a 30-km (19-mi.) day between Lisabeula and Wingehaven, and plan for paddling conditions to change at many points along the way, especially as you round Robinson Point on the east end of Maury Island.

TRIP 7 Southern San Juan Islands

SKILL:	Intermediate to advanced
TIME:	1–4 days
HAZARDS:	Traffic and currents
ACCESS:	Anacortes
CHARTS:	18421 · Strait of Juan de Fuca to Strait of Georgia · 1:80,000
	18423 · Bellingham to Everett including San Juan Islands · 1:80,000
	18424 · Bellingham Bay · 1:40,000
	18427 · Anacortes to Skagit Bay · 1:25,000
	18430 · Rosario Strait, Northern Portion · 1:25,000
TIDE TABLES:	Island Canoe San Juan

The San Juan Islands are known far and wide as a paddling paradise. Unfortunately, access to the waters of the San Juans is at a premium with the ever-increasing push of development and the annual summer rush. Don't despair, however, because islands such as Saddlebag, Cypress and Strawberry offer easy access and solace for the silent paddler.

LAUNCHING

The Cap Sante Marina, close to supplies and just off popular Route 20 in Anacortes, gets you in a nautical mood before you launch. This is a busy but well-sheltered marina. From Interstate 5 take the Highway 20 exit west about 24 km (15 mi.) to Anacortes. Go north on Commercial Avenue, which is lined with stores, then east on 11th Avenue. Do not go left on Highway 20 to the ferry terminal for the San Juans; this road takes you out of town. After leaving the hustle and bustle of the docks, you can head by Hat Island or, depending on tidal flow, brush the tip of Guemes Island. From put-in to Saddlebag Island is about 2.8 nautical miles.

SITES

Saddlebag Island The Cascadia Marine Trail site can be found just above the cove on the southern side of Saddlebag. When the wind is out of the south, you may wish to unload in the sheltered cove on the north side and carry your gear to the campsite. Saddlebag is a popular destination for other boaters seeking Dungeness crab, so expect company just about any time of year.

Cruising up the northeast side of Guemes Island for a stop at the Guemes Island County Park will get you started the next morning. This park is a beautiful stopping point for lunch and offers a good chance to check the tide tables and current guide. The county park is another excellent put-in site if Saddlebag Island is not on your itinerary. Note: There is no water at the park. The north end of Guemes Island, at Clark Point, should be watched carefully due to its tiderip areas. If in doubt, wait for slack tide to paddle around. After your break, plot a course towards the Cone Islands and check out the steep, nearly impassable shoreline as you paddle by.

Cypress Island Your second night's destination is Pelican Beach, on the northeast end of Cypress Island. It offers a pebble beach landing, room for up to 10 tents—and no fresh water. The site can be unpredictably busy at times; if so, head to the Cypress Head site about 4 km (2.5 mi.) south, which usually isn't as popular. Watch for the current, back eddies and tiderips off Cypress Head.

Although not all public land, Cypress Island is an incredible place offering extensive hiking and nature activities. It is crisscrossed by old logging roads that now serve as trails, and you can explore shoreline to mountaintop all in the same day. The diverse geography of the island supports equally diverse species of wildlife. You never know what you might see just around the next bend. Inland lakes and marshes attract varieties of bird life that you would not expect to see on an island surrounded by salt water. This island is truly deserving of more than one day if your schedule permits.

Strawberry Island If you have a third night available, try circumnavigating Cypress Island by stopping at Strawberry Island, on its western side. Once again, make sure to read and understand the currents. Timing is crucial if you want to take advantage of the water movement. Strawberry Island is a paddler's type of island. The steep shores and deep, swift currents prevent anchoring by larger boats, with just enough room for kayaks to land in a cove on the south end. Approach the island from the Strawberry Bay side at any time except slack tide to avoid being swept around the end of the island by the current. Terrific views of Rosario Strait can be found from each of the tent sites. No water will be found on this island, so bring what you need. Be sure to place your boats high on the beach, because passing tankers create huge breaking waves.

Returning to Cap Sante from Strawberry Island can either be a short or long trip, depending on the time of day. The current velocity in Guemes Channel can be swift; time it right to go with the flow or sit on the side until it changes. Be especially observant of other boaters as you pass through this area. Weekend traffic of all sizes is heavy during the summer season. Keep to the Guemes Island side of the channel to avoid most of the boat wakes and cross over to Anacortes, rounding Cap Sante, once you are clear of the channel. Safety first at all times in this are.

TRIP 8 Outer San Juan Islands
SKILL: Advanced
TIME: 3–5 days
HAZARDS: Variable weather, traffic and currents

ACCESS: Roche Harbor/San Juan County Park
CHARTS: 18421 · Strait of Juan de Fuca to Strait
                of Georgia · 1:80,000
            18423 · Bellingham to Everett including San Juan
                Islands · 1:80,000
            18431 · Rosario Strait to Cherry Point · 1:25,000
            18432 · Boundary Pass · 1:25,000
            18433 · Haro Strait—Middle Bank to Stuart Island ·
                1:25,000
            18434 · San Juan Channel · 1:25,000
TIDE TABLES: Island Canoe San Juan

The northwestern edge of the San Juans offers paddlers an incredible array of wildlife and scenery. Miles of rugged, undeveloped shorelines along Haro Strait provide habitat for a multitude of marine birds and mammals, including orca whales. Although this is a great environment for marine life, it is not one to be taken lightly by the paddler. The outer San Juans are for experienced paddlers who are capable of reading tide tables and current guides and are able to respond to the variable weather and water conditions likely to be encountered. Currents in Spieden and President Channels can be treacherous, at times exceeding 4 knots, and should be factored into your trip planning.

LAUNCHING

The logical put-ins for paddling this route are Roche Harbor or San Juan County Park on San Juan Island. To get to Roche Harbor or San Juan County Park, take a Washington State ferry from Anacortes to Friday Harbor. Check out the sailing schedule well in advance of your arrival and allow lots of time if you are attempting to do this trip on a summer weekend. Ferry traffic is very heavy on Fridays westbound and Sundays eastbound.

After reaching Friday Harbor, drive about 17 km (10.5 mi.) to Roche Harbor or about 22.5 km (14 mi.) to San Juan County Park. Friday Harbor is a little tricky; once you leave the ferry, go west on Spring Street for two blocks, turn right onto Second Street and travel three blocks, then turn left on Guard. Go one more block and turn right on Tucker at the stop sign. Bear to the left at an upcoming Y in the road. Now you are on Roche Harbor Road. Follow this road for the next 16 km (10 mi.) to Roche Harbor Resort. If you choose to put in at San Juan County Park, turn left after 13.5 km (8.5 mi.) onto West Valley Road and follow the signs.

These two sites offer the magic combination so hard to find on San Juan—overnight parking and launching. Deciding on which launch site to use is a matter of economics and distance. Roche Harbor Resort charges $5 per day per vehicle to park and $7 per kayak to launch, including the return use of the boat ramp. San Juan County Park rates vary with the season. The parking fee is $6 per day during the summer and less during the winter, but there is no launching fee. Launching at San Juan Park adds around 8 km (5 mi.) to the distance to Stuart Island, so plan accordingly.

SITES

Stuart Island State Park From Roche Harbor, paddle 1.6 km (1 mi.) northwest to Posey Island (described later in the trip). Then cross the 8.4 km (5.5 mi.) from Posey Island to the first night's campsite on Stuart Island. This region lies in the Vancouver Island rain shadow; you may notice the area is quite dry and even supports cactus, which is how the Cactus Islands, north of Spieden Island, got their name. Spieden even became an African game farm for a short period as entrepreneurs attempted to take advantage of the arid environment. With several of the smaller islands in the area designated as wildlife sanctuaries, there are opportunities to observe a variety of marine birds. Paddlers must remember that landing on these islands is prohibited due to the sensitive nature of local nesting activities. Watch and enjoy from a distance. Unfortunately, landing is also prohibited on Spieden Island because most of the shoreline is privately owned.

As you enter Reid Harbor on the southeast end of Stuart Island make your way to the head of the bay, where the water trail site can be found. There are several campsites in this area, so watch for the water trail sign. Many activities abound on Stuart Island. Explore the beaches and tide pools at low tide or try your luck with fishing. If you want some time away from the water, numerous trails and roads on the island can keep you busy exploring the area's history. For an extended hike, tour out to the Turn Point lighthouse for some spectacular views of Haro Strait.

For the next day's paddle, you will probably want to get an early start to avoid any afternoon wind, but check the current guide to determine that a sunup departure will have the water going in the right direction through President Channel. First, tour back through the Cactus Islands and cross over to the stark rocks off Point Disney. President Channel takes you north to Orcas Island, past Waldron Island to Point Doughty, about 18.5 km (11.5 mi.). Watch for bald eagles soaring overhead as you proceed northerly through President Channel. If you time the current correctly, the paddling will verge on being effortless.

Point Doughty (Orcas Island) Point Doughty at the northwest corner of Orcas Island is especially suited for kayaks and small, beachable craft, whereas its currents and lack of anchorage provide little protection for larger boats. The campsite does require a bit of an uphill climb, but the spectacular views westward to Boundary Pass make it all worthwhile. The point is not accessible by road, which usually provides the visitor with a somewhat secluded feeling. There are only a few tent sites, so large groups should avoid camping here. Land at the small beach on the south side of the point and be careful of the tiderips on nearby rocks and shoals. There is no fresh water, and the forest is closed to the public because the site is located within a Natural Area Preserve.

Posey Island State Park At this juncture in your trip, you have a few options depending on your schedule. It is about 19 km (12 mi.) to return directly to Roche Harbor; for those who put in at San Juan County Park, it is a long day of about 27 km (17 mi.). If you are destined for San Juan park, consider an overnight stop on Posey Island to make the journey a bit more manageable. Posey Island is off the northwest corner of San Juan Island, about 1.6 km (1 mi.) from Roche Harbor. The entire island is a designated marine trail campsite; however, there are 2 established campsites that should be used and a limit of 16 people per night. You cannot "hold" campsites for others, and reservations are currently not possible. The site is often crowded and has no source of fresh water.

Jones Island State Park If your trip allows for another day of paddling, plan for a sideline excursion to Jones Island State Park, located .8 km (.5 mi.) off the southwest corner of Orcas Island. You can then return to Roche Harbor or San Juan County Park the following day, with a much shorter distance to cover. Try to catch the President Channel "express" on its southbound trip, but watch for the eddy lines and waves that form as the water pushes out on the ebb tide. Watch for seals; you may even see some Dall's porpoise around Spring Passage.

Jones Island offers an excellent location for exploring the nooks and crannies of the many smaller islands nearby. The marine trail site on Jones is on the west side of the island. Guard your food and gear bags: the raccoons on the island are very curious and may decide that what is yours is theirs. Watch for the resident black-tailed deer as you explore the trails around the island. For a nice afternoon or evening paddle, tour the Wasp Group for a dip into an area rich in San Juan Island history.

As your paddling adventure comes to a close, you may be tempted to drift off with reflections of the past few days—but stay alert. This area of the San Juan Islands can surprise you at any time. Your last day of paddling should allow plenty of time to return to your vehicle, load up and make one of the afternoon ferries. Even with the ferry schedule in mind, don't miss out on the opportunity to carefully enjoy the remaining hours on the water, the wonderful scenery and the magnificent marine life of this special area.

TRIP 9 Metropolitan Seattle

SKILL:	Beginner to advanced
TIME:	Day trip
HAZARDS:	Traffic
ACCESS:	Numerous public launch sites
CHART:	18447 · Lake Washington · 1:25,000

Paddling within sight of downtown Seattle on fresh water may not be a wilderness experience. Just don't tell the occasional bald eagle or beaver you spot. The Lakes-To-Locks Water Trail, opened in 2000, makes possible trips from near the base of the Issaquah Alps east of Seattle. It allows paddlers to go from neighbourhood to shipyard, city park to spawning stream, and through the Ballard Locks to salt water and the Cascadia Marine Trail.

In the Lake Union vicinity, blocks north of downtown Seattle, head ashore for some of Ivar's take-out clam chowder, for the haute cuisine vegetarian cooking at Café Ambrosia or for any other food that may tempt you. Nearby, at the south end of Lake Union, the Center for Wooden Boats is a treat for all with boats to row and sail; it offers displays and special events. For shipbuilding and fishing aficionados, travel west through Ship Canal, or go east for houseboats, the University of Washington, and winding channels around the Washington Park Arboretum and Foster Island park.

Along Lake Washington the estates of millionaires and billionaires vie for attention with natural treasures such as the Mercer Slough and Seward Park; downtowns and marshes lie just a few minutes away from each other. Juxtapositions abound: you can dine on

v *Alki Point light and Mount Rainier, West Seattle,* joelrogers.com

fish tacos just yards from a fish hatchery or bird-watch under bridges carrying rush-hour traffic. Whether you have just a few hours or days to explore, you'll find plenty of interesting surprises.

Many streets end at the shoreline, where waterways, boat ramps, steps and beaches are a few of the possible launching sites for the Lakes-To-Locks Water Trail. There are kayak rental locations at Lake Sammamish, the Sammamish River, Lake Washington, Portage Bay and Lake Union, making it easy for travellers and locals alike to get on the water. In the Seattle area most boating is centred around these rental facilities; at times these street ends are filled to capacity with kayaks and canoes while paddlers fuel up or visit waterfront attractions.

We have included details for a trip in the Lake Union/Portage Bay area. For information on additional launch sites, visit WWTA's Web site or call and ask for the recently published Lakes-To-Locks map.

LAUNCHING

If you would like to explore the Lake Union/Portage Bay area and are approaching Seattle from the south on the Interstate 5, take exit 169, NE 45th Street, the University of Washington exit. Turn right on 45th and go straight until the intersection with Roosevelt Way. If you are approaching from the north, take the same I-5 exit (169) and turn left onto NE 45th Street and proceed to Roosevelt Way.

Turn right onto Roosevelt Way and travel three blocks. Take another right on NE 42nd Street followed by a left onto 7th Avenue NE. Travel to the stop sign, bearing to the right. Turn left onto 6th Avenue NE. Go underneath an overpass and turn right at the stop sign onto NE Northlake Way. After a couple of blocks you will see the sign for Waterway #15 Public Access and the narrow beach from which you can launch.

An alternative put-in site is just east of Waterway #15. Proceed eastbound on Northlake Way from the Waterway #15 site, turning right on NE Boat Street. Proceed to the intersection with Brooklyn Avenue NE, where there is a small public access ramp.

SITES

This paddle is very popular during the summer and gives you the opportunity to view urban life in a multitude of forms from the water.

Observe lakeshore living aboard the many houseboats in Lake Union or paddle down through Ship Canal into Fisherman's Terminal in Ballard to watch the fishing fleet that calls Seattle home. A growing number of businesses and restaurants have floats and docks that boaters can tie up to while visiting their establishment; look for these and plan to stop for lunch or dinner. Paddle quietly in the marsh areas of the Washington Park Arboretum (known locally as the Seattle Arboretum) to see the diverse bird life that resides there. Continue on via Portage Bay and the Montlake Cut into Lake Washington, or arrange a car shuttle and paddle through the Hiram M. Chittenden (Ballard) Locks out to Shilshole Marina and Golden Gardens. Whichever way you decide to paddle, there will be plenty to see and talk about as you cruise along the historic waterways of Seattle.

ADDITIONAL ROUTES

Heading north Close to Interstate 5 near Everett, you can combine fresh and salt water paddling along the Snohomish River Estuary Water Trail, a route set aside specifically for kayaks and canoes. Visit Jetty Island in Puget Sound or Otter Island on Steamboat Slough.

For those interested in travelling north into the Gulf Islands of British Columbia, your best bet is to cross from Stuart Island State Park to Isle-de-Lis Provincial Marine Park. Watch for ships and be sure to check in with Canada Customs when you arrive (tel.: 1-888-226-7277).

Heading south Willapa Bay, which is located in the southwest corner of Washington State, is a premier estuary experience. The area features sandy beaches, coastal pine forests, dune grasslands and camping in the Willapa National Wildlife Refuge on Long Island.

You can also check out the Lower Columbia River Water Trail discussed in chapter 2.

THE GULF ISLANDS

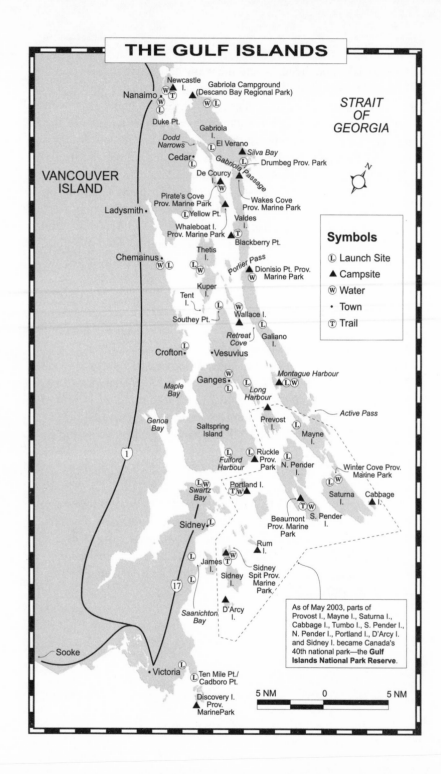

Nanaimo
Newcastle ▲ I.
Ⓦ Ⓣ
Ⓦ Ⓛ
Duke Pt.

Gabriola Campground
(Descano Bay Regional Park)
Ⓦ Ⓛ

*STRAIT
OF
GEORGIA*

Gabriola
I.
*Dodd
Narrows*
Ⓛ El Verano
Cedar•
Ⓛ
De Courcy
I.
Ⓦ

▲ Silva Bay
Ⓛ — Drumbeg Prov. Park
Gabriola Passage

Pirate's Cove
Prov. Marine Park
Ⓛ Yellow Pt.
▲
Wakes Cove
Prov. Marine Park
Whaleboat I.
Prov. Marine Park
Valdes
I.
▲ Ⓣ
Blackberry Pt.

Ladysmith •

Chemainus •
Ⓦ Ⓛ
Thetis
I.
Ⓛ Ⓦ
Portier Pass
▲ Dionisio Pt. Prov.
Ⓦ Marine Park

Kuper
I.
Tent
I.
Ⓛ
Southey Pt.
Ⓦ Wallace I.
▲
*Retreat
Cove*
Galiano
I.

Crofton•
Ⓛ
• Vesuvius

*Maple
Bay*

Ganges•
Ⓦ
Ⓛ
*Long
Harbour*
Montague Harbour
▲Ⓛ Ⓦ

▲
Active Pass

*Genoa
Bay*
Saltspring
Island
Prevost
I.
Ⓛ
Mayne
I.

Ⓛ Ⓦ Ruckle
▲ Prov.
Park
*Fulford
Harbour*
Ⓛ
N. Pender
I.
Winter Cove Prov.
Marine Park
Ⓛ Ⓦ
Saturna
I.
Cabbage
I. ◣

Ⓛ Ⓦ
*Swartz
Bay*
Portland I.
Ⓣ▲▲
▲
Ⓣ Ⓦ
Beaumont
Prov. Marine
Park
S. Pender
I.

Sidney •
Ⓛ

Ⓛ
James Ⓣ
I.
Ⓦ ▲ Rum
▲ I.
Sidney
I.
Sidney
Spit Prov.
Marine
Park
Ⓛ

Ⓛ
17
*Saanichton
Bay*
▲ D'Arcy
I.

Sooke

• Victoria
Ⓛ
Ⓛ Ten Mile Pt./
Cadboro Pt.

▲ Discovery I.
Prov.
MarinePark

1

Symbols

Ⓛ Launch Site
▲ Campsite
Ⓦ Water
• Town
Ⓣ Trail

N

As of May 2003, parts of
Provost I., Mayne I., Saturna I.,
Cabbage I., Tumbo I., S. Pender I.,
N. Pender I., Portland I., D'Arcy
I. and Sidney I. became Canada's
40th national park—the **Gulf
Islands National Park Reserve.**

5 NM   0   5 NM

VANCOUVER
ISLAND

4

The Gulf Islands

Alan Wilson

Carved from sandstone and marked by twisting, red-trunked arbutus, the Gulf Islands of southern British Columbia offer paddlers of all ages and abilities endless opportunities for exploration. They are a kayaker's paradise, with sheltered waters, infrequent summer rain, short distances between sites and easy access to services. Homes and cabins are tucked among the trees, provincial marine parks dot the shorelines—the lifestyle is rural and the pace a bit slow. There is no better place to take a quick break from urban life.

BACKGROUND
The Strait of Georgia is like a large inland sea, about 220 km (136 mi.) long, protected from the Pacific Ocean by the great length of Vancouver Island. Captain Vancouver first referred to the strait as the "Gulf of Georgia," which is why the islands here are called the Gulf Islands. Although each island has unique characteristics, they all offer a break from urban life—for a week or a weekend—with a pleasant ferry ride from Vancouver or Victoria. Saltspring is the largest of the lot, with a population of about 10,000. Its town of Ganges is considered the business centre of the south islands. The next largest

in population is Gabriola Island, with almost 5,000 people. Galiano, North and South Pender, Mayne and Saturna collectively house more than 5,000 residents.

All the islands are in the lee of the Vancouver Island Ranges and subsequently receive very little rain in the summer. The ensuing mild weather has attracted increasing residents over the years, creating development pressures and, in the opinion of some, eroding the quiet, rural lifestyle. But there is still an abundance of natural life, particularly in the waters and shores of the islands, with an estimated 3,000 species of plant and animal life. There are hundreds of seaweed and fish species, along with invertebrates such as octopus, starfish, oysters and clams, and large marine mammals such as seals, sea lions, river otters and porpoises. More than a hundred species of bird life, including bald eagles, great blue herons, ospreys, gulls, cormorants and a wide array of ducks, inhabit the islands year round.

Due to this abundance of wildlife and the sheltered conditions, people have been dipping their paddles into these waters for well over 5,000 years. Many shell middens can be seen throughout the islands, evidence of thousands of years of use, and native communities still exist in a number of traditional areas. Paddlers who are tempted to visit native lands should obtain prior permission from the Lyackson Band (Valdes Island), the Penelakut Band (Tent Island) or the Tsawout Band (Saturna Island).

In geologic terms, the Gulf Islands are fairly uniform, sharing a northwest to southeast orientation. Largely sandstone, with a thin soil layer and frequent outcrops of bedrock, their shores are often eroded in bizarre, picturesque shapes. Despite this rocky nature, and past and present logging, there is still considerable forest cover. To many, there is no sweeter moment than watching the islands' magnificent firs and twisting arbutus, perched on the sea-carved sandstone, glimmering in the setting sun. It is an image that will keep paddlers returning for generations to come.

GULF ISLANDS NATIONAL PARK RESERVE

The long-awaited Gulf Islands National Park Reserve was announced in May 2003. The park reserve consists of properties on 16 islands, plus numerous small islets and reef areas in the southern Gulf Islands, covering 26 sq km (10 sq. mi.) of the southern Strait of Georgia.

∧ *Blackberry Point, Valdes Island,* PETER MCGEE

Once full jurisdiction over the provincial lands is transferred to Parks Canada, undesignated camping on former provincial Crown lands will be reviewed. This will help park managers determine if some of the more fragile areas will require camping restrictions or the development of designated campsites rather than uncontrolled camping. This initial review should take place during the development of interim management guidelines for the park during its first year of operation. Kayakers are encouraged to participate in the public consultation process to make their views known, and to share their knowledge about kayaking routes with park managers.

These Crown lands include the small islands off Sidney such as Dock, Greig, Reay, Imrie and the Little Group; Isabella off Saltspring; the Channel Islets off Ganges; Red Islets, Bright Islets and Hawkins Island off Prevost Island; Georgeson, the Belle Chain, Pine and Java off Saturna; and Blunden off South Pender.

All existing provincial park campsites incorporated into the national park reserve will continue their current status for the next 4 to 5 years until a full management plan for the national park reserve is in place, with fees the same as those charged by BC Parks. The provincial parks being transferred are McDonald, Isle-de-Lis, D'Arcy Island, Beaumont, Princess Margaret, Prior Centennial, Winter Cove, Cabbage Island and Sidney Spit.

For more information on the new national park reserve, contact Parks Canada at (250) 654-4000 or gulfislands@pc.gc.ca.

Parks Canada has also begun to work on a feasibility study on a National Marine Conservation Area (NMCA) in the southern Strait of Georgia. This would complement and enhance the national park—which has primarily a terrestrial focus—by giving marine areas some level of protection. The NMCA study area extends from the Canada/U.S. border up to the north end of Gabriola Island and will likely include pockets of protected areas, for example, possible no-fishing zones to help conserve rockfish and other marine species.

GETTING THERE

By water Access to the southern Gulf Islands is provided by B.C. Ferries from the Tsawwassen terminal, 30 km (19 mi.) south of Vancouver, or from Swartz Bay, 32 km (20 mi.) north of Victoria, on Vancouver Island. To reach the north end of the Gulf Islands chain, take B.C. Ferries from Horseshoe Bay, 17 km (11 mi.) north of Vancouver, to Departure Bay in Nanaimo. There are also smaller ferry terminals for short trips to various Gulf Islands from Vancouver Island: Nanaimo for Gabriola Island, Chemainus for Thetis Island and Crofton for Saltspring Island. The southern Gulf Islands also have inter-island ferries that call at Saltspring, Pender, Galiano, Saturna and Mayne.

All ferries take vehicles, bikes and passengers. Kayak walk-ons are usually possible. Most terminals have potential launch sites nearby, although you are advised to check with local kayak operators for specific information or rentals. Overloads and waits are very common on holiday weekends and during the summer, so give yourself a bit of extra time. If you are taking a vehicle from the Tsawwassen terminal directly to the Gulf Islands, reservations are recommended. Call B.C. Ferries for information on routes, rates, schedules and reservations, or check www.bcferries.com.

In Washington State you can catch ferries from Anacortes and Port Angeles to Sidney and Victoria, respectively, or you can drive across the border and head to the Tsawwassen ferry terminal.

By land There are no bridges to the Gulf Islands and the islanders intend to keep it that way. It is possible, however, to reach the Gulf Islands by launching directly from Vancouver Island at Swartz Bay, Nanaimo and a number of points in between. Detailed launch information is provided later in the chapter. Occasionally people will paddle from the British Columbia mainland to the Gulf Islands; however, this crossing is not recommended due to the variable weather conditions and heavy vessel traffic.

By air Several float plane operations serve the islands, including Harbour Air and Tofino Air.

WEATHER AND HAZARDS

The Gulf Islands lie in the shelter of Vancouver Island and are well known for their low rainfall and calm conditions. Although the paddling season is generally considered to be May through September, those who live in the Gulf Islands take advantage of the mild climate to paddle year round.

The close proximity of land, short crossings and nearby services make for generally safe paddling. The main exceptions to this rule are the tidal passes, where water can run up to 8 knots as it rushes in and out of the Strait of Georgia. These include Gabriola Pass, Porlier Pass, Active Pass and any of the small passages that open into the strait. For information within the Gulf Islands, use the Fulford Harbour tide table. If you are travelling on the Strait of Georgia side of the islands, use the Point Atkinson table.

In addition to the ever-present fleet of B.C. Ferries, there is considerable small boat traffic in the summer, especially on long weekends. Remember that large objects appear to be moving more slowly than they really are and that large vessels have a very limited ability to manoeuvre. Due to the low visibility of kayaks, it is advisable to paddle defensively. Some paddlers mount a bicycle-type flag from a short mast at the stern of their boat to enhance their visibility.

SPECIAL CONSIDERATIONS

Paddlers are strongly discouraged, and at many sites prohibited, from having fires. The area is simply too dry during the summer and the risk too great.

As always, paddlers must take note of Indian Reserves (IR on charts) and contact the respective bands for permission to visit these territories. The Gulf Islands are largely privately owned, so try not to alienate landowners when stopping to rest on an attractive beach or point of land. Keep within the high tide zone and do not leave litter.

Kayakers are asked to refrain from camping on anything other than established campsites. Although many of the small islets look inviting, they are not able to withstand heavy use and often show noticeable signs of impact by the end of the summer. For their environmental well-being, please respect this voluntary closure.

Please don't paddle too close to cormorant colonies, especially during nesting season, when your approach can scare off adults and expose their young to danger. The same applies to seal haul-outs. Seals seem particularly sensitive to kayakers and can be spooked by your approach. Use your binoculars and try to stay at least 100 m (330 ft.) away. Of course, if you are being followed there isn't much you can do but enjoy.

It is best not to harvest shellfish given the uncertainty over red tide and paralytic shellfish poisoning (see chapter 1). Also be aware of areas leased for commercial shellfish growing; these are usually marked by shellfish lease signs.

TRIP 10   The Gulf Island Chain

SKILL:	Beginner to advanced
TIME:	1–10 days
HAZARDS:	Traffic and currents
ACCESS:	Numerous sites on Vancouver Island and the Gulf Islands
CHARTS:	3313 · Gulf Islands · Various scales
	3440 · Race Rocks to D'Arcy Island · 1:40,000
	3441 · Haro Strait, Boundary Pass and Satellite Channel · 1:40,000
	3442 · North Pender to Thetis Island · 1:40,000
	3443 · Thetis Island to Nanaimo · 1:40,000
	3462 · Juan de Fuca Strait to Strait of Georgia · 1:80,000
	3463 · Strait of Georgia, Southern Portion · 1:80,000
	3513 · Strait of Georgia, Northern Portion · 1:80,000
	3527 · Baynes Sound · 1:40,000
TIDE BOOK:	Canadian Tides and Current Tables, Vol. 5

Unlike the rest of this guidebook, there is no single excursion described in this chapter. The following trip is written in a south to north fashion—beginning on Vancouver Island near Swartz Bay and ending in Nanaimo—but multiple launching sites have been listed to allow you to plan an excursion suited to your time frame and abilities. Denman and Hornby Islands are briefly discussed at the end of the chapter.

Day trips, weekend excursions and weeklong explorations are all possible. Paddlers who wish to experience the entire chain of Gulf Islands can start their trip near Victoria or Sidney and paddle north to Nanaimo (or the reverse) over a period of 7 days or so. If time is a concern, a number of great 2–3-day paddling loops can be accessed from any of the launch sites listed in this chapter. Especially popular are the routes that launch from Sidney, Swartz Bay and Nanaimo. If you are a little unsure of your paddling skills, you may want to pick a central location, camp at a provincial park or stay at one of the many conveniently located B&Bs throughout the islands, and make day trips to the surrounding sites.

If you are having trouble planning a trip, call a local operator. Not only do they provide rentals, courses and instruction, some also offer shuttle service to and from ferry terminals.

LAUNCHING
The following three sites are common places to start a Gulf Islands exploration.

Swartz Bay You can launch kayaks by the government wharf near the ferry terminal at Swartz Bay on Vancouver Island; this gives you the option of leaving your vehicle behind and walking onto the ferry (with kayak wheels) at the mainland Tsawwassen terminal. At Swartz Bay, walk your boat through the loading area to the entrance of the employee parking lot. The road access for the government wharf can be seen from the upper left of this lot. Once at the wharf, you can launch from the beach to the left (facing the water). The distance from the ferry to this launch site is about 500 m (547 yd.).

If you are driving to Swartz Bay from Victoria, follow the signs to the passenger pick-up area at the Swartz Bay terminal. Continue beyond the final pick-up turnoff and take the next left to reach the government wharf. You can leave your car in a nearby lot. Be aware, however, that these lots are often full during the summer months.

Saltspring Island There are several good launches on Saltspring Island. At Long Harbour, after getting off the ferry from Tsawwassen, you can launch from the small park area to the southeast of the terminal or from the beach at Quebec Drive. You can also drive into the main town of Ganges and launch from the boat ramp in Centennial Park. Other launches are Drummond Park and Beddis Beach off Beddis Road (both excellent beach launches) or Ruckle Provincial Park, 10 km (6.2 mi.) from Fulford Harbour (a short carry down a hill that can be slippery when wet). It is possible to launch at Fulford but the beach is rough. Southey Point, at the north end of Saltspring, has an excellent beach launch, and there is another nearby via a trail off Arbutus Road. There is also a ramp .8 km (.5 mi.) north of the Fernwood dock on the northeast side of the island. At most of these sites, there is limited roadside parking. Please give consideration to the people who live in these areas.

Nanaimo The public boat ramp adjacent to the Departure Bay ferry terminal is the easiest launch point in Nanaimo, providing access to Newcastle Marine Park (immediately across a narrow channel) and to the chain of Gulf Islands running southward, beginning with Gabriola. The ramp is right beside the now defunct Sealand Public Market—the building and signage are still in place to help guide you to the boat ramp (on the north side). If you are driving off the ferry, turn left at the first set of lights as you leave the terminal, then make a quick right into the parking lot of the former market. If you walk your kayak (with a cart) onto the ferry at Horseshoe Bay, you will need to roll it approximately 500 m (547 yd.) out of the Departure Bay terminal (follow the cars that have just picked up foot passengers) and across the road to reach the public market ramp.

The new ferry terminal at Duke Point, for travellers arriving from Tsawwassen, provides kayakers with a poor launching opportunity. Although B.C. Ferries won't allow launching at the terminal itself, a kilometre or so away is a small park with flat sandstone ledges at the water's edge. If possible, you are much better off launching at the public market site in Nanaimo (above), which requires you to take the Horseshoe Bay to Departure Bay ferry rather than the Tsawwassen to Duke Point run. If you do choose to arrive by vehicle at the Duke Point terminal, you can access a nearby boat ramp at Cedar-by-the-Sea via Holden Corso or Barnes Roads from the Duke Point Highway.

SITES

Most of the sites listed below are managed by BC Parks, and the camping fees change from year to year. Many will have facilities for the deposit of a self-registered camping fee, and you should be fine if you plan on approximately $10 per night and bring adequate change. In addition, due to the creation of the Gulf Islands National Park Reserve, a number of campgrounds (including those on Prevost and Pender) will be managed by Parks Canada, and you may need to contact them for the latest fee information.

Discovery Island East of Victoria Harbour at the junction of Juan de Fuca and Haro Straits sits the 61-ha (151-a.) Discovery Island Provincial Marine Park, 3.2 km (2 mi.) from Oak Bay Marina. With toilets, trails and room for about 12 campsites, Discovery Island offers spectacular views of the Olympic Peninsula. Approach with caution, however, as there are many rocks and islets and the currents in Haro Strait and Baynes Channel can be extremely strong (consult the tables for Race Passage). Also note that the northern portion of Discovery Island, Chatham Island and some of the smaller islets are Indian Reserve lands and should not be entered without permission. Open fires are not permitted, and there is a self-registered camping fee.

Closest launches: Oak Bay ramp off Beach Drive; Cattle Point ramp off Beach Drive (ample parking); and Ten Mile Point's Smuggler's Cove on McAnally Road (park on roadside, launch from shore). All these launch sites are in or near Victoria.

D'Arcy Island Provincial Marine Park Established in 1961, D'Arcy Island Provincial Marine Park is a small, undeveloped island lying to the south of Sidney Island. It was a leper colony from 1896 to 1921, and ruins of the facilities are still visible. There are about 12 campsites, a beach landing and a pit toilet though no water. Little D'Arcy Island to the east is private property so please do not intrude. Open fires are not permitted, and there is a self-registered camping fee.

Closest launches: Island View Beach ramp off Island View Road, 5.5 km (3.4 mi.) from D'Arcy Island; public wharf in Saanichton Bay off James Island Road; and public beach access off Rothsay Road in Sidney.

Sidney Spit Provincial Marine Park Sidney Island, 4 km (2.5 mi.) off Sidney, has a very long sand bar, the main attraction to Sidney Spit Provincial Marine Park. Although Sidney Spit is a busy anchorage for boaters, the trail around the salt water lagoon and along the long log-strewn beach to the southeast sees much less use. A large, level, grassy camping area can be found at the old dock partway into the lagoon, too silted up to be used by pleasure craft though paddleable at higher tides. You will enjoy drifting along the current scant inches above eel grass, crab and other marine creatures. Toilets and water are available. Camp fees are collected by the park hosts. Walk-on ferry service is available from Sidney.

Closest launches: Sidney or Saanichton launches (see D'Arcy Island launches, above).

Isle-de-Lis Provincial Marine Park (Rum Island) Five kilometres (3 mi.) from Sidney is the 4.4-ha (11-a.) Rum Island known as Isle-de-Lis Provincial Marine Park. Rum Island apparently got its name from rum-running in the Prohibition era, as it borders on Haro Strait—the main shipping channel from the Pacific and site of the U.S.-Canada border. Rum Island was donated for a public park in 1978 with the owner's stipulation that it be called Isle-de-Lis for the wild lilies that grow there.

Rum Island is connected to Gooch Island by a steep gravel beach, the only place to land. Although it used to be hard to find a tent site on this rocky isle, BC Parks has recently installed several platforms. There is a small network of trails, and exploring will reward you with spectacular views to the south, especially of Mount Baker hovering in the distance. Watch for turbulent waters and swift currents off Tom

Point. There are toilets and a self-registered camping fee. There is no fresh water.

Closest launch: Sidney (see D'Arcy Island launches, above).

Princess Margaret Provincial Marine Park (Portland Island) Portland Island lies 4 km (2.5 mi.) to the north of Swartz Bay. The entire island was given to Princess Margaret, sister of Queen Elizabeth, in 1958, but was eventually returned to the people of B.C. and is now the aptly named Princess Margaret Provincial Marine Park. Portland is about 200 ha (494 a.) and well forested. Large ferries pass on either side of the island so be careful of ferry traffic and wash. There are a couple of beaches, each with designated campsites. Cross-island and perimeter trails offer pleasant hiking. Toilets and water are available, and there is a self-registered camping fee.

Closest launch: Beach launch near government wharf at the Swartz Bay ferry terminal.

Ruckle Provincial Park (Saltspring Island) Ruckle Provincial Park at Beaver Point on the south end of Saltspring has eight small coves and bays, miles of shoreline, rocky headlands and camping. It is an enormous site, accessible by land and water and hence quite busy during the summer. If you are arriving by boat, watch the ferry wake and unload quickly. One of the nicest beaches is at the south end of the park in the day-use area. A few bays to the north, you can find a suitable landing spot if you are spending the night. Currently, there is a day-use parking fee of $3. To park overnight you must be a registered camper and this can add up at $14 per night per party of 1 to 4 people.

Closest launches: On Saltspring Island, you can launch from the park itself (although the slope can be slippery), Fulford Harbour, Ganges and Long Harbour; on Vancouver Island, launch from the Swartz Bay ferry terminal.

Beaumont Provincial Marine Park (South Pender Island) Beaumont Provincial Marine Park is located on the west side of South Pender Island in Bedwell Harbour. Bedwell Harbour has a nearby full-service marine/resort that is busy in summer and acts as a Canada Customs office during those months. The two islands of North and South Pender are joined by a bridge over narrow Pender Canal, site of thousands of years of native habitation and extensive middens. There are good trail links on the way to the summit of Mount Norman Regional Park. Water and toilets are available, and a camping fee is collected by the park hosts.

Circumnavigation of South Pender is a nice 14-km (9-mi.) paddle but watch for turbulent waters off the south end, with whirlpools and standing waves when tide and winds oppose. Gowlland Point is a great viewpoint.

Closest launches: The Pender Island ferry terminal at Otter Bay prohibits launching, so your best bet is to drive to Port Washington on North Pender or to launch from Village Bay on Mayne Island.

Winter Cove Provincial Marine Park (Saturna Island) This park on Saturna Island does not allow camping but is worth a visit to watch the waters of the Strait of Georgia rush through narrow Boat Passage at up to 7 knots. Toilets and water are available, and there is a store at the inter-island ferry dock in Lyall Harbour. Fiddlers Cove at the south end of Saturna is on First Nations territory, and anyone wishing to visit should contact the Tsawout Band.

Closest launch: Lyall Harbour ferry terminal wharf on Saturna Island.

Cabbage Island Provincial Marine Park Beyond Boat Passage and out into the Strait of Georgia are Anniversary Island, Cabbage Island Provincial Marine Park and some unnamed islets west of Grainger Point. All but Cabbage Island have rocky landings, and weather conditions on the Strait of Georgia will dictate access. Cabbage Island has toilets, a wonderful sandy beach but no fresh water. There are approximately 6 campsites and a self-registered camping fee.

Closest launch: Cabbage Island is 9.6 km (6 mi.) from Lyall Harbour on Saturna Island.

James Bay (Prevost Island) Prevost Island, lying just off Saltspring Island, is a popular anchorage for boaters due to its long, shallow coves. Until recently it was privately owned, but two properties have been purchased under the joint provincial-federal program, the Pacific Marine Heritage Legacy fund, giving the public legitimate access to the shore. James Bay has a pleasant beach, an abandoned orchard and the potential for hiking trails to Peile Point. It is also only an hour's paddle from James Bay to the Hawkins Islets, a recreation site with rich intertidal life. James Bay can easily accommodate 10–15 tents. There is a toilet and a self-registered camping fee.

Closest launches: Ganges or Long Harbour on Saltspring Island (launch from small park area southeast of ferry terminal), or Montague Harbour on Galiano Island.

Montague Harbour Provincial Marine Park (Galiano Island) Across Trincomali Channel from Prevost and Saltspring Islands is Montague Harbour Provincial Marine Park on Galiano Island, one of the best protected and most popular anchorages in the Gulf Islands. The park has established, well-serviced campsites and a nearby store. It has a nice beach that is busy in summer due to its road access. Toilets and water are available, and a camping fee is collected by the park hosts. To explore the area, launch from the beach or the public wharf. The Ballingal Islets make a nice paddle some 5 km (3 mi.) north of Montague past a number of small private islands. A tradition among many Montague Harbour visitors is a ride to Galiano's Hummingbird Inn. Every evening from the May long weekend until the end of September a bus leaves the pub hourly to pick up campers and boaters who are ready for a pub meal. Keep in mind, there is no overnight parking unless you are a registered camper—$17 per night per party of 1 to 4 people. Day-use parking is $3 up to 11 P.M.

Closest launches: From the ferry terminal at Sturdies Bay, drive to Georgeson Bay Road and onto Montague Harbour Road. Launch from the government wharf near the ferry slip in Montague Harbour. You can also drive directly to the marine park to use the boat ramp; parking is available here.

Wallace Island Provincial Marine Park Wallace Island Provincial Marine Park just north of Montague Harbour is entirely public except for a couple of private homes. It has two coves popular with boaters, but there is limited camping available for paddlers (most sites are at Conover Cove). Chivers Point, a scenic site at the north end, consists of rocky fingers projecting north towards the adjacent Secretary Islands. At higher tides the reef and shallows off the southwest side of Wallace offer landings to a sparsely forested area where some

level spots can be found. A central trail runs down the length of the island, and there is a dock in Conover Cove. Open fires are not permitted. Water is available from a hand pump but should be boiled before
drinking. A camping fee is collected by the park hosts.

Closest launches: Southey Point on Saltspring Island or Retreat
Cove on Galiano Island.

Dionisio Point Provincial Marine Park (Galiano Island) Dionisio
Point Provincial Marine Park is at the north end of Galiano Island, on
the east side of Porlier Pass (wait out extreme currents), with nice
beaches, rocky headlands and rough road accessibility. There is a
hand pump for water and a self-registered camping fee.

Closest launches: A government dock and phone are located at
North Galiano before the entrance to Porlier Pass. You can also cross
over from Southey Point on Saltspring Island.

Tent Island Tent Island at the southern end of Kuper Island is a former provincial park on First Nations territory. The island has reverted
to First Nations control, and anyone wishing to visit is asked to contact the Penelakut Band on Kuper Island. For an interesting paddle,
enter the narrow, dredged canal that separates Thetis and Kuper Islands. Enter via Clam Bay or Telegraph Harbour, but be careful as
the canal is not passable at lowest water. Telegraph Harbour has marinas, toilets, water, a store, phone, pub and restaurant. The Rose Islets,
just to the north, are an ecological reserve with abundant bird life. Do
not go ashore.

Closest launches: Preedy Harbour on Thetis Island, which can be
reached by ferry from Chemainus; and Southey Point on the north
end of Saltspring Island.

Blackberry Point (Valdes Island) For years, the shell beach, large tenting area and beautiful views have made Blackberry Point on Valdes Island the most popular campsite for paddlers in the northern islands.
Although the site is privately owned by forestry giant Weyerhauser, the
B.C. Marine Trail Association secured access to the site in the late
1990s and set up a solar composting outhouse (built with the funds
from the first edition of this book). There has since been some vandalism to the facility but the BCMTA hopes to have it back in service by the

summer of 2004 or replace it with pit toilets. If you are interested in becoming a "volunteer warden," please contact the BCMTA.

Most other landings on Valdes Island are on First Nations territory. Permission may be sought there or by contacting the Lyackson Band in Chemainus on Vancouver Island.

Closest launches: Drumbeg Park or False Narrows on Gabriola Island, about 10 km (6 mi.) away. It is also possible to launch from the Vancouver Island communities of Cedar (a ramp at the end of Fawcett Road) or Yellow Point (the beach at Blue Heron Park), both located 20–25 minutes by car south of Nanaimo.

Whaleboat Island Provincial Marine Park Whaleboat Island is a tiny island on the east side of Whaleboat Pass, the narrows between Ruxton and Pylades Islands. Whaleboat provides anchorage for boaters failing to find space in nearby popular Pirate's Cove. We have also seen paddlers camped on Whaleboat, but very infrequently. The rocky landings are not particularly inviting and there are no facilities. Adjacent to Whaleboat is much larger Ruxton Island, with extensive walking trails accessible from the landing on the south end near Whaleboat Passage.

Closest launches: Drumbeg Park on Gabriola Island's south shores or Cedar or Chemainus on Vancouver Island.

Pirate's Cove Provincial Marine Park (De Courcy Island) Pirate's Cove Provincial Marine Park on De Courcy Island is a popular anchorage, but the south side of the park on Ruxton Pass is less busy and offers a wide beach with spacious camping areas and good walking trails around the adjacent peninsula. Toilets and fresh water are available, and a self-registered camping fee is in effect.

Closest launches: Gabriola Island or Cedar on Vancouver Island, both about 3.2 km (2 mi.) from De Courcy.

Gabriola Island As you continue north you will come across Drumbeg Provincial Park at the south end of Gabriola, on the Strait of Georgia side of Gabriola Passage. (Stay alert: this passage has serious currents.) This is a day-use only park. Even so, it is worth a stop as it has a pleasant beach, trails and toilets. Beyond Drumbeg, among the Flat Top Islands, is Brant Reef, a large seal haul-out so please keep your distance. Protected by the Flat Tops is Silva Bay on Gabriola, a popular yacht harbour with marinas, stores, laundry facilities, a pub and a restaurant.

For kayakers wanting to camp at the south end of Gabriola, your best bet is to head for Page's Marina and Resort next to the Silva Bay marina. They have grassy sites, showers, toilets, water and laundry facilities, and the paddling possibilities in the adjacent islands are lovely. Newly purchased Wakes Cove Provincial Marine Park on the northern tip of Valdes Island faces onto Gabriola Pass and should have camping available in the near future, once BC Parks has established a management plan for the area (due by the summer of 2004).

At the north end of Gabriola (some 16 km/10 mi. from the south end) is Descanso Bay Regional Park (formerly known as Gabriola Campground), a large camping and beach area accessible by kayak, which is not far from the Gabriola ferry terminal. The fee is $15 per tent per night. Coming north, you access this site by paddling through False Narrows or Dodd Narrows and up Northumberland Channel. Be sure to time the currents and watch for boat traffic. Don't forget to check out the weathered cliffs on Gabriola and the sea lions on the log booms off the Harmac pulp mill on the Vancouver Island side of the channel. If you are coming in the other direction, you can reach the campground from Nanaimo by kayak in about 45 minutes (but beware of the Duke Point and Gabriola ferries), or board the Gabriola ferry, take the first left off the ferry and drive about half a mile along Taylor Bay Road.

Closest launch: The public boat ramp adjacent to the Departure Bay ferry terminal offers great access to Gabriola and Newcastle Islands. See page 70 for details.

Newcastle Island Provincial Marine Park Finally, on your northward trip, there is Newcastle Island Provincial Marine Park just off Nanaimo. Newcastle Island is such a popular spot, it has its own passenger-only ferry as well as beaches, campsites, toilets and fresh water. The paddle between Newcastle and the launch site beside the Departure Bay ferry terminal takes only minutes, though be sure to keep your eyes open for ferry, float plane and small boat traffic. Pleasant trails cross the island. Newcastle Island has floats, a concession, a visitor's centre and almost 20 campsites; the camping fee is collected by the park hosts.

ADDITIONAL ROUTES

Heading north If you wish to paddle north from Newcastle, you will be exposed to the conditions of the Strait of Georgia until you reach Nanoose Bay on Vancouver Island. Nanoose is the site of the controversial Canadian Forces maritime base where the U.S. Navy tests ships and nuclear submarines. Maude Island and Southey Islands, off the tip of Nanoose Peninsula, are potential campsites; Winchelsea Island, the operational headquarters of the naval base, is offlimits. North of Nanoose are the sandbanks of Rathtrevor Beach and Parksville. Farther north, ferries depart from French Creek for Lasqueti Island and from Buckley Bay for Denman and Hornby Islands.

Denman and Hornby Islands are known as the undiscovered Gulf Islands. With large sections of unpopulated shoreline, the two islands combine with the protected waters of Baynes Sound to provide a tranquil setting that is ideal for the beginner paddler. Unfortunately, there is not much camping in the area, and overnighting is more or less limited to Fillongley Provincial Park and Sandy Island Provincial Park. Fillongley, located on the south end of Denman, is road accessible and has a designated tenting area. North of Fillongley Park, most of the shoreline is owned by logging companies so there is some potential to access these undeveloped lands. Sandy Island is a beautiful park just off Denman's northern tip that is only accessible by water. It has an outhouse but no fresh water, and camping is random. Helliwell and Tribune Bay Provincial Parks on Hornby are stunning but day-use only. Local operators are extremely helpful and will help you plan a trip to the area. It is worthwhile to call them before you arrive because parking and launching can be a little difficult, particularly on Hornby.

Heading south For those interested in exploring the northern part of Washington State, you can cross from Isle-de-Lis Provincial Marine Park to Stuart Island State Park. Watch for ships and be sure to check in with U.S. Customs when you arrive (tel.: 1-800-562-5943).

IN & AROUND VANCOUVER

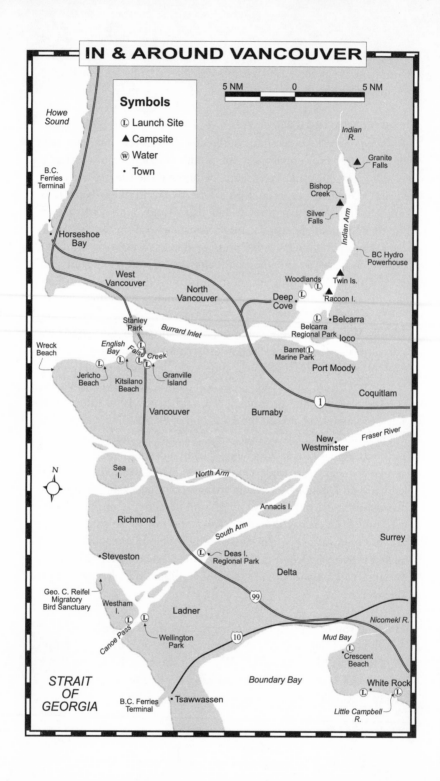

5 NM   0   5 NM

Symbols
- Ⓛ Launch Site
- ▲ Campsite
- Ⓦ Water
- • Town

Howe Sound

B.C. Ferries Terminal

• Horseshoe Bay

West Vancouver

North Vancouver

Stanley Park

Burrard Inlet

English Bay

False Creek

Wreck Beach

Ⓛ Jericho Beach

Ⓛ Kitsilano Beach

ⓁⓁ Granville Island

Vancouver

Burnaby

Indian R.

▲ Granite Falls

▲ Bishop Creek

Silver Falls

Indian Arm

BC Hydro Powerhouse

Woodlands ▲ Twin Is.

Deep Cove Ⓛ ▲ Racoon I.

Ⓛ • Belcarra

Belcarra Regional Park Ioco

Barnet Ⓛ Marine Park

Port Moody

99 1 Coquitlam

New • Westminster

Fraser River

Sea I.

North Arm

Richmond

Annacis I.

South Arm

Surrey

• Steveston

Ⓛ Deas I. Regional Park

Delta

Geo. C. Reifel Migratory Bird Sanctuary

Westham I.

Ⓛ Ⓛ Wellington Park

Ladner

Canoe Pass

99

10

Nicomekl R.

Mud Bay

Ⓛ Crescent Beach

White Rock Ⓛ Ⓛ

B.C. Ferries Terminal

• Tsawwassen

Boundary Bay

Little Campbell R.

STRAIT OF GEORGIA

N

5

In and Around Vancouver

Peter McGee, Catrin Webb
and Howard Zatwarnitski

L iving in Vancouver blesses the paddler with many things. The finest
boats and paddles in the world are made in our own backyard,
and many of the best paddling instructors and outfitters are based
here. Most importantly, we and our visitors have the ocean on our
doorstep, which means we can experience the joy of paddling 365
days a year. This chapter describes just a few of the trips you can take
in and around Vancouver. To find out about additional trips in the
Lower Mainland, consider joining the Sea Kayak Association of B.C.
or another club listed in Useful Contacts.

BACKGROUND
The influence of the Fraser River on the area in and around Vancouver cannot be overstated. Unlike the rest of the mountainous and
rugged B.C. coastline, the Lower Mainland is an area of unusually low
and flat land. Most of the region is actually a delta, formed by the
Fraser River after the last glacial ice sheet melted about 10,000 years
ago. Today the Fraser River basin is one of the largest food reservoirs

on the continent, home to millions of salmon, sturgeon, eulachon and trout; it touches, through an elaborate network of tributaries, over 200 000 square km (124,000 sq. mi.) of the province.

Not surprisingly, the magnificence of the Fraser River and the shelter of glacially sculpted Burrard Inlet did not go unnoticed by the First Nations, and several different peoples flourished in the area. Halq'emeylem is the language spoken by the people of the lower Fraser, and their histories reach back to the beginning of time, when certain individuals were transformed into the river's first salmon and first sturgeon.

Simon Fraser was the first European to experience the cultures of the Fraser River, in 1808. It wasn't until the gold rush of 1858, however, that any substantial immigrant population moved into the area. Even then, the 30,000 miners who came north were a transient folk, and most wintered in Victoria or San Francisco. In an effort to create some stability among the residents, Governor James Douglas introduced a law in 1860 that allowed settlers to claim land not currently "settled" by natives. Unfortunately, this law did not recognize sites that were used seasonally by the First Nations, and thousands of hectares of culturally significant lands were improperly claimed on the assumption they were vacant or abandoned.

Today the Halkomelem peoples are striving for greater self-definition and control over their traditional lands. As you journey in and around Vancouver, you will likely see the Halkomelem communities of the X'muzk'i'um (Musqueam), Tsawwassen and Semiahmoo strategically perched at the entrance of the Fraser River. These communities, as well as those of the Squamish Nation on the north shore and the Tsleil Waututh First Nation of Burrard Inlet, serve as a gateway to the city of Vancouver and remind us of a past that contains many lessons for our future.

WEATHER AND HAZARDS

The weather in and around Vancouver varies drastically due to the region's different geographic environments. From the flat Fraser delta to mountainous Indian Arm, paddlers need to recognize that, though close to a large city, you are ultimately at the mercy of the sea and of highly changeable conditions. Winds, currents and temperature are important considerations wherever you paddle.

Northwesterly winds tend to be dominant during the summer months but these can be strongly influenced by sea breezes, outflow winds from the Fraser Valley and the configuration of mainland inlets. Use care when travelling near the sand and shallows of the Fraser delta, White Rock and Spanish Banks on Vancouver's west side. In addition, be careful travelling near river mouths, particularly when wind and current are opposed.

Finally, be cautious of vessel traffic. In all but the smallest rivers or shallows, you are likely to encounter a number of different boats. Remember, large vessels cannot change course quickly, and you are advised to pick your route on the assumption that other boaters will not be able to see you.

SPECIAL CONSIDERATIONS

As paddlers we often travel in anonymity, but most of the areas in and around Vancouver place us in the company of local residents and other boaters. Please respect private property, be sure to give a wide berth to others while on the water and limit your impacts while on land.

TRIP 11 False Creek

SKILL:	Beginner to advanced
TIME:	2–4 hours
HAZARDS:	Traffic
ACCESS:	Granville Island/Coast Guard Station
CHARTS:	3311 · Sunshine Coast—Vancouver Harbour to Desolation Sound · 1:40,000
	3493 · Vancouver Harbour, Western Portion · 1:10,000
	3481 · Approaches to Vancouver Harbour · 1:25,000
TIDE BOOK:	Vol. 5

Situated in the heart of Vancouver, False Creek is about as urban as you can get without actually being on land. As the former home of the world fair, Expo 86, and the new home of a massive Concord Pacific development, the area has undergone dramatic changes over the years, but the essential qualities that made it a kayak destination have remained: it is easy to access and extremely well protected. Top this off with fantastic city views and you have the ultimate urban escape for the beginner and advanced paddler alike.

LAUNCHING

The most common launch sites for False Creek are the docks on Granville Island. Located under the Granville Street Bridge, Granville Island is home to numerous kayak builders and kayak stores including the Ecomarine Ocean Kayak Centre. Finding a kayak to rent is actually easier than finding a parking space (there is a 3-hour limit on free parking spaces) so if you are planning to rent, it might be worthwhile to park off the island and walk to the docks. If you are bringing your own boats, launch on Granville Island or beside the Coast Guard Station located in Vanier Park, at the northwest end of False Creek. To reach Granville Island, head north on Fir Street and take a right on 2nd Avenue; from there, follow the signs. To reach the Coast Guard Station from downtown, bear right once over the Burrard Bridge, turn right to Cypress, follow the signs to Vancouver Museum and park by Vanier Park. Most of the street parking is by permit, but you should be able to find space in the pay parking areas near the water.

Once on the water, keep an eye out for other boat traffic and stick to the sides of the inlet. Try to limit your crossings. Paddling the entire length of False Creek should not take more than a couple of hours, but you might want to leave a little time to visit the restaurants and stores that dot the shore.

Trip 12 English Bay

SKILL:	Beginner to advanced
TIME:	2–4 hours
HAZARDS:	Traffic and wind
ACCESS:	Jericho Beach/English Bay/Granville Island
CHARTS:	3311 · Sunshine Coast—Vancouver Harbour to Desolation Sound · 1:40,000
	3493 · Vancouver Harbour, Western Portion · 1:10,000
	3481 · Approaches to Vancouver Harbour · 1:25,000
TIDE BOOK:	Vol. 5

Paddling in English Bay quickly gives you a sense of Vancouver's beauty. To the north are the often snow-capped mountains, to the east are the forests of Stanley Park, to the south are the beaches of Kitsilano and Jericho, and to the west lie Pacific Spirit Regional Park and

∧ *Vancouver skyline,* NEIL GREGORY-EAVES

the Strait of Georgia. Watching the setting sun reflect off the city's downtown high-rises as you drift through this idyllic scene is a great way to finish the day.

LAUNCHING
English Bay can be accessed from a variety of launch sites. Jericho Sailing Centre, near the International Youth Hostel at Jericho Beach, is the site farthest west. Head west on 4th Avenue until the road forks; go right onto Discovery Road. Follow Discovery to the water, where you will see the Jericho Sailing Centre, an Ecomarine Ocean Kayak rental booth and a pay parking lot. In the West End, near downtown, you can launch and rent from the Old English Bay Bath House at the foot of Denman Street. You can also access English Bay from Granville Island, located under the Granville Street Bridge at the northern end of Fir Street. See False Creek (above) for details.

Early morning and evening are the best times to paddle in the bay as a fair-weather westerly kicks up most afternoons. If conditions are good, consider taking a trip out to the freighters anchored offshore or venture west to clothing-optional Wreck Beach and beyond for a picnic. Although this is an urban area, you are still at the mercy of the sea. It is not uncommon to experience some rather large breaking waves off the shallows of Spanish Banks and the beaches in Stanley Park, and there is quite a strong current in the bay. Plan your trip accordingly and be very cautious when paddling in the major shipping lanes (near the freighters). A final note: Although Burrard Inlet and the inner harbour may look tempting, it is illegal for kayaks, or any boat without power, to go under the Lions Gate Bridge.

TRIP 13 Crescent Beach

SKILL: Intermediate to advanced
TIME: Day trip
HAZARDS: Tidal currents
ACCESS: Wards Marina/Crescent Beach/White Rock
CHARTS: 3463 · Strait of Georgia, Southern Portion · 1:80,000
TIDE BOOK: Vol. 5

If you are looking to add adventure to your local paddling excursions, take the time to visit the communities of Crescent Beach and White Rock. The towns are quaint, and the shoreline between the two is exposed and an exhilarating paddle at any time of year.

LAUNCHING

This day tour begins at Blackie Spit, a sandy arm extending into Boundary Bay at Crescent Beach, or further up the channel of the Nicomekl River at the boat launch in Wards Marina. Take Highways 99 or 99A and follow the signs to Crescent Beach. If you choose to launch at Wards Marina and paddle the Nicomekl River out to the ocean, watch for a black iron gate on the right-hand side of Crescent Road, approximately two blocks past the 140th Street intersection. The boat launch is located behind the Stewart Farm house, a regional historic site. There is no charge for car-top boat launching. From this location you can paddle towards the ocean or up the Nicomekl River. If the main water is rough, try paddling east from the launch about 2 km (1.2 mi.) and portage around the small dam. The river area is calm and sheltered nicely by trees until 168th Street. After 168th, the river continues to Langley but is bluffed only by dyke banks.

If you choose to launch at Blackie Spit, follow the signs to Crescent Beach, heading over the railway tracks in the direction of the boat launch signs. After the tracks the road will come to a Y-intersection; keep to the right. Continue towards the water through a four-way stop and past Camp Alexandria. Prior to the road coming into a cul de sac, make a right on McBride Avenue, which will take you out to Blackie Spit (home of the Crescent Beach Sailing Club). There is no launch fee if you launch at the club. If you turn before the tracks, you will end up at the yacht club and will be charged.

The park at Blackie Spit is open from dawn to dusk. The gate is locked after dusk so if you expect to be late, move your vehicle in advance or it could end up getting locked inside until morning.

From the spit you can paddle up the Nicomekl River or around Crescent Beach, hugging the shoreline into White Rock. The Nicomekl River is a pleasant day trip that usually has calm, relatively protected water. Remember, if you ride the tide one way, you must leave yourself the energy to paddle back against it. With some advance preparation and a properly timed schedule, you can ride a flood tide into the river and catch the ebb out (or vice versa).

Paddlers heading from Crescent Beach to White Rock also need to be aware of winds and tides. In the summer months, most wind comes from the south to southwest. These winds shift to become more easterly in the winter months. At low tide the beach extends about 1 km (.6 mi.) from the shore and exposes a number of rocks. Watch for exposed or partly exposed rock once you round Kwomais Point and start to leave Boundary Bay to enter Semiahmoo Bay. Keep in mind, the large shallow sand shelf can result in steep breaking waves, especially if the wind is from the south to southwest.

The paddle along the shoreline to White Rock is anywhere from 1.5–2 hours if the tide is in. If the tide is out, add at least 1 hour to this trip. Dolphin markers outline the deep-water boating channel, where the tidal currents are strongest. If you paddle within the channel markers, watch for boats heading to and from the marina. From January to June you may be lucky to see some of the local gray whales that frequent the bay prior to their journey north. If the whales are not around, there are plenty of seals, herons, eagles, harlequin ducks and other shore birds to keep you occupied.

You can also paddle from White Rock to Crescent Beach by launching at the car-top boat launch off Marine Drive at Bay Street in White Rock. The car-top launch is approximately four blocks west of the pier on Marine Drive. There is a grassy section with picnic tables at the last pay parking lot, and the launch is over the tracks slightly below the promenade level. There is no charge for launching, but the city charges $1.25 per hour for parking. You can also drive west a few blocks on Marine Drive and park for free. This area can get crowded on summer weekends, but you can avoid the masses by leaving early in the morning.

TRIP 14 Little Campbell River

SKILL: Beginner to advanced

TIME: 1–3 hours

HAZARDS: River currents

ACCESS: White Rock

CHARTS: 3463 · Strait of Georgia, Southern Portion · 1:80,000

TIDE BOOK: Vol. 5

Located on the southwestern edge of B.C., White Rock is a bustling community that faces boldly onto the Strait of Georgia. Its shores are exposed, but escaping the salt, sand and wind is as easy as turning your kayak to nearby Little Campbell River.

LAUNCHING

Kayaks can be launched directly into the river at two locations: Semiahmoo parking lot by the baseball diamond off Marine Drive, or the walking bridge at the end of 160th (Stayte Road). Check the tides if you plan to use either location because the river is tidal fed and will not provide enough draft for kayaks if the tide is low. The Semiahmoo parking lot is operated by the local native band and is occasionally closed. If you launch at the bridge at 160th, you can avoid the coin meters by parking on the north side of Marine Drive, east of Stayte Road.

Kayaks can also be launched from the car-top boat launch located approximately four blocks west of the pier at Marine Drive and Bay Streets. Look for the last pay parking lot on West Beach, where the promenade comes to an end. Purchase parking tickets from the dispenser: you will need loonies and/or quarters. You are generally safe past the 4-hour parking limit as long as the meter is fed; however, on busy weekends the commissionaires can be more militant. Parking up the hill, west on Marine Drive, will require a walk, but the parking is free and there is no 4-hour limit.

Once on the water, paddle east towards the pier past the white rock and along the main beach promenade. On the left side you will notice a silver train bridge at the mouth of the Little Campbell River. The bridge is approximately 3 km (2 mi.) from the launch. Remember to avoid low tide, or the water in the river system won't be deep enough.

The Little Campbell River enters the Semiahmoo Indian Reserve, a beautiful example of the landscape prior to the encroachment of European civilization. People wanting to fish in this area should check with the Semiahmoo First Nation to obtain the necessary permits.

TRIP 15 Fraser Delta

SKILL:	Intermediate to advanced
TIME:	Day trip
HAZARDS:	Tides
ACCESS:	Canoe Passage/Deas Island Regional Park
CHARTS:	3463 · Strait of Georgia, Southern Portion · 1:80,000
	3490 · Fraser River—Sand Heads to Douglas Island · 1:20,000
TIDE BOOK:	Vol. 5

Westham Island, west of Ladner, is best known for the George C. Reifel Migratory Bird Sanctuary, a congregating place for a variety of marine and predatory birds. Each spring and fall, thousands of our winged friends rest here before their departures north or south, providing paddlers with endless hours of enjoyment. Be sure to bring a bird book and binoculars.

LAUNCHING

Several locations allow access to the Fraser River estuary, including a couple of launches close to one another off River Road in Ladner. From Highway 99, take exit 28 (Highway 17) south to the Ladner Trunk Road. Turn right and drive through Ladner on this street, which becomes 47A Avenue then River Road West. The preferred launch is at Wellington Point Park, about .5 km (.3 mi.) before the Canoe Passage bridge. There is a small sign a few hundred metres prior to the park entrance; keep your eyes open after you come to a large orange fish plant on the right. A large metal buoy will let you know you are near the park entrance; turn right, then follow the gravel road to the launch site, where you will find a cement pier, boat launch and a large fishing platform. There is no charge for landing and launching; however, the park gates are locked at night, so keep this in mind if you are paddling after dusk. Currently there are no public amenities such as washrooms or fresh water.

You can also launch on the north side of Canoe Passage by the bridge (parking on the side of the road is limited). This site can be tricky depending on the height of the tide, erosion of the bank and current. Although it gives direct access to Canoe Passage and the channel, the Wellington alternative is a little more convenient when parking and launching.

A circumnavigation of Westham Island takes most of the day with the tide in. The best paddling at high tide is on the west side of the island, even though it opens up to wind and waves. The opportunity to see migratory birds in the shallow water can be a treat for even the most ardent birders, but be sure to check the tides, wind, weather report and the stamina of your group before venturing out. This area is affected by currents running out of Canoe Passage and the Fraser River along the Steveston Jetty, and an opposing wind can quickly steepen the waves.

If the tide is low, you may want to paddle the east side of the island and the many inlets and tributaries of the Fraser delta. Paddling upstream takes you into Ladner and will give you a chance to see a number of maritime float houses as well as beavers, heron, seals, Steller's sea lions and a host of migratory birds.

Deas Island Regional Park is an alternative launch site accessed from River Road on the north side of Highway 99. Launch at the park and paddle west towards Ladner to explore this historic fishing village. The paddle from Deas to Ladner takes approximately 1–1.5 hours depending on tides.

Paddlers will definitely benefit from having a tide table, marine chart and topographical map of the area, for the tidal currents here can save time and simplify paddling. The area has many tributaries and islands, and a large-scale chart or map will minimize paddling up channels that lead nowhere.

TRIP 16 Indian Arm

SKILL:	Beginner to advanced
TIME:	1–4 days
HAZARDS:	Traffic and winds
ACCESS:	Deep Cove/Woodlands/Belcarra Regional Park/Barnet Marine Park
CHARTS:	3495 · Vancouver Harbour/Indian Arm · 1:80,000
TIDE BOOK:	Vol. 5

There is no better place within 30 minutes of Vancouver to experience wilderness paddling than Indian Arm. Whether you are day-tripping or planning to spend a few nights, Indian Arm has something for everyone.

Indian Arm has recently been protected in cooperation with the Greater Vancouver Regional District's (GVRD) Green Zone Plan and the provincial government's Protected Areas Strategy. In 1995, more than 9300 ha (23,000 a.) of wilderness in Indian Arm were designated provincial parkland. According to the government, this is the largest urban green-space initiative in recent Canadian history. BC Parks is currently managing the area and increasing the number of campsites, facilities and, likely, the crowds.

Crowded or not, Indian Arm is still a great location for paddlers of all abilities due to its protected waterway and surprisingly wild setting. Be aware, however, that the winds up and down the arm can cause problems, though your biggest concern may be the wakes from other boaters and water skiers. Make sure to allow extra time for the return portion of your trip, and take your tide table.

Bring fresh water—natural sources are unreliable due to the high volume of recreational activity in Indian Arm. Fires are not allowed.

For a great 2–3-day trip, launch from Deep Cove and travel up the western shore to Bishop Creek. After spending a night at Granite Falls near the Indian River, you can then paddle along the eastern shore and return to your vehicle, stopping at Twin Islands and Racoon Island along the way. Currently there are no fees associated with campsites in Indian Arm and reservations are not required—but this may change in the near future.

LAUNCHING

Deep Cove is the most common launch site for Indian Arm. Take Highway 1 north across the Second Narrows Bridge. Both the Dollarton Highway and Mount Seymour Parkway exits will get you to Deep Cove. Follow the Mount Seymour Parkway for 10–15 minutes, then turn left at the lights onto Deep Cove Road. If you are taking the Dollarton Highway, it eventually turns into Deep Cove Road. When Deep Cove Road becomes Gallant Avenue, you've made it.

Follow Gallant Avenue to the water and make a right onto Banbury Road. The first parking lot is just ahead to the left, on Rockcliff Road; another one is just up the hill. Both lots are near the Deep Cove Canoe and Kayak Centre.

Panorama Park also has a day-use parking lot. Follow Deep Cove Road to Gallant Avenue, then take the first left onto Panorama Drive. The parking lot is on your right. Unfortunately, overnight parking is limited to the street and can be difficult to find if you do not arrive first thing in the morning.

If you want to put in farther north than Deep Cove, drive to Woodlands, which has a government dock. To get there, drive along the Mount Seymour Parkway, turn left up towards Mount Seymour Road and then turn right on Indian River Road. Parking can be tricky because there is not much space.

It is also possible to launch on the eastern side of Indian Arm from the regional park at Belcarra. Approaching from Vancouver, take the Barnet Highway east until you reach Ioco Road in Port Moody and follow the signs to Belcarra. You can launch in the park but you will need to carry your boat a little ways. Nonetheless, the park is very kayak-friendly, with plenty of day-use parking and a seasonal kayak rental booth. Be warned: The gates to the park are locked every night and vehicles are towed. If it is essential that you launch from this side of the arm but need overnight parking, you can check in the village of Belcarra (at the time of writing there was not much available) or try the Reid Point Marina across Burrard Inlet or the Barnet Marine Park (off the Barnet Highway).

SITES

Belcarra/Jug Island Off Jug Island on the Belcarra side of the arm is a nice, small sandy beach. Located on the southeast tip of Indian Arm, the beach is part of Belcarra Regional Park. There are hiking trails and outhouses located up the path from the beach. Belcarra Beach, with its government dock, is farther south and is a great place to explore with kids and adults. There is no camping.

Raccoon Island This small island is a good place to stop and explore. Access is limited due to its rocky shoreline but it is close to Deep

Cove—30 minutes or so. Camping is permitted; however, there are no designated sites or water.

Twin Islands These islands get quite busy because they are easily accessible and close to Deep Cove—only 45 minutes one way. The best landing site is in between the two islands, depending on the tide. Be sure to pull your boat up as high as possible. Camping is permitted on 5 elevated wooden tent pads at the North Twin Campground, and an outhouse is provided. There is no water.

Silver Falls Silver Falls is a small waterfall located just south of Bishop Creek. This cool, lake-fed waterfall is a great refresher on a hot day. Stopping here can be a bit tricky due to limited pull-in space. There is no camping.

Bishop Creek The rocky shoreline of this alluvial fan provides a flat area frequently used by campers. Bishop Creek/Bergs Landing is located on the west shore, approximately a 3-hour paddle from Deep Cove. Currently the site has room for over 20 tents on grassy tent pads. There are two pit toilets and a few garbage cans but you are reminded to take out what you bring in.

Indian River The Indian River estuary is located at the top of the arm and is habitat for waterfowl and marine life. Harbour seals are plentiful due to the many species of Pacific salmon that live in Indian River. The river is accessible by kayak at high tide, and the estuary is a great place for observing wildlife. The Wigwam Inn, privately owned by the Royal Vancouver Yacht Club, is at the northern end of the arm. A short distance behind the Wigwam Inn is a small waterfall known as Spray of Pearls Falls. Those interested in exploring can access the narrow canyon via a primitive trail that follows Wigwam Creek. There is no camping.

Granite Falls This spectacular waterfall, 50 m (165 ft.) high, is located at the northeast end of the arm. Although the dock at the site has being designed for power boats, it is still a great spot for paddlers to take a break or pull out and spend a few nights. There are a number of small tent sites, four pit toilets and a spectacular view.

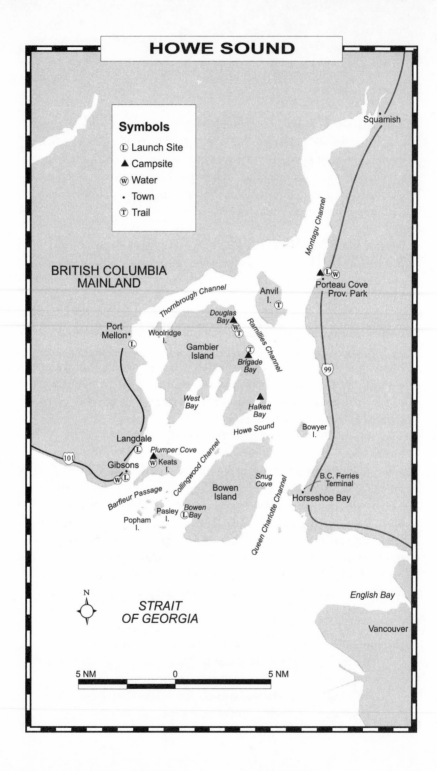

HOWE SOUND

Symbols

- Ⓛ Launch Site
- ▲ Campsite
- Ⓦ Water
- • Town
- Ⓣ Trail

Squamish

Montagu Channel

BRITISH COLUMBIA
MAINLAND

▲Ⓛ Ⓦ
Porteau Cove
Prov. Park

Anvil
I. Ⓣ

Thornbrough Channel

*Douglas
Bay* ▲
Ⓦ Ⓣ

Port
Mellon • Woolridge
Ⓛ I.

Gambier
Island

Ramillies Channel

Ⓣ
▲
*Brigade
Bay*

99

*West
Bay*

▲
*Halkett
Bay*

Howe Sound

Bowyer
I.

Langdale
Ⓛ

Plumper Cove
▲ Keats
Ⓦ I.

Gibsons
ⓌⓁ

Collingwood Channel

Bowen
Island

*Snug
Cove*

B.C. Ferries
Terminal

Horseshoe Bay

Barfleur Passage

Queen Charlotte Channel

Pasley *Bowen*
Popham I. Ⓛ *Bay*
I.

N

*STRAIT
OF GEORGIA*

English Bay

Vancouver

5 NM   0   5 NM

6

Howe Sound

Peter McGee

The first strokes I ever took in a kayak were in Howe Sound in the early 1980s. It was my godmother's Klepper, and I distinctly remember exploring every nook and cranny of the reef-strewn bays and coves that surrounded her cabin. Fifteen years later, while finishing a paddling trip that had lasted months and covered much of the coast, I had the opportunity once again to paddle through the sound as my group approached the city of Vancouver. For all I had just seen, Howe Sound still grabbed me as one of the most beautiful spots in British Columbia. Although it may not be wilderness, it still has its own special charms. Nestled among the coastal mountains, speckled with summer homes and flanked by the bright lights of Vancouver, West Vancouver and Gibsons, Howe Sound blends the beauty of the Gulf Islands with the rugged North Coast and places it all invitingly on our doorstep. It is a unique slice of West Coast life well worth exploring.

BACKGROUND

The history of the Howe Sound we see today began 20,000 years ago when a massive ice flow, 1500 m (5,000 ft.) thick, sculpted the fiord.

Although the environment was rugged, the Coast Salish peoples inhabited and prospered in the area for thousands of years after the ice
receded. The Squamish Nation still resides in the communities of
Squamish and North Vancouver; although their political voice is
gaining strength, it is the more recent European and Asian influences
that have made the most dramatic impacts on the region. The cities
and towns that border the sound are a testament to this fact, as are the
many European names attached to the islands, points, passages and
mountains. The region was named by Capt. George Vancouver in
1792 after Admiral Howe, a hero of the British navy known as the
"sailor's friend" for his fair treatment of his crew. On a more practical
note, Passage Island, on the south side of Bowen Island, was named
by Captain Vancouver for its use as a navigational aid. The island,
when "in one" or in line with the peak on Anvil Island, was used as a
mark to pass safely westward of the shoals, known as the Sandheads,
off the mouth of the Fraser River.

Yet for all the native and immigrant history in the sound, it is geologic forces that continue to shape its future—and if you plan on visiting, don't wait too long. The sands, silts and clays deposited by the
Squamish River and its seven tributaries are advancing the Squamish
delta, at the northern end of Howe Sound, at a rate of about 1 m
(3.3 ft.) a year. This may not seem like much, but if the present rate
continues, the entire sound could be filled in by a fertile valley as
early as AD 27,000. Paddle it while you can.

GETTING THERE
Getting to Howe Sound is not difficult: it is within easy reach of Vancouver (via Highways 1 and 99) and Gibsons. Local boat and float
plane operators can drop you off wherever you arrange, though this
added expense really isn't necessary. Prime launch spots can be found
on Bowen Island (accessible by B.C. Ferries from Horseshoe Bay), off
Highway 99, and near Gibsons and the Langdale ferry terminal on
the Sunshine Coast. For the more experienced, you can even launch
directly from Vancouver.

WEATHER AND HAZARDS
Although weather conditions here are usually quite moderate, paddlers need to be cautious of the winds that funnel down Montagu

Channel in front of Porteau Cove. During the summer there is a land/sea breeze (as described in chapter 1) that gathers strength around Squamish, often reaching speeds of 30 knots. The fact that there is a Squamish Windsurfing Society speaks to the winds' consistency. The period of the strongest onshore wind is between noon and early evening. In winter, particularly dangerous northerly outflow "Squamish" winds occur, as do strong, southerly inflow winds brought about by southeast gales in the Strait of Georgia. Do not let the relatively sheltered environment of northern Howe Sound fool you. In the past few decades, more than one winter paddler has perished as a result of these winds.

Tidal rapids are not a concern in Howe Sound, but paddlers should be aware of the gap leading into Gibsons from the Strait of Georgia. The funnelling effect of the channel increases the tidal flow, creating dangerously steep waves when the wind is against the tide and the water is shallow. Fog can also be quite common during the fall and spring, so be sure to bring a compass.

With any trip in Howe Sound, watch for boat traffic. Paddlers should be particularly cautious about the ferries that travel between Langdale and Horseshoe Bay, Snug Cove (Bowen Island) and Horseshoe Bay, and Nanaimo and Horseshoe Bay (affectionately called the bread slicer routes). There is also considerable small boat traffic.

Finally, you would be well advised to bring your own water on any trip in Howe Sound. There are several fresh water sources (on Gambier Island, for example), but heavy recreational traffic makes this water unreliable. Bring it, treat it or boil it.

HOWE SOUND TRIPS (17-19)

If you are planning a day trip, consider the Pasley Group of islands in the southwestern part of the sound. Although most of the islands are privately owned, they are great to explore from the water and easy to reach from Bowen Island. Unfortunately, there are no camping sites on the outer islands. If you are launching from Gibsons, you will be able to camp at Plumper Cove Provincial Marine Park on Keats Island and use it as a staging area to the Pasleys and Keats. For further overnight possibilities, your best bet is to take 2–3 days and explore the northern part of the sound around Gambier and Anvil Islands.

To avoid boat traffic and crowds, consider taking a trip in the fall or spring. The wildlife abounds and the snow-capped peaks provide a spectacular backdrop.

TRIP 17   The Pasley Group

SKILL:	Beginner to advanced
TIME:	Day trip
HAZARDS:	Traffic and winds
ACCESS:	Bowen Island/Gibsons
CHARTS:	3311 · Sunshine Coast—Vancouver Harbour to Desolation Sound · 1:40,000
	3512 · Strait of Georgia, Central Portion · 1:80,000
	3526 · Howe Sound · 1:40,000
TIDE BOOK:	Vol. 5

Perched on the edge of the Strait of Georgia, the Pasley Group provides the perfect setting to leisurely dip a paddle and enjoy the company of a few curious seals. Most of the islands are privately owned, and if you want to camp you'll need to paddle to Plumper Cove Provincial Marine Park on Keats Island. Don't let this deter you from some of the best day-tripping on the south coast, however, as access from Bowen Island is easy.

LAUNCHING

To launch from Bowen Island, take the Bowen ferry from Horseshoe Bay to Snug Cove and drive west across the centre of the island. The road snakes and splits a fair bit—just follow the main route. After about 15 minutes, you will approach the western shore of the island and a fork in the road that leads to Tunstall Bay or Bowen Bay. Keep to the right. At the bottom of the winding, steep hill is the public beach at Bowen Bay. Parking is extremely limited, but the bay is relatively protected and launching is easy. It is also possible to launch from the marina in lower Gibsons, but this will add a couple of hours to your trip.

SITES

As you leave Bowen Bay and head for Pasley Island, you will encounter Collingwood Channel. Although this is a short crossing, beware of boat traffic (particularly tugs with barges and booms in tow) and wind funnelling into Howe Sound from the Strait of Georgia. Once across, you will likely be looking at Pasley's East Bay or North Bay (distinguishable by its sand beach, numerous cabins, meadow and sizable wharf). Your decision to go south or north at this point is up to the winds. If a strong westerly is blowing, you are advised to head north towards Mickey Island, wrap around the north end of Pasley and venture off towards Hermit Island. Exploring Popham and Worlcombe Islands would be better left for another day. If conditions are calm, however, circumnavigating Pasley and exploring the smaller islands will give you a great afternoon of paddling.

You are likely to encounter numerous seals and birds among the islands; please respect their space. The seal haul-outs near Hermit and Popham Islands make for great wildlife viewing but the animals are easily disturbed; keep your distance when you see signs of agitation. If you need to stretch your legs, the northeast side of the small island connected to Hermit, locally known as Arbutus Island, is a designated picnic spot but fires and camping are *absolutely prohibited*. Keep in mind that if paddlers show that we are careful and responsible, more private land may be opened for public use. If you are not heading back to Bowen Bay, but instead crossing Barfleur Passage to Keats Island, take a peak into the passage before you cross, as the westerlies can bring extremely rough seas.

TRIP 18   Keats Island

SKILL: Intermediate to advanced
TIME: 1–3 days
HAZARDS: Traffic and winds
ACCESS: Gibsons
CHARTS: 3311 · Sunshine Coast—Vancouver Harbour
to Desolation Sound · 1:40,000
3512 · Strait of Georgia, Central Portion · 1:80,000
3526 · Howe Sound · 1:40,000
TIDE BOOK: Vol. 5

If you are approaching Howe Sound from Gibsons on the Sunshine Coast, exploring Keats Island is your best option for a day trip. Named after Admiral Sir Richard Goodwin Keats, a compatriot of Viscount Nelson, the island has many faces. Although much of the north coast is steep and inhospitable, Plumper Cove Provincial Marine Park and the community at Eastbourne show its more friendly side.

LAUNCHING

To get to the Sunshine Coast, take the ferry from Horseshoe Bay to Langdale (about 45 minutes). As you head off the ferry, turn left and follow the lower road. The best launch near the terminal is from the pier at Hopkins Landing, a minute or two from the ferry terminal. To launch from the marina in Gibsons, continue along the lower road until you reach Headlands Road and turn left towards the water. Parking is limited during summer. For boat rentals, Sunshine Kayaking has an office in lower Gibsons, and you can launch a couple of blocks from their door. Sunshine Kayaking will also pick you up at the ferry if you call ahead to arrange times. Look for the famed Molly's Reach restaurant from the *Beachcombers* television series and follow Molly's Lane for about a block until you see their sign.

v *Harbour seal*, PETER MCGEE

SITES

From Gibsons, it is a short hop (about 30 minutes) across Shoal Channel to reach Plumper Cove Provincial Marine Park on Keats Island. Although the crossing is relatively sheltered, paddlers still need to be cautious of the boat traffic and ferry wash. As you approach the western shore of the island you will see a number of cabins and the Shelter Islets. Tuck in behind the islets to find the public dock for the park. A park supervisor is there for much of the summer and nightly fees are collected. Currently the fee is $10 per night per tent site, and the park offers pit toilets as well as fresh water pumps. Call the BC Parks office in Brackendale to see if reservations are required.

Circumnavigating the island provides a good 4–5 hours of paddling and the opportunity to see some great bird life. Watch the weather, as the wave action at the southwestern end (near Home Island—also called Salmon Rock—*hint!*) can be quite severe. Similarly, there is a mile or so of cliffs on the north side that makes landing impossible.

For the truly adventurous, crossing Barfleur Passage puts you in the scenic Pasley Group and the land of many seals. Be sure to listen to the weather reports before you go. There is no camping on the islands, and the common summer westerlies can quickly turn Barfleur Passage into a blur of whitecaps, a tough crossing for even the most experienced paddler.

TRIP 19 Gambier and Anvil Islands

SKILL: Intermediate to advanced
TIME: 1–4 days
HAZARDS: Winds and traffic
ACCESS: Porteau Cove/Port Mellon
CHARTS: 3311 · Sunshine Coast—Vancouver Harbour
to Desolation Sound · 1:40,000
3512 · Strait of Georgia, Central Portion · 1:80,000
3526 · Howe Sound · 1:40,000
Tide Book: Vol. 5

In contrast to the islands and summer homes in the southern part of Howe Sound, surprisingly little development has occurred to the north. Although close to urban civilization and industrialization, with the mill at Port Mellon, Anvil and Gambier Islands provide a fantastic setting for day and weekend trips. Don't let the ease of access fool you, however, as the winds are notoriously strong in this part of Howe Sound (see Weather and Hazards at the beginning of this chapter) and the shores remarkably rugged. With mountains all around and log booms dotting many of the bays, this is truly coastal paddling.

LAUNCHING

To access the northern part of Howe Sound, launch from Porteau Cove Provincial Park on the mainland or at Dunham Road near Port Mellon. Porteau Cove can be reached easily from Highway 99 and is located about 30 km (19 mi.) north of Horseshoe Bay. There are a number of facilities at the park, including a dock, boat ramp, toilets and campsites. An extremely popular spot with divers and close to the road, Porteau Cove gets quite crowded on weekends and holidays. Nonetheless, it is a great launch spot.

To reach the launch site near Port Mellon, take the ferry from Horseshoe Bay to Langdale and head north past the ferry terminal for a few minutes; you will pass a small apartment development on your right. Look for Dunham Road soon after and follow it to the water. Be warned: Port Mellon is an active pulp mill and some days the smell is quite bad.

SITES

Heading out from Porteau Cove, your first challenge is crossing the often choppy Montagu Channel. As you approach Anvil Island, named by Captain Vancouver for the "shape of the mountain that composes it," you have a number of options: circumnavigating Anvil to the north, heading south into Ramillies Channel or taking a break on the eastern shore. Although there is little accessible public land on Anvil, a cleared area that may have been a scout camp sits midway up its east coast. This is a good place to stretch your legs, though No Trespassing signs have been popping up recently. Heading south towards Gambier Island provides better paddling and camping opportunities.

If you do stop on Anvil Island, you may want to check out the trail to Leading Peak that follows the north-south slope. The trail is marked and the view from the top is amazing.

∧ *The outer edge of Howe Sound and the Strait of Georgia,* PETER MCGEE

Gambier Island Approaching Gambier from the north, the first beach and campsite you will find is Douglas Bay, near the base of Gambier Creek. Farther along the shore is Brigade Bay, and on the southeastern tip of the island is Halkett Bay Provincial Marine Park, the only official campsite of the three. From any of these sites you are in a great position to explore the log booms around Gambier, the bird and seal colonies on Christie Islet, and the Pam Rocks. For those looking to take a break from paddling, several hiking trails on the island lead to destinations such as Gambier Lake and Mounts Liddell and Artaban.

Circumnavigating the rest of Gambier makes for great paddling, as the whole shore is a collection of interesting coves and bays. Unfortunately, most of the land on the southern side is private, and camping is limited to the sites listed above or to Plumper Cove on Keats Island. For paddlers starting their northern Howe Sound excursion near Port Mellon, crossing Thornbrough Channel should be relatively easy. For those making the paddle back to Porteau Cove, however, time your crossing carefully and be forever vigilant of changing wind conditions.

ADDITIONAL ROUTES

Heading north Howe Sound blends into the Sunshine Coast and the trips described in the following chapters.

Heading south The southern end of Howe Sound lies within sight of the Vancouver skyline and the trips described in chapter 5.

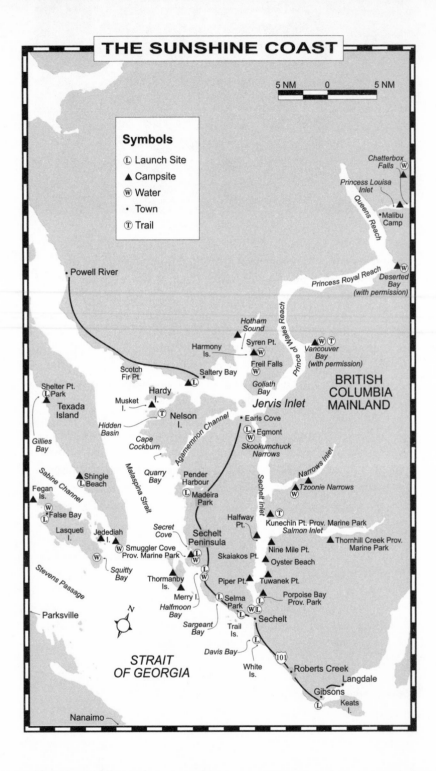

THE SUNSHINE COAST

Symbols

- ⓛ Launch Site
- ▲ Campsite
- ⓦ Water
- • Town
- ⓣ Trail

5 NM   0   5 NM

Chatterbox Falls ⓦ ▲

Princess Louisa Inlet

Queens Reach

• Malibu Camp

Princess Royal Reach

Deserted Bay (with permission) ▲ ⓦ

• Powell River

Hotham Sound ▲

Harmony Is.

Syren Pt. ▲ ⓦ

Freil Falls ⓦ

Prince of Wales Reach

Vancouver Bay (with permission) ▲ ⓦ ⓣ

BRITISH COLUMBIA MAINLAND

Scotch Fir Pt.

Saltery Bay ▲ⓛ

Goliath Bay

Jervis Inlet

Shelter Pt. ⓛ Park

Texada Island

Hardy I.

Musket I.

ⓣ Nelson I.

Hidden Basin

Cape Cockburn

Agamemnon Channel

• Earls Cove

ⓛ • Egmont

Skookumchuck Narrows

Gillies Bay

Quarry Bay

Pender Harbour

Narrows Inlet

Sabine Channel

Shingle ▲ Beach ⓛ

Malaspina Strait

ⓛ Madeira Park ▲

Tzoonie Narrows ▲ ⓦ

Fegan ▲ Is.

ⓛ • False Bay

Lasqueti I.

Jedediah ▲ I.

Secret Cove

Sechelt Peninsula

Halfway Pt. ▲ ⓣ

Kunechin Pt. Prov. Marine Park

Salmon Inlet

Sechelt Inlet

Thornhill Creek Prov. Marine Park ▲

Stevens Passage

ⓦ Smuggler Cove Prov. Marine Park ▲

ⓦ Squitty Bay

Thormanby Is. ▲

ⓛ ⓦ

Skaiakos Pt.

Nine Mile Pt. ▲

Oyster Beach ▲

ⓛ ⓦ

Piper Pt.

Tuwanek Pt. ▲

Porpoise Bay Prov. Park

Parksville

N

Merry I.

Halfmoon Bay

Sargeant Bay

ⓛ Selma Park

Trail Is.

ⓦⓛ • Sechelt

Davis Bay

101

White Is.

• Roberts Creek

Langdale

STRAIT OF GEORGIA

Gibsons ⓛ

Keats I.

Nanaimo

7

The Sunshine Coast

Bodhi Drope, Dorothy Drope
and Howard Zatwarnitski

The stretch of coastline from Gibsons north to Egmont along the
east side of the Strait of Georgia is known as the Sunshine Coast.
It is a region with a mild, dry and semi-Mediterranean climate that
has proved attractive to settlement and industry. Despite these pressures, the Sunshine Coast continues to provide a number of superb
wilderness experiences for paddlers of all abilities. From the ideal
learning environment of Sechelt Inlet to the exposed 32-km (20-mi.)
coastline between Gibsons and Sechelt, the Sunshine Coast offers
some of the best paddling experiences in southwestern British
Columbia.

BACKGROUND

Harry Roberts, the celebrated denizen of the first European family of
Roberts Creek, first coined the name "Sunshine Coast." In fact, he
originally called it "The Sunshine Belt" and painted these words in
large letters on his shed in the hopes of attracting the tourist trade.
Since that beginning in the 1920s, the name has evolved into the

more apt Sunshine Coast, and its application has crept north to include the Egmont–Jervis Inlet area with the advent of ferry service, and now the Powell River district.

Long before Harry Roberts, however, there were the Coast Salish peoples who lived off the bounty of the Sunshine Coast since time began. There were about 80 villages in the area, with major settlements of the Hunichin at the head of Jervis Inlet, the Tsonai in Deserted Bay, the Tuwanek at the head of Narrows Inlet and in Porpoise Bay, and the Skariakos in Garden Bay and on the Thormanbys. Large numbers of people would congregate for the winter in the Pender Harbour area.

The Sechelt people are now in the painful process of reclaiming their traditions. They are deservedly well known as the first natives of Canada to achieve self-government. Enacted by the federal government in 1986, the Sechelt Indian Self Government Act was modelled on municipal governments, with additional powers in several areas. A year later the provincial government also ratified this arrangement and, though the model has been criticized by other aboriginal groups, the Sechelts have apparently prospered under it. Like several native bands along the coast, the Sechelts are negotiating with the province to settle their land claims.

The immigrant history of the area is typical of others regions on the south coast, with logging, mining and agriculture the primary incentives for settlement. Evidence of this can be found in the mill town of Powell River and the lime mines of Texada Island.

GETTING THERE

By land and water Unless you already live on the Sunshine Coast you will need to access the area by vehicle and ferry. B.C. Ferries service runs from Horseshoe Bay (near Vancouver) to Langdale; Comox (on Vancouver Island) to Powell River; and French Creek (on Vancouver Island) to Lasqueti Island. Once on the Sunshine Coast, Highway 101 can take you to most launch sites. You will probably use additional ferry services between Earls Cove and Saltery Bay, and between Powell River and Texada Island. For people coming from Vancouver Island, paddling is an option that is not recommended due to weather and heavy marine traffic.

By air Check with the local float plane services such as Coval Air and Vancouver Island Air if you wish to arrange a charter.

WEATHER AND HAZARDS

Winds in this region follow the overall coastal pattern of northwesterly winds in the summer and southeasterly winds in the winter. In summer, west winds indicate warm and sunny conditions, although extremely strong west winds generated by a high pressure system can blow for days. Southeast winds indicate a change in the weather, usually for the worse.

Near Texada Island, winds and tides tend to be stronger due to channelling effects. Welcome Passage, between the Thormanby Islands and the mainland, is also subject to channelling. As always, expect the wind and tidal effect to increase on headlands: the so-called corner effects. Gusty winds and confused, steep seas can occur at the base of high cliffs, such as those found on South Thormanby Island and near Sargeant Bay. In all the inlets be aware of anabatic and katabatic winds as well as winter outflow winds (see chapter 1).

Tidal rips, overfalls and other nasty stuff occur in the Sechelt Rapids of Skookumchuck Narrows and the Malibu Rapids at the entrance to Princess Louisa Inlet. These rapids should only be attempted by *very experienced* paddlers who have a good handle on tide tables. In other areas the funnelling effect will increase tidal flow, creating steep waves especially when the wind is against the tide and the water is shallow, such as at the "gap" leading into Gibsons.

If you are accessing parts of the Sunshine Coast from Vancouver Island, be cautious of the local wind phenomenon known as a Qualicum. This gap wind, begins on the west coast of Vancouver Island and touches down with amazing force on the east coast near Qualicum Beach. During the morning the weather can be clear, with glassy seas on the Strait of Georgia, but very suddenly in the afternoon, southwesterly winds hit the Qualicum Bay area with speeds up to 40 knots. The winds often reach all the way across to the northern tip of Lasqueti Island, where they typically diminish and turn southward. One local bit of advice is to watch the cloud movement on summer days; if you see a southwesterly develop, head for cover.

Like much of coastal B.C., the Sunshine Coast is bear country, so be sure to handle your food (and self) appropriately.

Finally, be wary of fresh water sources in all regions of the Sunshine Coast. Even if the area you are visiting seems pristine and uninhabited, its proximity to the Lower Mainland means it is probably heavily used by recreationists of all kinds. Boiling or treating water is a good idea anywhere on the coast, and this is one area where you should make it a mandatory practice.

SUNSHINE COAST TRIPS (20–24)

There are many trips to choose from along the Sunshine Coast depending on whether you prefer sheltered or exposed paddling. If you are looking for an experience suited to beginner paddlers, consider taking a few days to explore the inside coast and Sechelt Inlet. For those with more experience, Hotham Sound awaits, providing fantastic scenery on the edge of magnificent Jervis Inlet.

If inlets and steep-sided hills are a little confining for you, paddling the outer Sunshine Coast will expose you to the beauty of the Strait of Georgia, Jedediah Island and Nelson Island. Most of these trips require a minimum of 3–4 days so, if time is short, you can take a few day trips from the numerous launch sites between Gibsons and Secret Cove. If you are venturing up Jervis Inlet to Princess Louisa Provincial Park, leave yourself at least 7–10 days.

People who love the Sunshine Coast ask that you be mindful of the impact of your presence in these waters. Help us to keep a comfortable relationship between the human population and the other creatures that share this space. Clean up after yourselves and respect the habitat of the birds and animals.

TRIP 20   Sechelt Inlet

SKILL: Beginner to advanced
TIME: 1–4 days
HAZARDS: Winds and Skookumchuck Narrows
ACCESS: Sechelt
CHARTS: 3312 · Jervis Inlet and Desolation Sound · Various Scales
3512 · Strait of Georgia, Central Portion · 1:80,000
TIDE BOOK: Vol. 5

Se-shalt, meaning "place of shelter from the sea," is the perfect name for the inlet that offers beginner paddlers a taste of coastal kayaking. More than 150 ha (370 a.) located along the shores of Sechelt Inlet, Salmon Inlet and Narrows Inlet are protected in Mount Richardson Provincial Park and Sechelt Inlets Provincial Marine Park, which together comprise nine marine parks and give you a chance to experience wilderness without travelling far.

The most common access points are located at the southern end of Sechelt Inlet, near the town of Sechelt. Although it is possible to access the inlet from Egmont in the north, this is not a recommended approach as extreme care must be exercised when crossing Skookumchuck Narrows. To get to Sechelt, take Highway 101 north from the Langdale ferry terminal, about a 30-minute drive.

LAUNCHING

The most popular launch site is on Porpoise Bay. There is a government wharf with a large parking lot at the end of Wharf Street in Sechelt. If you are heading north through town, turn right on Wharf Street and drive straight down to the water to get to the boat ramp. This launch site gives you the choice of paddling up either side of the inlet depending on winds and what you want to see. The west side is often quieter but has fewer camping opportunities.

If you prefer to launch a little ways from town, there are a number of sites located on the east side of the inlet, including Porpoise Bay Provincial Park. Turn right off Wharf Street onto Porpoise Bay Road and follow it to the park. Here you will find lots of parking, a nice flat beach to launch from and deluxe camping if you choose to stay. Be sure you have made reservations with BC Parks in the summer months as this is a very popular campground.

There are a few other launch sites farther up Porpoise Bay Road but, due to summer congestion and the objection of local residents, they are not listed here. If you are visiting in the late fall or early spring, you may want to check out these sites.

SITES—THE WEST SIDE

From the launch site at the Porpoise Bay wharf in town, paddle towards Poise Island, keeping to the left to avoid the float planes landing near and taking off from the wharf. There is a long mud flat beginning opposite Poise Island and running all the way to Snake Bay. These flats are rich with small fish and other marine life, so you can enjoy these creatures and all the birds that feed on them. Expect to see mergansers, cormorants and several other seabirds in their season. There is a pleasant beach in Snake Bay, which is a good place to head for a short day trip with some swimming. Subdivisions are creeping up this side of the inlet and now overlook the south side of Snake Bay. Past the bay there is only the odd summer cottage.

Around Carlson Point, where Carlson Creek enters the inlet, is the home of one of the coast's most colourful characters. The Solberg sisters were born and raised in the area and made their living as fishers, loggers and hunters. "The Cougar Lady" lives here, while her sister lives up Jervis Inlet at Deserted Bay. You will know her home by the animal hide nailed to the shed wall. Piper Point curves out here and features wilderness campsites with pit toilets. A few miles north is Skaiakos Point, another park, but completely undeveloped at this time.

From here, you can continue on to Halfway Beach, another marine park with wilderness campsites and a pit toilet tucked in behind Halfway Islet. This is one of the nicest camping areas in the inlet, with a mountain stream running through the site. Keep in mind that the water is not potable and should be boiled or treated.

At this point, cross the inlet if you plan to head farther north. If you are returning to Sechelt, double back or cross the inlet and explore Nine Mile Point, Oyster Beach and Tuwanek Point on your way home.

SITES—THE EAST SIDE

Tuwanek Point Tuwanek Point is about a 2-hour paddle from the Porpoise Bay Provincial Park launch site and a great place to stay if you get a late start. The park features a good beach, great swimming, nice campsites and a pit toilet. Fires should be laid below the high tide line in the dry season, otherwise use the fire rings on site.

Oyster Beach Not much farther along is the campground at Oyster Beach. Although Tuwanek Point is a nice site, many people paddle on to Oyster Beach or Nine Mile Point to put some distance between themselves and "civilization." There is still some evidence of past aquaculture at Oyster Beach, but the site was cleaned up by BC Parks and is now included in Mount Richardson Provincial Park. Tucked against a steep bank, the site has room for about 4 tents, a pit toilet, a good creek and a nice swimming beach. At the time of writing, there was no bear cache at this site but remember, the whole inlet is bear country so act accordingly. For those who need a little more room, you can press on for another 20 to 30 minutes along the east side to Nine Mile Point.

Nine Mile Point Nine Mile Point is where Salmon Inlet joins Sechelt Inlet, and the shoreline is a favourite of eagles, with plenty of snags to perch on and a good supply of food in the water. Watch for the Nine Mile Point park a short distance before the point. It has everything you could want including a fine beach with 8 to 10 tent sites, a pit toilet and a bear cache.

Winds whistle down the various stretches of water that converge at this point, and a look at the chart will tell you why this is the most dangerous part of this inland sea. In summer, the daily thermal winds move down the inlets and, meeting here, create confused waters and heavy chop. These winds can make for heavy work if you are paddling against them—and a false sense of ease if moving with them. More than one paddler has soared up the inlet on the wings of these winds only to despair at the ordeal of the return journey. Winter outflows are especially severe here.

Kunechin Point Provincial Marine Park From Nine Mile Point you are looking at an open water crossing to Kunechin Point, the next marine park on your journey. Be sure to assess conditions carefully before setting out. Experienced paddlers will not find too much difficulty, but the inlet often attracts people who are just beginning their paddling careers. If this is you, try to cross in the early morning.

Kunechin Point offers good camping with some hiking opportunities on the hills behind. The HMCS *Chaudière*, a decommissioned naval vessel, was sunk in front of the Kunechin Islets in 1992 and attracts a lot of scuba divers.

∧ *Salmon Inlet crossing,* SUNSHINE KAYAKING

Thornhill Creek Provincial Marine Park Salmon Inlet is less well travelled by paddlers for a couple of reasons. First, the shoreline is precipitous for most of its length, providing few good spots to land and camp. Second, there is a power line following the shoreline for miles and lots of logging activity. Having said that, there are some beautiful sights to see along this waterway, and you are more likely to have them to yourself. A marine park at Thornhill Creek, about halfway up the inlet on the eastern shore, provides about 5 tent sites and a pit toilet. There is also a short hike from the campground to the creek. At the end of the inlet, Clowhom River flows down from Clowhom Lake. Although the lake is quite beautiful, it is also the site of a hydro dam and a logging operation—not ideal if you are looking to "get away from it all."

Instead of heading up Salmon Inlet, you may opt to continue paddling west up Sechelt Inlet towards Narrows Inlet and the Skookumchuck Narrows. Proceeding west up Sechelt Inlet, you will paddle along a series of steep granite cliffs. Again, this is a good opportunity to see intertidal life, especially if the tide is low. Look for both green and purple sea urchins, lots of purple sea stars and tube worms. In the small stands of bull kelp on this stretch, watch for the graceful kelp crab clinging to the fronds with its triangular carapace.

Narrows Inlet As you round Cawley Point, Storm Bay opens to your right at the very mouth of Narrows Inlet. There is a long mud flat at the top of the bay where Storm Creek runs into it. The north shore is sprinkled with funky little dwellings, relics of the flower children of the sixties—Storm Bay was a haven for hippies heading back to the land. More prosaic dwellings are gradually supplanting them. Recently, some clearing has occurred and there are rumours of a private campground opening in the future.

Narrows Inlet is generally a kind and gentle place. The mountains rise less steeply here, leaving flats that invite the visitor to wander. Streams come coursing off the mountains, creating myriad waterfalls, especially in the rainy seasons. The stroke of the paddle is often accompanied by the sound of rushing water hidden in the bushes. These lovely spots are definitely worth a stop.

There is a very nice, though not pristine, private campground called the Tzoonie Wilderness Camp about halfway to the narrows along the eastern shore. You can enjoy tents on platforms, cabins, hot showers, a kitchen/dining area and, best of all, a sauna on the shoreline—pretty deluxe after a long day of paddling. Drop-ins are welcome but if the camp is full you're out of luck, so reservations are recommended.

Tzoonie Narrows The inlet narrows drastically, thus its name, at Tzoonie Narrows, creating a little tidal rapid that flows at a maximum of 4 knots—just enough to give you a bit of fun without too much work. Whenever water runs fast it encourages the proliferation of sea life, and Tzoonie Narrows is an excellent example of this.

The marine park runs along both sides of the narrows. The best campsites are on the grassy flat land of the bay beyond Tzoonie Point, on the south side of the rapid. This is the only developed part of the park.

The remainder of Narrows Inlet is a peaceful place to explore by kayak. Thermal winds are active from mid-morning to late afternoon on sunny days, but there is not enough fetch in any direction to generate much wave height. It can make for a lot of work though, so relax on a beach to wait out the wind if you prefer.

To continue your trip up Sechelt Inlet, exit Narrows Inlet and paddle northwest along the shore. You'll pass a tiny village called Doriston, consisting of one family and a logging operation on the south shore that harks back to old-time B.C.: no roads, no stores, not much of anything—but interesting to reflect on. Each little bay along here is filled with bull kelp, attesting to the increased tidal flow. As you approach Skookum Island at the top of the inlet, you will notice the water is becoming increasingly active. The Sechelt Rapids begin just beyond this island.

Sechelt Rapids *Do not paddle* in this area unless you know what you are doing! The full tidal exchange for all the waters you have paddled on to this point rushes through Sechelt Rapids, the tightest part of Skookumchuck Narrows, creating awesome and incredibly dangerous conditions. This is a tidal flow that will wax and wane depending on the time and size of the tide. Slack tide in these rapids is really a misnomer, as there is no time when water is not flowing one way or the other. Nonetheless, at "slack" the flow is much gentler, the water is flat, and very experienced paddlers can safely negotiate the rapids in a kayak. You must have a track record with this sort of paddling, however, because this is not an area for practice or play.

The best route for a kayak is along the northern shore. Once you have calculated the time of slack from the tide table, keep to the right so you can duck behind the many little islets and avoid the fastest moving water. The ebb continues for a while even after the flood tide begins on the south side of the rapids. After rounding the corner at the top of Sechelt Rapids, you will be heading into Egmont and then on to Jervis Inlet, Hotham Sound and the trip that follows.

TRIP 21 Hotham Sound/Jervis Inlet

SKILL: Intermediate to advanced
TIME: 3–10 days
HAZARDS: Winds and currents
ACCESS: Egmont/Saltery Bay

CHARTS: 3312 · Jervis Inlet and Desolation Sound ·
          Various Scales
          3512 · Strait of Georgia, Central Portion · 1:80,000
          3414 · Jervis Inlet · 1:50,000
TIDE BOOK: Vol. 5

Close to Vancouver, with great fishing and surreal beauty, this area is quickly becoming known in paddling circles. Exploring Hotham Sound requires 3–4 days. If you have more than a week, you might want to extend your trip to include the majesty of Jervis Inlet and Princess Louisa Inlet. Be forewarned: Although these inlets are beautiful, they are typically steep sided and provide few camping opportunities—you will have to keep your eyes open.

LAUNCHING

Hotham Sound and Jervis Inlet are best accessed from Egmont, a small community east of the Earls Cove ferry terminal. If you are coming from the Powell River area, launching at Saltery Bay Provincial Park is also an option.

v *Scotch Fir Point, Malaspina Strait,* PETER MCGEE

There are two launching locations in Egmont: the government wharf and the Egmont marina. The advantages of the marina are the store/pub and showers on site. There is a launch fee for kayaks and canoes, which is minimal, and a daily rate for parking. Long weekends are obviously the busiest time, and parking is limited. If you choose to launch from the wharf, ensure your vehicle is locked to avoid theft, especially if you plan to be away for a few days.

If the water conditions are not in your favour, consider driving up the road a short ways to a sign that outlines a hiking path leading to Skookumchuck Narrows. This area was named by the First Nations people and appropriately means rapid water. The area is a popular location for whitewater paddlers who choose to challenge their skills on a large surf wave that protrudes from the depths during certain tidal periods. Although not recommended for most paddlers, it can provide some great spectating while you wait out the weather.

SITES

From Egmont looking northwest, you can see the start of Hotham Sound, a paddle that takes 2–3 hours depending on wind, current and the speed of your group. The greatest tidal flow will be felt at the wharf or marina, where the current picks up speed when flooding or ebbing from Skookumchuck Narrows to the east. If timed right, you can catch the ebb out and reduce a struggle against the current. You can also hug the shoreline and catch the back eddies to make the paddling easier. The current is strongest towards the centre of the channel, and a tidal rip is usually present ahead of Sutton Islands.

Captain Island is a good paddling target and will give you an opportunity to have a rest while you assess the wind and water conditions prior to crossing Jervis Inlet. There isn't much in the way of camping, although it may be possible to squeeze in a tent or two on the Agnew Passage side, near the sandy spit by the lighted buoy off Nelson Island. At the very least, it is a place to wait out bad weather.

Jervis Inlet is exposed to westerly winds in the summer, which usually blow up in the afternoon. Be particularly sensitive to the winds and currents that can stir things up between Hotham Sound and Prince of Wales Reach. The shoreline at the east entrance to Hotham has steep cliff banks; if there is a west wind, paddling close to the Mount Foley side can expose you to rebound waves that may be uncomfortable for people with limited experience.

Harmony Islands Hotham Sound lies just north of Jervis Inlet. As you enter the sound, you will see Freil Falls plummeting from the top of the mountain fed by Freil Lake. Just ahead of the falls are a few places to camp on a gravel beach by a large boulder. The sites are on the side of a hill but will accommodate 2 to 3 tents in a pinch. Just past the falls is a cluster of islands, the Harmony Islands; the south island is a provincial marine park. Signs are obvious on those islands that are private land; please respect them. The marine park offers some small camping areas that are bear-free; groups larger than 6 people may have trouble finding a spot that can accommodate everyone. Landing at low tide can be quite rough.

On the mainland behind the islands is a small oyster-covered beach with 2 or 3 campsites tucked into the forest behind it. A stream runs by the campsite if you need water; Freil Falls is also a source of fresh water. Directly across from Syren Point is a large bay that has a few campsites and access to fresh water. A large grassy section once held up to 12 tents, but active logging has washed out the stream and eroded much of the camp. The beach is rocky but offers 2 to 3 tent sites and is a good location to use if you plan on venturing deep into the sound.

At this point, you may want to spend your time exploring or return to Egmont. If you are looking for a little more adventure, you can always head west to Nelson Island or east up Jervis Inlet.

Jervis Inlet The deepest of B.C.'s many inlets, Jervis Inlet reaches depths of 720 m (2400 ft.) though it is never more than 1.6 km (1 mi.) wide. As it zigzags 80 km (50 mi.) inland, each reach of the inlet commemorates a member of the British royal family, beginning with Prince of Wales Reach through Princess Royal Reach and Queens Reach. The inlet's banks are high cliffs with occasional pocket beaches, most of which have homes on them. Most of the land is tenured by forest companies as tree farms.

The winds in Jervis Inlet are notorious: they can pick up quickly and be deflected and funnelled off the steep-sided walls. Aside from

Malibu Rapids, the currents here are quite subtle, but it is best to paddle north with the flood and south with the ebb to give yourself a bit of a break. Jervis Inlet is not for beginners.

For those who do head up the inlet, be warned again: Campsites are few and far between. Goliath Bay has an old log sort where you will find flat ground when in need. Camping is possible at the mouth of High Creek on the north side of Vancouver Bay, if you first get permission from the Sechelt Indian Band; there is a beautiful hike up the creek featuring a few old-growth cedars. Deserted Bay, farther along, also has some gently sloping land and room for tents. Once again, however, this is Sechelt Indian Band land and permission must be obtained prior to visiting.

Princess Louisa Inlet Princess Louisa Inlet, a canyon 8 km (5 mi.) long and about .8 km (.5 mi.) across, opens up near the end of Queens Reach. This lovely inlet, whose towering cliffs are covered with myriad waterfalls, is an internationally known yachting destination beloved by generations of boaters. Its curious ability to inspire the imagination of those who see it is best characterized by Malibu Camp, which is situated at the tidal rapid at the entrance of the inlet. Built by Thomas Hamilton, the inventor of the variable pitch propeller, the camp was conceived as a retreat for the rich and famous, who visited in droves in its heyday in the 1940s. Constructed of local materials, the camp is an amazing structure complemented by the many totem poles that grace the grounds. Malibu Camp is now owned by Young Life International and operated as a summer camp for kids. Be sure to time your entrance and exit to the inlet with slack tide at Malibu Rapids, which can run up to 10 knots at full force.

Much of Princess Louisa Inlet—or *Suivoolot*, meaning sunny and warm—was once owned by James F. "Mac" Macdonald. In 1953, wishing to share and preserve its beauty, Mac turned the property over to the non-profit Princess Louisa International Society, which subsequently transferred it to the government of B.C. The property is now known as Princess Louisa Provincial Marine Park. Although there is little camping in the inlet, the site at Chatterbox Falls can accommodate people at 4 sites and is partially developed, with floats, picnic tables and toilets. A second campsite behind Macdonald Island, about midway down the inlet, also has 6 tent sites and a pit toilet.

TRIP 22 Nelson Island

SKILL: Intermediate to advanced
TIME: 3–5 days
HAZARDS: Winds and traffic
ACCESS: Pender Harbour
CHARTS: 3311 · Sunshine Coast—Vancouver Harbour
to Desolation Sound · 1:40,000
3312 · Jervis Inlet and Desolation Sound · Various
Scales
3512 · Strait of Georgia, Central Portion · 1:80,000
3415 · Jervis Inlet · 1:50,000
TIDE BOOK: Vol. 5

Named after Viscount Horatio Nelson, the hero of the British navy, Nelson Island sits at the mouth of Jervis Inlet guarding the secrets of Prince of Wales Reach and Queens Reach. Famous with the yachting crowd for the scenery and anchorages in Blind Bay and Hidden Basin, the area has a lot to offer paddlers. It is one of the few spots on the coast where you can feel the presence of the towering Coast Mountains while experiencing the expanse of the Strait of Georgia. To explore the west side of Nelson Island, it is best to launch at Pender Harbour.

LAUNCHING
The communities of Garden Bay, Madeira Park and Irvines Landing are known collectively as Pender Harbour, a well-known base for salmon sport fishing. Located 37 km (23 mi.) north of Sechelt, Pender Harbour provides all the necessary amenities to get you started on your trip. Launching at Irvines Landing is possible, but parking is extremely limited. Similarly, though Garden Bay is a 163-ha (403-a.) park, it has a small parking lot and less than 180 m (600 ft.) of beachfront. The day-use waterfront area is only accessible from a small footpath at the southern entrance of the park. In light of this, your best bet is to head out from Madeira Park. The Madeira Park government dock is located next to numerous stores and provides 480 m (1600 ft.) of moorage space and access to the shore. There is plenty of parking but be sure to lock your car. The downside to launching from Madeira Park is the boat traffic you will have to contend with as you cross the harbour and make your way towards Nelson Island.

SITES

Leaving Pender Harbour, you will see the two peaks of Mount Daniel rising behind you. The eastern peak is known as the site where puberty rites were practised by young Sechelt women, while young men performed similar rituals on Cecil Hill. Watch for traffic as you cross Agamemnon Channel and continue along the shore of Nelson Island. The shoreline, wrinkled by bays and lagoons, is filled with artifacts of the past that make for interesting paddling. Unfortunately, though movements are afoot to create more parks, most of Nelson Island is private property and is becoming more and more settled.

The first major bay you will encounter is Quarry Bay, the source of much of the granite used in the fine old buildings of Vancouver, the carved lions on the north steps of the Vancouver Art Gallery being a notable example. Be sure to explore this place; the land carries a record of the techniques used to quarry stone. Note that a stream runs out of little Quarry Lake onto the mud flats on the east side of the bay. The hike to the lake along the stream is lovely.

Cape Cockburn Continuing up the coast, you will find Cape Cockburn, named after Adm. Sir George Cockburn, who, in 1814, avenged the burning of York (later Toronto) by sailing up the Chesapeake and marching overland to burn the capitol buildings in Washington, D.C. This headland can see some pretty wild weather. SunRay, the homestead built by Harry Roberts, still graces the shores of Cockburn Bay. The land is now the property of B.C. Hydro and is the object of passionate local lobbying to turn it into another park. In the meantime, people continue to camp here during the summer months. Although there is no outhouse or water source, there is plenty of room for tents, and unless BC Hydro prohibits camping in the future, the site is worth a visit. Just a note: Cockburn Bay becomes dry during the lowest tides of the year.

A rock garden winds along the coast to the entrance to Hidden Basin. A narrow channel that shows on the chart as dry at low tide leads into an enclosed lagoon, a haven for all kinds of wildlife and yet another homestead.

As you move past Kelly Island, Blind Bay opens before you between Nelson Island and Hardy Island. There are lots of little islets and shoals here covered with oysters and other intertidal life. Ballet Bay on the eastern shore of Blind Bay features a walking trail to Hidden Basin, which is a long portage but worth it if you haven't explored the basin yet.

Musket Island Musket Island, just off Alexander Point on Hardy Island, is a provincial marine park in a quiet cove with a beautiful, dry arbutus landscape. The site is very small, however, and camping is limited to a few mossy flats. Fires are not recommended, but if you need to make one, do not burn on or near the moss. There is no camping fee.

TRIP 23 Jedediah Island

SKILL: Intermediate to advanced

TIME: 3–5 days

HAZARDS: Winds and traffic

ACCESS: Secret Cove/French Creek/Lasqueti Island/ Texada Island

CHARTS: 3311 · Sunshine Coast—Vancouver Harbour to Desolation Sound · 1:40,000

3312 · Jervis Inlet and Desolation Sound · Various Scales

3512 · Strait of Georgia, Central Portion · 1:80,000

3513 · Strait of Georgia, Northern Portion · 1:80,000

TIDE BOOK: Vol. 5

Jedediah Island is one of the newest provincial marine parks on the coast and a favourite trip for more experienced paddlers. Nestled between Texada and Lasqueti Islands, Jedediah is a 243-ha (600-a.) jewel with old-growth forests of Douglas-fir and arbutus, a variety of wildlife and a shoreline rich in marine life. In the early 1990s the owners and residents of Jedediah, Mary and Al Palmer, decided it was time to move on and agreed to sell it to the province. The Palmers were committed to the dream of the island being protected as a park, and their price tag of $4.2 million was well below market value. Nonetheless, the province was strapped for cash. Contributions from the federal government under the Pacific Marine Heritage Legacy program, from the estate of Dan Culver and from numerous individuals, groups and corporations helped raise the full purchase price.

LAUNCHING

You can reach Jedediah from a number of areas including Vancouver Island, Lasqueti Island, Texada Island and the Sunshine Coast.

If launching from Vancouver Island, you can put in at various boat launches between Nanoose Bay and Parksville; the best spot is French Creek. Here you have the choice of paddling the 13 km (8 mi.) of potentially treacherous water to reach Sangster Island and points beyond or of taking the B.C. ferry to False Bay on Lasqueti Island. If you decide to paddle, be very cautious of the vicious and sudden Qualicum wind as well as the usual southeasters. This crossing should not be attempted by beginners.

If you are taking the Lasqueti Island ferry, you will have to deal with its awkward schedule and restrictive capacity. Once on Lasqueti, launching is easily done from the beach by the ferry dock. There is also a store if you need to pick up last-minute supplies. Although it is about 20 km (12.5 mi.) to Home Bay on Jedediah Island, there is some camping on Finnerty Island and the Fegan Islets just north of False Bay, though the sites are small. From here, Long Bay at the north end of Jedediah is an easy day's paddle, and Home Bay is only a few more kilometres away.

Launching from Texada Island puts you in one of the best positions to access Jedediah. If you are coming from Vancouver Island, take the Comox ferry to Powell River and then the 35-minute ferry to Texada. Once on Texada, you can drive across the island and launch at the Shelter Point Park in Gillies Bay or travel farther south along a gravel road to the free Forest Service recreation site at Shingle Beach. You will need local information or a Ministry of Forests recreation map (from the Powell River office) if you are heading to Shingle Beach, because the road takes quite a few turns.

To launch from Secret Cove on the Sunshine Coast, follow Highway 101 north from Sechelt and past Halfmoon Bay until you see signs indicating the turnoff. Shortly after exiting the highway, turn onto Secret Cove Road and follow it to the government dock. There isn't a lot of parking, but the atmosphere is a little easier to deal with than the surrounding marinas.

A final option for launching is to hire a charter service or kayak operator to shuttle you and your boats to Jedediah Island. Considering the dangerous crossings involved, this is a good idea for beginners. There are a number of services in French Creek, Nanoose Bay and Gibsons.

The following trip description is written as though you are paddling from Secret Cove. If this is not the case, simply use the camping information to help customize your journey from any of the launch sites.

SITES

The Thormanbys Starting from the mainland, head for the light at Epsom Point at the northwest corner of North Thormanby Island. The Thormanbys are great islands to explore, and they provide two marine parks for people wishing to camp (see the following section on trips in the Strait of Georgia for more information). From North Thormanby, paddle directly across to Texada, heading for the point that, at the time of writing, was easily identified by a navigation light just off it. As your mother would say, look both ways before you cross. This is a major shipping lane, and no matter what the rules of the sea may state, most ships have the right of way over the kayaker by virtue of their size. Expect lots of tugs, log booms, the occasional cruise ship and all manner of other vessels.

Texada Island The crossing to Texada Island of about 10 km (6 mi.) is through some of the most treacherous water along the coast. Because you are exposed to the full fetch of the strait to the south, weather here can descend on you rapidly. Tidal currents diverge around the various islands and passes, creating unexpected conditions. The trip is best made in the early morning or late afternoon; evaluate carefully before setting out. Although there are many shallow bays on this shore of Texada Island, they are private and must be treated with respect if you are forced to seek refuge.

As you round the south end of Texada, you will enter Sabine Channel, an area of consistent winds. Note: There is virtually no water on Jedediah Island. If you need extra water, there is a large stream in a shallow bay just around Texada's south end. There is also an abandoned homestead just up from the beach where you can camp, if necessary.

Jedediah Island Across Sabine Channel you'll find a cluster of islands. The first are huge, bare granite peaks punching out of the water with shoals at their base, followed by Jedediah Island, the largest of the group. Follow the east shore of Jedediah south until you find the entrance to Home Bay. This narrow defile is hard to see until you are right on top of it. If the tide is low when you arrive, the lagoon may be dry. You can land on the rock beach before the entrance to the bay or wait till the tide comes in before unloading your boat and setting up camp.

Home Bay offers the paddler a sand beach with a grassy upland for camping. An old horse and a flock of sheep, remnants of an old homestead, share the island with goats reportedly left there by the original explorers of the coast. Although free from bears, the island is home to many a raccoon that will enjoy picking through your camp given half a chance. Take advantage of the walks available through the grassland and over rocky crags. BC Parks is developing the site, so call them for the latest camping information.

Although Home Bay is a favourite camping spot, many of the little bays along the west side of the island offer good camping, as does Long Bay at the north end. A lot of these bays dry at low tide leaving long mud flats, so time your landings and launchings. Be sure to explore the deluxe paddling in and around the island. Little Bull Passage on the west of Jedediah has a nice tidal flow between high granite cliffs, and the trip to Squitty Bay on the southernmost tip of Lasqueti is a feast for the senses. Although camping is not allowed in Squitty Bay Provincial Park, some of the best paddling around is found at the head of the bay.

Shingle Beach (Texada Island) If you don't want to head directly home, you can explore the southwest shore of Texada Island a little more closely. Shingle Beach is a road-accessible Forest Service recreation site (see Launching, above). To find it from the water, look for Texada's Mount Davies and head just to the south. A mile or so away you should be able to recognize the sweeping pebble shoreline of

Shingle Beach. There are often cars parked at the north end of the beach—another tip that you are in the right spot. The beach is beautiful but a little exposed, and landing can be a tricky. There is plenty of room for camping up the road if you can't find anything by the water. If you continue heading north along Texada, you will start to see prominent signs of development and the odd pay-for-use campground.

Whichever route you take, remember that southeast winds will be at their strongest on the open strait and can keep you in camp for a day or two, especially in the spring and fall. You are particularly vulnerable at Squitty Bay and around the tip of Lasqueti. Sabine Channel funnels wind and tide, producing severe chop augmented further when the wind is against the tide. By waiting for slack you will avoid the worst conditions. Remember: These islands are in the middle of shipping lanes from both Powell River and Campbell River, and all that traffic is bigger than you in your kayak. Enjoy one of B.C.'s newest parks but stay alert!

TRIP 24 Strait of Georgia

SKILL:	Beginner to advanced
TIME:	Day trip
HAZARDS:	Winds and traffic
ACCESS:	Numerous sites on the Sunshine Coast
CHARTS:	3311 · Sunshine Coast—Vancouver Harbour to Desolation Sound · 1:40,000
	3512 · Strait of Georgia, Central Portion · 1:80,000
TIDE BOOK:	Vol. 5

The Strait of Georgia trip described below can be used either by long-distance paddlers travelling the coastal marine trail, from the south or the north, or by paddlers out for day trips. The following launch sites are listed in a south to north fashion.

LAUNCHING

Leaving from Gibsons is quite easy, using either the marina or Hopkins Landing, near the Langdale ferry terminal. For more information, see chapter 6.

∧ *Merry Island,* PETER MCGEE

To launch from the beach at Davis Bay, follow Highway 101 through Gibsons northwest towards Sechelt. As you are nearing town, just after crossing the Chapman Creek bridge you will see a small lot off the highway at Mission Point. Park in the lot and launch from the beach.

The Selma Park boat ramp is another possibility. Look for the boat ramp sign between Davis Bay and Sechelt. Exit the highway and follow Mason Road to the breakwater. The concrete ramp and small beach offer protected access to the water, and the Trail Islands are only a couple of miles away. There is ample parking.

Sargeant Bay Provincial Park is located a few minutes north of Sechelt. The cobble beach at this day-use area is excellent for launching; you may also want to relax for a few minutes and check out the abundant sea and intertidal life. There is a picnic area and pit toilet, but no overnight parking.

Halfmoon Bay is accessed off Highway 101 about 7 km (4.3 mi.) north of Sechelt. You can launch at the government wharf at the apex of the bay or at Frenchmans Cove at the end of Brooks Road. Limited parking is available.

Secret Cove is located just north of Halfmoon Bay. Turn off the highway where indicated and turn onto Secret Cove Road to reach the government wharf. Limited parking is available.

SITES

The first thing you encounter after leaving Gibsons and heading up the Strait of Georgia is "The Stretch." The 32-km (20-mi.) coastline between Gibsons and Sechelt has no offshore islands and only rare bits of sand along the rocky shore, which leaves you open to the full fetch of the strait. The estuary of Roberts Creek, the new marina at Davis Bay and the boat ramp at Selma Park offer respite in need. A one-way trip up or down the whole Stretch is a 7–10-hour paddle.

White Islets Look for the White Islets, a number of granite peaks thrusting out of the water with windswept austerity, about a mile offshore opposite the Wilson Creek estuary. Although inhospitable in human terms, these rocks offer a welcome haven for a variety of seabirds and mammals. This is a designated bird sanctuary so stay on the water and keep your distance. For a day trip, launch from the beach at Davis Bay.

The next large bay along the coast is Trail Bay, which encompasses the smaller Davis Bay, Selma Park, the Sechelt Indian lands and the town of Sechelt. The Trail Islands are nestled in the northwest corner of the bay. These islands are home to a great variety of wildlife, considering their proximity to town. Although the islands are private property, look for the spit on the inland side of the most southerly island if you need to land, and enjoy the flocks of oystercatchers that favour this spot. These islands also make a wonderful day trip when you launch from either the Selma Park boat ramp or Sargeant Bay.

Sargeant Bay Sargeant Bay opens off to the north, a lovely little pocket of protected water with a beach and a park at the apex, though no camping. Take the time to walk through the wetlands at the creek mouth where a wildlife refuge has been developed and maintained by local people and BC Parks. The high bank at the mouth of Sargeant Bay creates a long flat stretching out into the sea, a favourite habitat for herons and other fish-loving birds.

Merry Island Heading north you will encounter Halfmoon Bay, Merry Island and the Thormanbys. Merry Island has the quintessential lighthouse with its high, white tower topped by the flashing light, red roof and railings—a classic photo opportunity. It guards the entrance to Welcome Passage, the narrow channel between South Thormanby Island and the mainland. Be careful: This channel is notorious for nasty weather when the funnelling effect picks up the wind and waves, especially when the wind is against the tide. Unfortunately, due to liability concerns, the lightkeepers no longer tour visitors around the island. Nonetheless, there is plenty to see from the water, for many varieties of duck patrol the shores of Merry Island due to its great fishing opportunities. Franklin Island, which hugs the western shore of Merry Island, is another sanctuary for nesting seabirds. A number of the older homes on Merry Island are gradually falling down, leaving room for potential campsites. The ongoing Coast Guard shuffle regarding light stations will have to be sorted out, however, before a site is created here.

The government wharf at the apex of Halfmoon Bay is a good place to stop off to replenish supplies at the great little general store just up the road.

North and South Thormanby Islands The Thormanby Islands lie just west of Halfmoon Bay and are a study in opposites. South Thormanby is the usual pile of granite with lots of sheer cliffs indented by tiny bays and cobble beaches. North Thormanby, on the other hand, is one enormous sand dune falling into long, shallow flats.

Simson Provincial Marine Park covers the entire southeastern side of South Thormanby so camping spots are easy to find, although they are all undeveloped. The small bay that sports the marine park sign will lead you to the interior of the island, which was formerly a homestead. Great camping, hiking and birding abound.

North Thormanby arcs out from the western shore of its companion island, creating the wide Buccaneer Bay between them. The apex of the bay is a narrow isthmus that connects the two islands. The public campground is on this little lick of land in Buccaneer Bay Provincial Park, which also provides lots of sand with great swimming. Mind your feet when walking here as the bay is home to a unique cactus-like plant. During big tides, water will flood the spit so you can paddle right through. Resist the impulse to climb the sand cliffs: they are very unstable. The beaches on the open strait offer an opportunity for some gentle kayak surfing.

Smuggler Cove Buccaneer Bay opens off the western end of Welcome Passage, whereas Smuggler Cove Provincial Marine Park lies on the mainland side. The end of a narrow pass marked by the familiar marine park sign reveals a completely enclosed cove sprinkled with tiny islands and shoals.

A favourite with the boating crowd, Smuggler Cove is rich with tales of the booze trade during Prohibition and the often tragic stories of thousands of Chinese workers from the CP Railway who came here looking for illegal passage to the United States. Camping is best at the far end, where there is a small beach for landing and some facilities. The beach ends up as a long mud flat at low tide, so try to arrive and leave at high tide. The cove is also accessible from a 1.3-km (.8-mi.) trail that leads to a parking lot located just off Highway 101, and you can expect company during the summer.

Secret Cove is at the top of the next wide bay on the mainland. Another enclosed patch of water with a couple of marinas, Secret Cove also features a small store with supplies for visiting boaters. Local kayakers often use this cove as the jumping-off place for the trip to Jedediah Island.

ADDITIONAL ROUTES

Heading south The southern end of the Sunshine Coast blends into Howe Sound and the paddle routes described in chapter 6.

Heading north Continuing up the coast towards Powell River from Musket Island Provincial Marine Park will take you to Scotch Fir Point, an area of great camping potential though individual sites have not been developed. If you head into Jervis Inlet, you will soon come across Saltery Bay Provincial Park—a nice, though developed, park that sits by the roadside. If you paddle in the opposite direction, towards Texada Island, check out Pocahontas and Raven Bays. Although they are road accessible, there are plenty of flat areas for camping and reasonably protected landings. Pocahontas Bay is an old log dump and considerably more industrial in feel than Raven Bay.

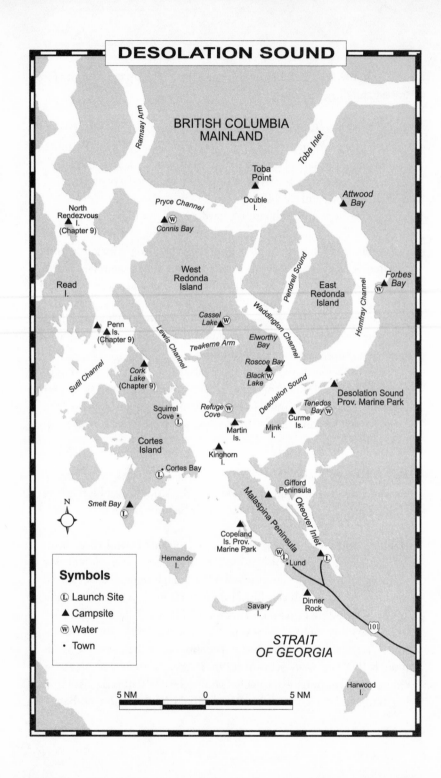

DESOLATION SOUND

BRITISH COLUMBIA MAINLAND

Ramsay Arm

Toba Inlet

Pryce Channel

Toba Point ▲

Double I.

Attwood ▲ Bay

North Rendezvous ▲ I. (Chapter 9)

▲ⓦ Connis Bay

West Redonda Island

Pendrell Sound

East Redonda Island

Forbes ⓦ Bay

Read I.

Cassel ⓦ Lake ▲

Homfray Channel

▲ Penn Is. (Chapter 9)

Teakerne Arm

Lewis Channel

Elworthy Bay

Waddington Channel

Sutil Channel

Cork Lake (Chapter 9) ▲

Roscoe Bay ▲

Black ⓦ Lake

Desolation Sound

▲ Desolation Sound Prov. Marine Park

Squirrel Cove ▲ •ⓛ

Refuge ⓦ Cove ▲

Martin Is.

Mink Is.

▲ Curme Is.

Tenedos ⓦ Bay

Cortes Island

Kinghorn I. ▲

ⓛ • Cortes Bay

N

Smelt Bay ▲ ⓛ

Gifford Peninsula

Malaspina Peninsula

Okeover Inlet

Copeland Is. Prov. Marine Park ▲

Hernando I.

ⓦ ⓛ •Lund

Symbols

ⓛ Launch Site
▲ Campsite
ⓦ Water
• Town

Savary I.

▲ Dinner Rock

(101)

STRAIT OF GEORGIA

Harwood I.

5 NM   0   5 NM

8

Desolation Sound

Ralph Keller

Located beyond the northern terminus of Highway 101, Desolation Sound greets thousands of boaters every summer with its spectacular scenery and unusually warm waters. Bordered by the Coast Mountains of mainland B.C. to the east and the Discovery Islands to the west, Desolation Sound offers paddlers of all abilities a wilderness unscarred by the development that is so common in southern B.C. It is here that paddlers often gain their first taste of the North Coast.

BACKGROUND

When you paddle in Desolation Sound, you are in Sliammon territory and the territories of their friends and relatives, the Klahoose people. As Cheryl Coull writes, the people have always lived here and the winds have always blown. In the very earliest of times, the people of Sliammon tell us, Raven and some other people journeyed north, killed the tiresome Wind-Maker and his wife, and brought their gusty son home with them. Something to remember on your trip.

Capt. George Vancouver referred to Desolation Sound as "a dark and gloomy place." The summer paddler is unlikely to notice that particular effect, though Homfray Channel and Pendrell Sound with their high mountains might well take on a "gloomy" appearance in bad weather. Desolation Sound only receives about 102–152 cm (40–60 in.) of rainfall per year—little of that during the summer.

One of the most interesting facts about Desolation Sound is that it marks the junction of the two tidal streams entering the inside coast of Vancouver Island—one via Juan de Fuca Strait to the south and one via Johnstone Strait to the north. This junction limits the flushing effects of the tides and dramatically increases the water temperature, creating some of the best swimming on the coast. Pendrell Sound, at the north end of East Redonda Island, the most notable example of this phenomenon, has actually reached temperatures of 26°c (78°f) during the summer, earning it the title of the warmest ocean temperature north of the Gulf of Mexico.

The junction of the two tidal streams also creates inconsistent tides throughout the area. Water wrapping around the north end of Vancouver Island floods in a southerly direction, and water entering from Juan de Fuca Strait floods in a northerly direction (and vice versa for an ebbing tide). It is this change in tidal direction that first tipped Captain Vancouver and his crew to the possibility that the land mass to the west of them—Vancouver Island—was in fact an island.

GETTING THERE

To reach Desolation Sound, it's best to launch from Lund or from Okeover Inlet. It is also possible to access the area by launching from Cortes Island, a good option if you are travelling from Vancouver Island or intending to explore the Discovery Islands as well.

By land From Vancouver, head to Horseshoe Bay and catch the Langdale ferry (45 minutes). The ferries run frequently but expect delays on long weekends. Head north along Highway 101, past Sechelt, to the Earls Cove ferry terminal. Catch the ferry to Saltery Bay (35 minutes) and once again head north along Highway 101 through the town of Powell River, until you reach Lund. Total travel time from Vancouver is about 5 hours.

If you are coming from Vancouver Island, drive to Comox, take the ferry to Powell River and follow Highway 101 north to Lund. The trip from Comox to Lund takes about 2 hours.

If you plan to launch from Cortes Island, drive to Campbell River, take the ferry to Quadra Island (15 minutes), drive across Quadra Island to Heriot Bay (15 minutes) and board the ferry to Cortes Island (40–45 minutes).

By water Remote water drop-off service, including kayaks, is available from Discovery Launch Water Service, Sutil Charters and Coast Mountain Expeditions, which specializes in remote kayak charters (up to 12 paddlers and kayaks per trip).

By air There are scheduled flights to Campbell River from Vancouver and Seattle with stops in Victoria, Nanaimo and Courtenay. There is also float plane service available from Seattle via Kenmore Air. Coval Air and Island Air/Rush Air out of Campbell River provide drop-off service to remote outlying areas (a maximum of two hard-shelled boats per trip).

WEATHER AND HAZARDS

Desolation Sound is known for both its fair weather and warm waters. In the summer, air temperatures hover around 22°C (72°F). Winds during June, July and August tend to be reasonably light, though be sure to review the note on anabatic and katabatic winds in chapter 1 if you plan to venture up any of the inlets. In addition, exercise caution, for even a fair-weather westerly can catch you off guard when it is redirected within the convoluted channels of the Discovery Islands. Fog is not typically a problem. There is usually good VHF weather reception on channel 21 International throughout the region.

Although the paddling environment in Desolation Sound is fairly benign, other boaters can make certain areas unsafe for kayakers. The danger from larger high-speed powerboats cannot be overstated, so you are best to limit your crossings as much as possible and never assume you are seen. Finally, paddlers should take the necessary precautions against bears when camping on the mainland and the larger islands.

SPECIAL CONSIDERATIONS

As you paddle around Desolation Sound, you will likely notice the striking profile of Mount Addenbroke on East Redonda Island. This is

B.C.'s tallest offshore mountain, aside from those on Vancouver Island, and it has a wonderful array of ecosystems. Because of this, much of East Redonda is an ecological reserve, and paddlers are asked to refrain from camping anywhere on the island.

Due to the dry climate, campfires and beach fires are not allowed on most of the islands of Desolation Sound without a burning permit. We ask that paddlers use caution at all times with fires of any kind—a major fire would be devastating.

DESOLATION SOUND TRIPS (25–26)

The paddling possibilities of Desolation Sound are limitless. For beginners, there are great 3–4-day trips that begin in Lund or Okeover Inlet and explore the Desolation Sound Marine Park—perfect for a long weekend. If you have a week or so, and a bit more experience,

v *Heading into the Copeland Islands,* PETER MCGEE

the spectacular vistas, rugged beauty and peace of the Redonda Islands and Toba Inlet await. For those who like to mix things up a little and have the time, see the note at the end of the chapter on combining trips in Desolation Sound and the Discovery Islands. The logistics are a little hard to work out, but the adventure is worth the effort.

TRIP 25 Desolation Sound

SKILL: Beginner to intermediate
TIME: 3–5 days
HAZARDS: Boat traffic
ACCESS: Lund/Okeover Inlet/Cortes Island
CHARTS: 3312 · Jervis Inlet and Desolation Sound · Various Scales
3538 · Desolation and Sutil Channel · 1:40,000
TIDE BOOK: Vols. 5 and 6

This trip passes through Desolation Sound and Homfray Channel. The route leaves from Lund, although there is an alternative and more protected launch site in Okeover Inlet, on the eastern side of the Malaspina Peninsula.

Paddlers looking for a 3–4-day beginner-to-intermediate exploration of Desolation Sound should limit their paddling to the area south of, and including, Desolation Sound Provincial Marine Park. Please keep in mind that exploring farther north and into Toba Inlet requires more time and more skill.

LAUNCHING

Launching from Lund provides you with the greatest number of amenities although it also leaves you somewhat exposed to the Strait of Georgia. To reach the best launching site, follow Highway 101 to the centre of Lund. Facing the water, you will have the Lund Hotel to your right and the government wharf in front of you and to your left. The best option is to unload all your gear at the wharf and arrange for Dave's Boat Rental to valet park your car. The cost, about $4 per day, saves you the virtually impossible task of finding an overnight parking space. Finally, don't forget to have a few dollars handy to stock up on the cinnamon buns from Nancy's Bakery—perhaps the best start to any kayak trip. Kayak rentals are available in Lund.

To reach the provincial park and launching site in Okeover Inlet, turn right at Malaspina Road, 6 km (3.7 mi.) before Lund, and drive 4 km (2.5 mi.) to the government wharf at Okeover Inlet. Parking here is also hard to find, and there have been a few incidents of vandalism. You are advised to park in one of the private pay lots such as the Y-Knot Campsite. Okeover Arm Provincial Park has vehicle accessible campsites for $14 per night.

Although Okeover does provide relatively sheltered access to the Desolation Sound Provincial Marine Park, the wind has been known to howl quite nastily down the inlet. If you choose to launch in Okeover, please note that Portage Cove at the mouth of the inlet is private land; no matter how tempting, avoid crossing the property. If you need a place to camp near the launch site, look for the small beach on the Malaspina Peninsula that sits directly across from Kakaekae Point on the Gifford Peninsula.

SITES
As you paddle away from Lund, you will be able to see Savary Island to the south and a number of smaller islands to the north. These are the Copeland Islands, a provincial marine park that offers campsites, pit toilets and anchorages. Although it is a short half-hour to an hour's paddle to reach the Copelands, be sure to keep an eye on the winds and boat traffic.

Copeland Islands The Copeland Islands were named after Joe Copeland, a hand logger who lived here during the early part of the century. It seems this character was a rather unscrupulous officer in the Confederate army during the American Civil War. After the war, he became an outlaw who specialized in holding up stagecoaches. He was chased by U.S. officials over the border and into Canada. Fearing apprehension, he lived out the rest of his life in the Copelands.

The islands are beautiful and well known so don't be surprised if you are not alone. Perhaps the best campsite is on the middle island in a west-facing bay. A gently curving beach, lined with arbutus trees, provides access to plenty of tent sites. Watch the setting sun or climb the steep, short hill behind camp to watch the rising moon. There is no fresh water.

Leaving the Copelands and heading north, you will round Sarah Point and enter Desolation Sound. The point is steep-sided, and landing can be difficult; plan this leg of the journey with care—you might be in your boat for a few hours. If the Curme Islands are your next destination, head directly for Mink Island and work your way to its eastern shore. If you are into exploring, a number of sites lie nearby including Kinghorn Island and the Martin Islands (discussed below).

Curme Islands They may not be big but they sure are pretty. During the high season you can expect to share these gems with other paddlers. Tent and landing sites are a little difficult to find on the rocky shores, but you can find both in the centre of the northern cluster of islets. The Curmes have no fresh water, and the nearest supply of drinking water is a small stream flowing out of Unwin Lake at the top of Tenedos Bay. If you are a large group, avoid camping on the Curmes due to the limited space. All paddlers should be aware of the nearby seal haul-outs and try to maintain a reasonable distance.

It is a short jump from the Curme Islands into Desolation Sound Provincial Marine Park. Although popular with the big-boat crowd, the park offers a number of camping spots for kayakers, including sites in and around Prideaux Haven. Another provincial park, Roscoe Bay, is located close by on the southwestern end of West Redonda Island.

Roscoe Bay and Black Lake (West Redonda Island) When you first paddle into Roscoe Bay, you'll notice it is wall-to-wall (shore-to-shore) pleasure craft, and you may wonder why it is included in this guide. The truth is, the busyness of the place does not completely diminish its beauty. There are great campsites here and pit toilets compliments of BC Parks. Most noteworthy is Black Lake. There couldn't be a warmer lake anywhere else in B.C., and it is definitely worth the paddle (a few kilometres). Black Lake is a great place to brush up on rescues, rolls or any other kayak-related activity that involves getting wet.

The most obvious place to get water is the small stream running out of the lake past the campsites. Because of the number of people using the lake, however, drinking the stream water is not recommended. The best place to get good drinking water is to paddle about 100 m (330 ft.) to the north side of the bay, where a delightful spring splashes over a small cliff. Often, someone will have rigged up a water line to facilitate filling containers.

At this point in the trip, people with time constraints or little paddling experience should begin working their way back to Lund or Okeover Inlet. Those wanting to carry on can head east and begin the journey up Homfray Channel towards Forbes Bay.

TRIP 26 Toba Inlet

SKILL:	Intermediate to advanced
TIME:	5–14 days
HAZARDS:	Boat traffic and wind
ACCESS:	Lund/Okeover Inlet/Cortes Island
CHARTS:	3312 · Jervis Inlet and Desolation Sound · Various Scales
	3538 · Desolation and Sutil Channel · 1:40,000
	3541 · Approaches to Toba Inlet · 1:40,000
TIDE BOOK:	Vols. 5 and 6

SITES

The following trip assumes you have already reached Homfray Channel via the Desolation Sound trip described above.

Forbes Bay Two good campsites exist at Forbes Bay. The first is in the middle of a large rocky beach right at the top of the bay, about 300 m (990 ft.) north of Forbes Creek; the second is in an adjacent watershed at the extreme south end of the bay. Pleasure craft tend to anchor at the latter site, which is somewhat more protected than just off the main beach. Both sites are close to the wonderful water of Forbes Creek.

Part of the rocky beach and surrounding watershed belongs to the Klahoose Nation, and you'll notice that the watershed has more or less all its trees intact. You are enjoying much of this extraordinarily beautiful place courtesy of the Klahoose Nation, and their permission should be sought before camping on the northern beach.

Finally, a sobering thought: Forbes Bay is grizzly bear habitat. It is not prime habitat but they are there. This is no place to become complacent about bear protocol. Be careful and do everything right. If you don't remember how to cache your food, read chapter 1 again.

∧ *Bourassa Falls, Toba Inlet,* DALE DUFOUR

Attwood Bay If you are continuing up Homfray Channel, be sure to check out Attwood Bay. On the south side of the bay is a flat, albeit exposed, clearing that used to be a log dump. It is a nice campsite even though the bay can get quite busy with sport-fishing boats.

Toba Point Unnamed on your chart—we gave it this name—Toba Point is distinguishable by a navigational light about 300 m (990 ft.) to the west and by Double Island to the east, in the entrance to Toba Inlet. It has a great, steep gravelly beach—easy on your kayak and a short carry to the high tide line. This site was a real gem until it was clear-cut a few years ago. Still, it is a great find in an area where the mountains tend to rise straight out of the ocean. There is good camping on the nearby point just to the west. This is prime bear country so take appropriate measures.

In the early part of the summer season, you will probably find water in a small stream just above the beach but don't plan on it. Because of the mountainous terrain, however, there are literally dozens of good-sized creeks tumbling down the hills all along your route. During a lunch or bladder break, fill your water containers from one of these. Not only is the water here potable, at least one major company bottles the stuff and sells it internationally at premium prices. So drink up!

Heading farther up Toba Inlet requires quite a commitment since campsites become scarce and the weather more temperamental. Nonetheless, experienced paddlers will be rewarded with spectacular vistas and wonderful solitude. For the less adventurous, heading west towards Connis Bay will start you on the path home.

Connis Bay (West Redonda Island) Connis Bay is several hundred metres west of Connis Point. When you see Connis Point, you'll understand why we prefer to stay at Connis Bay. There are plenty of good campsites among the alders just above high tide. If you're energetic and don't mind doing a little bushwhacking, you can hike up to a small lake about 2 km (1.2 mi.) back into the hills. Be warned: This part of West Redonda Island seems to have a rather healthy black bear population, and you will need to adopt bear protocol during your stay.

Spilling out into the bay is a wonderful creek that is always brimming and bubbling with cold, pure water. If you follow the creek back into the tree line just above the beach—wade up the creek from the beach—you'll discover a wonderful pool fed by a 3-m (10-ft.) waterfall.

Teakerne Arm and Cassel Lake (West Redonda Island) As you head south down Lewis Channel, you will come across Teakerne Arm. The journey to the top of this arm on the west side of West Redonda Island is a little out of the way—an 8-km (5-mi.) round trip. Still, the time and energy spent getting here is easily worth it. The setting is as idyllic as anything you will find on the coast: a deep, protected bay whose top is graced by a waterfall—not just any waterfall, a *warm* waterfall that spills out of an equally warm lake. This is also a campsite if a day's visit is not enough.

Leaving Teakerne Arm and continuing south, you soon end up back in Desolation Sound. There are a number of campsites including the Martin Islands, where Lewis Channel and Desolation Sound meet.

Martin Islands Although the chart shows two islands, for practical purposes there is just one. Evidently the neck that joins the two islands floods during the big winter tides but this never happens in the summer. This relatively flat neck is where most people put their tents. If it is occupied when you arrive, don't be dismayed: there are other good sites nearby. Be advised that you are once again entering the very heart of Desolation Sound—an international pleasure craft destination. A lot of big yachts can be seen cruising by, especially in the pass between the Martin Islands and West Redonda Island. These big boats love to blast through the pass at high speed, throwing off huge amounts of wash. If you're unloading your kayak for the day, be sure to put it well up on shore so it does not get slammed around on the rocky beach whenever a member of the afternoon double-martini crowd zips by.

Unfortunately, there is no fresh water here. The closest source is at Refuge Cove on West Redonda Island, about 1.5 km (1 mi.) away. They not only have water but ice cream, pop and espresso coffee. So if you haven't had a sugar or caffeine fix in a while...

If the Martin Islands seem a little crowded or exposed, check out the north end of Kinghorn Island. Although it has no designated campsites, there are a number of rocky beaches to land on and roomy trees to camp among. From here, it is a short jump back to Okeover Inlet or the Copeland Islands and Lund.

ADDITIONAL ROUTES
Heading north This leads to the Discovery Islands (chapter 9).

Heading south Savary and Hernando Islands, both extremely beautiful, are essentially private. Dinner Rock just south of Lund is a Forest Service recreation site but the rest of the coast to Powell River is pretty developed. Farther south, sites appear on Texada and Nelson Islands (chapter 7).

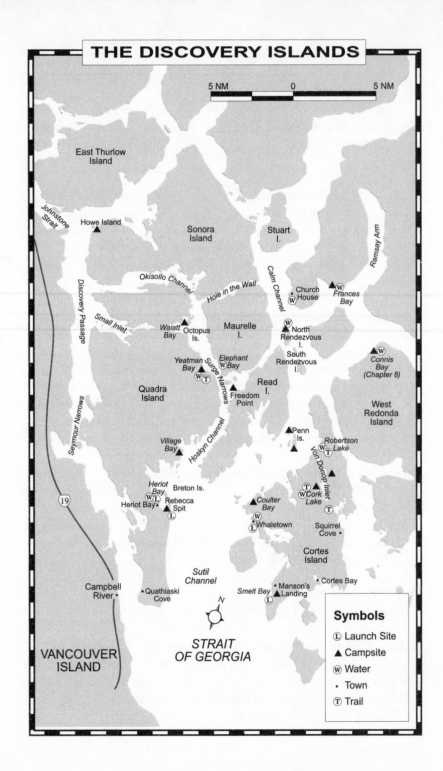

THE DISCOVERY ISLANDS

5 NM · 0 · 5 NM

East Thurlow
Island

Johnstone Strait

Howe Island ▲

Sonora
Island

Stuart
I.

Ramsay Arm

Discovery Passage

Okisollo Channel

Hole in the Wall

Calm Channel

Church
House ●
Ⓦ

Frances
Bay ▲Ⓦ

Small Inlet

Ⓦ North
Rendezvous
I.

South
Rendezvous
I.

Connis
Bay
(Chapter 8) ▲Ⓦ

Waiatt
Bay ▲
Octopus
Is.

Maurelle
I.

Elephant
WBay

*Yeatman
Bay* ▲
Ⓦ Ⓣ

Surge Narrows

Read
I.

▲
Freedom
Point

West
Redonda
Island

Quadra
Island

Hoskyn Channel

Seymour Narrows

Village
Bay ▲

▲Penn
Is.

▲

*Robertson
Lake* Ⓦ
Ⓣ

▲

Von Donop Inlet

(19)

Heriot
Bay ▲ⓌⓁ
Heriot Bay ●
Rebecca
Ⓛ▲ Spit

Breton Is.

▲Coulter
Bay

Ⓣ
Ⓦ*Cork
Lake*

Ⓣ

Ⓦ
Ⓛ Whaletown

Squirrel
Cove ●

Cortes
Island

Campbell
River ●

*Sutil
Channel*

● Quathiaski
Cove

Smelt Bay

Ⓝ

● Manson's
▲Landing
Ⓛ

● Cortes Bay

*STRAIT
OF GEORGIA*

VANCOUVER
ISLAND

Symbols

Ⓛ Launch Site
▲ Campsite
Ⓦ Water
● Town
Ⓣ Trail

9

The Discovery Islands

Ralph Keller

Steps away from urban civilization, the Discovery Islands are gems of tranquillity at the threshold of a majestic wilderness. Guarded by swift ocean currents, the islands offer spectacular vistas, remote beach camps and a solitude that will make each day a journey of discovery.

BACKGROUND

The Discovery Islands or, more technically, the Northern Gulf Archipelago, are in fact the foothills of the highest mountains in the province, some with snowy peaks rising thousands of metres. Nowhere else on the coast will you find a more dramatic backdrop for a kayaking trip. The waterways between these islands are recent glacier tracks that only 15,000 years ago were scoured out to incredible depths—in some instances, to more than 1500 m (5,000 ft.).

Thousands of years ago, the first people moved into this area. Eventually, three distinct groupings formed: the Klahoose, the Homanthko and the Kwakwaka'wakw (Kwakiutl). They still occupy lands within these islands and the mainland coast, and their ancient pictographs still decorate the cliffs of these islands, their traditional homeland.

In the late 1800s, almost a century after European exploration of the area by Capt. George Vancouver and the Spanish navigator Quadra, among others, settlers began to build homesteads using logging and whaling as their means of support. The warm, calm waters of the southern islands were home to about 300 gray whales, and the entire group was hunted out in just three years. The whale population has never recovered, truly one of the world's great tragedies—all for a few barrels of oil. Whaletown, Lund and Refuge Cove were the three principal whaling stations.

In 1996, a number of dedicated locals successfully lobbied the B.C. government to recognize the rare and outstanding qualities of the region. This led to a significant increase in protected areas, bringing the regional total to about 8000 ha (20,000 a.). On your next trip, consider buying your groceries here, renting a kayak or staying in a B&B as a way of contributing to the local economy and thanking the residents for being the guardians of this magnificent area.

GETTING THERE

By land Take the ferry from Vancouver to Nanaimo (via either the Horseshoe Bay or Tsawwassen terminals) and drive north along Highway 19 (the Island Highway). You can drive from Nanaimo to Campbell River in 1.5 hours and then take the 15-minute ferry ride to Quadra Island. On Quadra, the best place to put in is the beach by the Heriot Bay government dock or at Rebecca Spit Provincial Marine Park. Public parking is available.

By water Remote water drop-off service, including kayaks, is available from Discovery Launch Water Service, Sutil Charters and Coast Mountain Expeditions, which specializes in remote kayak charters (up to 12 paddlers and kayaks per trip).

By air There are scheduled flights to Campbell River from Vancouver and Seattle with stops in Victoria, Nanaimo and Courtenay. Kenmore Air of Seattle offers a limited number of seasonal flights onto Quadra. See chapter 8 for charter information.

WEATHER AND HAZARDS

Desolation Sound and the Discovery Islands are uniquely situated in that they are affected by currents from the Strait of Georgia to the south and from Johnstone Strait to the north. The result is two very different climates. All of the Okisollo Channel, from Surge Narrows north, lies within the Johnstone Strait Oceanic Ecosection, whereas South Quadra, Read Island and Cortes Island fall into the Georgia Basin Ecosection. When you paddle north through Surge Narrows, you paddle through a bioclimatic door and enter a different world. The Okisollo Channel is clearly a much colder, foggier, rainier place even though it is only a few kilometres away from the sunnier and milder Georgia Basin. Most of the trip suggested in this chapter occurs in that warmer setting, where summer temperatures generally range from 19–26°C (66–78°F).

Two notable natural hazards occur in this region: heavy tidal overfall or tidal rapids, and the anabatic, katabatic and outflow wind conditions of the mainland inlets. There is nothing trivial about tidal rapids or the local wind conditions of the inlets. *Under certain conditions, they are guaranteed to be fatal.* With intelligence and humility, however, they can be negotiated by an experienced paddler. For general information on these phenomena, please refer to chapter 1.

There are six distinct sets of tidal rapids in the Discovery Islands, some of which are considered to be the most powerful in the world: Yuculta Rapids, Dent Rapids, Upper and Lower Rapids of the Okisollo, Hole in the Wall, Surge Narrows (Beazley Passage) and Arran Rapids. They run at between 7 and 14 knots. Your Official Canadian Tide and Current Tables: Volume 6 (Discovery Passage and West Coast of Vancouver Island) contains appropriate current table information for Surge Narrows, Hole in the Wall and the Arran Rapids. Any of the region's tidal rapid passes can be negotiated within 15–20 minutes at slack current. You must have current tables—*not tide tables*—with you, and you must understand how to read them and the current direction indicators on your marine chart. (Remember, times listed are Standard Time; add one hour to compensate for local Daylight Saving Time.)

Surge Narrows has a 40-minute window for safe passage—20 minutes either side of slack. Stay out of Beazley Passage, the main shipping route, and take one of the secondary passages. Your journey will be more interesting and you'll have fewer boats to contend with. Unless you intend to stay put for a tide (6 hours), don't stop or get out in the tidal rapids pass. Right at slack current, the pass appears unusually benign but this will change very quickly. You may choose to get out on one of the smaller islets within the pass and watch the tide build to maximum current—a truly eye-opening and humbling experience.

Negotiating Hole in the Wall is a serious undertaking. On large summer tides, the safe passage window is only 10 minutes either side of slack. If you want to go through this passage, your timing has to be bang-on and don't even think about getting out anywhere! A half-hour into a 14-knot flood tide, conditions are unmanageable in a sea kayak.

Use the current tables for Hole in the Wall to predict current movement in the Upper and Lower Rapids of the Okisollo, just north of the Octopus Islands. The current speed will generally be lower but the times relatively similar.

Sometimes you or your group will arrive late at a given pass and, rather than wait 5 or 6 hours for slack current, be tempted to try to get through anyway. Or, sometimes advanced paddlers simply want to play around in the current to see what it is like. Whether you are a beginner paddler or a hotshot whitewater paddler turned sea kayaker, you need to understand two things: The Pacific Ocean is not a river, and you are not in a whitewater boat! I once cautioned an experienced whitewater kayaker (a trained guide) about entering a local tidal rapids. He looked at me and exclaimed, "I can't remember the last time I blew a roll!" He was later fished out of the Upper Rapids of the Okisollo by a local who was alert enough to see him and save not only his life but his kayak too. The bottom line is this: No amount of skill—rolling, bracing or paddling—will guarantee you a safe passage through any of the region's rapids. Even in the best conditions, this is no place for beginners. For the latest information, check out a tidal rapids instruction site at www.discovery-islands-lodge.com/tidal_rapids.pdf.

TRIP 27 The Discovery Islands
SKILL: Intermediate to advanced
TIME: 4–14 days
HAZARDS: Tidal rapids and winds
ACCESS: Quadra Island/Cortes Island

CHARTS: 3312 · Jervis Inlet and Desolation Sound · Various
Scales

3538 · Desolation Sound and Sutil Channel ·
1:40,000

3539 · Discovery Passage · 1:40,000

3541 · Approaches to Toba Inlet · 1:40,000

3537 · Okisollo Channel · 1:20,000

TIDE BOOK: Vol. 6

The trip through the Discovery Islands described in this chapter begins at Heriot Bay on Quadra Island and passes through Hoskyn
Channel and Hole in the Wall as it circumnavigates Maurelle and
Read Islands. It is possible to finish this trip in as little as 4 days, but it
is best to leave time to explore.

Although there are maintained campsites at locations such as Rebecca Spit on Quadra Island and Smelt Bay on Cortes, kayakers are
free to camp most anywhere with a few notable exceptions. Most of
the southern half of Quadra is private, as are the western and southern shores of Cortes. Read Island's shoreline is peppered with large,
undeveloped industrial lots; by and large, these are unmarked and appear to be public land. To date, most industrial landowners have not
seemed to mind having kayakers on their land as long as fundamental
concerns are addressed. Take your garbage with you, deal properly
with your human feces and do not make any fires!

Fresh water is available at some sites and not at others; you are advised to bring your own supply and, as always, to treat or boil any
water from local streams.

LAUNCHING

To launch at Heriot Bay, drive across Quadra Island towards the
Whaletown (Cortes Island) ferry and turn left onto Cramer Road a
few hundred metres before the terminal. Drive a few hundred metres
more to Antler Road and then down to the Heriot Bay government
dock. There is usually adequate and relatively safe parking. The
Quadra Island Harbour Authority manages the dock and has
discussed implementing a parking fee. Currently, however, parking is
free. Rebecca Spit, another launch site, is located just south of the
ferry terminal.

If you are launching from Whaletown, catch the ferry from Quadra Island to Cortes Island. Once on Cortes, you'll see the Whaletown government dock and a store to the right of the ferry terminal. To get there, turn right at each of the two major stop signs. There is safe parking available.

SITES

Hoskyn Channel From Heriot Bay, begin your trip by heading north towards Hoskyn Channel. At the bottom of the channel you will see a number of smaller islands called the Breton Islands. The southernmost island has a fantastic pebble beach on its southwest side that makes a great spot for stretching your legs. At the time of writing, the island is believed to be privately owned, though undeveloped, and camping is not permitted without permission. Please, no fires of any kind.

As you paddle north, you have the option of following Quadra Island or Read Island to Surge Narrows. Both routes offer a number of potential campsites including Village Bay and a beach 1 km (.6 mi.) north of Sheer Point, which is known locally as Freedom Point. For people wanting to mix hiking with paddling, you may want to press on through Surge Narrows to Yeatman Bay. Remember: Surge Narrows is for *very* experienced kayakers only.

Yeatman Bay Although it is not especially picturesque, Yeatman Bay offers lots of campsites. Only .5 km (.3 mi.) north of Surge Narrows (Beazley Pass), it is also a great layover spot for kayakers coming or going through the rapids of the narrows. A time-worn trail starting at the head of the bay will take you on a very short forested walk to a secluded part of Main Lake. If you're just passing through and don't plan to stay overnight, try to leave enough time to hike up to the lake for a swim—it's well worth the time and effort. All the lakes found within the Discovery Islands become unbelievably warm in July and August. At the very top of the bay you'll find a small cold stream that always tastes great—even in the driest summer.

Keep in mind that Yeatman Bay is only marginally protected and is open to the summer westerlies that can blow down Okisollo Channel. Since there is little fetch, the bay rarely ever poses a problem for

∧ *The Octopus Islands with Hole in the Wall in the background,* PETER McGEE

the kayaker, but any boat left on the beach is prey to a rising tide and battering waves.

Okisollo Channel Continuing north you will enter upper Okisollo Channel. The water temperature here is noticeably colder—too cold for anything more than a quick swim or a splash. You'll notice huge beds of kelp whereas farther south there were few, if any. Here the ocean floor is covered with spiny sea urchins. The Okisollo contains prolific numbers of harbour seals and Dall's porpoises, not to mention huge flocks of gulls, especially Bonaparte's gulls, that congregate by the thousands on the kelp beds of the tidal passages. Expect early morning fog, notably in the latter half of summer. It usually burns off by 10 AM.

Octopus Islands Also to be found in this part of Okisollo Channel are the enchanting Octopus Islands. Most of the eight Octopus Islands are suitable for hauling out and camping on, with one exception: the large island right in the middle of the group, which is private and well marked. The smaller islands are actually more open and better suited for the kayaker's purpose. Once inside the island group, it should not take you long to locate a pleasant campsite, but don't expect any sandy beaches.

It should also come as no surprise to find there is no water on these islands. During an average summer, however, the small streams in Waiatt Bay—in particular, the large one on the south shore as indicated on the chart—do have good water. If you are desperate, there are two other reliable sources, both 4 km (2.5 mi.) away: Yeatman Bay on Quadra Island and Elephant Bay on Maurelle Island.

Just north of the Octopus Islands lie the Upper and Lower Okisollo Rapids. Similar to Surge Narrows, these are not to be taken lightly. Anyone passing through should be experienced and have had a good look at the tide and current tables. A rough 1.5 km (.9 mi.) portage trail runs between Waiatt Bay and Small Inlet, and may negate the need to pass through the rapids if heading north into Johnstone Strait. Since the trail is not suitable for wheels, however, and the walk is reasonably far, this is recommended only as a backup plan.

To continue your trip in the Discovery Islands, you will most likely want to pass through Hole in the Wall. This is also an area of extreme tidal activity, standing waves and whirlpools, so use caution. If you have the necessary skills, plan carefully—and don't let fear ruin the delightful thrill of being whisked between enormous rock cliffs to the sanctuary of Calm Channel. It is an experience not unlike river travel and gives your aching arms a brief respite. Not far away is a fantastic campsite just off North Rendezvous Island.

North Rendezvous Island Although most of North Rendezvous Island is private, a 4-ha (10-a.) park at the very northern tip of the island includes a small islet 50 m (165 ft.) farther north. A small grassy road runs up the interior of the island past several homesteads and cabins. There are a number of good campsites on the islet and a few more near the beach on North Rendezvous.

North Rendezvous has a wonderful spring that is dependable even in the driest summers. Although the spring is quite small, the water is clear and cold. You may have a little trouble finding it but don't give up: it is about 150 m (500 ft.) east of the island road in dense salal. You'll also find some small human-made pools 20 m (65 ft.) or so upstream from the beach.

If the site is full, you can try South Rendezvous Island, where one or two old homesteads provide excellent ground for pitching a tent, and the surrounding old growth provides a great place to stretch your legs after a day in the boat. Although South Rendezvous Island is now a provincial marine park, there are no facilities at this site. Frances Bay, north and just west of Ramsay Arm, also has a couple of campsites and streams. There is plenty of room at both sites; the one at the entrance to Frances Bay is the most attractive. If these are not to your liking, you can try Von Donop Inlet on Cortes Island or the Penn Islands, just south of Read Island.

Von Donop Inlet Von Donop Inlet is extremely well protected and subsequently a favourite anchorage for boaters, which may turn you off at first. Pleasure craft or not, the inlet is beautiful and well worth checking out. Once inside Von Donop there are some attractive clearings and perfect kayak haul-outs. Although a provincial marine park (Háthayim), there are no designated campsites or fees but random wilderness camping is allowed. There is one pit toilet. If you don't want to put up with the boaters, try your luck going up into the lagoon and camping where the larger vessels can't go. This is a tidal lagoon, and depending on the tide, you may have trouble getting through its rather small and turbulent entrance. At any rate, it is not considered dangerous.

Cork Lake Farther up the west side of Van Donop Inlet is a bay that is extremely shallow and impassable by larger vessels. At the base of the creek running out of Cork Lake is an old Forest Service recreation site. Although it needs a little work, the site still has room for a few tents. The remnants of the Cork Lake trail are visible for those who want to stretch their legs.

Aside from the creek at Cork Lake, fresh water is limited in Von Donop Inlet during the summer. At Robertson Bay, .5 km (.3 mi.) to

^ *Relaxing in the meadows of South Rendezvous Island,* PETER MCGEE

the east of the inlet entrance, you will find good drinking water at a small, reliable stream. At the stream mouth is a trail leading up to Robertson Lake, where you can enjoy a refreshing plunge into this very picturesque and usually warm body of water. Logging activity has left the near end of the lake completely plugged up with logs, and you may have to walk a few hundred metres to find a good place to get in. Fortunately, Robertson Lake is now a protected area.

If you want to explore Desolation Sound, the region described in chapter 8, you can attempt a portage across Cortes Island to Squirrel Cove. This is a fairly quick way to get across the island, and there are signs marking the trailhead at the southern end of Von Donop Inlet; the distance is about 1 km (.6 mi.) with very little gain in elevation. If you decide to do this, be sure to time your departure on a high tide, especially at the Squirrel Cove side, where you can add an extra .5 km (.3 mi.) of carrying on a low tide.

Penn Islands If you are heading back to Heriot Bay, exit Von Donop Inlet and paddle for the nice campsites among the Penn Islands. One such site is located in a small bay with a gravelly beach on the southeast corner of the most northerly island. The other good site is located

.5 km (.3 mi.) from the first campsite almost due south on the extreme eastern point of the next island. The first campsite has the best beach for the kayaker's purpose, but each is beautiful. In late April or May the islands are host to dozens of varieties of wildflowers, some rather rare. Nearby are two seal haul-outs whose inhabitants will likely be your constant companions as you paddle through the adjacent islands.

As can be expected of most smaller islands, there is no drinking water on these two sites. The closest reliable supply is the small stream at Robertson Bay. From the Penn Islands to Heriot Bay is about 14.5 km (9 mi.).

ADDITIONAL ROUTES

Heading north You can pass through the Okisollo Rapids with extreme caution and continue north towards Johnstone Strait. For great camping, be sure to stop at these campsites, about a day's paddle apart: on Sonora Island tucked in behind Howe Island, in the grassy meadow at Camp Point on West Thurlow Island and on the southern shore of Yorke Island.

Heading south Paddling south through Discovery Passage and Seymour Narrows is not recommended due to the extreme currents and heavy shipping traffic. Instead, cross to Cortes Island and work your way south along the shores of Texada Island or the mainland. Paddling towards Desolation Sound opens up a number of possibilities. See chapter 8 for more information.

A Discovery Islands–Desolation Sound combination The Discovery Islands are situated very close to Desolation Sound, and overlapping the two regions in your planning can produce some great routes. The ultimate trip begins in Lund and finishes at Heriot Bay on Quadra Island (or vice versa). Unfortunately, the pick-up and drop-off logistics are a little hard to work out for this route. If you decide to explore both regions at once, another possibility is to take the ferry to Cortes Island and depart from there. Depending on where you want to go, there are numerous public launch sites, the best ones being Whaletown, Squirrel Cove, Smelt Bay, Cortes Bay and Coulter Bay. Parking is available at all these locations.

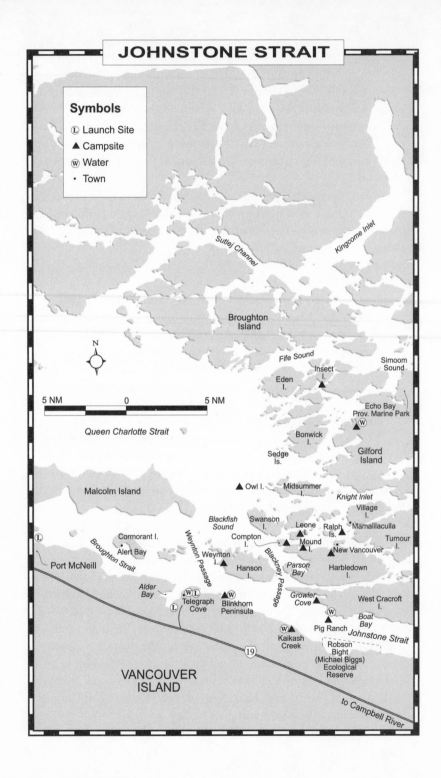

JOHNSTONE STRAIT

Symbols

ⓁLaunch Site
▲ Campsite
ⓦ Water
• Town

Sutlej Channel

Kingcome Inlet

Broughton
Island

Fife Sound

Eden
I.

Insect
I. ▲

Simoom
Sound

Echo Bay
Prov. Marine Park
ⓦ

N

5 NM   0   5 NM

Queen Charlotte Strait

Bonwick
I.

Sedge
Is.

Gilford
Island

Malcolm Island

▲ Owl I.

Midsummer
I.

Knight Inlet

Village
I.

*Blackfish
Sound*

Swanson
I.

Leone
I. ▲

Ralph
Is. ▲

Mamalilaculla

Cormorant I.

Alert Bay

Compton
I.

▲ Mound
I.

New Vancouver ▲

Turnour
I.

Ⓛ

Broughton Strait

Weynton Passage

Weynton
I. ▲

Hanson
I.

Blackney Passage

*Parson
Bay*

Harbledown
I.

Port McNeill

*Alder
Bay*

ⓦⓁ

Ⓛ Telegraph
Cove

ⓦ▲
Blinkhorn
Peninsula

*Growler
Cove*

▲

West Cracroft

ⓦ
▲
Pig Ranch

*Boat
Bay*

ⓦ▲
Kaikash
Creek

Johnstone Strait

Robson
Bight
(Michael Biggs)
Ecological
Reserve

19

VANCOUVER
ISLAND

to Campbell River

10

Johnstone Strait

Fran Hunt-Jinnouchi, Marc Jinnouchi, Peter McGee and Tessa van Scheik

Each summer, pods of resident orcas and lone transients congregate in the waters of Johnstone Strait to feed on salmon, socialize and rub on the pebble beaches of Robson Bight. Similarly, each summer thousands of boaters, kayakers and whale watchers congregate to watch these magnificent mammals in the wild. As paddling experiences go, nothing rivals paddling with the orcas—an awesome event that mixes inspiration, exhilaration and even fear. The area, however, offers a lot more for the true explorer, and a journey into the protected waters north of Johnstone Strait will unleash a world of small bays, protected coves and ancient village sites. It is an area rich in history, wildlife and, above all, beauty.

BACKGROUND

In the early 1900s, Johnstone Strait thrived, full of coastal villages established in response to the booming logging and fishing industries. Apart from Telegraph Cove, however, little is left of these villages today. Sadly this also applies to many of the native sites in the area—the islands are dotted with Kwakwaka'wakw ruins, middens and the odd house but little else. One of the villages still visible is Mamalila-culla, a truly special place located on Village Island. The last major potlatch, held here in 1921 by Emma Bell and Dan Cranmer, was halted by the RCMP under the infamous anti-potlatch laws. The now dilapidated village holds signs of a once-stately village. There are remnants of large fluted house-posts and massive beams, and totem poles, some fallen and some still standing. Nearby Telegraph Cove, a thriving tourist destination and the site of a new international resort, presents a very different picture.

Established in 1911, Telegraph Cove served as the terminus of a telegraph line to northern Vancouver Island built by the government. The small town became home to a saltery business, dry-salting salmon for the Japanese market, and then, in 1929, a tiny sawmill. Today an attractive boardwalk links more recent homes and structures with the old village, but the town's popularity is threatening to erode the quaint atmosphere. In the summer Telegraph Cove becomes a bustling sport-fishing community with an RV campground, tourist shops, whale-watching businesses and a new condo development rumoured to have a golf course in its plans. Nonetheless, Telegraph Cove is still a highlight to any visit to Johnstone Strait and continues to be the launching spot for almost every kayaker heading into the area.

Kayak instruction, guided tours and water taxis are now available right in the cove as well as rentals of kayaks, marine radios and underwater hydrophones. In addition, a new launching area has eased the congestion that was associated with launching from the cove in the past. The new marina has showers, laundry facilities and toilets as well as the amenities available within the original resort. A sani-dump is available for those who use portable toilets to reduce impact.

Aside from the modern conveniences there are, of course, the whales. During the summer months, pods from up and down the Pacific Coast congregate in the strait to rub on the beaches of Robson Bight and feed on the salmon of the Inside Passage. Two different forms of orcas swim in these waters—residents and transients. They never associate with each other and seem to specialize in different prey—fish for residents and mammals for transients. The social structures of the two also differ, and it has been determined that each resident pod has a unique vocal dialect. Pods with similar dialects form a clan and are most likely to have descended from a common ancestral group. The only other mammals known to have dialects are humans.

There were plans in the early 1980s to turn Robson Bight into a log-booming area, which would have greatly threatened this important whale habitat. Fortunately, lobbying efforts by researchers and conservationists led to the 1982 creation of the Robson Bight (Michael Biggs) Ecological Reserve for whales. Research stations were set up in the islands nearby, producing an enormous amount of information on the four major activities of the whales: foraging, resting, socializing and travelling. The ecological reserve is closed to recreational traffic, and landing in the area is prohibited; however, orcas are easy to view in the surrounding waters throughout June, July, August and September. In 1995, an additional 3745 ha (9,254 a.) of the lower Tsitika was set aside as the Lower Tsitika River Provincial Park to protect the areas upland of the ecological reserve. There is, however, no water access to this park or the ecological reserve.

GETTING THERE

By land From the south along Highway 19 (the Island Highway), the turnoff to Telegraph Cove is 345 km (214 mi.) from Nanaimo and is clearly marked. Drive down the paved road until a T-junction. Turn left onto the gravel road and follow the signs to Telegraph Cove, about a 20-minute drive.

By water and air If you want to charter a boat or plane into the region, check out the possibilities in Port McNeill or contact North Island Kayak for assistance. Telegraph Cove has a number of small fishing boats available as well as several water taxi services.

WEATHER AND HAZARDS

The Johnstone Strait Oceanic Ecosection is a much colder, foggier and rainier place than its Georgia Basin counterpart (see chapter 9) and will give you a feel for the rest of the northern B.C. coast. Nonetheless, summer is usually quite pleasant, with warm, sunny days and cool nights. The prevailing winds during summer months are westerly, and it is very important that you take this into account: these winds pick up almost every afternoon, often reaching gale force conditions. The strait also has significant tidal currents that cause hazardous paddling conditions, particularly when an ebb tide mixes with a late afternoon westerly.

Generally Johnstone Strait has a current of 1–2 knots, but some areas have significant currents of 2–3 knots during full flow. An example of this is the northern shore of Johnstone Strait from Hanson Island across to Boat Bay on West Cracroft Island. Blackney and Weynton Passages are even more extreme and are not to be taken lightly: they have very strong currents on big tides and moderate currents on smaller tides. Experienced kayakers can use the ebb and flood to help them, but most paddlers should pass through these areas at slack.

When travelling in Blackfish Sound, you will need the current tables for Weynton Passage, Johnstone Strait and Seymour Narrows. The slack current for Blackney Passage, located between the east side of Hanson Island and West Cracroft Island, is at a different time than Weynton Passage on the west side of Hanson Island. The slack and maximum currents for Weynton Passage are calculated by reading the Weynton Passage current table.

However, figuring out Blackney Passage is more of a challenge. The turn here is 70 minutes before Seymour Narrows. For example, if the turn at Seymour Narrows is at noon during the summer, you would add 60 minutes for daylight savings and then subtract 70 minutes; slack would be at 11:50 AM. However, the turn at Blackney Passage is often 15–45 minutes early (and almost never late). To allow for this local variance, you may wish to attempt your crossing 30 minutes before the official turn.

Calculating the maximum current is done by reading the Johnstone Strait Central current table; there is no variation on maximum flow and time between Johnstone Strait Central and Blackney Passage. If you travel at slack current, you will avoid the dangerous standing waves and whirlpools that form at Blackney Passage and Weynton Passage.

Marine traffic is another hazard, as virtually every ship heading north is funnelled through this 3.2-km (2-mi.) wide area. Do not underestimate the danger posed by marine traffic in this area. Watch for boat wakes and avoid crossing in the fog. Remember, cruise ships move quickly and have no way of detecting kayaks by radar. They also produce unusually large wakes, so you need to ensure that your boat is secure and well up from the tide line at night. Blackney Passage is an area of high shipping traffic. It is also a blind corner. On several occasions kayaking parties have been split by a large ship while crossing Johnstone Strait from Vancouver Island to West Cracroft Point and while crossing Blackfish Sound. Many of the commercial sea kayak guides in the area can be called on to help or to give advice on crossings in this region.

Finally, there are numerous black bears on all but the smallest islands, so you should take the appropriate measures to bear-proof your camp.

SPECIAL CONSIDERATIONS

The effects kayakers and other boaters have on orcas have yet to be fully understood. Nonetheless, Straitwatch, a stewardship-based marine mammal monitoring and education group (www.straitwatch.org), patrols the area enforcing the guidelines and suggestions listed below:

- Never enter the Robson Bight (Michael Biggs) Ecological Reserve.
- Paddle no closer than 100 m (330 ft.) to whales.
- Approach whales from the side, not from the front or rear. Approach and depart slowly. Avoid disturbing a "line" of resting whales. Resting whales are typically grouped tightly together, travel slowly and dive synchronously every 4–5 minutes. Resting episodes usually last 2–3 hours.
- Try to be conscious of the effect of your actions on whales, and do not engage in any activity that will disturb or interfere with them. Under section 71(a)(2) of the federal fisheries regulation it is illegal "to disturb or molest orcas." Although orcas can travel more than 45 kph (28 mph) and easily escape a kayak, your presence can still affect feeding or socializing activities. Keep in mind that leaving shore when whales appear can easily be interpreted by the animals as approaching or harassing behaviour.
- Limit the time spent with any group of whales to no more than 30 minutes.

Telegraph Cove also overlooks the traditional home of many Kwakwaka'wakw (Kwakiutl) tribes, including the Mamaleleqala, the Matlipi and the Tlowitsis. These tribes have a tradition of welcoming respectful visitors but also need to protect their lands and resources in light of the growing numbers of paddlers. Please check with the appropriate band offices prior to your trip to ensure your paddling

∧ *Bull orca off Kaikash Creek,* PETER MCGEE

journey will not upset this balance. A few sites listed in this chapter are midden sites; although currently open for camping, they are susceptible to closures in the future. Please respect any future management changes in these areas. Call the appropriate bands for the most recent information.

TRIP 28 Johnstone Strait

SKILL:	Intermediate to advanced
TIME:	3–14 days
HAZARDS:	Winds, currents and traffic
ACCESS:	Telegraph Cove
CHARTS:	3515 · Knight Inlet · 1:80,000
	3545 · Johnstone Strait—Port Neville to Robson Bight · 1:40,000
	3546 · Broughton Strait · 1:40,000
	3547 · Queen Charlotte Strait, Eastern Portion · 1:40,000
TIDE BOOK:	Vol. 6

A number of day trips are possible from Telegraph Cove, including visits to Bauza Islet, the Wastell Islets and the Blinkhorn Peninsula. If you have a couple of nights to spend in the area, however, consider paddling down to Kaikash Creek and exploring the south side of the strait and the waters outside the Robson Bight (Michael Biggs) Ecological Reserve. If you are able to spend several nights in the area, it is worth crossing the strait and exploring Harbledown Island, Village Island and Blackfish Sound; this trip is described below. Regardless of the route you choose, be prepared to sit out bad weather and rough sea conditions. For those crossing the strait, allow for the afternoon winds and ensure you have extra food and water in case you need to sit them out. Never paddle in conditions above your ability simply to keep to a schedule.

LAUNCHING

Telegraph Cove is by far the most popular launching site for Johnstone Strait. Fees for launching are $6 per boat, payable at the Telegraph Cove Resort or the Telegraph Cove Marina. Since Telegraph Cove has had problems with kayakers avoiding payment, please be sure to pay or we may all lose our launching privileges. Parking is $5 per day at both the marina and resort, or $15 per week at the marina. Telegraph Cove facilities and amenities now include a liquor store, general store, the Old Saltery Pub, the Killer Whale Café, showers, and laundry and washroom facilities.

Those looking for a little more peace and quiet may prefer to launch from the Alder Bay campsite, 2.4 km (1.5 mi.) before Telegraph Cove. The turnoff is on your left, 10 minutes after leaving the highway, and is well marked. Alder Bay has an easy launch site and a $5 launching fee and parking. Unfortunately, the paddle between Alder Bay and Telegraph Cove is a tedious 1.5 hours of log booms and unspectacular scenery.

If you have time, it is also possible to launch from a few different locations in the town of Port McNeill, a full day's paddle north of Telegraph Cove. For people who would like to avoid Telegraph Cove and Johnstone Strait altogether, it is possible to launch from Simoom Sound or Echo Bay on Gilford Island.

SITES

Soon after leaving Telegraph Cove you will encounter the currents of Johnstone Strait at the head of Bauza Cove. In this part of the coast, ebb tides flow north and flood tides flow south as the ocean wraps around the north end of Vancouver Island. Bauza Cove was once a nice picnic spot but is now part of the ongoing development in the area.

Blinkhorn Peninsula Within an hour you will reach Blinkhorn Peninsula. For reference, there is a light on the eastern side of the small island just off the point. Paddle around the island, or across the spit if the tide is high enough, and land on the east-facing beach. Blinkhorn is not the most attractive site in the area but it is large, has a year-round water source and some older buildings to explore. Recently, the east-facing campsites have been improved and a composting toilet has been added.

Kaikash Creek Farther south is Kaikash Creek, the most popular site on Johnstone Strait. An enormous site, Kaikash has room for 30 or so tents and is quite often near capacity. Due to pressure from groups such as the B.C. Marine Trail Association, the Ministry of Forests has installed a composting toilet to help with the heavy use. The creek is large, providing year-round water that needs to be treated.

Pig Ranch and Growler Cove For people wanting to explore a little more, head across the strait to the west end of West Cracroft Island and a camping area known locally as Pig Ranch. (As discussed in Weather and Hazards, use caution crossing the strait.) This is a great spot to watch for whales and is occasionally used by research teams. Camping is best on the point, near or even on the old tent pads. Some of the adjacent small bays have great landings but a lot of salal. If you have time, venturing up Eagle Bluff will give you a spectacular view of the strait. There is a small creek in the northern bay. If camping is limited, try the site in Growler Cove one inlet over. Growler Cove is quite sheltered but much of the area has been logged, allowing winds to funnel over the end of the inlet. For those looking to continue south, camping is possible at nearby Boat Bay though the shore is a little rugged.

Venturing north of the strait lessens your chances of encountering whales but gives you a break from boat traffic. This area has some great inlets, waterways and cultural sites. Heading north from Growler Cove, you can paddle around the western end of Harbledown Island, across Parson Bay and through the numerous islands and islets that guard Knight Inlet.

Village Island For many, the primary reason for venturing into these waters is to visit the Kwakwaka'wakw village site of Mamalilaculla. Located at the western end of Village Island, the remnants of this significant village are definitely worth exploring. Tom and Kathleen Sewid of Village Island Tours charge for camping on Village Island—$5 per person per night or $25 per group. Visitors to Village Island can also take part in a narrative cultural tour for $12 per person. If the cultural riches of Village Island don't interest all members of your group, there are lots of berries and a huge, fat black bear to keep them occupied.

Mound Island If you want to camp near Village Island, the islets just off Ralph Island have room for a few tents, though your best bet is the midden site at the western end of Mound Island. This is one of the most beautiful sites in the area and is heavily used in the summer. It is well protected from the wind and has a large grassy area that can accommodate upwards of 10 tents. Although not an officially designated Indian Reserve, evidence of past use is obvious. Recently, a camping fee was introduced and then retracted by the band, and you are best to check with the band office in Campbell River before using this site. Since this site is a midden, be extremely careful and practise zero impact camping. If this does not occur, closure of the site may result. There is no water on-site. If you need an overflow area, check the small island immediately off the midden site or Dead Point on Harbledown Island, a few hundred metres due west.

Harbledown and Compton Islands Dead Point, on the north side of Harbledown Island, was once used by the Kwakwaka'wakw as a winter village and is also worth exploring. In 1914 there were at least 10 houses standing; in later years the village moved to the west side of the point. Today it consists of a pier and a couple of houses and is known as New Vancouver. Camping can be found in the little bay just south of New Vancouver.

Nearby Compton Island in Blackfish Sound is an Indian Reserve that can be used for camping if permission is granted and a fee is paid. Again, contact Village Island Tours or the band office in Campbell River for more information. Compton Island is often used by large commercial groups.

If you're looking for something a little different, a paddle into the Parson lagoon won't disappoint. This is not the typical kayaker's site — it has an extremely rugged landing and a long haul at low tide — but the surrounding forest and lagoon provide an incredibly serene setting. There is also a new toilet and campsite on Leone Island, off the back of Berry Island.

Hanson Island For paddlers with little time left, you can head back to Telegraph Cove the way you came or work your way west to Hanson Island. The northern side of Hanson is full of little coves, streams and pretty good campsites for small groups. Keep your eyes peeled for the orca research stations as well as beaches lined with cottonwoods, a sure sign of an old homestead. Double Bay, though it may look tempting on the chart, is home to a fish farm and various amenities for the yachting crowd. However, tucked in behind Weynton Island at the western tip of Hanson is a small site if needed. The currents here can run up to 5.5 knots, causing some steep waves when opposing the wind, so it is best avoided by inexperienced paddlers. Commercial groups use this site so expect company.

Broughton Archipelago If you are not ready to head home, consider taking a trip into the Broughton Archipelago and its maze of intricate islands and waterways. Camping can be difficult for large groups but don't let that deter you: this is some of the nicest paddling B.C. has to offer. Highlights include the Sedge Islands to the west of Bonwick Island and the massive camping area on the southern tip of Insect Island. Owl Island and the Echo Bay Provincial Marine Park on Gilford Island provide additional campsites, though the park may be too developed for some. There is a large grass field to camp on in

∧ *A calm day heading north up Johnstone Strait,* PETER MCGEE

Echo Bay as well as a dock, water supply and store at the adjacent Echo Bay Resort.

ADDITIONAL ROUTES

Heading north From the Broughton Archipelago, you will enter the exposed waters of Queen Charlotte Strait. Once again, camping spots for more than 1 or 2 tents are sparse. For larger groups, check out Robinson Island near Blunden Harbour, Shelter Bay just off Richards Channel and Burnett Bay south of Cape Caution.

If you are heading towards Port Hardy from Telegraph Cove, there are a number of great campsites in the islands just off Fort Rupert. For those venturing north of Port Hardy, see chapter 11 on Queen Charlotte Strait.

Heading south Down Johnstone Strait provides some surprisingly good camping. Just south of the ecological reserve (make sure you are well south of the sign marking the ER) is a pebble beach at the mouth of a creek with some camping above the high tide line. On the north side of the strait are great sites at the Broken Islands and, farther along, at Yorke Island. From here you begin to venture into the territory discussed in chapter 9, the Discovery Islands.

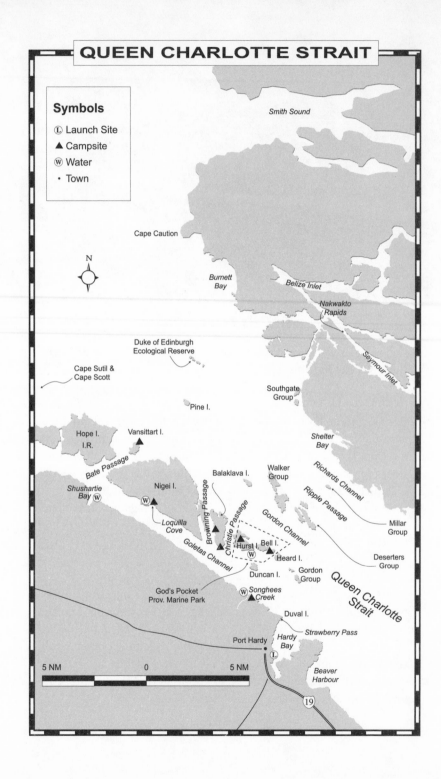

11

Queen Charlotte Strait

Debbie Erickson

Tucked between the northeast coast of Vancouver Island and the mainland is a little-known paddling area with a colourful history. Shaped by hurricane-force winter storms, the archipelago of islands that sprawls across Queen Charlotte Strait offers wild, rugged shorelines for kayakers to enjoy.

BACKGROUND

Just north of the 51st Parallel, cold, nutrient-rich water is drawn inland from the Pacific Ocean and flows through an expanse of water called Queen Charlotte Strait. Four times a day the tidal flow picks up speed as it is split and diverted through Richards Channel, Ripple Passage, Gordon Channel and Goletas Channel—the waterways that separate the island groups. With this movement of water comes an astounding volume of nutrients that sustain a diverse and concentrated intertidal and invertebrate community. The marine life is so big and so prolific in this area that it grows in mounds underwater—fish live atop shells that house crabs, and these sit next to barnacles that comb the water for food. Gigantic white plumose and brooding anemones sprout up from the sea floor, and a broad selection of the 300 known species of sea stars live here. There is no doubt about it, the water is cold—about 9°C (48°F) at depth in August—and a wet suit is a good idea, but the underwater visibility can range from 12 to 36 m (40 to 120 ft.), depending on currents and seasons, which means lots of glimpses at the astounding world below.

The strait is a major commuter route for huge schools of Pacific whiteside dolphins and the largest resident orca population in North America. It is also home to humpback whales, sea lions, harbour seals, porpoises, blacktail deer, bald eagles, mink and occasionally gray whales and black bears. Bring your bird identification book too, as the area supports a wide variety of unusual seabirds such as auklets, guillemots and puffins. Both Queen Charlotte and Johnstone Straits are part of the "Pacific Flyway" for the bufflehead, surf scoter, harlequin duck, scaup and many more birds—incredibly, over 81 species have been recorded in the area.

Queen Charlotte Strait contains two designated protected areas: God's Pocket Provincial Marine Park and the Duke of Edinburgh Ecological Reserve, which supports internationally and/or nationally significant populations of seabirds and marine mammals, as well as a Sasquatch-like creature that is said to live on the islands. This entire group of islands is considered to be haunted by spirits and is truly an enchanting place to visit.

The area is rich in cultural and coastal history of the Kwakwaka'wakw (Kwakiutl) people, and many archeological sites mark where villages once stood or legends took place. Kanekelak, champion of the Transformer myth, appears in many of the stories about this area. His powers were incredible but so was his wrath.

Centuries later, the Spanish and English came in their great sailing vessels and then in steamships. Suwanee Rock is named for the wreck of a U.S. war steamer that foundered there in 1868. A once-thriving sea otter population, which is slowly making a comeback, brought fur traders and the Hudson's Bay Company as well as settlers. At one time a hotel, post office, cannery and several ships were built on these remote islands.

GETTING THERE

By water If you are arriving from Prince Rupert, see B.C. Ferries information under General Contacts.

By land Coming from the south along Highway 19 (the Island High-way), Port Hardy is 391 km (242 mi.) from Nanaimo—approximately 4–4.5 hours. Extensive improvements to the final 45 km (28 mi.) be-fore Port Hardy are currently taking place, as well as stretches of high-way between Sayward and Campbell River, so travel time should be reduced a little bit over the coming years. Port Hardy has full facilities for outfitting and provisioning.

WEATHER AND HAZARDS

The prevailing winds in the summer are westerlies and they usually increase in strength in the afternoon, so try to make your crossings in the morning. If you arrive at your launch site late in the day, consider spending your first night along the Vancouver Island shoreline, then paddle over to the islands the next morning to ensure a safer crossing.

When the tide opposes the wind, Goletas Channel can quickly get rough as can Gordon Channel, which lies farther out in the strait. Currents in the main channels can be strong during full flow but they are mainly in the same direction as the tide. Pay particular attention around the outside of Duval Point, where wind, waves and current can exaggerate conditions.

Christie Passage, Browning Passage and Bates Passage all have fast-er currents and upwelling and should be avoided at maximum flow. Gordon Channel is the route for all major marine traffic, including cruise ships whose wake can create dangerous paddling conditions.

SPECIAL CONSIDERATIONS

Full-time residents live on these islands, so please respect their pri-vacy. Hope Island is an Indian Reserve, and visitors are not permitted. Kayakers should also stay away from the private float dwellings in Clam Cove on the southern end of Nigei Island. Scarlett Point Light-house on the north side of Balaklava Island welcomes visitors. A beach just in behind the lighthouse offers a landing spot.

Queen Charlotte Strait is often used as a foraging ground for the resident orcas, and humpbacks are also very common here. Please ad-here to the whale-watching guidelines in chapter 10 when paddling in this area.

God's Pocket Provincial Marine Park protects a seabird breeding colony, a bald eagle habitat and known archeological sites. This park contains no developed facilities, but fresh water is available. Use "no trace" practices when visiting the park.

TRIP 29 Queen Charlotte Strait/God's Pocket

SKILL:	Intermediate to advanced
TIME:	4–8 days
HAZARDS:	Winds, currents and exposed coast (optional)
ACCESS:	Port Hardy
CHARTS:	3548 · Queen Charlotte Strait, Central Portion · 1:40:000
	3549 · Queen Charlotte Strait, Western Portion · 1:40,000
TIDE BOOK:	Vol. 6

Twenty km (12.5 mi.) northwest of Port Hardy lies a group of small islands, including Hurst, Bell, Boyle and Crane, that make up God's Pocket Provincial Marine Park. This 2025-ha (5,004-a.) park also contains a number of islets and, combined with exceptional campsites on nearby islands just outside the park, your paddling options are unlimited. If you are short on time, consider leaving Port Hardy early in the morning (and only in calm seas) and crossing Goletas Channel to the park. Spend a few days exploring Bell, Hurst and Balaklava Islands, then retrace your route to Port Hardy. If you have more time, circumnavigating Nigei Island will give you a great taste of the area as well as a little more exposure to Queen Charlotte Strait. You may also want to consider a one-way trip and arrange to have a water taxi ferry you back from any of the areas mentioned above.

LAUNCHING

From Port Hardy, you can launch for free from the beach along the sea walk near Tsulquate Park. The best launching site is at the bottom of Central Street. Parking is available at the Northshore Inn—a 2-minute walk away. The Town of Port Hardy also has public pay parking at the Fishermans Wharf, 6600 Hardy Bay Road, which is a more suitable location for those venturing out by water taxi. The Scotia Bay RV Campground is located just beyond the town and is the closest launching point to the Gordon Group Islands. Access is left off Market Street at the northern end of the street and straight through the

Tsulquate Reserve. Signage marks the route well. Camping, showers and secure parking are available but it costs $5 to launch and $5 per day for parking.

If you are looking for information regarding charts, water taxis, rentals and guide services, you can go to the shared building of North Island Kayak and Adventure Centre, just off Market Street at the head of the Seagate Pier. For other information, you are best to check with the visitor information centre at 7250 Market Street.

SITES

Strawberry Pass As you are leaving Hardy Bay, you will notice a small opening to the northeast between Duval Island and Vancouver Island. This is Strawberry Pass and it's worth a short detour, both for the scenery and for the emergency campsite (and fishing lodge), where you can hole up if you are having any last-minute doubts. It is also the setting of a legend. Tsakame lived on the mainland north of here and had an infant son. At Duval Island, Tsakame caught the mythical double-headed sea serpent, Sisiutl, in his salmon weir and washed his son in its blood to give him mythical powers. His son's skin became as hard as stone, and he was called Stone Body. A dispute between his tribe and the Nimpkish led to an ambush at Duval Point. As Stone Body passed through narrow Strawberry Pass on one of his journeys, he was easily attacked. At first he hid, but soon he was found and killed, and his murderer's cry of victory was heard all the way to the Nimpkish River. In celebration, Stone Body's head was set up on a pole decorated with feathers at the mouth of the Nimpkish.

From Strawberry Pass you can see the entrance to Goletas Channel and the southernmost of the Gordon Group Islands. It is about an hour's paddle from Vancouver Island to the Gordon Group via this route. Doyle Island lies ahead, its 126-m (415-ft.) high Miles Cone and a sister cone clearly visible. These tall bluffs were aptly called Gilsgiltem (long heads) by the Kwakwaka'wakw (Kwakiutl). The backside of the island has remnants of a small plane crash.

Leaving Strawberry Pass, you can either cross Goletas Channel to the Gordon Group and the park or follow the Vancouver Island shoreline to Songhees Creek. If the wind has kicked up, or if you got a late start, you may want to leave the crossing for the following morning and enjoy Songhees Creek for the afternoon.

∧ *Spring time, Browning Passage,* PETER McGEE

Songhees Creek Located on Vancouver Island on the south shore of Goletas Channel, Songhees Creek offers a beautiful pebble beach that the orcas love. It also makes an excellent campsite and, although there are no facilities, fresh water is available.

From Songhees you will cross Goletas Channel in the vicinity of Duncan Island. Once again, be careful of wind. Just in behind Duncan Island is Bell Island and one of the prettiest campsites on the coast.

Bell Island With its white shell beach and protection from wind on all sides, Bell Island is like having a private lagoon to yourself. The little cove is hidden behind the Lucan Islands and the gap is barely visible until you are close to the entrance. The campsite itself is about 5 m (16 ft.) higher than the beach and is a large midden. This site is within God's Pocket Provincial Marine Park, which protects archeological sites, so take care not to damage the midden. Use the log at the far end of the beach as a ramp rather than walking on the bank itself. There is no fresh water or toilets on Bell Island although there is room for at least 12 people.

At this point in your trip, take a few days to explore the remarkable area you are in. If you feel the need to move camp, try Harlequin Bay, on Hurst Island just to the west of Bell Island.

Harlequin Bay Hurst Island is 200 wooded ha (500 a.) and is also part of God's Pocket Provincial Marine Park. A trail goes across the island, ending at God's Pocket Resort. Although the resort—which is known as a base for scuba diving—has changed owners recently, it still sells pie, which is worth a trip either on foot or by boat.

Named after the bird, the site at Harlequin Bay has a long beach at low tide, so try to time your arrival on the higher part of the tide. The campsite is at the head of the bay. Fresh water is available at various sources on the island but tends to be seasonal so you are best to bring your own.

To start a counterclockwise circumnavigation of Nigei Island from here, head towards the southern end of Browning Passage. Counterclockwise is preferable as it keeps you sheltered longer so you can turn back if necessary and also allows less experienced paddlers to do a portion of the trip. It will also have you travelling down Goletas Channel with the prevailing winds, a bonus that should not be underrated.

Nolan Point (Balaklava Island) Nolan Point is located at the southern end of Balaklava Island. This great historic site was home to the mythical champion Kanekelak for a time. More recently, Nolan Point was the site of an old trading post, and remnants of the cabin foundation and fences are easy to see. For those who visit in the late spring, daffodils abound! Although campsites are plentiful, water is scarce.

Browning Passage A little farther along, between Balaklava and Nigei Islands, is Browning Passage.

At the south end of the passage, on Nigei Island, is Clam Cove. There is much to look at here, but please do not disturb the private float dwellings. From the head of the cove a short hike leads through the forest to the beaches of Port Alexander (which is also accessible by water at the other end of Browning Passage). Try to avoid going ashore at low tide, when the flats are very "sinky" mud. However, once on land there are fossil beds in the area, and Cardigan Rocks nearby has interesting "holey" stone formations made by rock-boring clams.

Browning Wall is a vertical face along the southeastern side of Nigei Island. The wall is so sheer that it begins as a 61-m (200-ft.) granite cliff that plunges through the waterline and doesn't even hint of levelling until it reaches another 61 m (200 ft.) below the surface.

Paddling along the wall at a low tide reveals why the region is such an incredible diving area.

Midway through the passage, on Balaklava Island, is an excellent campsite. What was once the site of an A-frame log dump is now a grassy field with scattered second-growth timber that provides additional shelter as needed. From the campsite, an old logging road leads up into the interior of the island, where there are lots of places to explore.

Vansittart Island As you leave Browning Passage and wrap around the north side of Nigei Island, you will come to Vansittart Island. The campsite on this island faces towards Pine Island, in the middle of the strait. The nearby burial island (actually connected at low tide to Vansittart) belonged to the village Chumdasbe on Vansittart and is the scene of one of Kanekelak's magic contests, with a man named Omal. The village of Chumdasbe was a fortified camp as were many of the villages in the area. Although no longer visible, wooden stockades used to surround Chumdasbe to protect the people from a Haida raid or local warfare. Be sure to bring your own water to this island.

Loquilla Cove Heading home, follow the shore of Nigei Island into Goletas Channel. As always watch the winds in the channel, but also keep an eye on the currents as you can make your trip a little easier if you catch the flooding tide.

Three km (2 mi.) from the southeastern tip of Nigei Island, on Goletas Channel, was the fortified Indian camp Chuselas Dwechagila (fort of the Kwechagila). Nowadays it is more commonly known as Loquilla Cove, and it offers a pretty and protected place to spend one of your last nights. The site is in the part of the cove that faces towards Hope Island. There is fresh water but no toilet.

From Loquilla Cove, it is possible to make Port Hardy in a day, or you can slow your pace and revisit Songhees Creek.

ADDITIONAL ROUTES
Heading west Paddling around Cape Scott is a rewarding but challenging trip for advanced kayakers with experience on exposed coast-

line and with strong currents. To get there from Port Hardy, travel west up Goletas Channel towards Cape Scott Provincial Park.

On Vancouver Island opposite Bate Passage, which separates Nigei and Hope Islands, is Shushartie Bay, which was a busy community around the turn of the century when ships were built here and settlers established a general store, hotel and post office. It was deserted mid-century but now has a log-loading area and is to be the terminus for the proposed North Coast Trail, which will connect with the Cape Scott Trail. The huge estuary is a great source of fresh water and is full of wildlife and waterfowl. Unfortunately camping is limited. Continue to Jepther Point, a steeper pebble beach that is popular with orcas and that flattens out quickly to make for good tenting areas on top. Beyond here, be especially careful when navigating the Tatnall Reefs and the Nahwitti Bar. Watch the tides, since you may find yourself in standing waves if you paddle at the wrong time. The Nahwitti River estuary has longer pebble beaches, with fresh water and flat areas for tenting across the river from the old cabins. Cape Sutil also offers very protected sand and pebble beaches and is a favourite stopping spot. Rounding the northernmost tip of Vancouver Island and heading southwest there are numerous beaches all the way to Cape Scott. These are Shuttleworth Bight (where there is fresh water), Laura Creek, Nissen Bight (Fisherman Bay), Nel's Bight and Experiment Bight. Most of these beaches have great camping areas and incredible sunsets, and sea otters are quite numerous around there once again. Pay particular attention to the strong currents in Scott Channel when paddling in this area.

Heading east From the Gordon Group Islands, you can cross to the Walker Group and the Deserters Islands before making the last crossing to the mainland. This is a trip for advanced paddlers. Campsites are few. Conditions can change quickly in the strait and cruise ship traffic can make the crossing quite tense, but the scenery is spectacular. Beyond the islands, be aware of strong currents and overfalls in Ripple Passage. Shelter Bay, Burnett Bay, the Southgate Group of islands, Nakwakto Rapids and many gray whales await you on the other side.

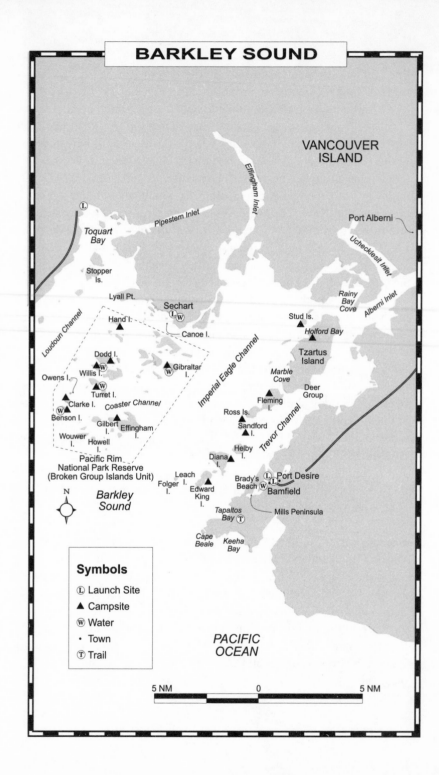

BARKLEY SOUND

VANCOUVER
ISLAND

Port Alberni

Effingham Inlet

Pipestem Inlet

*Toquart
Bay*

Uchecklesit Inlet

Alberni Inlet

Stopper
Is.

*Rainy
Bay
Cove*

Lyall Pt.

Sechart

Stud Is.

Loudoun Channel

Hand I.

Canoe I.

Holford Bay

Dodd I.

Gibraltar
I.

*Tzartus
Island*

Owens I.

Willis I.

*Marble
Cove*

*Deer
Group*

Turret I.

Coaster Channel

Clarke I.

Fleming
I.

Benson I.

Ross Is.

Gilbert
I.

Effingham
I.

Sandford
I.

Wouwer
I.

Howell
I.

Helby
I.

Pacific Rim
National Park Reserve
(Broken Group Islands Unit)

Diana
I.

Brady's
Beach

Port Desire

N

Leach
I.

Bamfield

Folger
I.

Edward
King
I.

Mills Peninsula

*Barkley
Sound*

*Tapaltos
Bay*

*Cape
Beale*

*Keeha
Bay*

Imperial Eagle Channel

Trevor Channel

Symbols

Ⓛ Launch Site

▲ Campsite

Ⓦ Water

· Town

Ⓣ Trail

*PACIFIC
OCEAN*

5 NM   0   5 NM

12

Barkley Sound

Liz Johnston, Edwin Hubert
and Bill McIntyre

The pounding surf and relentless swells of Vancouver Island's west coast breed fear in the minds of many kayakers. Yet within Barkley Sound lie two clusters of islands that tame the ruggedness of the open ocean: the Broken Group Islands and the Deer Group. These are places where advanced paddlers can test their skills among outer islands and sea arches, and where beginners and families can discover the joys of ocean kayaking while drifting through a maze of protected coves and passages. Barkley Sound encompasses all that is special about the West Coast and lets everyone enjoy its treasures.

BACKGROUND
Barkley Sound is the traditional home of the Nuu-chah-nulth people. The name *Nuu-chah-nulth* can be loosely translated as "all along the mountains" and refers not only to the natives of Barkley Sound but to all the bands living alongside the mountains on Vancouver Island's west coast, from Cape Cook to the Jordan River.

Although the area was explored and named in 1787 by Capt. Charles William Barkley of the British trading ship *Imperial Eagle*,

European settlement in the Barkley Sound area did not occur until the 1850s. As the European population and exploration of the land and marine resources expanded, disease and government intervention forced native peoples to abandon their traditional way of life and relocate in permanent villages near stores and mills. Indian Reserves and the tragedies of missions and residential schools followed. Today, the Nuu-chah-nulth reserves of the Broken Group Islands are limited to Effingham, Nettle and Keith Islands, but the more than one hundred culturally significant sites scattered throughout the islands remind us of a more prosperous time when close to 10,000 native people lived here. As always, please treat all archeological sites with proper respect and remember that Indian Reserves are private property, so please avoid trespassing.

In 1970, close to 50 000 ha (123,500 a.) of land and ocean on the west coast of Vancouver Island were set aside to create Pacific Rim National Park Reserve, made up of the Broken Group Islands, the West Coast Trail and the Long Beach Units. The Broken Group Islands consist of about one hundred islands and islets between Loudoun Channel to the west and Imperial Eagle Channel to the east, encompassing an area of 10 607 ha (26,200 a.), of which only 1350 ha (3,335 a.) are land.

On February 19, 2001, Pacific Rim National Park Reserve was proclaimed under the Canada National Parks Act. Due to the comprehensive claim of the Nuu-chah-nulth Tribal Council, the park will remain a reserve until the treaty is settled. In the interim, the National Parks Act, and all the rules and regulations associated with it, apply to the Broken Group Islands.

To the east of the Broken Group Islands are the Deer Group islands, the smaller chain of islands dividing Imperial Eagle Channel from Trevor Channel. Although not within the Pacific Rim National Park Reserve, these remote islands offer incredibly diverse paddling options and, best of all, are easily accessed from the quaint coastal community of Bamfield.

Romantically known as "the Venice of Vancouver Island," Bamfield is a village of approximately 400 people. Bamfield Inlet splits the village into east and west sides, with no road access to the west side. The village is known for its famous boardwalk along the harbour, small art galleries and shops where you can sit and watch the boats go by. The Bamfield Marine Station on the east side was previously the site of the historic Bamfield Cable Station and is known worldwide for its contribution to marine biology and education. The Bamfield Coast Guard and Rescue Training Station also contribute to the unique flavour of the village.

Truly the jewel of the west coast of Vancouver Island, this little fishing village is still magical, wild and relatively untouched—the perfect jumping-off point for paddlers headed for the Deer Group islands.

GETTING THERE

THE BROKEN GROUP

By land and water For most paddlers, the easiest way to get to the Broken Group Islands is by freighter from Port Alberni on Vancouver Island. The MV *Frances Barkley* travels to Sechart, a site outside the Broken Group Islands about 1.6 km (1 mi.) north of Prideaux. A former whaling station, Sechart is now used as a land base by Alberni Marine Transport Ltd.; phone them for schedules and reservations. Reservations are strongly advised during July and August.

To reach Port Alberni from the mainland, catch the ferry to Nanaimo from either Horseshoe Bay or Tsawwassen. From Nanaimo, head north along Highway 19 (the Island Highway) towards Qualicum Beach. Exit at the Qualicum Beach/Port Alberni turnoff and follow the signs for Highway 4 to Port Alberni.

If you are approaching from Seattle, you can also catch the ferry from Seattle to Victoria, then drive north 2 hours to Nanaimo. From Nanaimo, follow the directions above.

Island Coach out of Nanaimo offers bus service to Port Alberni.

For experienced paddlers, the islands can be reached by launching from Toquart Bay and crossing Loudoun Channel to Hand Island, a distance of 8 km (5 mi.). A logging road connects Toquart Bay to Highway 4. From Port Alberni follow Highway 4 west for 88 km (55 mi.). Look for the gravel turnoff to your left—you will have just come down a steep hill, and Kennedy Lake will be on your right. (The turnoff is about 12 km [7.5 mi.] before the junction of Highway 4 and the Tofino-Ucluelet highway.) Follow the logging road to the Forest

∧ *Leaving Bamfield for the Deer Group*, PETER MCGEE

Service recreation site and boat launch at Toquart Bay. It is a large site that fills up with RVs and power boaters during the summer months. Be sure to lock your vehicle. If weather and time permit, take to the water and make the passage to the Broken Group Islands — where the camping is far superior.

THE DEER GROUP

By water Alberni Marine Transport offers day trips aboard the famous MV *Lady Rose* into Bamfield on a summer schedule. The vessel, one of the favourite means of transportation for tourists, transports kayaks and freight into Bamfield, Ucluelet and the Broken Group Islands. The company also rents kayaks and equipment. The Bamfield Express Water Taxi will make special passenger trips from Port Alberni to Bamfield or the Deer Group on request.

By land In earlier years, Bamfield could be accessed only by water via the Port Alberni Inlet or by the dangerous, exposed "Graveyard of the Pacific" route from Victoria. The famous West Coast Trail starts 5 km (3 mi.) south of Bamfield at Pachena Bay. Even today, accessing the town from logging roads and waterways is definitely part of the challenge of these expeditions.

By vehicle, you can reach Bamfield by either the Lake Cowichan route or the Port Alberni route. It is a 3-hour drive from Nanaimo to Bamfield via Port Alberni, including 80 km (50 mi.) of gravel logging road. It is a 4-hour drive from Victoria to Bamfield via Cowichan Lake, with 90 km (56 mi.) of logging road after Youbou or Honeymoon Bay; you can use either side of the lake. The logging roads are fairly good, but they are very active, rough and often dusty. Two spare tires are recommended; before leaving, check that your car jack works and your wheel nuts can be loosened. If you can make the journey in the evening or on a Sunday, after the logging crews are off, chances are you will have a more relaxing drive. Forestry maps are helpful though there are directional signs on the roads. Always drive with your headlights on.

Two bus services are available to Bamfield: Western Bus Lines, which travels between Port Alberni and Bamfield, and the West Coast Trail Express, which travels between Victoria and Bamfield. These bus services run during the summer only, and you need to make a reservation.

By air There is a small, privately owned airstrip in Bamfield. There is no scheduled air service, but charters can be arranged from any major town, by land or float planes.

WEATHER AND HAZARDS

From July to September, prevailing high pressure systems in Barkley Sound create warmer air temperatures with westerly winds, building typically in the late morning and subsiding overnight. Be prepared, however, as storm conditions can occur unexpectedly. Low pressure systems, dominated by strong southeast winds and heavy rain, can produce dangerous seas and extreme exposure conditions along the southeast shores of the islands. Storms can occur at any time of year but are more common from October through June.

Fog is also a serious concern. Always travel with a compass and GPS as fog banks can move in with alarming speed, even in the absence of wind. Paddlers are advised to avoid surge channels, sea caves and submerged rocks.

Sea lions are present in both the Broken Group Islands and the Deer Group, especially off Wouwer, Howell and Folger Islands.

Although these animals are not usually aggressive, they are territorial and it is best to keep your distance. If the smell and pounding surf that surround their haul-outs haven't already alerted you to their presence, 900 kg (2,000 lb.) of growling blubber probably will.

Near Bamfield, the Cape Beale headlands are very hazardous. Strong tidal currents from Barkley Sound create very large and steep waves to the point of breaking. Combined with excessive rebounding waves from boomers, exposed rocks and a strong rip tide, these currents make this one of the most hazardous spots on the west coast of Vancouver Island. Westerly winds on an ebb tide can also cause steep waves in Trevor Channel. In the summer, winds usually build to moderate during the late morning and often die down in the evening, making the crossing of Trevor Channel best in the early morning or evening.

Paddling across Imperial Eagle Channel to the Broken Group Islands from Bamfield via the Deer Group islands is not recommended for any skill level. Similarly, crossing Loudoun Channel from Ucluelet is dangerous and not recommended for anyone but the most experienced paddler.

Parks Canada advises paddlers in the Broken Group Islands that they are expected to be self-sufficient and responsible for their personal safety.

SPECIAL CONSIDERATIONS

Park wardens patrol the Broken Group Islands and are based at the floating warden station located at Nettle Island, due north of the Gibraltar Island campsite. To preserve the delicate wilderness character of the Broken Group Islands, Parks Canada has various rules and guidelines.

- The maximum stay in the Broken Group Islands is 14 days; maximum stay at any one campsite is 4 days. Maximum group size allowed in the Broken Group is 10 persons. This applies to private, commercial and non-profit groups alike.
- All island users and visitors must camp in the designated campsites located on Hand, Turret, Gibraltar, Willis, Dodd, Clarke, Benson and Gilbert Islands. Camping fees are $5 per person per night from May 1 to September 30. Fees are collected at the campsites and a use permit

issued. Fees are payable in cash or by credit card and are subject to change.

- Campfires are allowed only on beaches and only below the high tide line; driftwood may be used but collecting wood from forested areas is not permitted.
- You must pack out all items you bring to the islands, including garbage.
- Limit your travel in and around sea caves due to the nesting of cormorants and other seabirds.
- It is illegal to collect and remove natural or cultural objects.
- It is unlawful to feed wildlife.
- There is a no angling/no harvest policy in effect for the entire Broken Group Islands.
- Never knowingly enter a burial cave. Should you inadvertently do so, leave immediately without disturbing anything or taking photos.

Also note, federal regulations concerning marine mammal viewing are being drafted—until formalized, stay 100 m (328 ft.) away.

To further protect the fragile ecosystems of the Broken Group Islands, Parks Canada is considering a quota and reservation system. For more information, contact the information officer at Pacific Rim National Park Reserve.

TRIP 30 The Broken Group Islands

SKILL: Beginner to advanced
TIME: 3–7 days
HAZARDS: Outer coast, fog and winds
ACCESS: Sechart (MV *Frances Barkley*)/Toquart Bay
CHARTS: 3671 · Barkley Sound · 1:40,000
3670 · Broken Group · 1:20,000
TIDE BOOK: Vol. 6

There are 8 official campsites in the Broken Group Islands, but the islands are so close together it is unlikely you will use them all on any one trip. Setting up a base camp and exploring for a few days is a popular option. Experienced paddlers will undoubtedly want to visit the outer islands, and staying at Gilbert, Clarke, Benson and Turret Islands will give you easy access to the open ocean. For beginner paddlers or those with children, the campsites on Hand, Willis, Dodd and Gibraltar Islands make great base camps for exploring some of the more sheltered waterways. Make sure to bring your own fresh water and treat any water you find, as all surface water is subject to coliform contamination from wildlife. For more information on the Broken Group Islands, see the *Official Guide to Pacific Rim National Park Reserve*. Much of the following information is used with permission of Parks Canada and was extracted from this guide.

LAUNCHING

Most paddlers will approach the Broken Group Islands via the MV *Frances Barkley* from Port Alberni. You will be dropped off at Sechart Lodge, located just behind Canoe Island, a mile or so from the northern park boundary. Kayak rentals and lodging are available at Sechart, though food and additional supplies weren't being sold at the time of writing.

If you launch from Toquart Bay, you will need to cross Loudoun Channel, a body of water that is open to the Pacific Ocean and subject to strong winds and ocean swells. Once again, this access is not recommended for inexperienced paddlers or those travelling with children. As you cross, it is worthwhile to use the Stopper Islands and the light on Lyall Point to help find you bearings. Your first stop in the park will likely be Hand Island.

SITES

Hand Island The site at the north end of Hand Island is the largest of the designated campsites, accommodating up to 20 tents, and it is a favourite among paddlers for its shell and sand beaches and unobstructed views. Be sure to keep an eye out for native fish traps but please do not disturb. These traps consist of a circular wall of stones, placed in the shallow bays, that acts as a corral at high tide, trapping fish when the tide recedes. Another item you might notice on Hand is the outhouse. These solar composting units, at many national park campsites throughout B.C., are particularly important to the Broken Group Islands. Not only are they clean and efficient, they are raised above ground so as not to disturb the archeological record contained within the soil and middens.

Dodd and Willis Islands Leaving Hand Island and heading south puts you in the natural harbour created by Dodd, Willis and Turtle Islands, one of the most sheltered spots in the Broken Group. Crossing Peacock Channel to reach the harbour should be done with care, as strong westerlies can kick up in the afternoon. Once in the harbour, however, there is little to worry about, and examining the abundant sea life and exploring the intricate maze of islets nearby make for a great afternoon. Bald eagles are common on Dodd Island so don't be surprised if there are more than a few pairs of eyes on you as you drift by. Campsites are located on Dodd and Willis.

Turret Island Thiepval Channel, named after a fisheries patrol boat that sank here in 1930, is quite small, but its western end is exposed and paddlers should exercise caution when crossing. The most direct route from the campsite on Willis to the campsite on Turret is to work your way through the tiny islets off the western end of Trickett Island, as tides permit. It is here the paddler begins to feel some of the energy of the open ocean—both an intimidating and exhilarating experience. Heading back towards the southern side of Turret, you will soon see the campsite tucked in behind a small unnamed islet. Land on the south-facing beach and head into the giant Sitka spruce forest to pick your site for the night.

Clarke and Benson Islands From here on, the seas can get quite nasty, and continuing south should only be attempted by paddlers with experience. Owens, Clarke and Benson Islands sit just across from Turret Island and, though their eastern sides are normally sheltered, the western shores of all three are fully exposed to the pounding Pacific. Clarke has a stunning sand beach and campsite at its northern end; camping on Benson takes place in a large meadow, remnants of an orchard Capt. John Benson planted in 1893 when he built a hotel on the island. The hotel shut its doors in 1922. Benson is also the site of a blowhole near the water catchment station at the island's south end. It takes a bit of hiking to reach but is worth the effort.

Gilbert Island The campsite at Gilbert Island lies across Coaster Channel, an area subject to Pacific swells and strong winds that should only be accessed by more experienced paddlers. Once across the channel, exploring the extremely rugged shores and watching the sea lions off Wouwer and Howell Islands will give you a taste of the wild Pacific in all its glory. Fittingly, the Nuu-chah-nulth name for nearby Dicebox Island is "a place you don't want to leave." Keep in mind that, some days, you actually *can't* leave due to fog, so be sure to allow yourself a little time for waiting it out. Due to the sensitive nature of Dicebox Island, please restrict your movements to the pocket beach.

Look for the beach at the southeastern end of Gilbert to find the campsite. The forest can seem quite dark yet is worth wandering through; many of the trees have been "culturally modified"—stripped of their bark by native peoples to make clothing, blankets, baskets, rope and even diapers. These culturally modified trees are distinguished by a bare patch on the side of an otherwise normal living cedar. Effingham Island, the largest of the islands, sits right next to Gilbert and is

v *Low-tide exploration, Turret Island,* PETER MCGEE

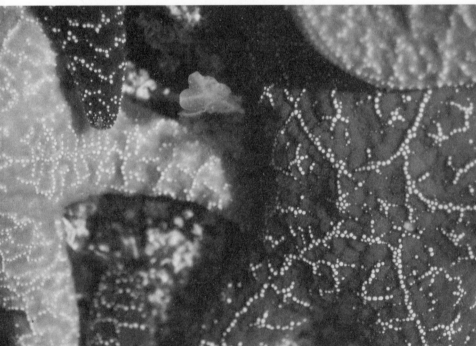

home to one of the Nuu-chah-nulth reserves. Meares Bluff, over 100 m (330 ft.) high with a large sea arch spanning the foreshore, is truly spectacular—the island's most prominent feature. Heading north from Effingham will take you to Wiebe and Dempster Islands and, finally, to Gibraltar, the last campsite in the Broken Group Islands circuit.

Gibraltar Island The eastern shores of all these islands are constantly pounded by the storm-driven waters of Imperial Eagle Channel, and previous paddling experience is a must. If you are looking for a less intense experience, the quiet lagoon between Jacques and Jarvis Islands is an excellent place for exploring marine life and a number of ancient fish traps. Please do not land on the beaches on the south side of Nettle Island, as they are part of the Tseshaht First Nation reserve. Gibraltar is a short jump to the launch site at Sechart Lodge, and a good 3–4-hour paddle to the launch site at Toquart Bay.

TRIP 31 Bamfield and the Deer Group

SKILL:	Intermediate to advanced
TIME:	2–5 days
HAZARDS:	Outer coast, fog and winds
ACCESS:	Bamfield
CHARTS:	3671 · Barkley Sound · 1:40,000
	3646 · Plans Barkley Sound—Bamfield Inlet · 1:12,000
TIDE BOOK:	Vol. 6

The trips in the Bamfield area are numerous and range from a few hours in the inner harbour to a few days in the Deer Group. Although campsites in the Deer Group are generally quite small and will only accommodate a few tents, the views over Barkley Sound and the Pacific Ocean make them some of the best on the coast. The trip described below begins in Bamfield and covers most of the islands in the Deer Group. For paddlers looking for a shorter excursion, a couple of day trips around Bamfield are described at the end of the chapter. If you plan on visiting any Indian Reserves in the area, make sure you have received prior permission and a visitor's pass from the Huu-ay-aht (Ohiats) First Nation.

LAUNCHING

There are a few options for launching boats in and around Bamfield. The best spot is the boat ramp in Port Desire. To get there, turn right at the four-way stop when you first get into Bamfield and follow Grappler Road to the government wharf at Port Desire. Parking is on the side of the road. There is also a government wharf in east Bamfield but it doesn't have the convenience of a boat launch.

There is a summer information centre, store and campground when you arrive by road on the east side of the inlet. If you arrive by boat on the west side of Bamfield Inlet, information is available at the Coast Guard Station or the Bamfield General Store.

SITES

Day trips to the Deer Group are easy if wind and weather are steady, but it is best to leave yourself a few days. The crossing from Bamfield to the islands should be undertaken in the morning, with winds and tides taken into account. Crossing Trevor Channel to Helby Island usually takes about 30 minutes. Although Helby Island is private, you can land and stretch your legs at Self Point if necessary.

Diana Island Much of Diana Island is an Indian Reserve, but camping is possible at the sand beach on the northern point. For people hoping to explore the island by foot, or wanting to land at the beaches near Kirby Point on the island's south end, you must have a pass from the Huu-ay-aht First Nation. Although you can usually find sheltered waters in Dodger Channel, Kirby Point and Voss Point are exposed and should only be attempted under the right conditions. From here, intermediate paddlers should start to head east (see Sandford Island, below). Those with more experience may want to include Folger Island and Leach Islet to the west in their trip.

Folger, Leach and Edward King Islands It is among these islands that sea and land meet in full fury, carving and twisting the shore into beautifully bizarre shapes and providing an ideal environment for birds, seals and sea lions. Always use caution when approaching sea lions and keep a reasonable distance from their haul-outs and rookeries. This is the wild West Coast so be prepared for anything, especially fog.

The closest camping spot in the western end of the Deer Group is on the northeast corner of Edward King Island. The island was named for Capt. Edward Hammond King, who was accidentally killed here in 1861, unloading his rifle from a boat while on a deer hunting expedition. It is quite rugged, though beautiful, with few sheltered landings.

Sandford Island Heading back to Diana and Helby Islands will put you into calmer waters again, and you can continue your journey east by crossing over to Sandford Island from Helby. This crossing can also be rough, with Satellite Passage open to the ocean swell. Please do not land at Wizard Islet; there are often breeding seabirds on this islet and any disturbance can have a large impact on their success. For people looking to camp, head to the eastern shore of Sandford, where there are a number of good campsites tucked above a small sandy beach. The nearby Ross Islets also have a few small sites; don't be surprised if you have company.

v *Testing the water near Fleming Island, Deer Group,* PETER MCGEE

From the Ross Islets, paddle around the western corner of Fleming Island and into the large bay on the north side. Use caution: the southwest point of Fleming can be quite rough under certain conditions. A beach on the northwest side of the island is suitable for camping, though it is quite a small area when the tide is high.

Tzartus Island The last of the major islands in the Deer Group to explore is Tzartus. Named from a native word for "place of the seasonal or intermittent waterfall" or "place where the water flows inside the beach," Tzartus has much to offer the paddler, including the absolutely stunning sea arches of Marble Cove and the intricate Chain Group of islands off its northern shores. In and around Robbers Passage and Marble Cove are a number of floating cabins and the Canadian King Lodge, which leaves little in the way of campsites. This shouldn't deter you from extending your trip to include Tzartus, however, as the largest of the Stud Islets and Holford Bay each have room for a few tents.

From this point you can either retrace your strokes back to Bamfield or head directly across Trevor Channel to Vancouver Island and work your way west along the shores.

ADDITIONAL ROUTES
In and around Bamfield For those less inclined to venture to the Deer Group but still looking for some paddling adventures, consider the following suggestions.

Mills Peninsula offers terrific day trips both in and right outside Bamfield Harbour. The inside waters of Bamfield and Grappler Inlets are calm in most weather and offer lots of little inlets and side coves; the estuaries at the heads of the inlets are a treasure-trove of wildlife. Beyond the harbour, the peninsula has magnificent white sand beaches and rugged rock formations with numerous caves. The coast can be rough, with a constant swell—experienced paddlers only!— but it is spectacular. This paddle is best started in the morning because the wind from the open Pacific Ocean picks up towards the afternoon, and it is always exhilarating riding the swells home accompanied by a brisk westerly. Brady Beach is the most famous beach along this southward route; it offers an easy landing.

As you continue south, you will come to the Blow Hole, an impressive phenomenon at the right tide, spraying cascades of ocean up to 15 m (50 ft.) into the air, creating rainbows. Past the Blow Hole you will find incredible beaches, including First Beach, Second Beach and Keeshan. These three are on Indian Reserve 9, and visits to First and Second Beaches require a pass. Keeshan is off limits completely: it is one of the region's most sensitive historic village sites. The lookout here, with its commanding view of the entrance to Barkley Sound, is known as Execution Rock and is rich in native lore and history. The cliffs and caves are breathtaking and the waters very turbulent as ocean swells smash and reverberate off the rugged coast.

The last large beach before Cape Beale is in Tapaltos Bay (located in the West Coast Trail Unit of Pacific Rim National Park Reserve). This is a most inviting crescent-shaped beach about 1 km (.6 mi.) long with a spectacular double sea arch at the southwest end. Landings are more often than not treacherous as the surf can be wicked. The Tapaltos Bay Hilton is a rough little shack at the south end of the beach. With its beach treasures, rainbow graffiti and stunning view, this is a place to enjoy lunch and relax. From the Tapaltos Beach, trails lead to Keeha Beach and the Cape Beale lighthouse.

To paddle beyond this point and around Cape Beale requires extreme caution and experience. There is a slip of an entrance into a magical cove just before reaching Cape Beale. The cove is used to bring in supplies by boat to the lighthouse, and there is a trail from the beach up to the lighthouse. You can paddle through the cove or portage your kayak across the mud at low tide and do the "shortcut"; this will bring you to the other side of Cape Beale, avoiding the reef and famous breakers. However, you will still find it tricky negotiating the rocks and surf before reaching open ocean—experience is a must. From here you can paddle around into Keeha Bay, a spectacular 2-km (1.25-mi.) beach with wonderful caves at the west end. Floats in the middle of the beach mark the Keeha trail back to Bamfield.

Heading north or south from Barkley Sound Neither direction is recommended. Both shorelines are exposed to the full fury of the Pacific and should only be attempted by paddlers very familiar with the open ocean.

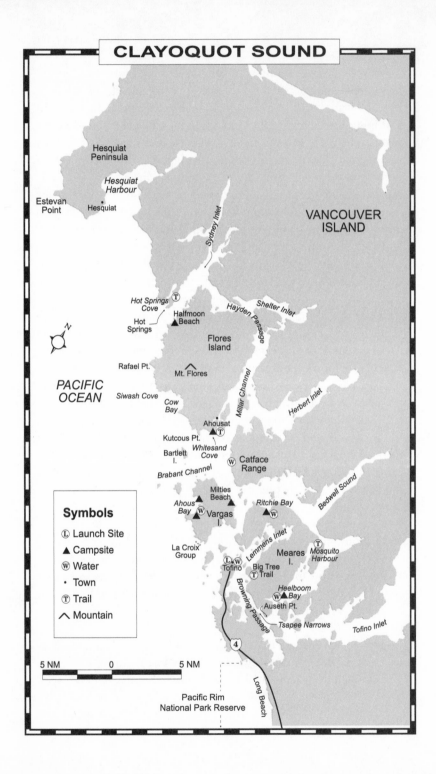

CLAYOQUOT SOUND

Hesquiat
Peninsula

*Hesquiat
Harbour*

Estevan
Point

• Hesquiat

**VANCOUVER
ISLAND**

Sydney Inlet

*Hot Springs
Cove* Ⓣ

▲ Halfmoon
Beach

Shelter Inlet

Hayden Passage

Hot
Springs

Flores
Island

Rafael Pt.

⌃
Mt. Flores

*PACIFIC
OCEAN*

Siwash Cove

*Cow
Bay*

Millar Channel

Herbert Inlet

Ahousat
▲ Ⓣ

Kutcous Pt.

Bartlett
I.

*Whitesand
Cove*

Ⓦ Catface
Range

Brabant Channel

Bedwell Sound

Milties
Beach
▲   ▲

*Ahous
Bay* Ⓦ

▲
Vargas
I.

Ritchie Bay

▲ Ⓦ

Lemmens Inlet

La Croix
Group

Meares
I.

*Mosquito
Harbour*
Ⓣ

Ⓛ Ⓦ
Tofino

Big Tree
Ⓣ Trail

Browning Passage

Heelboom
Ⓦ▲ *Bay*

Auseth Pt.

Tsapee Narrows

Tofino Inlet

④

Symbols

Ⓛ Launch Site

▲ Campsite

Ⓦ Water

• Town

Ⓣ Trail

⌃ Mountain

5 NM   0   5 NM

Long Beach

Pacific Rim
National Park Reserve

13

Clayoquot Sound

Bonny Glambeck and Dan Lewis

Home to ancient rain forests and white sand beaches, Clayoquot Sound is a gem on the rugged West Coast. Once known only for its stunning scenery, hot springs and whales, the area was flung into the international spotlight during the infamous summer of 1993. Over 12,000 people attended the Clayoquot Sound Peace Camp that summer to protest the provincial government's decision to open up 62 per cent of the sound to clear-cut logging. It was the largest civil disobedience action in Canadian history and led to the arrest of 932 people. Although the future of the area is still uncertain, the summer of 1993 highlighted a very clear and important message supported by people around the world: The temperate rain forests of Clayoquot Sound must be protected from industrial logging.

BACKGROUND

Located halfway up the west coast of Vancouver Island, Clayoquot Sound encompasses 262 000 ha (647,390 a.) between Tofino and the Hesquiat Peninsula. Its 10 major river systems support the largest lowland temperate rain forest remaining on Earth.

Clayoquot Sound is also the traditional home and unceded territory of three Nuu-chah-nulth First Nations: the Hesquiaht, Ahousaht and Tla-o-qui-aht peoples. Clayoquot (pronounced Klak-wit) is an anglicization of the native term *tla-o-qui-aht* (pronounced tla-oo-quee-at), meaning "different or changing." The provincial and federal governments have recognized the ancestral claim of the Nuu-chah-nulth Tribal Council and are now in the process of negotiating a treaty. In 2003, the local native population was approximately 1,100, largely concentrated in the village sites of Opitsat on Meares Island, Ahousat on Flores Island and Hot Springs Cove north of Flores. Most of the 1,600 non-native residents in Clayoquot Sound live in Tofino.

First incorporated as a village municipality in 1932, the town of Tofino has served as the gateway to Clayoquot Sound since the lifeboat station was established in 1913. Named after Vincente Tofino, a Spanish rear-admiral and prominent astronomer, Tofino has undergone some dramatic changes over the past decade, transforming itself from a quiet coastal community into a booming tourist destination. This change comes as no surprise, however, as Tofino sits just north of Long Beach and the Pacific Rim National Park Reserve, an area that receives more than half a million visitors annually, most of them between June and September. The high number of visitors means that you must book any accommodations well in advance. In 2000, Clayoquot Sound was designated a UNESCO Biosphere Reserve. Although this does not protect any of the pristine watersheds for which Clayoquot is so famous, it is yet another sign of the global significance of this rare ecosystem.

GETTING THERE

By land Tofino is approximately 250 km (155 mi.) from Nanaimo at the end of Highway 4 (the Pacific Rim Highway). Coming from the mainland, catch the ferry to Nanaimo from either Horseshoe Bay or Tsawwassen. Once in Nanaimo, head north along Highway 19 (the Island Highway) towards Qualicum Beach. Exit at the Qualicum Beach/Port Alberni turnoff and take Highway 4 to Port Alberni. Follow the signs to Tofino as you head west, through the town of Port Alberni and beyond. When you run out of road, you've reached Tofino. Total driving time from Nanaimo is roughly 3 hours, though some sights along the way (such as the MacMillan Provincial Park/Cathedral Grove) and a few curves in the road may slow you down a bit. There are also several bus services to Tofino.

If you are approaching from Seattle, you can also catch the ferry directly from Seattle to Victoria, then drive north for 2 hours to Nanaimo along Highway 19. From Nanaimo, follow the directions above. If you are approaching from Port Hardy, head south on Highway 19 until you reach the turnoff at Qualicum Beach for Port Alberni, and follow the directions above.

By air North Vancouver Air, based at the Esso Avitat Terminal in Richmond, flies daily to Tofino, landing at the Long Beach Golf Course. Flight time is approximately 1 hour.

WEATHER AND HAZARDS

Winds typically blow northwest or west in the summer in this region, particularly on sunny days. Westerly winds of 20–30 knots are common on most fair-weather afternoons, quickly blowing fog away but also kicking up a chop. Do not be caught midway on an exposed crossing by this predictable phenomenon. Another potential hazard is the presence of fog during July and August. Although this fog generally lifts by the early afternoon, do not count on it clearing—and avoid crossings while it persists. On shore, fog makes for cool, damp camping conditions so be prepared with the appropriate clothing. Clayoquot Sound receives 250 cm (98.5 in.) of precipitation annually, though the summer months tend to be relatively dry with temperatures ranging from 10–25°C (50–77°F).

Because of the dangers of the exposed coast, beginner paddlers should only plan trips on the protected waters behind Meares Island. If you do not have experience landing in surf, pull over at Long Beach in Pacific Rim National Park Reserve, and get out and play in the surf. Best of all, take a kayak surfing course from a reputable instructor.

Regardless of the trip you decide upon, you will likely face currents of 2–3 knots around the harbour at Tofino. These currents can be particularly dangerous if running counter to the prevailing winds and/or mixed with the heavy boat and plane traffic in the area. Tofino

Harbour is a beehive of activity, especially during the summer. Water taxis, float planes, whale watchers and fishing charters all add to the excitement. As at other locations throughout the province, locals affectionately refer to kayakers as "speed bumps," so stay together in a tight pod and make your presence known.

No matter how visible you are, however, two areas still require extra caution. The first is the harbourfront traffic flow running along the shore of Tofino. Cross this area in a tight group perpendicular to traffic. The other area is the traffic route between Tofino and Opitsat Village on Meares Island, marked by red and green buoys. This is the main route for all traffic coming and going in Clayoquot Sound. If you are heading for Vargas or Flores Islands, avoid this fairway by paddling out towards Stubbs (Clayoquot) Island. If the tide is too low to do this, paddle down the right side of the lane in single file, keeping clear of traffic.

SPECIAL CONSIDERATIONS

Gray whales migrate past Clayoquot Sound every spring, and several stay each year as summer residents. Encountering whales while paddling is a thrilling experience. The kayak, however, is not the ideal craft for whale watching. Although grays appear to be gentle and slow-moving creatures, they are powerful wild animals that deserve space and respect. If you encounter whales of any kind, please keep these guidelines in mind.

- Always approach slowly from the side, no closer than 100 m (330 ft.). (The same distance applies to sea lion haul-outs.)
- Make noise by tapping on your kayak frequently so that the whales know where you are at all times.
- Do not restrict or interrupt a whale's normal movement.
- Do not disturb a motionless or sleeping whale on the water surface.
- Do not split up groups, especially mothers and calves.
- Do not box whales in with other boats or in shallow water.
- Keep in mind: The best encounters with whales are the ones where they choose to visit you.

Finally, please remember that all of the beaches you land on, camp on and explore have been home to the Nuu-chah-nulth since time immemorial. Some of them are designated Indian Reserves. Do not land at an IR without permission from the appropriate band office.

∧ *Morning mist, Meares Island*, GRANT THOMPSON/TOFINO EXPEDITIONS

CLAYOQUOT SOUND TRIPS (32–34)

There are several popular trips in Clayoquot Sound. If you have only a day, the Big Tree Trail on Meares Island is a must-see. Three to 4 days will provide enough time to circumnavigate either Meares Island or, for more advanced paddlers, Vargas Island. Finally, for those of you lucky enough to have at least 7 days on the water, the increasingly popular trip to the natural hot springs north of Flores Island awaits. Each trip departs from, and returns to, Tofino.

TRIP 32 Big Tree Trail (Meares Island)

SKILL:	Intermediate
TIME:	Day trip
HAZARDS:	Traffic and currents
ACCESS:	Tofino
CHARTS:	3673 · Clayoquot Sound, Tofino Inlet to Millar Channel · 1:40,000
	3685 · Tofino · 1:20,000
TIDE BOOK:	Vol. 6

This spectacular hike through a grove of giant cedars is an essential ingredient for any visit to Clayoquot Sound. A short paddle, the trip is suitable for all but complete novices. If you have never kayaked before, consider taking a guided trip—it makes dealing with the harbour traffic, complex currents, float planes and potential winds a lot easier. If you are heading out into the sound for a longer trip, plan on working Meares Island into your schedule; it is one of the best hiking opportunities into Clayoquot Sound's ancient forests.

LAUNCHING

As you approach the town of Tofino, Pacific Rim Highway turns into Campbell Street. Go all the way to 1st Street, turn right, go to the bottom of the hill and turn left. You will see the kayak launch sign. This site is conveniently near the Common Loaf Bakery, in case you need to make a last-minute dash for treats, and the Tofino Sea Kayaking Company, a good local resource centre for kayakers.

The municipality of Tofino is working on a strategy to deal with the shortage of parking space in the summer. Parking in the downtown core is limited to 1 hour. Your best bet is to park on Main Street between 2nd and 4th Streets. If you have questions about parking, call or visit the village office.

Big Tree Trail If you leave Tofino on a rising tide, the currents will push you over to Meares, making for a relaxed paddle. The trailhead can be a little hard to find: it is located in the passage between Morpheus and Meares Islands, about halfway down the Meares side. In summer there will likely be other boats coming and going, which makes the trail easier to find. Be sure to beach your boats up high and tie them to a tree; tides and currents have been known to strand the occasional visitor. Overnight camping is not permitted.

The trail was originally built in 1984 by the Friends of Clayoquot Sound. Local photographer Adrian Dorst thought that more people would be motivated to help save Meares Island if they saw for themselves the awesome forests at stake. In 1992, a boardwalk was developed in a joint effort between the Tla-o-qui-aht First Nation and the Western Canada Wilderness Committee. The boardwalk was built to protect the forest, especially the tree roots, from the damage caused by thousands of visitors each year. Please stay on the boardwalk and do not pick or remove anything.

The boardwalk winds its way through a varied forest of cedar, hemlock and spruce. The trail ends at the famous Hanging Garden

Tree, a huge cedar with hundreds of smaller plants, shrubs and trees growing on it. All of this lush rain forest would have been clear-cut in the 1980s were it not for the valiant efforts of concerned locals, native and non-native alike. The fate of Meares Island is still in limbo. Although the Nuu-chah-nulth won a court injunction that halts all development on the island, the future of Meares depends on how the native land question is settled. In the meantime, the Nuu-chah-nulth declared Meares Island a tribal park in 1984, set aside for continued traditional use and for the recreational enjoyment of all who wish to visit the island and leave it as they find it.

TRIP 33 Meares Island

SKILL:	Intermediate
TIME:	3 days
HAZARDS:	Traffic and currents
ACCESS:	Tofino
CHARTS:	3673 · Clayoquot Sound, Tofino Inlet to Millar Channel · 1:40,000
	3685 · Tofino · 1:20,000
TIDE BOOK:	Vol. 6

Circumnavigating Meares Island is an excellent 3-day trip, especially if you are a less experienced kayaker and want to ease yourself into West Coast paddling.

See the trip above for launching details. It is best to leave Tofino on a rising tide, no more than 4 hours after low tide; this way you will have the current pushing you down Browning Passage. There is a small tidal rapids at Tsapee Narrows—another good reason to be going with the tide. If you are paddling against the current, creep along the shore of Meares Island in the back eddies. Tsapee Narrows is a popular sport-fishing location and can be busy with local traffic, so stay close to shore.

Rounding Auseth Point, head north. You will note on the charts that the rapids at Dawley Passage flow north on the ebb, not on the flood as you might logically expect. If you have timed things right, you can picnic in the vicinity of Auseth Point at high tide and then allow the current to push you through Dawley Passage. Again, watch for traffic in these narrow passages and stay close to shore. Unfortunately,

∧ *Many hands make light work, Flores Island,* GRANT THOMPSON/TOFINO EXPEDITIONS

Dawley Passage Provincial Park has no camping or water. It is simply a scenic corridor connecting Fortune Channel and Tofino Inlet. The closest camping is at Cis'a'quis.

SITES

Heelboom Bay/Cis'a'quis As you head north from Dawley Passage, Heelboom Bay is the first big bay on your left. Known locally as Cis'a'quis, this was the site of the 1984 confrontation between MacMillan Bloedel and local natives and environmentalists. A sign declaring the area "Meares Island Tribal Park" can be seen on your left; a cabin built for the blockade is located on the west side of the bay. There is good camping across the little bridge behind the cabin. Water can be gathered from creeks on either side of the cabin, though following the creek up the left side of the cabin will reward you with the purest water. In adverse weather the cabin can be used. Sign in to the logbook, even if you camp outside.

Mosquito Harbour is a day's paddle away from Cis'a'quis and a great place to visit. The harbour has a trail that leads to the largest cedar on Meares: 19 m (62 ft.) in circumference.

Milties Beach and Ritchie Bay From Heelboom Bay or Mosquito Harbour, you can head back to Tofino the way you came, catching the tides in reverse, or continue to circumnavigate Meares. A careful look at the charts will show the steep, cliff-lined coast along the north side of Meares Island that makes camping impossible. One option is to go all the way to Milties Beach on Vargas Island (see the route to Hot Springs Cove below). Another is to camp at Ritchie Bay at the base of a couple of old clear-cuts; a creek runs down the middle of the beach. Both these beaches may be under water at spring tides (full and new moons), but otherwise there should be enough room to fit a small to medium-sized group.

TRIP 34 Hot Springs Cove

SKILL: Intermediate (inside route) to advanced (outside route)
TIME: 5–10 days
HAZARDS: Traffic, currents and open coast
ACCESS: Tofino
CHARTS: 3673 · Clayoquot Sound, Tofino Inlet to Millar Channel · 1:40,000
3674 · Clayoquot Sound, Millar Channel to Estevan Point · 1:40,000
3685 · Tofino · 1:20,000
TIDE BOOK: Vol. 6

Few trips along B.C. waters combine as many pleasures as the trip from Tofino to Hot Springs Cove. Not only is the scenery beautiful and the wildlife abundant, but at the end of it all you can soak away your troubles in one of the most picturesque hot springs on the coast. To reach the hot springs, you can either take an exposed route along the outside of Flores and Vargas Islands or travel the protected inside passage. As mentioned earlier, intermediate paddlers who do not have surf experience should choose the protected route.

LAUNCHING

As you leave Tofino for Vargas Island, be careful of the harbourfront traffic flow and the designated traffic lane between Tofino and Opitsat Village on Meares Island (as mentioned earlier). You can avoid much of this traffic by paddling out towards Stubbs (Clayoquot) Island, but only attempt this if the tide is high. If not, paddle down the right side of the lane in single file. Once on Vargas, hug the eastern shore to stay out of the way of boat traffic travelling inside of Elbow Bank, then follow the northern shore to Milties Beach. Leave yourself at least 3 hours to reach Milties from Tofino and be particularly careful about other boat traffic in the event of fog.

SITES

Milties Beach (Vargas Island) This is a good destination for the first day of a trip into the sound: a sandy beach with a western exposure, far enough removed to feel you are "out there" yet not too far for the frenzy of last-minute runs to the bakery and packing to catch the tide. This site is often busy in the summer so bring along your common courtesy and patience. There can be a bit of a surf landing here. Be prepared for a dunking, and make sure loose bits of gear will not be scattered along the beach should you tip.

At the north end of Milties Beach, a cabin has recently been built on the former campsite. Otherwise there is .4 km (.25 mi.) of sandy beach for you to camp on; just check the tide tables carefully to ensure a dry night's sleep. There is no water source. Just north of Milties, across Brabant Channel, lies an alternative spot at Whitesand Cove.

Whitesand Cove (Flores Island) As the name suggests, this area is a heaven on earth. Gibson Provincial Marine Park covers most of the beachfront, which is where you should plan to camp and where BC Parks has installed an outhouse. Similar to Milties Beach and other spots throughout the sound, you may find that you are not the first to discover this prime campsite. If you do appear to be alone, keep your

∧ *Fall sockeye salmon*, PETER MCGEE

camp compact and avoid spreading out in case more paddlers show up later in the day or evening. There is no water source here.

Nearby is the Ahousat Walk the Wild Side Trail. The result of a 1996 collaboration between the Ahousat First Nation and the Western Canada Wilderness Committee, this trail runs along the outer coast of Flores Island, from Ahousat to Mount Flores, and offers paddlers a great chance to stretch their legs. You can start the trail at Ahousat or pick it up on any of the nearby beaches.

If you are day-tripping in the area of Whitesand Cove, a couple of cautions. First, Bartlett Island is an Indian Reserve in its entirety: do not plan on landing here, even for a picnic. You can picnic at the nearby Whaler Islets, an ideal location to play *Gilligan's Island* for a few hours. Second, the unprotected coastline west of Kutcous Point is not a good place for less experienced paddlers. The beaches require surf landings and the entire area is exposed to the typical afternoon westerly winds, as well as to the infrequent summer storms with southeast winds.

Flores Island (Inner Coast) There is not a lot of camping along the inside of Flores Island, though several small sites are scattered along Millar Channel and Shelter Inlet. If you can, plan to go up Millar Channel on a flood, arriving at the south end of Hayden Passage at high tide. The current races through Hayden Passage—try to go with it. Take the ebb through the pass then carry on around Flores to Half-moon Beach.

Halfmoon Beach and the Hot Springs Although there is no water, Halfmoon Beach is an excellent base camp for a day at the hot springs. The springs themselves lie within a part of Maquinna Provincial Marine Park where camping is not permitted. The surf is usually quite small by the time it works its way up Sydney Inlet and into the bay. Give yourself a full day to visit Hot Springs Cove. Paddle around Sharp Point and up into the cove. Note: Rounding Sharp Point in big swell or strong winds is not recommended. There is a steep cobble beach half a mile along, or you can leave your boats at the government wharf (it is difficult to land at the peninsula near the springs) and hike the easy, well-marked boardwalk to the springs. Once there, you get to shed your gear and enjoy one of the finest natural pleasures known to paddlers around the world.

Flores Island (Outer Coast) Paddling down the outside of Flores Island can be a thrilling trip, but only attempt this route if the conditions are good to excellent and you are experienced and prepared. If you are not, the trip can be harrowing, as more than one paddler has found out. Conditions to avoid include seas greater than 2 m (6.5 ft.), winds above 15 knots, fog and nighttime. What makes this paddle especially challenging is that there are no safe landings between Rafael Point and Siwash Cove—you are 100 per cent committed out there and will feel it. What makes this paddle special, however, is that a huge area (7113 ha/17,500 a.) of land and foreshore on the island is protected in Flores Island Provincial Park, which offers wilderness campsites and a pit toilet at Cow Bay. If you are not an experienced open-coast paddler, it is better to learn in a relatively safe setting such as the outside of Vargas Island.

Ahous Bay On the exposed outside of Vargas Island, Ahous Bay is another kayaker's dream come true. A 1.6-km (1-mi.) sand beach looks out over Blunden Island and the open ocean beyond. This is a surf beach, and on a large swell you can actually get out and practise your surfing skills—if you brought a helmet.

Camping can be found at both ends of the bay. This makes the landings a little easier, as the surf is smaller at the edges than at the middle of the beach. BC Parks has installed an outhouse behind the main beach at the south end. There are also a few small creeks at the southern and northern ends of the bay. The southern point is an Indian Reserve and is off limits.

If you decide to paddle around the southern end of Vargas Island on your way back to Tofino, be sure to take care passing through the La Croix Group. Not only are the islands exposed to surf, but reefs, fog and sport-fishing boats can make them particularly dangerous.

ADDITIONAL ROUTES

Heading north and south There is currently a tourism moratorium in Hesquiat territory, so we cannot recommend a route north towards Hesquiat Peninsula. We also don't recommend a route heading south: the coastline is rugged and completely exposed to the full fury of the Pacific Ocean for 20 nautical miles. The Hesquiat Band plans to keep the moratorium in effect until it is able to develop some of its own tourist facilities. Paddlers who wish to enter the area, whether to visit Cougar Annie's Garden in Hesquiat Harbour or Hesquiat Peninsula Provincial Park, should check with the band office and confirm their travel plans.

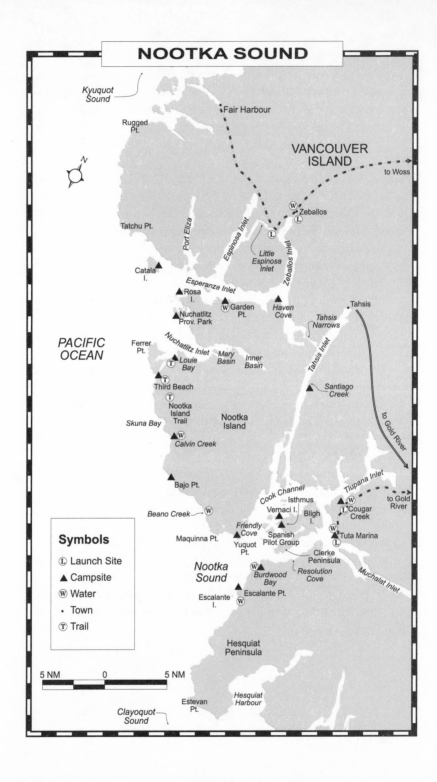

NOOTKA SOUND

Kyuquot
Sound

Fair Harbour

Rugged
Pt.

VANCOUVER
ISLAND

to Woss

Tatchu Pt.

Port Eliza

Espinosa Inlet

Ⓦ Zeballos
Ⓛ

Ⓛ

Little
Espinosa
Inlet

Zeballos Inlet

Catala
I.

Esperanza Inlet

▲ Rosa
I.

Ⓦ Garden
Pt.

▲ Haven
Cove

Tahsis

▲ Nuchatlitz
Prov. Park

Tahsis
Narrows

Tahsis Inlet

PACIFIC
OCEAN

Ferrer
Pt.

Nuchatlitz Inlet

Mary
Basin

Inner
Basin

Ⓣ Louie
Bay

▲ Santiago
Creek

▲ Ⓣ
Third Beach

Ⓣ
Nootka
Island
Trail

Nootka
Island

to Gold River

Skuna Bay

Ⓦ
Calvin Creek

▲ Bajo Pt.

Tiupana Inlet

Cook Channel

Isthmus

Ⓦ
▲ Cougar
Ⓛ Creek

to Gold
River

Beano Creek → Ⓦ

Vernaci I.

Bligh
I.

Friendly
Cove

▲ Ⓦ
Ⓛ Tuta Marina

Maquinna Pt.

Yuquot
Pt.

Spanish
Pilot Group

Clerke
Peninsula

Muchalat Inlet

Nootka
Sound

Ⓦ
▲ Burdwood
Bay

Resolution
Cove

Symbols

Ⓛ Launch Site

▲ Campsite

Ⓦ Water

• Town

Ⓣ Trail

▲ Escalante
Escalante ▲ Pt.
I.

Ⓦ

Hesquiat
Peninsula

5 NM   0   5 NM

Estevan
Pt.

Hesquiat
Harbour

Clayoquot
Sound

14

Nootka Sound

Jamie Boulding

For all its natural beauty, it is the history of Nootka Sound that makes this area unique. Nootka Sound is where Capt. James Cook first set foot in British Columbia and where the sea otter fur trade began. Most importantly, Nootka is the ancestral home of the Mowachaht/Muchalaht people. As the Mowachaht/Muchalaht have said, it is not just a place: Nootka is a feeling, and if you listen closely as you paddle the shores and walk the beaches, you might just hear the elders talking.

BACKGROUND

Long before Europeans arrived in Nootka Sound, the area was populated by dozens of Mowachaht communities. On March 29, 1778, Capt. James Cook, commander of the ships *Resolution* and *Discovery*, moored off the Mowachaht village of Yuquot/Friendly Cove. Believing the area to be officially Spanish, based on the voyage of Juan Perez in 1774, Cook did not bother to claim it for the British Empire. Instead, while repairing his ships he explored the area and traded European goods for sea otter furs. Many of these furs were later sold for outrageous prices in China, and the transpacific trade between Nootka and China began.

In light of this sudden interest in the area, the Spanish felt their rather dubious claim was being threatened and, in a show of force, seized American and British ships. The seizure caused an uproar in London, and Britain mobilized its forces for war. Spain, not wishing to embroil itself in yet another conflict, relinquished her claim to the region in the Nootka Convention of 1790. Shortly after gaining title to the northwest coast of the continent, however, the British withdrew from the area, concentrating their forces on the defence of the homeland. For the next 80 years following the abandonment of the Spanish fort at Yuquot/Friendly Cove, no Europeans occupied any land on the west coast of Vancouver Island.

When Europeans once again started to settle the area, the sea otters were long gone and livelihoods were created from fish, forests and mines. Logging still makes its mark on Nootka Sound, with many slopes visibly scarred. Recognizing the importance of the region, the provincial government has finally started to look more closely at the protection and management of Nootka Sound and Nuchatlitz Inlet. There are four new parks in the district—Catala Island, Nuchatlitz, Santa-Boca, Bligh Island—though there is still very little information on the plans for their management. The Mowachaht/Muchalaht Band has development plans for Yuquot/Friendly Cove including a museum, rental cabins (these are in place) and improvements to the west coast hiking trail on Nootka Island. Although the Mowachaht/ Muchalaht are encouraging tourism at Yuquot/Friendly Cove, it is best to obtain permission and information from the Band office (formerly the Ahaminaquus Tourist Centre), near Gold River, if you plan on stopping there.

GETTING THERE

By land Most visitors to Nootka Sound and Nuchatlitz Inlet will pass through the town of Gold River, approximately 1.5 hours west of Campbell River along Highway 28. Campbell River lies about 153 km (95 mi.) north of Nanaimo along Highway 19, the Island Highway.

If you are heading to Nootka Sound, you can launch from Ahaminaquus, approximately 14 km (8.7 mi.) west of Gold River on Pulp Mill Road. Closer launch sites to the sound can be found at Cougar Creek and Tuta Marina, which can be reached via the logging road that connects Gold River to Tahsis. The total driving time from Gold River to either site is about 1.5 hours, but you will avoid the long paddle down Muchalat Inlet that is necessary if you launch at Ahaminaquus.

If you are heading directly to Nuchatlitz Inlet, drive 125 km (76 mi.) north along Highway 19 from Campbell River to Woss and then head west 60 km (37 mi.) to Zeballos. It is possible to launch from Zeballos, but your best bet is to take the logging road leading to Fair Harbour and stop short at the bridge that crosses Little Espinosa Inlet. From here you can avoid the winds and extra paddling associated with Zeballos Inlet.

By water and air For paddlers who want to customize a trip into Nootka Sound or want a quick drop-off, head to Ahaminaquus (see above). From here the region can be accessed by the MV *Uchuck III*, Maxi's Water Taxi, Air Nootka or a private boat. *Uchuck* owner Fred Mather reports that reservations are essential for the weekly summer passage.

WEATHER AND HAZARDS

The weather in Nootka Sound is typical of the southern section of the west coast of Vancouver Island and a little less severe than its northern counterpart. The paddler must be continually aware of boat and ship traffic, large swells, changing wind patterns, surf landings, breaking waves and boomers. Various inlets funnel and redirect the winds, particularly in Muchalat and Tlupana Inlets, and afternoon winds typically become quite strong during the summer. On the outer coast expect serious weather. Ocean swell and fog can combine at any time of year to make a deadly combination. Many stretches of the exposed coastline have limited take-outs, so plan your routes carefully.

Animals are not generally a problem here, but cougars can be a danger to small children left unattended. Half of the more than 60 recorded cougar attacks in North America have taken place on Vancouver Island. There have been a few problems with bears getting into people's boats and food, most recently on Strange Island, so remember to cache your food unless you are on a small island. It only takes one careless kayaker to create a problem bear. Also be on the alert for wolves.

NOOTKA SOUND TRIPS (35–36)

The paddling possibilities in and around Nootka Sound are seemingly endless. The route from Cougar Creek or Tuta Marina along the west side of Bligh Island and through the Spanish Pilot Group is ideal for intermediate paddlers who want a feel for the West Coast. Those with more experience can lengthen their trip with excursions to Yuquot/Friendly Cove, Burdwood Bay and beyond. North of Nootka Sound lie the Esperanza and Nuchatlitz Inlets. From the launch site at Little Espinosa Inlet, paddlers can easily spend a few days exploring the new marine parks at Catala Island and Mary Basin (in Nuchatlitz Provincial Park). For the truly adventurous, a circumnavigation of Nootka Island is possible, but both experience and time are essential.

TRIP 35 Nootka Sound

SKILL: Intermediate to advanced

TIME: 3–7 days

HAZARDS: Open coast

ACCESS: Gold River/Cougar Creek/Tuta Marina/
MV *Uchuck* III

CHARTS: 3675 · Nootka Sound · 1:40,000
3676 · Esperanza Inlet · 1:40,000

TIDE BOOK: Vol. 6

Exploring the Spanish Pilot Group is a great 2–4-day tour that will give you a good taste of Nootka Sound and most likely whet your appetite for further adventures. For the more experienced, taking a few more days to explore Yuquot/Friendly Cove and Burdwood Bay is time well spent.

LAUNCHING

The most convenient put-ins for a short trip in Nootka Sound are either the Cougar Creek Forest Service recreation site or Tuta Marina. To drive to these sites, take the gravel road from Gold River towards Tahsis. (The road from Gold River to either of the put-ins is gravel, and vehicles with high clearance are recommended.) After you come down the steep pass from the obvious high point, look for a left turn marked Nesook Log Dump and take that road. Watch for logging trucks along the road and at the dump itself: this is an active logging area and drivers should be wary at all times. When you reach the paved dryland-sort area at the Nesook dump, stay left and continue along the Tlupana Inlet road. This is perhaps the most confusing part of the drive, and many newcomers to the area have turned around here thinking they were lost. Cougar Creek, approximately 6 km (3.7 mi.) past the dump, is well marked and will be obvious especially in summer, when up to one hundred RVs, filled with overzealous sport fishers, arrive on their annual migration. Tuta Marina is another 6 km (3.7 mi.) past Cougar Creek on the same road. This private marina was opened in 1995 and offers a boat ramp, store, showers, moorage and a campground. Although there is a small parking fee at Tuta Marina, the site allows you to put in on Hanna Channel, where you can avoid the head winds that blow up Tlupana Inlet most afternoons.

SITES

Spanish Pilot Group The most common route from these put-ins is to paddle around San Carlos Point at the northern tip of Bligh Island and then down the west side of the island. The most desirable destination for the first night out is at a location commonly called the Isthmus, or Charlie's Beach, located on the southwest tip of Bligh Island directly north of Clotchman Island. This is a very special campsite with two beaches that offer great morning and evening light. The downside of the Isthmus is that it is too popular, hence crowded and occasionally dirty. There is a pit toilet but no water. The most popular backup site is in the small bay on the east side of Vernaci Island. This site is a little buggy but has good flat places to camp and some beautiful culturally modified trees.

Water is hard to find in the Spanish Pilot Group unless it has been very rainy before your trip. Your best plan is to carry lots of water and/or make water collection trips to Bligh Island streams, which are marked on the chart.

On the second day of this short tour, if weather reports for the seas and winds are moderate or less, head to the Yuquot/Friendly Cove area. If the weather is not agreeable, fishing and exploring in the Spanish Pilot Group are excellent. If you travel to Yuquot/Friendly Cove, the Cook Channel crossing should not be taken lightly. In low visibility conditions, your major consideration will be the large ocean-going ships that, though infrequent, are still a significant hazard. You should also consider other boat traffic in Cook Channel and around the Saavedra Islands. If there is any chance of challenging conditions, try crossing Cook Channel from the north end of Narvaez Island, heading directly for the north end of the Saavedra Islands—or don't cross at all. This route will minimize your time in the channel and allow you a scenic paddle through McKay Passage south towards Friendly Cove. There is a nice campsite in the southwest corner of Santa Gertrudis Cove.

Yuquot/Friendly Cove Yuquot/Friendly Cove is part of the Mowachaht Indian Band Reserve. If you plan to stay at Yuquot/Friendly Cove or on any part of the reserve property in this area, call or write the Mowachaht/Muchalaht Band Office in Gold River for permission and reservations. The band charges a $10 per person landing fee, so be sure to bring cash. If you arrive without prior arrangements with the band, talk to Ray and Terry Williams, band members who reside permanently at Yuquot/Friendly Cove.

You can easily spend a whole day exploring and visiting Yuquot/Friendly Cove. The highlights include the pebble beach on the west coast, the church (with permission), a swim in the lake (the water is surprisingly warm) or a walk along the exposed beach on the west side of the cove. A visit to the lighthouse is also recommended. The view is excellent, and the keepers are always friendly and keen to inform citizens of their views regarding Ottawa's plans to destaff the stations. It is also possible to camp or even stay in a small rental hut at Yuquot/Friendly Cove. Again, call the band to make the appropriate arrangements and for a list of current fees.

Resolution Cove After visiting Yuquot/Friendly Cove, the safest route out is to retrace your strokes back to Narvaez Island. Once back in the Spanish Pilot Group, you can return to your vehicle via San Carlos Point, the easiest way back, or circumnavigate Bligh Island. If you plan to paddle around the island, be wary of the headlands on the tip of Clerke Peninsula: they can cause nasty rebound waves with even moderate swells. History buffs may want to stop in Resolution Cove to look at the plaques that commemorate Captain Cook's first landing

∧ *Bligh Island*, GRANT THOMPSON/TOFINO EXPEDITIONS

on the west coast of North America. Although Cook made contact with the Mowachaht at Yuquot, Resolution Cove is the site where British explorers first actually set foot in what is now British Columbia. The native name for Resolution Cove is Kathni-aktl, meaning "a place of driftwood."

It is possible to cross from Yuquot/Friendly Cove directly to the southern tip of Clerke Peninsula, but paddlers must exercise caution during such a long and exposed crossing. This option is not recommended if there are any concerns about weather, wind or visibility.

Burdwood Bay For paddlers who are comfortable in open water, try a trip to the beautiful beach in Burdwood Bay. The bay will likely require you to execute a surf landing, and the size of the surf will vary depending upon the wind speed and direction of the waves. The best campsite on the Burdwood beach is on the far left side of the bay when coming in. A dependable water source is inland about 50 m (164 ft.); follow the trail that leaves from the corner of the beach — you will likely have to cross over a section of piled driftwood to find the trailhead.

If you arrive in Burdwood Bay and the surf landing looks like more than you bargained for, paddle instead to the little bay due west on Burdwood Point. This is the easiest beach to land on near the bay.

Escalante Island Advanced paddlers can also consider making a trip down to Escalante Island from Burdwood Bay. This trip involves paddling 5 km (3 mi.) of exposed coast. The best route south along the coast is to stay inside the two groups of islets while weaving through the boomers. The chart accurately shows the rocks that are likely to boomer, but you should not attempt this route unless you are comfortable and experienced with these types of challenges.

In the Escalante area, the easiest landing and standard campsite is called Jim's Refuge. To get there, travel around Escalante Point and land on the beach between the rock shelves directly inland from the centre of Escalante Island. Other possible landing and camping sites in the area are on the inside of Escalante Island, Escalante River (the landing into the mouth of the river should only be attempted in very small swell) and the south end of the beach beside Escalante River before you round Escalante Point. Also noteworthy in the Escalante area are the prospector's cabin at Escalante River and the trail overland to avoid the headlands at Escalante Point.

TRIP 36 Nuchatlitz Inlet and Nootka Island

SKILL: Intermediate to advanced
TIME: 3–14 days
HAZARDS: Open coast
ACCESS: Little Espinosa Inlet/Zeballos
CHARTS: 3676 · Esperanza Inlet · 1:40,000
TIDE BOOK: Vol. 6

Paddling the bays, basins and islands around Nuchatlitz Inlet is a great 4–5-day trip. Those with the skill and mental preparation needed for the open coast can try the waters of Nootka Island's west side. The beaches at Skuna Bay, Calvin Creek and Beano Creek are some of the nicest on the coast, rewarding paddlers who are able to negotiate surf landings and quickly punishing those who are not. Travelling the inside of Nootka Island is a little less exciting. Nonetheless, a circumnavigation of Nootka Island will give you the best feel for the area and may bring a certain closure to your trip.

LAUNCHING

If you are planning road access, the best places to start a tour of the Nuchatlitz area are at Little Espinosa Inlet or the town of Zeballos. From the put-in at Little Espinosa, you have a shorter and more protected paddle into the sound, avoiding the winds that are so common in Zeballos Inlet. For this reason it is the favoured launch site even though Zeballos is a little more secure.

To reach the launch site at Little Espinosa, follow the road that leads from Zeballos to Fair Harbour. A few kilometres out of town the road crosses a small bridge over the inlet. There is no sign, but it is a fairly obvious launching area. Park on the side of the road. Be sure to lock your car and remove all valuables, as this area is quite isolated.

SITES

Garden Point After launching from Little Espinosa Inlet, a good objective for the first day is the Forest Service recreation site at Garden Point. Paddling out of Espinosa Inlet, stick to the east of Centre Island and head for the sand and pebble beach at the base of Brodick Creek. There are a number of tent sites in the old growth and the setting is relatively wild.

Catala and Rosa Islands From Garden Point, you can head to either Catala or Rosa Islands. Catala is a provincial marine park that offers some nice camping and plenty of beach to explore. The most sheltered site is near the sandy spit on the Rolling Roadstead side of the island. A more exposed site can be found on the south side of the island, opposite the twin islands. Rosa Island is contained within the larger provincial park, Nuchatlitz. You may want to use the camp on the centre of Rosa for a base when exploring the park. Although there are some pleasant little islands to camp on in Nuchatlitz, there are also numerous private holdings, Indian Reserves and burial sites that should be avoided unless you have permission. Check the BC Parks Web site for the latest information and maps.

Continuing past Nuchatlitz involves paddling in some exposed areas. The three options in order of increasing difficulty are to head up Nuchatlitz Inlet to Mary Basin, cross Nuchatlitz Inlet to Louie Bay or paddle around Ferrer Point and continue along the outside of Nootka Island.

The trip into Mary Basin and the Inner Basin is a good choice for a couple of days of exploring. This section of coast has an impressive sea cave to visit in calm conditions, but watch out for the boomers between Belmont Point and Benson Point. If you are planning to explore Nuchatlitz Inlet for a few days, you can also use Belmont and Benson Point as base camps. It is possible to avoid some of the exposed paddling en route to Port Langford by taking either of the two narrow portages from Nuchatlitz Provincial Park.

Louie Bay The crossing to Louie Bay from Nuchatlitz is 5 km (3 mi.) long and receives huge seas at times. Louie Bay has some good campsites on the sand beaches just south of Florence Point. There is a derelict radar station that was formerly used as a Christian camp by the Esperanza mission near Tongue Point. Do not try to paddle to the outside coast through the passage from Louie Bay; it is only covered in extremely high tides, and you will likely end up stuck in a mud flat. If you venture into the small inlet directly south of Louie Bay, try to catch the tide midway between high and low or you will be dragging your boat over some very slippery rocks. At the far end of this inlet is a trail that leads to a very beautiful beach camp on the west side of Nootka Island. This trail is actually the north end of a trail that runs down the outside coast of Nootka. Hiking parties often fly into this small inlet and hike down to Yuquot/Friendly Cove.

Nootka Island (West Side) Only expert paddlers should attempt the trip down the exposed coast of Nootka Island. It is best paddled from north to south to take advantage of the fair-weather westerlies. The route takes you around Ferrer Point, with the first possible landing at what is sometimes called Third Beach (the beach described above as the spot to hike to from Louie Bay). Landing at Third Beach is only possible if the swell is not very big; the swell direction will dictate which side of the rocks in front of the beach you should come in on. If the landing looks bad, you must be prepared to paddle down the coast to Skuna Bay or Calvin Creek. Both of these landings can be attempted in large swell without much danger, as long as you are comfortable in surf. The beach at Calvin Creek is one of the most spectacular on the B.C. coast. Calvin Creek has a 10-m (33-ft.) waterfall called Crawfish Falls that creates a little swimming hole right on the beach.

The next landing on this coast is inside the reef at Bajo Point. This is the easiest landing on the outside of Nootka Island and the only place where a skilled operator who knows the area can land a power-boat. There is also a landing at Beano Creek, another spot you would not want to land on if the swell is too big. The final stretch from Beano Creek around Maquinna Point to Yuquot/Friendly Cove is the most dangerous part of the trip. Even in moderate swell, you should expect unstable rebound waves if you get too close to Maquinna Point.

Nootka Island (East Side) The paddle along the inside of Nootka Island, though not exciting, should be your route unless you have the weather window and expertise to attempt the outside. Recommended camps include Santa Gertrudis Cove, the Spanish Pilot Group, Santiago Creek (between Tsowwin Narrows and Tahsis), then through Tahsis Narrows, west to Haven Cove and on to Garden Point.

ADDITIONAL ROUTES

Heading north This advanced paddle route puts you on the dramatic and exposed coastline between Tatchu Point and Kyuquot Sound. The odd pebble beach breaks up an otherwise rocky shore, and much of the area has been subjected to substantial logging. At the northern edge of this stretch of coastline lies Rugged Point Provincial Marine Park (see chapter 15).

Heading south The route south should only be attempted by advanced paddlers. Rounding Estevan Point in strong winds and heavy seas or swell is hazardous as waves steepen on the strong tidal currents close to the point. Once around the point, you are on the way to Clayoquot Sound (see chapter 13).

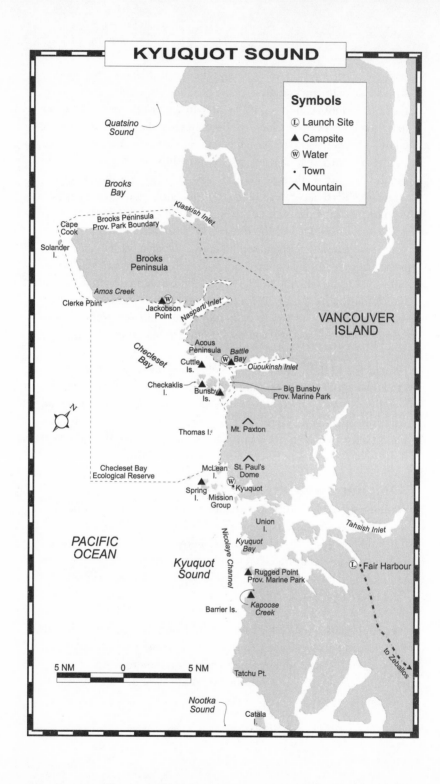

KYUQUOT SOUND

Symbols

- Ⓛ Launch Site
- ▲ Campsite
- Ⓦ Water
- • Town
- ⌃ Mountain

Quatsino Sound

Brooks Bay

Klaskish Inlet

Cape Cook

Brooks Peninsula Prov. Park Boundary

Solander I.

Brooks Peninsula

Amos Creek

Clerke Point

Ⓦ Jackobson Point

Naspartí Inlet

VANCOUVER ISLAND

Acous Peninsula

Battle Bay

Ⓦ ▲

Ououkinsh Inlet

Checleset Bay

Cuttle Is. ▲

Checkaklis I.

▲ Bunsby Is. ▲

Big Bunsby Prov. Marine Park

Thomas I.

⌃ Mt. Paxton

McLean I.

⌃ St. Paul's Dome

Checleset Bay Ecological Reserve

▲ Spring I.

Ⓦ • Kyuquot

Mission Group

Union I.

Tahsish Inlet

PACIFIC OCEAN

Nicolaye Channel

Kyuquot Bay

Kyuquot Sound

Ⓛ • Fair Harbour

▲ Rugged Point Prov. Marine Park

Barrier Is.

⌃ *Kapoose Creek*

to Zeballos

5 NM   0   5 NM

Tatchu Pt.

Nootka Sound

Catala I.

N

15

Kyuquot Sound

Rupert Wong

When a local sea kayak guide was asked once why she loved returning to Kyuquot every season, she closed her eyes, inhaled the salty air, smiled and said it was the bone-coloured nights when moonlight bathes the moss-covered trees, the sound of smacking as sea otters dine while nothing else is stirring, the fascinating stories and people of Kyuquot, and the way the place changes people in a matter of days.

BACKGROUND

Fewer than 5,000 people live in the northwest quadrant of Vancouver Island, with approximately 300 in the Kyuquot area. The coastline is rugged and folded with fiords, and the surrounding waters are strewn with reefs. The village of Kyuquot is one of the only communities on Vancouver Island's 400-km (250-mi.) long outer coast that remains isolated and without road access. For recreationists, the key attraction of the Kyuquot wilderness area is the Checleset Bay Ecological Reserve for sea otters and the Brooks Peninsula Provincial Park northwest of the community of Kyuquot. These protected areas are in proximity to coastlines and watersheds that have been logged since the 1940s, with most of the harvesting in the Kyuquot region taking place before the implementation of the Coastal Fish Forestry Guidelines in 1988. Visitors are often shocked by the dramatic contrast between remaining pristine coastlines and extensively logged slopes.

Some clear-cuts, such as those on the slopes of Mount Paxton, are so extensive that *National Geographic*'s 1992 article on temperate rain forests highlighted them as among North America's most ugly faces. It was such articles and the passionate lobbying of locals like Sam Kayra and Cindy Lee that alerted a stunned public to the devastation and ultimately heightened awareness to what remained. Although present-day logging practices have improved, the steep slopes are struggling to recover as erosion and blow-down, the byproducts of logging, continue.

Considering this recent history, it comes as no surprise that many locals remain wary of outsiders. The abundance of food on land and in the sea has sustained the Che: k' tles7et'h' (Checleset) and Ka:' yu: 'k t 'h' (Kyuquot) First Nation culture and traditions for many centuries. They were great hunters and traders who travelled the ocean in open canoes, navigating the same waters presently used by recreational paddlers. The powerful link to land and sea continues for the Che: k' tles7et'h' and Ka:' yu: 'k t' h' First Nation today and it is important for visitors to respect this relationship. Although the Che: k' tles7et'h' and Ka:' yu: 'k t 'h' First People generally welcome outsiders, they ask that you tread softly.

The paddling routes suggested in this chapter should be approached with a generous degree of care, and all travellers should be mindful of the many natural forces that have humbled locals for centuries. Today, Kyuquot is in flux with impending First Nations treaty negotiations, forestry issues and a growing tourism industry. The fate of Kyuquot is in everyone's hands.

GETTING THERE

By land The most economical means of reaching Kyuquot is to drive the 220 km (137 mi.) of Highway 19, the Island Highway, and logging roads from Campbell River to Fair Harbour. Once a forestry-based community, Fair Harbour now acts as a parking lot for people who live and work beyond. During the summer, there is some space for tents, though paddlers generally launch immediately after finding parking. It is often worth spending the evening in Campbell River or Courtenay so you can get a morning start for Fair Harbour.

Drive 125 km (78 mi.) north along Highway 19 from Campbell River to Woss. (Woss and Zeballos are the only places to stop for fuel en route to Fair Harbour.) From Woss to Zeballos is about 60 km (37 mi.) and usually takes about 1 hour. Take the Zeballos turnoff, approximately 22 km (14 mi.) north of Woss, just past the Steele River bridge along Highway 19. This is the start of the gravel logging road to Fair Harbour. Use your headlights and be aware of logging trucks. From Zeballos, follow the main logging road along the 35-km (22-mi.) stretch (roughly 30 minutes) to Fair Harbour. Forks in the road are usually well marked, but if you encounter one that is not signposted, follow the route most travelled until you reach the gravel parking lot of Fair Harbour.

If you want to avoid the paddle from the parking lot, a water taxi service can be arranged whereby all your gear, including kayaks, is moved from Fair Harbour to almost any drop point of your choice.

By water You could also drive to Gold River and board the 24-m (80-ft.) freighter MV *Uchuck III*. The *Uchuck* serves northwest coastal communities between Gold River and Kyuquot, and reservations are essential. The romance of the 7-hour *Uchuck* sail into Kyuquot is well worth the effort. Should you choose to use the *Uchuck*, bear in mind that your travel plans will be dependent on her return schedule.

By air Finally, you can always fly. Air Nootka presently holds the contract to deliver mail to Kyuquot on scheduled flights departing from Gold River. For $130 one way, you can join the mail run after carefully lashing your kayak onto the pontoon. This is an excellent way to gain a lofty perspective on forestry, the coastline and the lay of the land. Ask about air and water packages that combine charter service using Air Nootka and the *Uchuck III*.

WEATHER AND HAZARDS

The remote and rugged nature of Kyuquot can be a hazard in itself, and paddlers are reminded that this is not an area for beginners. Even during the popular summer months, you may encounter storms or fog. Storms generally approach from the southeast or northwest.

During the summer there are the added local effects of katabatic and anabatic winds amplified by inlets and warmer weather. Storms are usually accurately forecast by Environment Canada and broadcast on the area weather channel (WX1). Southeast storms pose the most serious threat to paddlers, as wind and wave energy easily and quickly develops to unsafe levels. Northwest storms seem to be deflected to some degree by the hulking mass of the Brooks Peninsula, which protects Checleset Bay in its lee. The challenge in Kyuquot Sound is weighing the risks of negotiating a certain exposed body of water in light of the forecast. It is always best to err on the side of caution and build ample contingency measures into your travel plan.

For inexperienced and unprepared paddlers, fog can present an insurmountable challenge. Familiarity and confidence with navigation can make fog less of a problem, but there is always the concern of ensuring your own visibility to oncoming motor vessels. See chapter 1 for more information on fog and wind.

Finally, some of the emergency resources typically available in more populated communities cannot be found in Kyuquot. There is no regional hospital within striking distance and the Coast Guard's nearest port is Tofino. Nonetheless, the Coast Guard can often be reached on channel 16 with a transmitting VHF radio, and there is a Red Cross outpost hospital attended by a registered nurse located outside the southeast entrance of Kyuquot. Since 1996, an RCMP officer has been posted in Kyuquot.

SPECIAL CONSIDERATIONS

As with any other First Nations traditional territory, you should seek permission to visit the area as part of your trip-planning process. The Che :k' tles7et'h' and Ka:' yu: 'k t 'h' traditional territory includes Checleset Bay to Kyuquot Sound, south of Rugged Point, and points inland including channels, inlets and watersheds. The key concern, particularly with elders in the community, is the degradation of heritage sites. Trespassing on mortuary sites, including burial caves and sacred islands, is strictly forbidden. Most of these sites are virtually unknown except to family members and the odd visitor who has accidentally stumbled upon them while exploring. As for uninhabited village sites, hereditary chiefs and their families usually do not mind sharing their beauty, but travellers should secure permission first, limit their

visits to day use only and minimize their impacts by not destroying vegetation, removing materials, building fires or constructing structures.

If you have not prearranged your visit with the Che: k' tles7et'h'
and Ka:' yu: 'k t 'h' Nation, visit the band office to check. At the time of
writing, recreational use permits and registration were not mandatory,
but this is being considered by both BC Parks and the First Nations. A
2000 pamphlet titled "Checleset Bay/Kyuquot Sound — Protected Areas" provides information on heritage sites, environmental etiquette
and sea otter viewing guidelines, among other things.

Garbage disposal is another serious issue in the community of
Kyuquot. At present, there are limited garbage disposal and recycling
options, and garbage generated by the community is sometimes
dumped directly into the ocean for lack of better alternatives. Domestic
sewage from Walters Island is piped straight into the cove. Untreated
sewage from Houpsitas is discharged into Nicolaye Channel. Although
there is a dumpster on the government wharf, it is often brimming
with waste. In short, do not plan on leaving your garbage in Kyuquot.

Unique to the B.C. coastline is the 34 650-ha (85,620-a.) Checleset
Bay Ecological Reserve established in 1981 for sea otters and their
habitat. The reserve is located immediately south of the Brooks Peninsula and encompasses such prime paddling destinations as the Bunsby
Islands and the Cuttle Islets.

It was once thought that the B.C. coast had been completely
stripped of sea otters (not to be confused with river otters) during the
greed-driven fur trade of the late 1700s. The last sea otter was reportedly shot near the village of Kyuquot. Through recolonization efforts
largely initiated by Ian MacAskie, then director of the West Coast
Whale Research Foundation, sea otter populations have begun to
make a dramatic recovery. The Checleset Bay area was selected as the
recolonization site for its remoteness, sheltered waters and extensive
shallow beds for feeding.

Sea otters rank at the top of the food chain, their only threat being
humans, eagles and orcas. When a marine ecosystem such as the one
in Checleset Bay is in equilibrium, the sea otter plays a key role in
controlling the numbers of kelp-grazing shellfish. An average adult
sea otter weighs about 30 kg (66 lb.) and will eat a quarter of its body
weight per day, a diet that consists of sea urchins, abalone, clams,
crabs, snails and other invertebrates collected on dives to the bottom.

∧ *Exploring the Bunsby Islands,* RUPERT WONG/WEST COAST EXPEDITIONS

The presence of the sea otter is so significant that whole ecosystems are altered by their positive influence on kelp growth in inshore waters. Like a terrestrial forest, kelp provides both food and shelter for its inhabitants. Kelp forests also act as natural breakwaters, absorbing the force of waves and currents. When these forests disappear, inshore productivity diminishes as beaches become exposed, and fish and other animals dependent on kelp become less abundant.

At the time of her study in the Kyuquot area in 1993, Dr. Jane Watson estimated the growth rate of the local sea otter population at 19.2 per cent per year from the original 89 sea otters re-introduced between 1962 and 1972. Today the Kyuquot sea otter population numbers about 400 to 450 individuals, which is an optimum population for the available habitat. The otters may be encountered singly, in small groups or in large colonies called rafts. They are very cautious animals and difficult to observe in the wild. If their space is intruded upon, they will disappear by either diving, swimming underwater or porpoising along the surface.

Since sea otters are usually above water, grooming or eating, a kayaker's presence can be stressful to them. If you observe sea otters in an upright position with head and shoulders above the water, they are most likely assessing their surroundings and possibly you. Many other marine mammals do this "spy hopping," especially orcas.

Kayakers should approach sea otter habitats carefully, observing the animals from a distance that will not startle them. This distance will vary, so use common sense. Female sea otters caring for pups, though entertaining to watch, are also the most vulnerable due to their protective nature. Stay clear of crying sea otter pups. A mother will temporarily leave her dependent pup while foraging for food, and your presence may prevent them from reuniting.

In addition to Checleset Bay, there are four other ecological reserves in the area that paddlers should avoid when camping: Solander Island, Klaskish River, Tahsish River and Clanninick Creek.

TRIP 37 Kyuquot and the Bunsby Islands

SKILL: Intermediate to advanced
TIME: 5–14 days
HAZARDS: Open coast and winds
ACCESS: Fair Harbour/MV *Uchuck III*
CHARTS: 3623 · Kyuquot Sound to Cape Cook · 1:80,000
3682 · Kyuquot Sound · 1:36,700
3683 · Checleset Bay · 1:36,500
TIDE BOOK: Vol. 6

The most common trip leaves from Fair Harbour and heads north towards the Bunsby Islands and the south side of the Brooks Peninsula. Due to the exposed coast and the varying weather conditions, it is wise to leave at least 1 week for this trip. If you are short on time, consider establishing a camp in the Mission Group or at the Rugged Point Provincial Marine Park and taking day trips to explore Kyuquot Sound.

LAUNCHING

Launching at Fair Harbour is easy: there is good water access and plenty of room for parking. Be prepared, however, as there are no facilities—only the large gravel parking lot used by logging companies and residents of Kyuquot. Lock all vehicle doors and do not leave valuables inside. Theft is uncommon but you never know.

SITES

The paddle to Kyuquot Sound from Fair Harbour is approximately 4–6 hours depending on inflow or outflow wind strength and tidal exchange. (The unofficial record of 2.5 hours is held by Bill Noble, who started from Spring Island.) Although there are no choice camping spots en route to Kyuquot, small groups can certainly improvise without too much difficulty. The best site at the southern edge of the sound, and the first camp on this route, is at Rugged Point.

Rugged Point Provincial Marine Park Precariously balanced between extensive mountainside clear-cuts and the open ocean, this park represents the way the exposed coastline between Rugged Point and Tatchu Point appeared before logging. Relentless surf over a shallow shoreline helps to maintain this stretch of fine sand beach, interrupted only by the occasional rock outcrop. The area is used frequently by boaters, with the highest concentration of use at the northwest end, where a protected anchorage exists. Paddlers capable of surf landings and launchings can venture southeast of Rugged Point towards Kapoose Creek, where more secluded camping can be found. Creeks that run through the park are not reliable for drinking without some method of treatment. It should also be noted that black bear, cougar and wolf are not uncommon, and care should be taken not to intrude upon their space if you suspect they are in the vicinity.

The Rugged Point geology is characterized by tilted seabeds dating back to the Jurassic Period, and marine fossils can be found in most rock outcrops. For the enjoyment of others who come after you, and in the spirit of conservation, BC Parks advises visitors not to remove or destroy specimens.

Gray whales find the subtidal habitat offshore of Rugged Point park ideal for feeding grounds, and they use them each spring and winter during their annual migration. Occasionally, non-reproductive whales take up residence here.

Union Island and Nicolaye Channel The paddling routes between Rugged Point and the Mission Group depend on the weather. On calm days, it is feasible and fun to travel offshore between the largest of the Barrier Islands. A more conservative approach is along Union Island and through Nicolaye Channel. Kyuquot Bay on Union Island offers protection and a place to beach if necessary. Both routes are about 13.5 km (8.4 mi.) and leave you vulnerable to wind and waves. If you must push the journey to Kyuquot or the Mission Group, taking the 21-km (13-mi.) inside passage around Union Island can be accomplished in all but extreme weather.

Mission Group and Spring Island Located approximately 13.5 km (8.4 mi.) northwest of Rugged Point is Spring Island, the largest of the Mission Group. Spring Island historically provided many resources for the Che :k' tles7et'h' and Ka:' yu: 'k t 'h' community that resided on the neighbouring islands of Aktis and Kamils.

More recently Spring Island served as a military radar station until the mid 1970s. An old roadbed, building remnants and other debris are evidence of this previous occupation. The old service road is now a Forest Service recreation site that provides easy access between Spring Island's exposed coast and the more protected bay on the northeast side. Both protected and exposed aspects of the island offer good camping, with the most breathtaking vistas facing the open ocean. The finest sand, and certainly the least damaging to the hull of your kayak, can be found on the central and eastern portions of the more protected, shallow bay. On the exposed side of Spring Island, winter storms leave steep gravel beaches that offer suitable camping on flat terraces, which get wet only on the most extreme summer tides.

Spring Island is 3.2 km (2 mi.) from Houpsitas Village and the community of Kyuquot, which has such modern conveniences as restaurants, a general store, post office, telephones and fax machines. Spring Island was not named for its water, so paddlers must either bring water from Kyuquot or collect it from Clanninick Creek, located 3.5 km (2.2 mi.) north of Spring Island.

Day-tripping around the tightly knit Mission Group of islands is richly rewarding, with shallows teeming with life and sea otters displaying their curious antics. Due to the proximity of Kyuquot, however, this region has more powerboat traffic than you will find elsewhere in the area. Avoid paddling in powerboat corridors wherever possible. Certain islands in the Mission Group, such as Aktis,

Ahmacinnit, Sobry and Kamils, are off limits to visitors without prior permission from the hereditary chiefs. Other islands located between Favourite Entrance and Minx Rocks offer suitable beaches for resting or camping for small groups.

Checleset Bay Perhaps the most daunting leg of a paddler's journey to Checleset Bay is the 13-km (8-mi.) stretch between the Mission Group and Bunsby Islands. The first portion of your paddle should be made close to outer McLean Island. Except in extreme weather, this water is protected by offshore islands, extensive kelp beds and shallow reefs. While paddling you can observe the exposed water and make an informed judgement regarding the more open portion of the journey to the Bunsby Islands.

The 5-km (3-mi.) shoreline along the base of the Mount Paxton clear-cut is characterized by inhospitable bedrock, steep cliffs and beaches—an exposed body of water with few opportunities to seek refuge. Rebounding waves can cause localized confused water that should be avoided by travelling offshore, where wave patterns are more predictable. Thomas Island is approximately halfway to the Bunsbys and offers some leeward protection from wind, but the island is often too rough to land on safely. On calm water days, watch for large feeding groups of gulls, murres and cormorants or the harbour porpoises that frequently play in the area.

Bunsby Islands Ranked high in kayaking circles as a must-do destination, the Bunsby Islands are nothing short of a paddler's paradise. However, growing popularity and the Che :k' tles7et'h' people's recent interest in returning to occupy traditional village sites may soon change the character of this cherished place.

The 2 primary campsites in the Bunsby Islands can comfortably accommodate medium-sized groups of 6 to 8 people. One is located in a sandy cove near the southeast entrance to Gay Passage. The other is located on an outer Bunsby Island with a chart elevation designation of 59 m (195 ft.). Both sites offer camping on or above the beach, but it is critical for the conservation of these sites that any necessary fires be below the high tide line and that campers follow basic minimum impact principles. Big Bunsby is now a provincial marine park, and camping can also be found on its southwest and northeast shores.

∧ *Spring Island,* PETER MCGEE

Wherever you camp in the Bunsby Islands, please take measures to minimize disturbances to black bear, deer and other wildlife.

In years past Checkaklis Island has been a favourite spot to visit. Historically, it was a Che :k' tles7et'h' village site. Its proximity to excellent clam beaches and channels for trapping fish provided ample resources to sustain people through the winter. Since 1998, Che :k' tles7et'h' elder Lucy Pawio has been living on Checkaklis Island year round to re-establish occupancy of her traditional territory. As with any private property, visitors to Checkaklis Island should respect Lucy's privacy and seek permission to land. Lucy is a very talented weaver who often sells her traditional art through galleries.

Acous Peninsula, Battle Bay and Cuttle Islets The Cuttle Islets are located less than 8 km (5 mi.) northwest of the Bunsby Islands. Crossing the entrance of Ououkinsh Inlet is generally manageable except against headwinds or extreme weather. Two of the larger Cuttle Islets offer suitable camping for small groups.

Acous was the largest of the traditional Che :k' tles7et'h' village sites. Also known as Byers Cone, its proximity to Battle Creek made it an ideal village location. It is a popular heritage site with more new paths created every year by foot traffic; there is even evidence of excavation by people searching for artifacts to take home. For this regrettable reason, it is fortunate that this is not a suitable campsite for sea kayakers due to the presence of black bears and mosquitoes. To help preserve the quality of this heritage site, access has been restricted to day use only.

Beaches at the northeast end of Battle Bay are good for beachcombing and also suitable for camping. Water can be collected from Battle Creek above the estuary. Look for wolf and elk prints along the streambanks. Be cautious of black bears.

Brooks Peninsula and Nasparti Inlet The Brooks Peninsula and Nasparti and Battle watersheds make up Brooks-Nasparti Protected Area, proclaimed in 1995. For many paddlers it is the unfragmented view of this 51 631-ha (127,578-a.) protected area that makes the paddle from the Bunsby Islands worthwhile.

The Brooks Peninsula appears as a mountainous obstruction protruding from Vancouver Island's otherwise uniform coastline. Cape Cook, at the peninsula's outermost extremity, is regarded by many as the worst section of water on the West Coast. Winds either accelerate around Cape Cook or push over the top, generating cloud en route. This wild domain separates the traditional territories of the Nuu-chah-nulth and Kwakwaka'wakw First Nations. For botanists and ecologists, the Brooks is endlessly fascinating. Evidence collected from botanical and geological samples suggests that parts of the Brooks may have escaped the ice that deeply blanketed Vancouver Island during the Fraser Glaciation, ending about 10,000 years ago. As a glacial refugium, the Brooks likely supported hardy plant communities unchanged throughout the millennia.

Roosevelt elk are the largest ungulates found on Vancouver Island. They prefer browsing in primary forest and inhabit larger watersheds such as the Tahsish River, Battle Creek and the Nasparti River. The Brooks Peninsula Provincial Park will further ensure the protection of Roosevelt elk habitat.

Few beaches on the Brooks Peninsula guarantee launching after you manage to land. Peddler's Cove, inside of Jackobson Point, is the only refuge from extreme weather on the south side of the Brooks. A BC Parks interpretive sign at the head of a small trail greets you with insightful information about the area before showing the way to an outer beach. Several camping sites can be found along the stretch of beach west of Jackobson Point. You can choose between accessing a beach from the outside or taking the more conservative approach of hiking your gear over the trail from the protected side of Peddler's Cove. Water sources on the rarely visited Brooks Peninsula are usually reliable.

ADDITIONAL ROUTES

Heading north Venturing north of the Brooks Peninsula from Checleset Bay is nothing short of exhilarating. This area is for advanced paddlers only. If you can land at Amos Creek, a strenuous day's meander up the drainage will take you to fascinating alpine zones and breathtaking vistas. Off Cape Cook lies monolithic Solander Island, often circled by birds such as tufted puffins and rhinoceros auklets. Solander is off limits to humans as an ecological reserve for marine birds; it also bears the brunt of the weather that accelerates around the cape. North of the Brooks Peninsula, on its wild and rain-swept coast, the watersheds of Klaskish and East Creek are being threatened with large-scale clear-cut logging by two forest companies. At the time of writing, roads have been built in the area but timber removal has yet to begin. Unfortunately, it appears to be only a matter of time. Learn more about how you can help the Quatsino First Nation continue stewardship of this area at www.saveeastcreek.com.

Heading south Immediately south of Rugged Point is an expanse of sand beach interrupted by rocky outcrops. Rugged Point Provincial Marine Park includes this remote beach up to Kapoose Creek. Prior to the establishment of the Rugged Point park, a forestry reserve protected the line of trees that provide a scenic backdrop for the popular destination. Behind this veil of trees, however, you will find large clear-cuts and tree farms. South of Kapoose Creek, clear-cut logging has reached the water's edge. The dramatic coastline towards Tatchu Point is mostly rocky, with pockets of gravel beach constantly being worked by the swell and surf of the Pacific; this area is for advanced paddlers only. A few hours of paddling down this exposed coast will put you in Esperanza Inlet and the waters described in chapter 14.

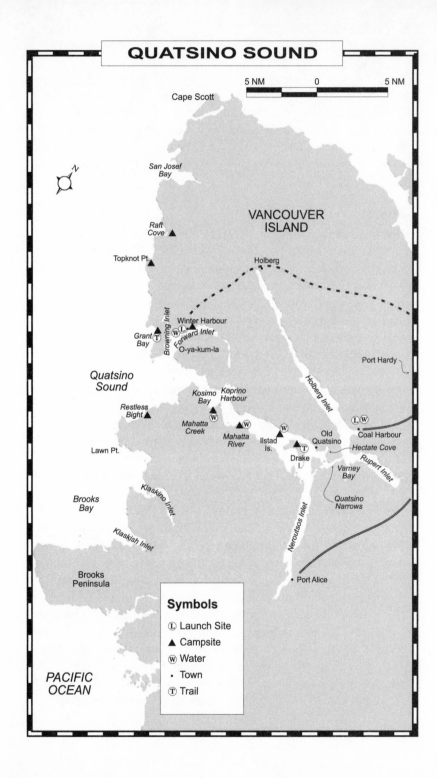

QUATSINO SOUND

5 NM   0   5 NM

Cape Scott

San Josef
Bay

N

VANCOUVER
ISLAND

Raft
Cove ▲

Topknot Pt. ▲

Holberg

Winter Harbour ▲
Ⓦ Ⓛ
Forward Inlet

Browning Inlet

Grant Ⓣ
Bay

O-ya-kum-la

Port Hardy

Quatsino
Sound

Holberg Inlet

Kosimo   Koprino
Bay   Harbour

Restless
Bight ▲

Ⓦ

Ⓛ Ⓦ

Mahatta
Creek

Ⓦ

Coal Harbour

Mahatta   Ⓦ
River   ▲ Ⓦ
Lawn Pt.   Ilstad Is. ▲   Old
                        Quatsino   Hectate Cove
                       Ⓣ
                     Drake   Rupert Inlet
                      I.
                                    Varney
Klaskino Inlet   Bay

Brooks   Quatsino
Bay   Narrows

Klaskish Inlet

Neroutsos Inlet

Brooks
Peninsula

• Port Alice

Symbols

Ⓛ Launch Site

▲ Campsite

Ⓦ Water

• Town

Ⓣ Trail

PACIFIC
OCEAN

16

Quatsino Sound

Fran Hunt-Jinnouchi

Despite the presence of major forestry and mining operations, the wild coastline and steep rock face in Quatsino Sound remain much the same as they have for thousands of years. The sound offers both pristine wilderness and rigorous paddling, but most interesting is that Quatsino is still distinctly unpopulated by kayakers, and paddlers rarely cross paths. With the rugged shoreline on one side and the brilliant, unrestrained blue Pacific Ocean on the other, one cannot help but realize that the picturesque and tranquil sound will soon be discovered.

BACKGROUND

Quatsino Sound encompasses about 113 km (70 mi.) of waterways and has countless harbours of interest scattered along its shores. The most northern of the five main sounds on the west coast of Vancouver Island, Quatsino Sound has three arms: Neroutsos, Rupert and Holberg Inlets. Quatsino has been interpreted to mean "people of the outside."

There were four native tribes throughout and to the north of Quatsino Sound: the Koskimo, Giopino, Klaskino and Quatsino. Prior to the mid 1800s, there was also a tribe called the Hoyalas. Today, the main communities are Coal Harbour, Quatsino, Port Alice, Winter Harbour and Holberg (Quatsino and Winter Harbour were important village sites of the Koskimo people). During fishing season, the area is abuzz with activity, primarily in and around Grant Bay and Winter Harbour. There are marinas at Coal Harbour, which has a government dock, and at Quatsino. Winter Harbour also has a government dock.

With an unfortunate impact on scenery, major industries have developed in the sound, such as the BHP copper mine in Rupert Inlet (closed in 1996) and the Western Forests Products pulp mill in Neroutsos Inlet. Logging activity has been extensive and ongoing, though somewhat scaled down today. Thankfully the birds don't seem to mind, and puffins, oystercatchers, murres, ducks, gulls, eagles and murrelets can be seen by those with a keen eye.

GETTING THERE

By land You have to go through Port Hardy to reach Coal Harbour. Port Hardy is a community of 5,000 at the northern terminus of Highway 19, the Island Highway. The drive from Nanaimo is approximately 4.5 hours. There is little in the way of amenities beyond Campbell River, especially if you are travelling in the evening, so be sure to have a full tank of gas. Securing accommodations can prove to be difficult without early reservations.

There are three First Nations in the immediate Port Hardy area: the Gwa'sala-Nak'waxda'wx, the Kwakwaka'wakw and the Quatsino. Calvin Hunt, a renowned Kwakwaka'wakw carver, owns and operates a native art gallery on the Kwakwaka'wakw reserve. The reserve is a 10-minute car ride from Port Hardy. Shops in Port Hardy carry almost everything you will need for your kayaking adventure, including charts, groceries and camping gear. Coal Harbour is a tiny community approximately 18 km (11 mi.) or 15 minutes from Port Hardy. The road is paved and in good condition.

Winter Harbour is approximately 75 km (47 mi.), or 80 minutes, from Port Hardy. The gravel road is usually kept in good shape though after heavy rains the potholes can be quite bad.

By air The flight from Vancouver to Port Hardy on Pacific Coastal takes approximately 1 hour, and there is limousine service from the airport to town. It is possible to fly to Coal Harbour by float plane, but it is better to fly to the Port Hardy airport and take the shuttle to town or Coal Harbour.

WEATHER AND HAZARDS

The weather in the Quatsino area is more or less typical of the west coast of Vancouver Island. Summer temperatures are mild, from a low of 8–10°C (46–50°F) at night to 16–20°C (61–68°F) during the day. May can be wet, whereas July and August are the driest months. The prevailing winds are generally from the west and in the afternoon. Wind funnelling down the sound creates a bit of chop. Rounding the point into Forward Inlet can be hazardous because of its openness to the Pacific Ocean; this area should be approached with caution. In late summer and early September, fog can appear but will usually dissipate before noon. Kayakers are cautioned to negotiate Quatsino Narrows during slack tide only.

There are some bears in the region, but they tend to avoid humans. Nonetheless, you should always approach bears and camping in bear country with extreme caution, particularly in Winter Harbour and Ahwhichaolto Inlet. A local garbage dump not too far inland seems to attract bears that are prone to disturb campers. Many years ago at a Rediscovery Children's Camp near Winter Harbour, seven bears came into the camp and made off with some food, and a cub got into the outhouse and stole a roll of toilet paper. In the past few years, however, tours in the Winter Harbour area have had no bear encounters. Either we have been lucky or the sound of all the drumming, singing and dancing has been scaring them off.

SPECIAL CONSIDERATIONS

I had the privilege of growing up in Quatsino Sound. My childhood was spent in the isolated Indian village Quattishe, more recently known as Old Quatsino. My family and community made seasonal migrations to Winter Harbour to fish for halibut and salmon.

We have not lived in Old Quatsino since the early 1970s, and prior to that time many of our people had begun their journey to larger centres in search of modern life and employment. My family was the very last to leave the village. During our last few weeks, grave robbers began to enter our shores and desecrate the gravesites in search of valuables. It was disturbing to watch, especially through my 12-year-old eyes. My community's experience with people entering our land has not always been pleasant, so for this reason and because of common courtesy and respect, kayakers are encouraged not to enter Old Quatsino. If you feel strongly about going ashore, please contact the Quatsino Band Council in writing.

TRIP 38 Quatsino Sound

SKILL: Intermediate to advanced
TIME: 4–10 days
HAZARDS: Winds, currents and open coast (optional)
ACCESS: Coal Harbour/Winter Harbour
CHARTS: 3679 · Quatsino Sound · 1:50,000
3681 · Plans Quatsino Sound · Various scales
3686 · Approaches to Winter Harbour · 1:15,000
TIDE BOOK: Vol. 6

With Quatsino Sound as your destination, you can depart from Coal Harbour and paddle west to Winter Harbour, or vice versa. Paddling the east to west route will sometimes place you in a head-on position with howling winds, but either direction works. If you are launching from Coal Harbour, make sure your departure coincides with slack tide so you can run with an ebb tide.

A return trip between Coal Harbour and Winter Harbour usually takes about a week at a relaxed pace. Eight to 10 days would allow for full exploration of the area; if you are paddling one way, 3 to 4 days is sufficient. The main factor that can slow you down is the wind.

LAUNCHING

You can easily launch from Coal Harbour right off the beach or government dock; parking is nearby on the main road. You can also launch from the boat launch for $5 per kayak; there is a small fee for parking. The person who arranges parking and launching works inside the huge hangar that was once used to cut up whales. Coal Harbour also has a small store with a limited supply of goods, a post office and a restaurant. Fuel and water can be obtained at the dock.

∧ *Bald eagle, Winter Harbour,* GRANT THOMPSON/TOFINO EXPEDITIONS

In Winter Harbour, you can launch from the beach at the campsite just before town. Parking is inside the camping area, no charge. You can also go another mile into town and launch off the docks, or go to the end of the road and launch off the beach at "C" Scape B&B (tel.: 250-969-4240), where Helen and "Winter Harbour" Bob Cake will put you up for the night and keep your car safe. You can also park in and around the small village as long as you are not impeding the commercial fishing operations.

The following trip describes the route from Coal Harbour to Winter Harbour.

SITES

The whaling ramp and gigantic whalebone in the centre of town are testament to the whaling station that was active in Coal Harbour right up till the 1960s. DH Timber Towing and Salvage now operates chartered runs from the dock. You would be wise to talk to their very capable employees as to weather conditions, emergency channels and procedures; you can also advise them of your route—they are very helpful.

Departing from Coal Harbour, Quatsino Narrows quickly sets the tone for what lies ahead. Most paddlers do not venture off to Neroutsos or Holberg Inlets, though both offer interesting exploration points. Day trips may be considered for these destinations.

Just before entering Quatsino Narrows is Varney Bay, on the south side of Rupert Inlet. This is where the Marble River enters the inlet. Varney Bay is an excellent site for bird- and otter-watching enthusiasts and a popular crabbing area. To enter the river, paddle through the narrow, attractive gorge in the bay; if time permits, you can follow the gorge to the bottom end of Marble River.

Quatsino Narrows Quatsino Narrows is approximately 150 m (500 ft.) wide and 3.2 km (2 mi.) long, with steep rock walls on both sides. The rip tides and eddies at the northern entrance of the narrows are treacherous. Currents can run as fast as 8 knots and even the most experienced paddler is cautioned not to paddle the narrows during running tides. However, paddling during slack tide or a slow-moving tide provides you with one of the most enjoyable and attractive sites in

v *Bull kelp near Grant Bay*, PETER MCGEE

Quatsino Sound. Eagles perch on low craggy trees, and with luck you may chance to pass just metres under one of these magnificent creatures. Be sure to have your camera within reach: it is not unusual to spot up to 50 bald eagles while paddling the relatively short narrows.

Coal Harbour is a former Royal Canadian Air Force base, and a gun was once mounted at the narrows to restrict access. The warring aspect of the narrows goes back even further: as you pass through, look up the steep cliffs and try to imagine the Koskimo people luring their enemies to the harbour only to roll heavy logs down on them, smashing their canoes and drowning the paddlers. You can sometimes hear their cries if you paddle close enough to the cliffs' jagged walls.

If you are fond of cod or black bass, you are almost guaranteed a catch. Just toss your hook in along the steep wall and troll as you paddle. Black bass sizzled in soy sauce and garlic is extremely tasty. On the beaches of Hecate Cove you will find wild sea asparagus in abundance.

Old Quatsino was once a thriving community but it has been reduced to a place of memories that sits eerily quiet. One small house remains along with a few hints of the people who inhabited the land not too long ago. As mentioned above, kayakers are asked not to enter Old Quatsino.

Drake and Ildstad Islands A little farther west is the formidable Drake Island. Drake was once inhabited, and there are remnants of a homestead and meadow in the middle of the island. Pamphlet Cove sits in the centre of Drake Island on the north side and is a great place to stop overnight, as it provides protection from the winds. For those inclined to hike, a short trail leads to the south side of the island. Berries are plentiful and you are likely to stumble upon planted mistletoe. Drake Island has no fresh water. A small portion of Drake Island, approximately 8 ha (20 a.), is designated as a recreation map reserve, or UREP, under BC Parks. (The Ministry of Sustainable Resource Management is also developing a coastal plan for the area, so we may see some more protected areas designated in the near future.) Do not camp on the exposed eelgrass beach unless tides are very low.

Kayakers will find a good picnic spot on the Ildstad Islands. There is no major water source, but you can access a limited water supply at the creek on the north bank of the inlet behind Ildstad. You can camp in between the two small islands but only during extreme low tidal periods.

Cleagh Creek should be avoided. It is a noisy area with logging activity, and waste is emitted into the ocean here. Mahatta River, or more specifically, the knoll just beyond Mahatta River, offers a nice campsite though the nearby generator hums constantly. A bonus feature of this area, however, is that there is usually plenty of fresh water. Koprino Harbour should be avoided because it is a busy log-booming site.

Mahatta Creek Mahatta Creek is magnificent, truly breathtaking on a warm summer night when the moon glistens overhead. There is an excellent campsite to the east of Mahatta Creek, and the vast sandy beach and grassy areas provide plenty of camping spots, especially for large groups. Driftwood is usually at your disposal, and there is a fresh stream in the east corner of the beach. (Obtaining the water can be difficult, however, because the creek ends in a waterfall that tumbles into the sea.) Nonetheless, Mahatta Creek is an ideal spot. Berries of all varieties are bountiful, and the salmon fishing is excellent. Take a few minutes to paddle to the falls—the clear, icy water is beautiful and offers a refreshing cleanse. You will have to wait for high tide but the wait is worth it.

Try to arrange an early departure from Mahatta Creek because Forward Inlet can be difficult to negotiate. When you depart, be sure to cross immediately to the north side. The paddle to Forward Inlet can involve some large swells; there are also interesting rock formations along the wall. There are no places to stop except for emergency landings, so be prepared. Combine the swells with afternoon winds, and this area can spell trouble for less experienced paddlers. Expect to paddle for a few hours to reach your next destination, O-ya-kum-la.

O-ya-kum-la O-ya-kum-la is beautiful and offers fantastic camping. Known locally as Picnic Beach, O-ya-kum-la is located on the northeast side of Forward Inlet as you make your way to Winter Harbour. It is discernible by its pebble beach. This is Quatsino Band reserve land, and permission to visit should be confirmed in writing with the band. If you haven't received advance permission from the band, don't ruin the experience for others by camping illegally. You are only about 1.5

hours from Winter Harbour, where campsites are available. On the east side of O-ya-kum-la is a river with a great waterfall at the top. You can go for a day paddle to Grant Bay from here.

Grant Bay An easy route to Grant Bay is to make the approximately 1-hour paddle from O-ya-kum-la to Browning Inlet. Entry into Browning must occur at high tide, otherwise the marsh area at the end of the inlet will be difficult to navigate. A path on the left side of the marsh is indicated by a float tied to the branch of a tree. The hike into Grant Bay is about 35 minutes and not too difficult to manoeuvre. (This trail to Grant Bay also starts in Winter Harbour.) Grant Bay is splendid with its virgin white sand, high rushing waves, vast amounts of driftwood, berries and the odd glass ball.

Winter Harbour The first houses in Winter Harbour date to the early 1930s when settlers lived on floats, fishing in the summer and hand logging in the winter. The harbour historically provided shelter for ships waiting out Pacific storms, and it continues to house a large commercial fishing fleet in the summer. Camping is available at the campsite just before town, where you'll find a memorial pole in memory of my grandparents, who were lost at sea: Jessie and Billy George. You can pull out at the beach by the campsite or at the docks in town.

ADDITIONAL ROUTES

Heading north and south Both directions offer some of the most challenging paddling along the entire coast. The stretches from Winter Harbour around the Brooks Peninsula and from Winter Harbour around Cape Scott should be attempted by very experienced paddlers only. Although it is usually possible to tuck in behind a point or a rock to avoid the swells, always be prepared for surf landings and, before you go, read the section on the open coast in chapter 1.

If heading north, look for camping just past Topknot Point and at the north end of Raft Cove. If heading south, look for camping just north of Restless Bight and on the beaches of Brooks Bay.

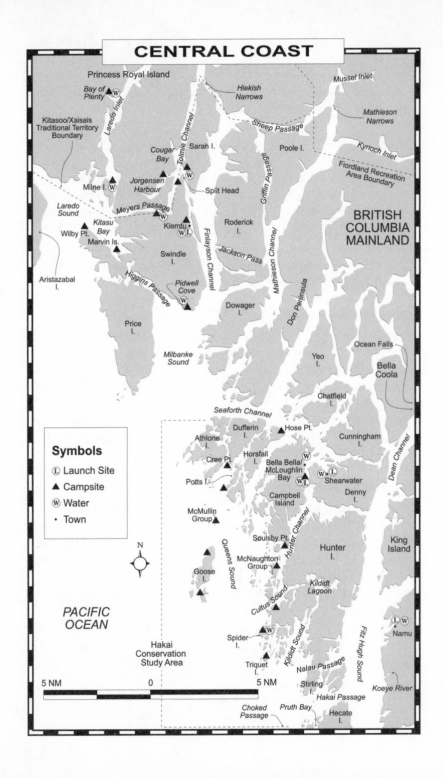

CENTRAL COAST

Princess Royal Island

Hiekish Narrows

Mussel Inlet

Bay of Plenty (W)

Laredo Inlet

Mathieson Narrows

Sheep Passage

Kitasoo/Xaisais Traditional Territory Boundary

Cougar Bay

Sarah I.

Poole I.

Kynoch Inlet

Tolmie Channel

Fiordland Recreation Area Boundary

Jorgensen Harbour (W)

Milne I. (W)

Split Head

Griffin Passage

BRITISH COLUMBIA MAINLAND

Meyers Passage (W)

Roderick I.

Mathieson Channel

Laredo Sound

Kitasu Bay

Klemtu (W)(L)

Finlayson Channel

Jackson Pass

Wilby Pt.

Marvin Is.

Swindle I.

Higgins Passage

Aristazabal I.

Pidwell Cove (W)

Dowager I.

Don Peninsula

Price I.

Milbanke Sound

Yeo I.

Ocean Falls

Bella Coola

Chatfield I.

Seaforth Channel

Dufferin I.

Hose Pt.

Cunningham I.

Athlone I.

Horsfall I.

Bella Bella/McLoughlin Bay (W)

Dean Channel

Symbols

(L) Launch Site
▲ Campsite
(W) Water
• Town

Cree Pt.

Potts I.

(W)(L) Shearwater
(W)(L)

Campbell Island

Denny I.

McMullin Group ▲

N

Soulsby Pt.

Hunter I.

King Island

McNaughton Group

Queens Sound

Goose I.

Kildidt Lagoon

Hunter Channel

PACIFIC OCEAN

Cultus Sound

Kildidt Sound

Fitz Hugh Sound

(L)(W) Namu

Hakai Conservation Study Area

Spider I. (W)

Triquet I.

Nalau Passage

Stirling

Koeye River

5 NM   0   5 NM

Choked Passage

Pruth Bay

Hakai Passage

Hecate I.

17

The Central Coast

Frank Brown, John Nelson
and Evan Loveless

The Central Coast is the ancient and contemporary homeland of
the Heiltsuk, Kitasoo, Oweekeno and Nuxalk First Nations. For
thousands of years, these peoples have derived their sustenance from
the land and sea, with marine resources forming an integral part of
their diet and economy. An intimate knowledge of these resources
and environment is the basis of their survival and unique cultural
achievements. Others have joined them more recently in their traditional territories, which are blessed with an amazing diversity of
wildlife and landscapes including the beautiful Great Bear Rainforest, the world's largest remaining intact temperate rain forest and one
of the richest, most diverse ecosystems on earth. This area is a paddler's paradise. From towering inland fiords to spectacular white
sandy beaches, this largely unpopulated area will feed your soul with
the sights and sounds of the unspoiled Pacific Ocean and the power
of ancient cultures that live on today.

BACKGROUND

The Central Coast has just seven towns with 3,500 permanent residents in a 3 million-ha (7,410,000-a.) area. Most residents are native

and live at the villages of Bella Bella, Bella Coola, Klemtu and Oweekeno. Ocean Falls, Shearwater and Hagensborg are the other communities in the area.

The Central Coast is bound by Tweedsmuir Provincial Park to the east, the Fiordland Recreation Area to the north and the Hakai Conservation Study Area to the west. Tweedsmuir is one of B.C.'s largest parks but it is landlocked and not of much interest to paddlers. Fiordland Recreation Area is located northeast of Klemtu and occupies 76 500 ha (189,000 a.). The Hakai Conservation Study Area, located on the outer coast south of Bella Bella, is an archipelago of small islands, well suited to exploration by kayak. Its 123 000 ha (304,000 a.) of ocean and islands make it the largest marine park on B.C.'s coast.

The Central Coast also contains five small marine parks, selected for their values as strategic anchorages and safe havens: Penrose Island, Codville Lagoon, Oliver Cove, Jackson Narrows and Green Inlet.

A recently completed Central Coast Land Resource Management Plan (LRMP) reviewed the recreation area status of Hakai and Fiordland, and accorded Hakai status as a protected area. Both Hakai and Fiordland areas are the subject of outstanding land claims, and the First Nations of the Central Coast are very concerned about their issues being properly resolved.

The Central Coast, however, is not just a place of politics. It is also a place of celebration, and in the summer of 1993 the Heiltsuk people hosted what may be the greatest gathering ever on this coast. Thousands of participants converged on Waglisla (Bella Bella) in ocean-going cedar canoes to celebrate indigenous maritime nations. The event was *Qatuwas*, "people gathered together in one place," and it renewed much of the cultural energy of communities up and down the coast.

GETTING THERE

By water The Discovery Coast Ferry, the newest addition to the B.C. Ferries fleet, leaves from Port Hardy on Vancouver Island and stops in McLoughlin Bay (Bella Bella), Shearwater, Klemtu, Ocean Falls and Bella Coola. Port Hardy is 500 km (310 mi.) from Victoria or 391 km (243 mi.) from Nanaimo along Highway 19, the Island Highway. Pay parking is available 2 km (1.2 mi.) away at Wildwoods campsite for $2 per day. Overnight camping is prohibited on B.C. Ferries property, so stay at a local hotel or campground the night before, as most sailings depart early in the morning. A shuttle bus operated by North Island Transportation runs from all accommodations to the ferry terminal. If you rent boats from North Island Kayak, they will deliver their kayaks to the ferry terminal free of charge.

Check the ferry schedule very carefully to determine when and where the ferry arrives and departs at each spot. Some ports are not available on all sailings, though the ferry can launch kayaks directly from the ship without docking. Mid-channel launches or recoveries are at the discretion of the captain, subject to weather, and must be requested prior to sailing. Those kayakers wishing to do mid-channel launches or pick-ups should have a VHF radio. Contact the ferry on channel 11 north of Cape Caution and on channel 71 south of Cape Caution.

You can park your vehicle in Bella Coola or Port Hardy and take your kayak on board. Kayak wheels are handy. Ferry facilities include a licensed bar, storage lockers, a cafeteria, showers and a gift shop. Seats in the lounge recline to a semi-sleeping position; you can also pitch a tent on the deck, though room is limited. Sleeping bags are allowed on the floor in the lounge or solarium. Tents and binoculars are available for on-board use only. Water is also available.

Whether you are boarding the ferry at Port Hardy or at Bella Coola, be sure to arrive at least 1 hour before departure, preferably 2 hours if your gear is disorganized. You will need the time to unload your gear, park your car and place your kayaks on the luggage racks. The length of voyage varies from 8 hours between Port Hardy and Bella Bella, to as long as 33 hours between Port Hardy and Bella Coola. If you are taking a vehicle from Port Hardy to Bella Coola, you will need a reservation.

For information on the launching conditions at the ferry stops, see the section below on launching.

A water taxi from Port Hardy is also an alternative to get to the area. These ocean-going boats can carry up to 12 people, kayaks and equipment and drop you directly at your first campsite.

By land Bella Coola is the only community on the Central Coast that can be reached by road. From Vancouver, the journey starts with either Highway 99 (via Whistler) or Highway 1 (via Lytton) and goes to Cache Creek, where the roads meet Highway 97 to Williams Lake. From Williams Lake, it is a 456-km (283-mi.) drive to Bella Coola along Highway 20, which is paved for approximately the first 400 km (250 mi.). Be careful when driving through Tweedsmuir Provincial Park and its notorious descent known as "the Hill." The narrow gravel road has very steep grades and numerous switchbacks, so you must drive slowly, keeping a watchful eye for oncoming traffic and wildlife.

In Bella Coola, you can either take the ferry to your paddling destination (see Launching below) or start your trip at the end of the road. Potential routes are only limited by time, ability and expectations (fiord routes versus outer coastal routes). There is pay parking at the Bella Coola launch site.

By air A number of small airlines, including Wilderness Air, Pacific Coastal Airlines and Air B.C, service the Central Coast.

WEATHER AND HAZARDS

The Central Coast is the home of the world's largest continuous area of intact coastal temperate rain forest, the Great Bear Rainforest. It has a generally wet and mild climate, and winds are predominantly westerlies in the summer and easterlies in the winter. During the summer, sea breezes occur in most of the mainland inlets and fiords, beginning in the morning and often increasing to 20–25 knots in the afternoon. Winds typically decrease in the early evening though occasional gusty drainage winds can develop at night. Summer winds should not be taken lightly, as many of the west to southwest winds funnelled into Milbanke Sound and other east-west channels along the Central Coast generate rough seas on ebbing tidal currents.

Visibility in the Central Coast is best in the spring. In late summer and fall, sea fog spreads over the area from the west and occasionally lowers visibility to less than 3.2 km (2 mi.). This fog can persist for several days until stronger, drier winds flush it out of the area.

The Central Coast also has many localized hazards that directly affect kayakers. Currents often create tidal rapids in narrow passages, and tiderips occur where the waters of Fitz Hugh Sound drain into the open ocean, such as at the western end of Hakai Passage. Open ocean swells can create boomers when they hit a submerged rock or reef, surf can make for dangerous landings, and campsites are few and far between. Be particularly cautious about the boat traffic in Fitz Hugh Sound, Hunter Channel and Milbanke Sound, and the potentially vicious water of Queens Sound.

Many of the offshore islands have black bears, and many of the mainland rivers, like the Koeye, have an ample supply of grizzly bears and the occasional wolf.

Help is often very far away, and passing fishing boats and pleasure craft may be your only chance for human contact. Do not attempt any journey if you cannot handle these conditions. None of the trips on the Central Coast are for beginners, and they should only be attempted by experienced sea kayakers who have done similar trips in wilderness areas. Kayak guiding companies provide excursions to this area for people who lack the necessary experience.

SPECIAL CONSIDERATIONS

Kayakers should be sensitive to the challenges their increasing numbers present to the Central Coast and be respectful of their potential impact on its natural and cultural sites. Regardless of whether these sites are on or off Indian Reserves, they are protected by law and very important to First Nations. Please avoid camping on any midden sites in the area unless you have the approval of the Heiltsuk.

Coastal First Nations have a long history of extensive trade networks and family ties up and down the coast and into the interior. The Heiltsuk and Kitasoo have always welcomed visitors into their territory as long as they, and the resources and landscape that have sustained them for countless generations, are treated with respect. Local residents hope that mutual respect and reciprocity between themselves and visitors will be established. All visitors to Klemtu and the Kitasoo/Xaixais Traditional Territory are asked to register with the tourism office (see Useful Contacts) before conducting any activities in the area. You will be expected to adhere to local protocol, which includes a Visitors Code of Ethics and trip guidelines. We would like to acknowledge and thank the Heiltsuk Cultural Education Centre (Jennifer Carpenter, director) and the Heiltsuk Fisheries Co-Management Program (John Bolton, former director) for the information and perspectives they contributed to this chapter.

∧ *Western entrance to Higgins Passage,* PETER MCGEE

The Heiltsuk, and particularly the Kitasoo, are taking active steps to manage their territory in a sustainable manner. The Kitasoo have developed a land use plan for their traditional territory that sets aside 43 per cent of their land as protected area with the intent to preserve fish, wildlife, and cultural and biodiversity values. The Spirit Bear Protection Area, mostly on Princess Royal Island, forms the corner-stone of these protection areas. It is designed to ensure the long-term protection of the Spirit bears and their habitat, and it forms a historic agreement between environmental campaigners, forest companies and First Nations that will protect a large chunk of the Great Bear Rainforest.

As always, try not to disturb any wildlife you may encounter on your travels. Be particularly cautious around Princess Royal Island, home to the Kermodei, or Spirit bear, a white black bear. This distinct coloration of the black bear is not albino, but a genetically distinct subspecies. These bears are unique, so it is important that they are not disturbed or harassed in any way. Pick kayaking routes that avoid Princess Royal Island; if you must camp on the island, be sure to hang your food, properly dispose of your dishwater and pack out all your garbage—as always!

Fecal contamination has been found in clam beds around Bella Bella. In association with the development of the Heiltsuk commercial clam fishery, Environment Canada has monitored water quality at commercial beaches since 1993. Beaches that tested clean in the past—and are today popular with kayakers—were found to be contaminated. The correlation is compelling, so you are asked to be very conscious of how you dispose of your waste. Clam beds are a source of both food and much-needed employment for local residents.

One way kayakers can help reduce their impact is by supporting the construction of outhouses and composting toilets. Currently, no sites have outhouses except those in the Hakai Conservation Study Area. The Heiltsuk have expressed their support for constructing waste facilities as part of long-term management of recreational tourism in their traditional territory. Contact the Heiltsuk Tribal Council or the B.C. Marine Trail Association if you would like to contribute to this cause. (The BCMTA is currently pursuing a protocol agreement with the Heiltsuk Tribal Council.)

CENTRAL COAST TRIPS (39–40)

There is no shortage of kayak trips in the waters of the Central Coast. From the surf beaches of Cape Caution to the intricate island archipelagos of Hakai Passage, your options are only limited by your skill and imagination. The first trip described in this chapter is based around Discovery Coast Ferry stops; the second leads you to the island archipelagos, sandy beaches and abandoned native villages around Klemtu. These trips cover a mere fraction of what the region has to offer. Feel free to explore the other paddling possibilities that exist throughout this isolated and wild stretch of the Pacific coast.

LAUNCHING

Namu Namu is an ancient village and processing site of the Heiltsuk and the oldest dated location on the coast. More recently it was a cannery site, and evidence of the old outbuildings can still be seen today. The Heiltsuk are currently seeking to regain this property and have it designated as a Canadian and World Heritage Site. In its current condition, don't expect much in the way of services when you arrive. Due to the fragility of the dock, B.C. Ferries no longer has scheduled stops here although they will "wet" launch paddlers if arrangements are made in advance. We've kept Namu in the guidebook simply because it is a great place to explore and a great place to launch if you are exploring the southern part of the Hakai Conservation Study Area. For those interested in trout fishing or simply walking through a very beautiful forest, Namu Lake is a 10-minute walk from the dock. Cold Creek, just south of Namu, has a long pebble beach suitable for camping and is a source of fresh water.

Bella Bella/McLoughlin Bay Bella Bella, also known locally as Waglisla, is the home of the Heiltsuk First Nation and the largest native community on the Central Coast. With a population of 1,800, the present-day community of Bella Bella is located on the northeast coast of Campbell Island, just north of the Discovery Coast Ferry stop at McLoughlin Bay. The Bella Bella band store can be accessed from the government dock and offers dry goods, souvenirs and groceries. Bella Bella also has a post office, fuel station, hospital, clinic and RCMP detachment. Be sure to visit the Heiltsuk Cultural Centre, located in the Bella Bella Community School just up from the wharf; you will find a wealth of information about Heiltsuk history, language, culture and community. A number of B&Bs and charter operations are also located in Bella Bella. The Bella Bella Coast Guard Auxiliary is on standby for marine emergencies.

At McLoughlin Bay, kayaks are unloaded from the ferry on special carts that can be walked directly to the shore. There is a commercial waterfront campsite with a few rustic cabins, and fresh water can be obtained from outdoor hoses at the fish plant and at the Bella Bella wharf. An interpretive centre offers Heiltsuk cultural sharing, traditional arts and crafts as well as guided nature walks and ocean canoe tours or expeditions. A number of different charter companies will provide pick-up and drop-off service for kayakers.

Shearwater Shearwater is a community of 75 people with two hotels, a restaurant pub and a small marine store. The community is located across from Bella Bella on Denny Island, and a sea bus runs on a regular schedule between the two towns. Kayak carts are offloaded at the head of the ferry wharf. You then simply walk your kayak down the adjacent boat launch right into the water. There is water at the pub. Note: Shearwater is sometimes referred to as Bella Bella, since mail addressed to Bella Bella ends up in Shearwater. Mail addressed to Waglisla ends up in Bella Bella—confusing maybe, but it has been that way for years so the locals are used to it.

Klemtu Located on the east coast of Swindle Island, Klemtu is home to the Kitasoo First Nation. There are 400 residents, two grocery stores, a post office, campground, a bank machine, showers and laundry facilities, a B&B and a medical clinic. The Discovery Coast Ferry docks next to the government wharf. The ferry crew is happy to bring your kayak cart either to a float beside the ferry ramp or to the adjacent beach, which is a little rocky. There is water at the tourism office and at the fuel dock.

Ocean Falls Ocean Falls, a community of 50 people if you include the nearby town of Martin Valley, is located at the head of Cousins Inlet. There is a grocery store, post office, pub, restaurant, cafe and accommodation. For those looking for a new kayak, check out Rain Raven Handbuilt Boats, which sells locally made hand-built kayaks and canoes. Please note that Ocean Falls has no medical facilities. Martin Valley is located 3 km (2 mi.) from Ocean Falls. Your kayak cart will be left at the top of the wharf when unloaded from the ferry. To launch, walk down to the adjacent government wharf.

Bella Coola Bella Coola is the main town for the Nuxalk First Nation and has numerous hotels, B&Bs, restaurants, grocery stores, a post office, an RCMP detachment and a hospital. The Bella Coola Valley has 2,500 permanent residents, including the community of

Hagensborg, located 18 km (11 mi.) from Bella Coola. You can launch from the government wharf immediately adjacent to the ferry dock. There are pay phones here but no other facilities; the actual town of Bella Coola is 3 km (2 mi.) away. Water can be obtained from the gas station in town or you can try the fuel dock.

TRIP 39 **Bella Bella and the Hakai Conservation Study Area**

SKILL: Intermediate to advanced

TIME: 7–21 days

HAZARDS: Open ocean, tidal currents and boat traffic

ACCESS: Discovery Coast Ferry/Bella Coola

CHARTS: 3744 · Queen Charlotte Sound · 1:365,100
3727 · Cape Calvert to Goose Island · 1:73,600
3728 · Milbanke Sound and Approaches · 1:76,600
3936 · Fitz Hugh Sound to Lama Passage · 1:40,000
3937 · Queens Sound · 1:40,000
3787 · Queens Sound to Seaforth Channel · 1:36,400

TIDE BOOK: Vol. 6

This trip to the Hakai Conservation Study Area starts in Bella Bella and is located entirely within Heiltsuk traditional territory. The journey begins at the ferry stop in McLoughlin Bay and heads west up Seaforth Channel. Rounding Horsfall, Dufferin or Athlone Islands places you in the north end of Queens Sound and provides great access for those looking to camp in the McMullin Group or, for the truly adventurous, the Goose Group. Farther south, campsites in Cultus Sound and on Triquet and Stirling Islands create ideal bases for venturing into the surrounding lagoons. For people with more time, camping on the wind-swept beaches of Calvert Island or the rugged coast of the mainland offers a chance to get off the beaten path. At least this is usually true; you may find yourself on the doorstep of a fishing lodge—such is the West Coast. Paddling back to Bella Bella via Hunter Channel provides you with a change in scenery and a sheltered last leg to your journey.

Please note that unless you are prepared for outer coastal conditions, including surf landings and launches, as well as open ocean swell, you should avoid paddling the western end of Seaforth Channel and any shorelines exposed to the full force of Queens Sound. If you are unsure of your abilities, limit your paddling to the waters easily accessed from Hunter Channel. Be prepared to carry an ample supply of water, as there are few water sources in this region. Use VHF channel 2 for continuous weather broadcasts. Residents use channel 6, so this is a good channel to listen to for local chatter or to call for assistance. There is currently a BC Parks headquarters at Pruth Bay from May to September; visitors are encouraged to drop in for information. Rumours are that this cabin may be moved north, closer to Princess Royal Island and the new Spirit Bear Protection Area, but we couldn't confirm this at the time of writing. Check the BC Parks Web site for the latest information (see Useful Contacts).

SITES

Hose Point Leaving McLoughlin Bay, you will briefly enter Lama Passage heading north and pass Dryad Point before heading west up Seaforth Channel. Just past Hose Point, at the north end of Horsfall Island, is a gently sloping gravel beach. There is room for 3 tents just up from the beach and a small creek at each end. Please note that clam digging is prohibited, and there is no toilet. Also, avoid camping on any shell middens in the area.

Cree Point If you paddle south on the west or east side of Dufferin Island and have your timing quite right, you will likely encounter tidal rapids. Don't let these be a deterrent, however, as rapids often mark the presence of island lagoons, and exploring in these parts is bound to uncover some gems. The campsite at Cree Point is in a sheltered cove at the extreme southern tip of Dufferin Island. The boulders that cover the beach at low tide have been moved to make for easy landing and launching on the sand. There is room for 3 tents, but no water or outhouse. Please do not realign any of the rocks, as this can disturb the Heiltsuk historical record and the pattern of traditional use sites.

The clam fishery in nearby Gale Passage is very sensitive, and kayakers should avoid the area completely if possible. Camping is off limits as is any discharge of waste in transit.

Louise Channel There is a great white sand beach located on the east shore of a very small island at the southwest end of Louise Channel, just south of Potts Island. Hazards include currents, surf and reefs as you approach the island. The waters outside the basin are exposed to the pounding seas of Queens Sound, but a ring of islets protects the bay, and the landing is relatively easy. Look for the short trail that leads up from the beach to the tent spots. Once again, there is no drinking water or outhouse.

McMullin Group For paddlers prepared to negotiate the perils of Queens Sound, the beaches of the McMullin Group will be your just reward. These small islands sit just north of the Goose Group and often appear as an oasis, fading in and out of the haze of the horizon. Exposed to the full brunt of the open Pacific Ocean, they are rugged, isolated and incredibly beautiful. Head for the lee side of the largest island if you want to land and camp. The beach is large, with a couple of different approaches, and you should have no trouble avoiding surf. There is no water, and weather can keep you pinned here for a few days. Be prepared.

If you are not comfortable with this sort of exposed paddling, work your way south and through the maze of intricate islands that border Queens Sound to the east. For a place to camp, try the north island in the McNaughton Group; the site has an easy landing at high tide. There is no toilet or water but there is room for a few tents.

Goose Group A short hop from the McMullin Group, and even more exposed, is the Goose Group. So far from the rest of the Hakai Conservation Study Area, these islands truly have a character all to themselves. Their bogs, beaches and lagoons can keep you occupied for days while the stunning vistas of the distant Coast Mountains act as a reminder of where you must ultimately return.

There is camping at two sites: Snipe Island (often called Little Gull), which is between Gull and Gosling Islands, and on the west side of Goose Island, just below the northern tip. Please do not use the beach right at the north end of Goose: it is a Heiltsuk Rediscovery Camp. The Indian Reserves on the south end of Goose Island and the north end of Duck Island are private property and also off limits to the public. Bring your own water—sources on the islands are questionable.

Cultus Sound Heading east from the Goose Group towards Cultus Sound is an exposed 9-km (5.6-mi.) crossing. Check the weather forecasts and time your crossing carefully. As you approach Cultus Sound, be cautious of tidal activity and rebounding waves. The sea can be extremely tricky in these parts, often rocking your boat in one direction and throwing it in another. Thankfully, the campsite in Cultus Sound, on the west side of Hunter Island, is well protected with an easy landing.

As you enter the sound, look for a beautiful sand beach flanked by two rocky shores. There is great beach camping here, as well as 6 tent sites in the woods and a box toilet. Fishing in the surrounding area is excellent, and exploring the nearby lagoons reveals a whole new coastal environment. Take some time and study the amazing intertidal life that flourishes at the entrance to these lagoons. If possible, paddle in and drift about the serene waters. A few of the streams that flow into the lagoons lead to lakes, and a short hike can often bring the reward of a fresh water bath. Don't forget, however, that as the tide drops, your doorway to this world will quickly close, only to open again at the next high water slack.

The paddle south to Triquet Island is delightful. Around headlands the waters can get a little tricky, particularly at the mouth of Cultus Sound, but for the most part you are protected from the raging Pacific and are free to enjoy the charms and passages of the many islets. If fog rolls in, these islets can quickly transform into a harrowing maze, so use care as there are not a lot of landing sites. On the way south, you might want to stop at Spider Island to explore the wooden road, remnants of a World War II military base, and fill your water bottles in the creek at the northeast end of the island.

Triquet Island If the sun is shining when you reach Triquet Island, the scene will be blissfully tropical. On the northern side of the island are a number of large, sandy beaches and plenty of room for camping. Landing is easy as the island is protected from the surf and southerly winds, though a few of the beaches become muddy, even quicksand-like, at low tide. There is no fresh water, but BC Parks has provided a box toilet. *Please avoid the shell midden at the north end.* There is plenty of camping on the adjacent beaches.

∧ *Afternoon sun, Triquet Sound,* PETER MCGEE

Stirling Island Plan carefully when you head west across Kildidt Sound. Not only is the area exposed, but the seas can get nasty at the western edge of Nalau Passage and Hakai Passage. Try to avoid the combination of strong west winds and a falling tide. Also, keep your distance from the schools of sport-fishing boats in the area. When $500 per day is the going rate, the last place you want to be is between a fisher and his catch. Although BC Parks lists Stirling Island as a campsite, a number of shell middens on the eastern shore should be avoided.

Choked Passage beaches Farther south, the west coast of Calvert Island offers little shelter but many rewards for the intrepid paddler. At the northwest tip, beaches line the shores of Choked Passage and provide great camping just above the high tide mark. On the downside, a large fishing lodge is nestled in the nearby woods; on the upside, the lodge is actually quite nice. Nonetheless, you will likely want to camp a good distance away. There is a hiking trail across private land to Pruth Bay and a BC Parks ranger station staffed during the summer. Although there is no drinking water, there is a pit toilet at the Wolf Beach site.

At this point, you may want either to continue south to Port Hardy via the wild and stunning waters of Cape Caution or to cross over to the magnificent Koeye River en route to Namu and the Discovery Coast Ferry. For those heading back to Bella Bella, your best bet is to retrace your strokes to the site at Cultus Sound. From here, heading up Hunter Channel offers the most direct route to McLoughlin Bay and gives you a chance to try one more campsite before heading home.

Soulsby Point Graced with spring wildflowers, the small island off Soulsby Point has a white shell beach and room for 2 or 3 tents. There is no water or outhouse on the island but you are now in a great position for the final leg of your journey. Of course, this might just be the starting point to a whole new paddling adventure...

TRIP 40 Klemtu

SKILL:	Intermediate to advanced
TIME:	5–10 days
HAZARDS:	Open coast, wind, currents and traffic
ACCESS:	Discovery Coast Ferry/Klemtu
CHARTS:	3902 · Hecate Strait · 1:250,000
	3726 · Laredo Sound and Approaches · 1:72,200
	3728 · Milbanke Sound and Approaches · 1:76,600
	3737 · Laredo Channel including Laredo Inlet and Surf Inlet · 1:77,400
TIDE BOOK:	Vol. 7

The village of Klemtu on Swindle Island is the staging area for most kayak trips in the Kitasoo territory, which includes most of Princess Royal Island, north to Aaltanhash Inlet, east to the Fiordland Recreation Area, west to Aristazabal Island and south to Lady Douglas

Island. Some of the southern extremities of the Kitasoo territory are considered shared territory with the Heiltsuk First Nation. Klemtu, which means "blocked passage," is a close-knit community of 400 people, mostly Kitasoo who are related to the Tsimshian and the Xaixais people who originate from Kynock Inlet. Many, many years ago, the Kitasoo and Xaixais who lived in smaller villages throughout the territory came to settle in Klemtu (Klemdulxk). The area first served as a camping site on a trade route, and was later used as a base for trading and for providing cordwood to fuel the steamships that travelled the Inside Passage. Eventually Klemtu became a cannery village, and even today the main employer in the village is the new processing plant, which processes salmon, sea cucumbers and herring roe.

Klemtu is now a thriving modern community, but life here is as it's always been—simple and timeless—and residents welcome visitors. Please respect the area's rich cultural history. There are over one hundred documented ancient cultural sites, including abandoned native villages, fish traps, culturally modified trees and middens. If your timing is right, you may be invited to participate in a traditional potlatch or another cultural event in the newly constructed Big House, the most beautiful of its kind on the West Coast.

SITES
The Kitasoo territory offers many undeveloped wilderness campsites for kayakers. Most have good water sources, but treatment is recommended. And although none of the sites have toilets, with the exception of the Marvin Islands, the Kitasoo plan is to put in toilets, and in some cases composting toilets, at some of the popular sites. Klemtu Tourism has also been building a few wilderness huts, which are available for rent. These huts are situated in areas of the territory that provide great opportunities for wildlife and cultural exploration as well as sea kayaking. Currently there is one on Marvin Island at Kitsu Bay and another in Mussel Inlet, on the beach just east of David Bay. Each hut holds up to 12 people in bunk-style accommodation and is outfitted with a wood stove for heating and a propane stove for cooking. The rental fee is $25 per person per night.

Tolmie Channel Leaving Klemtu, most paddlers head north through Klemtu Passage and into Tolmie Channel. Be careful, as the current in Tolmie Channel can reach 3 knots and some tiderips can occur near Boat Bluff and Split Head. Directly north of Split Head, on Sarah Island, you will find an unnamed bay behind a small island. There is space for up to 3 tents in the trees above the gently sloping rocky beach. Water can be found in the creek to the right, but there is no toilet. Watch for boat traffic crossing Tolmie Channel.

Meyers Passage Heading south from Split Head, you will enter Meyers Passage. On the east side of the passage is a nice shell beach behind a small island. This site is a good lunch stop, and there is room for up to 3 tents on the beach during most summer tides. You can also find camping options in Jorgensen Harbour, on the west side of the passage. At the end of Meyers Passage, before heading west through Meyers Narrows, in the eastern corner, is a gently sloping gravel beach. You will find spaces for 5–6 tents in the trees above the beach, and water is available at one end.

Milne Island As you exit the west end of Meyers Passage, head north to Milne Island. In a small bay on the northeast corner of the island, you will find a sand and rock beach. There are two open camping areas above the beach with space for 3–4 tents, and space for up to 3 more in the trees. Tents can also be set up on the upper beach during most summer tides. There is a very small creek with water most of the summer.

Laredo Inlet/Bay of Plenty For paddlers wanting to journey up beautiful Laredo Inlet, Bay of Plenty offers the most likely campsite (although there are a few other sites along the way that will hold 1–2 tents). The Bay of Plenty is aptly named. It was traditionally a food-gathering village, and it is still known for its abundance of salmon, crabs and other seafood as well as for its berries and edible plants. The campsite is on the south side of the bay next to a small creek. Another 1–2 tents can be set up in the grass above the high tide mark, and there are a few more sites in the trees. Water can be taken from the creek.

Marvin Islands At the end of Kitasu Bay are the Marvin Islands, a group of three islands connected by beautiful sandy beaches at low tide. On the biggest island is one of the new rental huts built by

Klemtu Tourism. The other, older cabins built by local Kitasoo are not recommended for use; however, to the right of the buildings, above the beach, is camping space for several tents. There is no obvious water source on Marvin Island, but there are seasonal sources in Kitasu Bay and there is great water in Kwakwa Creek. Look for the makeshift outhouse to the left of the new hut.

Wilby Point At the west end of Kitasu Bay is Wilby Point. This spot boasts several sand and pebble beaches where paddlers can find suitable tent sites. At low tide, Wilby Point is a great place for intertidal exploration, and the beaches on either side of the po int provide several kilometres of beachcombing. Water can be scarce at this site, though a couple of outflow seepages flow during most of the summer.

Pidwell Cove If conditions in Milbanke Sound are calm enough, paddle south from Wilby Point past Abrams Island and into Higgins Passage. Pay close attention to your chart and your direction, as the entrance to Higgins Passage can be hard to find. There are a few small campsites in Higgins Passage, but you may want to press on to the beautiful sandy beach at Pidwell Cove near Pidwell Reef. There are plenty of tent sites on the beach during most summer tides. Water can be found in the creek at the west end of the beach.

ADDITIONAL ROUTES

Heading north Paddling towards Mussel and Kynoch Inlets and the fiords on the mainland puts you in the Fiordland Recreation Area. This area is known for very steep cliffs that soar hundreds of feet above the ocean. Mountain goats grace the cliffs, while grizzly bears roam the rivers pouring into the inlets. A handful of kayakers paddle this route each year, a difficult trip due to the very few camping spots. BC Parks prohibits camping on estuaries within the recreation area because of the danger of bear encounters. This leaves only two small beaches where you can camp, but for paddlers up to the challenge, the scenery is the reward.

Look for the pebble beach east of David Bay, where a small creek flows into the south side of Mussel Inlet. There are a couple of rough tent spots in the woods as well as a wilderness hut (described earlier), which is available for rent from the Kitasoo Nation. Waking up to the view of a large waterfall flowing out of Lizette Lake amid the towering fiord walls that surround you is an amazing experience. David and Oatswish Bays are two delightful places to explore in Mussel Inlet, and the estuaries of Mussel River and Poison Cove Creek will yield trout as well as bear sightings.

The small pebble beach at Heathorn Bay is the only other place we know of where you can camp in the Fiordland Recreation Area. Be aware that there can be currents and turbulence at Mathieson Narrows. Heathorn Bay has a couple of rough tent spots in the woods but lacks any facilities, including water.

Take time to explore Kynoch Inlet, which has incredible views, including a large waterfall flowing directly into the ocean. Pick Desbrisay Bay as a lunch spot but not as a campsite—it is frequented by bears. Paddlers should also be aware of wolves, especially in Duthie Creek and James Bay.

Heading south Paddling towards Port Hardy is one of the most enjoyable and challenging trips on the coast. If you decide to paddle south from Namu along the mainland, as opposed to the outside of Calvert Island, you will quickly encounter the magnificent Koeye River. The estuary of the river is prime grizzly habitat and must be approached with caution; camping is currently available near the river mouth. Farther south, camps at Penrose Island/Fury Island Provincial Marine Park and Cranston Point allow you to rest up before attempting Cape Caution. Camping can be found at Burnett Bay and many of the smaller beaches near Cape Caution, though it is likely you will have to execute a surf landing. For those mentally and physically prepared for such conditions, you won't be disappointed: the massive sand beaches are some of the most impressive in the Pacific Northwest and home to many gray whales during the summer. Please keep in mind that the weather and exposure on this stretch of the coast is severe and should only be attempted by advanced paddlers. Be sure to leave yourself plenty of time. Continuing south will place you in the waters described in chapter 11.

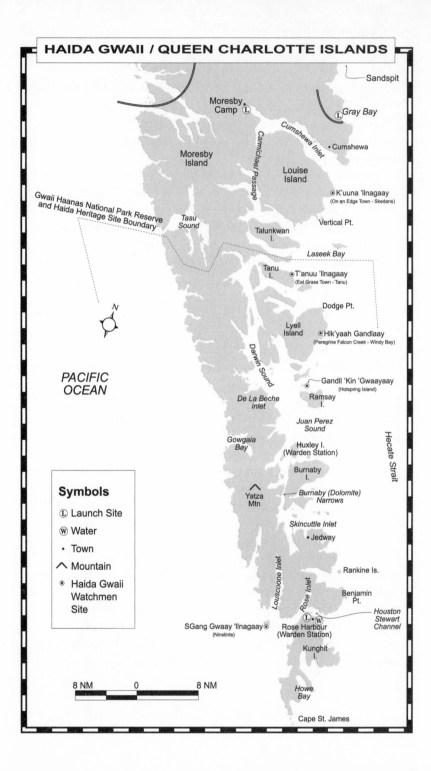

HAIDA GWAII / QUEEN CHARLOTTE ISLANDS

Sandspit

Moresby Camp Ⓛ

Ⓛ Gray Bay

Cumshewa Inlet

• Cumshewa

Moresby Island

Camichael Passage

Louise Island

◉ K'uuna 'Ilnagaay
(On an Edge Town - Skedans)

Gwaii Haanas National Park Reserve and Haida Heritage Site Boundary

Tasu Sound

Talunkwan I.

Vertical Pt.

Laseek Bay

Tanu I.

◉ T'anuu 'Ilnagaay
(Eel Grass Town - Tanu)

Dodge Pt.

Lyell Island

◉ Hlk'yaah Gandlaay
(Peregrine Falcon Creek - Windy Bay)

Darwin Sound

PACIFIC OCEAN

De La Beche Inlet

◉ Gandll 'Kin 'Gwaayaay
(Hotspring Island)

Ramsay I.

Juan Perez Sound

Gowgaia Bay

Huxley I.
(Warden Station)

Burnaby I.

Hecate Strait

Burnaby (Dolomite) Narrows

Yatza Mtn

Skincuttle Inlet

• Jedway

Rankine Is.

Symbols

Ⓛ Launch Site

Ⓦ Water

• Town

⌃ Mountain

◉ Haida Gwaii Watchmen Site

Louscoone Inlet

Rose Inlet

Benjamin Pt.

Ⓛ•Ⓦ

Houston Stewart Channel

SGang Gwaay 'Ilnagaay ◉
(Ninstints)

Rose Harbour
(Warden Station)

Kunghit I.

8 NM   0   8 NM

Howe Bay

Cape St. James

18

Haida Gwaii | Queen Charlotte Islands

Peter McGee and Michele Deakin

Not long ago the notorious stretch of water known as Hecate Strait was paddled by the Haida during raids on mainland tribes. Legend has it that following an attack, the Haida canoes would turn and head towards Haida Gwaii, the Queen Charlotte Islands, leaving their less seaworthy adversaries bound to the mainland for fear of crossing the strait. Times have changed, but even today the isolation of the islands continues to preserve their natural and cultural wealth. Nowhere is this more apparent than in Gwaii Haanas National Park Reserve and Haida Heritage Site in the southern third of the archipelago. Here paddlers can travel through sheltered bays and inlets, explore ancient forests and Haida villages, and gain a sense of the wilderness and society that have lived together since time began. Gwaii Haanas is an area so distinctive, both culturally and biologically, that it is often referred to as the Canadian Galapagos. It is truly one of the world's great paddling destinations.

BACKGROUND

A variety of cultures and nationalities has recently shaped the history of the Haida Gwaii/Queen Charlotte Islands, but the culture that has truly reigned is that of the Haida. At points in their 10,000-year history, it is estimated that the Haida population on the islands was upwards of 20,000; by 1870, however, several epidemics in quick succession came close to decimating them. The Haida who survived, roughly 1,500 people, left their traditional villages and congregated in Skidegate and Old Massett. Since then, the Haida have regained their political voice, though Spanish, French, British, American and Canadian influences have forever altered many of the 140 islands.

As elsewhere in the province, the logging industry thrived in the Queen Charlotte Islands for the better part of this century, largely unchecked by environmental concerns. In 1974, a small but dedicated group contested the logging plans of Burnaby Island, situated 120 km (75 mi.) south of Sandspit, and the struggle to save "South Moresby" began.

Fourteen years later, following a preservation campaign that reached people around the world, the provincial government signed a deal with the federal government that transferred the rights of the land from the province to Ottawa and established the national park reserve in the southern third of the archipelago. The total cost to the federal government for the preservation of Lyell Island to Cape St. James, a wild and remote area that stretches 90 km (56 mi.), was $106 million.

Although native land claims have yet to be resolved and ultimate authority over the land yet to be determined, the area is currently co-operatively managed by Parks Canada as a national park reserve and by the Council of the Haida Nation as a Haida Heritage Site. The legal agreement that created Gwaii Haanas as a cooperatively managed/protected area recognizes that long-term protective measures are essential to safeguard the archipelago as one of the world's great natural and cultural treasures. Gwaii Haanas also reflects the desire to sustain Haida culture and provides for the continuation of cultural activities and traditional renewable resource harvesting activities.

GETTING THERE

There are two considerations when going to the Queen Charlotte Islands: how much time you've got and how much money you want to spend. In general, getting to the islands is neither quick nor inexpensive.

You can either drive to Port Hardy or Prince Rupert and take a B.C. ferry to Skidegate Landing, with or without your vehicle, or you can fly to Sandspit. It is possible to rent a car on the islands, but this tends to be quite expensive. However, getting around the Charlottes without a vehicle is difficult, so you should make arrangements for the appropriate transportation. A third option for reaching the islands is to take an Alaska Marine Highway ferry, from either Washington State or Alaska to Prince Rupert, and then board a B.C. ferry.

By land It is about a 20-hour drive to Prince Rupert from Vancouver, along Highways 1 and 97 to Prince George, then through the picturesque interior of the province on Highway 16 (the Yellowhead). With a car full of people, this is by far the cheapest way to go. Once in Prince Rupert, follow the signs to the B.C. Ferries terminal and catch the sailing to Skidegate Landing.

If you are on Vancouver Island (or want to spend more time on a boat than in a car), your best bet is to drive to Port Hardy and catch the ferry to Prince Rupert. See chapter 17 for information about the ferry terminal at Port Hardy. Often people will take the ferry one way and drive the other—a good way to mix up the scenery.

If you have extra time, you can also try the train; VIA Rail leaves Vancouver three times a week for Prince Rupert. The trip takes three to five days, with overnights in Jasper and Prince George at your own expense (including hotel charges for layovers). Greyhound Bus Lines operates a two-day service between Vancouver and Prince Rupert.

By water B.C. Ferries sails from Port Hardy to Prince Rupert, then from Prince Rupert to Skidegate Landing. Alaska Marine Highway ferries sail from Washington State and Alaska to Prince Rupert. These trips are a great way to see the coast and meet people. You must have advance reservations for all ferry rides, and reservations should be made for both directions, even though standby spots do come available.

By air In high season, Air Canada flies twice daily to Sandspit from Vancouver. The flight time is approximately 1.5 hours. From Sandspit, Harbour Air and South Moresby Air can fly you into Gwaii Haanas. Over the years, several new airlines have also tried to service the islands, so you are best to check with the visitor information centre for current details.

WEATHER AND HAZARDS

The climate of the Queen Charlottes is typical of B.C.'s West Coast: cool and wet at virtually any time of year. May, June and July are generally the driest months. The rainy season can begin as early as mid-August. The east side of the islands is considerably drier than the west, which can receive 500–800 cm (200–315 in.) of rain a year. Northwest and westerly winds prevail in summer and can blow hard for lengthy periods of time. These winds often funnel over Moresby Island and down the inlets of the east coast, creating sudden gusty conditions that can be a hazard to kayakers. Storms associated with the passage of a frontal system hammer the islands from the southeast and southwest. These occur frequently throughout the winter and are not uncommon in the summer. There are no guarantees here, but, in general, the best months for paddling are from mid-June through mid-August. As always, make sure you build enough time into your plans for the days you may be "weathered in" and unable to travel.

Use caution travelling around exposed points of land, as there are often strong tidal currents, swells and winds. Tidal currents occur elsewhere throughout the islands, so be sure to check the charts and tide tables, especially in the Houston Stewart Channel area. Sea fog occurs frequently during the summer along the west coast and throughout the Houston Stewart Channel area.

You should also use proper bear etiquette in Gwaii Haanas (see chapter 1). Although there are no grizzlies on the islands, the black bears here are among the largest in North America: their snouts tend to be longer, their jaws and teeth heavier. In the event of problem encounters between bears and people, the park reserve's policy is to close areas to public use. They will not remove any bears. Don't ruin the experience for others—be sure to bear-proof your camp. Please be particularly careful around Burnaby Narrows and Rose Inlet.

Please note: Wardens patrol Gwaii Haanas throughout the summer and stay at the warden stations at Huxley and Ellen Islands. They monitor channel 16 and a radiophone interconnect number in case of emergencies. Nonetheless, although there are regular patrols, the area is extremely isolated and help may be a long way off. In addition, if you are travelling to a warden station for assistance, please keep in mind that the wardens are usually in the field between 8 AM and 8 PM.

SPECIAL CONSIDERATIONS

Reservations, registrations and orientations Gwaii Haanas has several visitor management systems for reservations, registrations and orientations. These are intended to reduce crowding during the peak season, increase public safety and ensure environmental impacts are reduced in the protected area. User fees are also in place.

If you are planning a trip into Gwaii Haanas as an independent traveller, contact the Gwaii Haanas office for information on how to make an advance reservation. If you choose not to make an advance reservation, you and the members of your group must travel into Gwaii Haanas using daily standby space; there is no guarantee that space will be available. Reservations are highly recommended, and group size is limited to 12 people.

Everyone travelling into Gwaii Haanas *must* take the orientation session and register each trip they take. Registration provides information that is essential to managing the protected area. The orientation is also a means for you to get updates, the latest safety or closure information, and interesting new research findings that will make your trip safer and more enjoyable. Visitors travelling with an operator will receive their orientation from that operator.

The information on campsites in this chapter is limited, as requested by Parks Canada and the Council of the Haida Nation, to ensure that the necessary exchange between paddlers and Gwaii Haanas personnel occurs. We all believe this will allow the area to be managed in the best possible way.

Haida Gwaii Watchmen The Haida Nation started the Watchmen program in 1981 when the number of visitors to the area started to increase. Parks Canada began funding the program in 1990 and continues to work jointly with the Haida Gwaii Watchmen.

Haida Watchmen live at five of the village sites in Gwaii Haanas during the visitor season. There are often two to four people at each site, including elders. The Watchmen are not there as attendants or servants but as guardians and hosts who provide basic assistance to visitors. The village sites are K'uuna 'llnagaay (Skedans, which is actually outside Gwaii Haanas), T'anuu 'llnagaay (Tanu), Hlk'yaah Gandlaay (Windy Bay), Gandll 'Kin 'Gwaayaay (Hotspring Island) and SGang

Gwaay (Anthony Island). The village of SGang Gwaay 'llnagaay (formerly Ninstints) on SGang Gwaay is considered to have the world's finest display of standing Haida mortuary poles, all of which are more than 100 years old. In consultation with the Haida people, UNESCO declared SGang Gwaay a World Heritage Site in 1981.

Trip 41 Gwaii Haanas

SKILL:	Intermediate to advanced
TIME:	7 days and up
HAZARDS:	Isolation and frequent weather changes
ACCESS:	Moresby Camp/Gray Bay/boat and plane charters
CHARTS:	3807 · Atli Inlet to Selwyn Inlet · 1:37,500
	3808 · Juan Perez Sound · 1:37,500
	3809 · Carpenter Bay to Burnaby Island · 1:37,500
	3825 · Cape St. James to Houston Stewart Channel · 1:40,000
	3853 · Cape St. James to Cumshewa Inlet and Tasu Sound · 1:50:000
	3855 · Houston Stewart Channel · 1:20,000
	3894 · Selwyn Inlet to Lawn Point · 1:73,000
TIDE BOOK:	Vol. 7

Please note: A backcountry management plan review is underway and some of the finer details in trip planning may have changed. Check with Gwaii Haanas for the most current information package before you go.

Most of the paddling that occurs in the Queen Charlotte Islands takes place in the Gwaii Haanas National Park Reserve. From Sandspit you can paddle to the beginning of Gwaii Haanas, but conditions can be quite treacherous and most people choose to launch from Moresby Camp. A one-way trip from Moresby Camp to SGang Gwaay (at the south end of Gwaii Haanas) can take as little as a week, but allow at least two so you have time to enjoy yourself. The ultimate journey is a trip from Moresby Camp to SGang Gwaay and back, paddling both inside and outside the smaller islands on the east coast of Moresby Island.

However, laying out an agenda is not true wilderness travel in Gwaii Haanas, and some careful spontaneity is encouraged. When too many people follow a predetermined, predictable itinerary, the results are overcrowding at Watchmen sites and campsites and heavy user impacts. Paddlers looking to experience the real Gwaii Haanas should pick an area based on the charts and explore it. Slow down to the rhythm of the tides, poke in and out of the little bays and be open to the "whole" of Gwaii Haanas. To travel the area and check sites off a list is to miss the connection between humans and the land. Let Gwaii Haanas dictate your pace.

Paddlers who do not have time to cover the whole Gwaii Haanas tend to focus trips either around Gandll 'Kin 'Gwaayaay and the centre of Gwaii Haanas or around SGang Gwaay and the village of SGang Gwaay 'Ilnagaay. It is also worth noting that, though more expensive, customizing your trip to Gwaii Haanas is relatively easy, and boat and plane charters can make drop-offs and pick-ups at the destination of your choice. The northern boundary of Gwaii Haanas lies a good 2 days' paddle (under reasonable conditions) from the closest road access at Moresby Camp, so arranging a charter makes sense if you are short on time. The boundary for Gwaii Haanas begins near Talunkwan Island. Some options:

- Explore T'anuu 'Ilnagaay, Juan Perez Sound, Gandll 'Kin 'Gwaayaay and Burnaby Narrows, with put-in and pick-up sites to be determined by your charter.
- Explore the southern end of Gwaii Haanas, visiting SGang Gwaay and using Rose Harbour as a put-in and pick-up site.
- Limit your charter costs by paddling one way from Moresby Camp to Juan Perez Sound, or vice versa. Another possibility is to take a commercial trip, many of which are only a week in length and simplify the logistics of dealing with charters and rentals. Licenced operators offer kayaking or kayak mothershipping trips.
- With two weeks, your options open up a little. One possibility is to simply take more time to paddle one of the trips described above. For those who want to cover a little more ground, consider launching from the north end of Gwaii Haanas, around T'anuu 'Ilnagaay, and paddling to SGang Gwaay, or vice versa. If you want to cut down your charter costs, you can always put in or take out from Moresby Camp or Gray Bay.
- If you have three weeks or more, paddling from Moresby Camp to SGang Gwaay and back will give you the best sense of the area.

Ironically, though this is the longest trip, it is also the cheapest as there are no charter costs involved. This is the trip described below.

LAUNCHING

Moresby Camp is the closest road access to Gwaii Haanas and the preferred launching spot for independent paddlers. Most tour companies have designated drop-off and pick-up spots within the park reserve. Other options include launching at Gray Bay or taking a boat or plane into Gwaii Haanas to the launch site of your choice.

To reach Moresby Camp or Gray Bay, you need to travel on active logging roads. Moresby Camp is about 32 km (20 mi.) from the Alliford Bay ferry terminal. (A ferry runs regularly between Skidegate and Alliford Bay. The crossing takes 30 minutes.) To reach the camp, turn right as you leave the terminal and drive for about 10 km (6 mi.) to South Bay. Continue for 7 km (4.5 mi.) along the Main Line and turn right onto the Moresby Main. Another 11 km (7 mi.) will take you to the Moresby Camp recreation site. There is an outhouse, dock and creek, but the site is quite industrial so you are advised to bring your own water.

To reach Gray Bay from Sandspit, drive south past the golf course and along the gravel Main Line. At the 14-mile marker (22.5 km), turn left and drive another 11 km (7 mi.) until you reach the sand beach of Gray Bay. There are a number of Forest Service campsites and a small creek, but the water is not drinkable.

From May to the beginning of September, check with the visitor information centres upon arrival for further information on the state of the logging roads. In the off-season you can call Teal Jones Logging. It is also possible to paddle directly from Sandspit, but the seas here are shallow and confused, creating hazardous conditions.

SITES

Undesignated camping is practised in Gwaii Haanas. You camp where you please though there are exceptions: camping is not permitted at T'anuu 'llnagaay or on Gandll 'Kin 'llnagaay (Hotspring Island), Ata Naa (House Island and islets), the Rankine Islands, the Copper Islands, Jeffrey Island, Slug Islet, SGang Gwaay, Burnaby Narrows, the Bolkus Islands, Bowles Point peninsula, the Kerouard Islands and the isthmus between the Swan Islands. Maximum group size is 12, and

∧ *An unusually calm Juan Perez Sound,* GRANT THOMPSON/TOFINO EXPEDITIONS

you are asked to limit your stay at any one campsite to a maximum of 3 nights. Water is plentiful throughout the islands, but it is not available at every campsite and creeks do dry up. Fill up when you can.

Launching from Moresby Camp puts you at the head of Cumshewa Inlet, an area of active logging. You will probably want to head south around the exposed side of Louise Island or through Carmichael Passage as quickly as possible. Try to catch the ebb tide from Moresby Camp and, if you are taking the outside route, exercise caution as you pass over the shoal and kelp bed near Skedans Point.

K'uuna 'Ilnagaay (Skedans) If you have chosen the outside route, don't miss the chance to visit the village of K'uuna 'Ilnagaay (On an Edge Town). Traditionally a Raven site, it is estimated that K'uuna 'Ilnagaay had upwards of 30 houses and 738 inhabitants prior to 1860 when, aside from seasonal use, the residents moved to a site on Maude Island and then to Skidegate. Most of the totems at K'uuna 'Ilnagaay that were not taken to museums or private collections have fallen, but dramatic carvings can still be detected amidst the moss and decay. According to George F. MacDonald's *Haida Monumental Art: Villages of the Queen Charlotte Islands*, the head chief of K'uuna 'Ilnagaay, Gida'nsta, was friends with Chief Tsebassa of Kitkatla, which led to the introduction of many new crests and stories from the mainland. The three dominant Raven families shared the same crests, with the exception of the moon, which was the exclusive right of the chief. The shared crests included the mountain goat (a crest obtained from the Tsimshian as a result of the relationship with Kitkatla), the grizzly bear, the killer whale, the rainbow, the sea-grizzly and the child of Property Woman.

The village faces south onto Skedans Bay and, though located just north of the park reserve boundary, is a Haida Watchmen site. The small peninsula is bordered by a high rocky bluff at one end and a rocky prominence on the other. There is no camping at K'unna 'llnagaay.

Vertical Point Continuing along the outside of Louise Island, you will come across Vertical Point and a narrow spit connecting the impressive limestone bed of the point with Louise Island. The area has been used consistently over the years, first as a site of a Xa'lanit village and then during the Depression as a refuge for hand loggers. The people who chose to make the spit their home left a legacy of apple trees, honeysuckle and rose trees. The remains of log cabins lie nearby as does a fine well.

If you want to camp, check out the cabin on the south side of the spit. According to author Kathleen Dalzell, it was built by Benita Saunders, a young artist from New York, in the early 1970s. Head for the meadow where the point narrows and tuck your boats in behind the kelp. The cabin is only a few hundred feet from the shore, and its logbook provides some great reading to get you ready for the remainder of your trip.

Farther south you will still see many logging scars until you enter Gwaii Haanas, just south of Talunkwan Island. From here on, aside from Lyell Island and Jedway Bay, signs of recent logging and mining are virtually nonexistent, and the ancient history of the islands slowly begins to envelop you.

T'anuu 'llnagaay (Tanu) T'anuu means Eel Grass Town in Haida. The village site is the next Watchmen camp you will encounter and a hauntingly beautiful place. Moss and time have disguised much of its greatness, but the remaining house pits, numbering over 20, are signs that T'anuu 'llnagaay was one of the most flourishing villages on the islands. Like most Haida villages, T'anuu 'llnagaay was struck by several epidemics. Over the course of 10 years, beginning in 1880, the population dwindled from over 500 to less than 80. When approaching T'anuu 'llnagaay, land on the southeastern beach. There is a posted map of the house-pit sites at the landing area and great camp-ing on the nearby islands and beaches.

Hlk'yaah Gandlaay (Windy Bay) If you continue taking the outside route, you will come across Hlk'yaah Gandlaay, which means Pere-grine Falcon Creek, near Gogit Point. The 1985 standoff between the Haida and Western Forest Products occurred nearby and, as a result, the bay is still home to one of the most spectacular watersheds on the coast. Although the B.C. minister of forests gave the go-ahead to log Lyell Island after the arrests of 1985, the blockade created a wave of in-ternational support for the Haida cause and led to the direct involve-ment of the federal government, a critical step in the ultimate creation of Gwaii Haanas. Images of Haida elders being arrested for non-violent protest struck a chord with people around the world and shamed the provincial government for its actions. Hlk'yaah Gandlaay is a joyous place to visit these days, with the beauty and spiritual forces of the streams and the forests of immense Sitka spruce, hem-lock and cedar.

If you do visit Hlk'yaah Gandlaay, and it is highly recommended, keep in mind that camping is only allowed for 1 night unless weather conditions make it dangerous to continue paddling. Even in the best of weather, the access to the village is exposed and not appropriate for beginners. Be particularly cautious of the winds and waves near Dodge Point. Hlk'yaah Gandlaay is a Watchmen site. A little farther south is the beloved Gandll 'Kin 'Gwaayaay.

Gandll 'Kin Gwaayaay (Hotspring Island) Unofficial place names like Smoke Bay, Volcanic Island, Island of Fire and now Hotspring Island leave little doubt as to what makes this area one of the most visited spots in Gwaii Haanas. Francis Poole, a civil and mining engineer with the Queen Charlotte Mining Company, was told by Chief Klue of T'anuu 'llnagaay that soaking in the miracle waters would cure him of every ailment. The year was 1862. How much of that claim is true is difficult to verify, but the numerous pools on the island continue to work wonders on the aching muscles of paddlers and fishers alike.

Popularity has a price, and it is quite likely you'll be sharing your bliss with people from around the world. Please be considerate of their experience. The Watchmen cabin is located near the pools as is the new solar-composting toilet. The pools are on the southwest corner of the island, but landing is also encouraged at the north end as a trail runs across the island. Alcohol is not allowed in or around the pools, and you should refrain from using soap in anything but the bathing hut. There are great campsites on nearby islands, so you won't have to travel far to set up for the night.

Paddling in Juan Perez Sound gives you access to some stunning scenery but also exposes you to some extreme weather. When a southeaster is blowing, it is best to sit it out for the day. A little less predictable are the gap winds that funnel over the San Christoval Range on Moresby (see chapter 1). Some afternoons you will encounter ferocious headwinds and steep waves paddling west from Gandll 'Kin 'Gwaayaay. These winds should always be treated with respect, no matter how short your passage.

If you have the time and desire, hiking through the open alpine of the San Christovals provides a fantastic view of the remote west coast of Moresby and gives your arms a break from the daily grind. One of the more popular day hikes begins in Island Bay, across from the northern tip of Burnaby Island, and summits the 707-m (2,330-ft.) Yatza Mountain. Sections of the hike are difficult, but the biggest concern is a quick change in the weather. Be prepared and don't assume the sun (if you are so lucky) will hold for the whole day. It's easy to get lost (especially in the fog), and all hikers should have strong compass skills and use them.

Burnaby Narrows Continuing south, you will soon find yourself in a passage 50 m (164 ft.) wide that cuts between Moresby and Burnaby Islands. Burnaby Narrows is officially called Dolomite Narrows on the charts and is one of the most significant intertidal areas in North America. Less than 10 per cent of all coastlines support intertidal life, and most of those areas do not come close to the abundance of the narrows. The seabed is reputed to contain more protein per square metre than anywhere else in the world, and it is virtually impossible to walk here at low tide without stepping on living creatures of many kinds. As a result, visitors are asked to float through the narrows to see the intertidal life. However tempting, rearranging intertidal life for photographic purposes is strongly dis-couraged as this exposes animals to predators or takes them away from their food source; photos are possible through the water even without specialized camera equipment. Camping is not permitted in the narrows, but you won't have a problem finding suitable spots at either end.

At this point in the trip, you are making a big commitment if you choose to continue south. Rounding Benjamin Point and heading into Houston Stewart Channel puts you in an area of incredible beauty that is also extremely rugged and isolated. Weather and currents in this part of Gwaii Haanas can have you shorebound for several days, so be sure to leave ample time in your trip planning. Cautions aside, however, visiting the village site of SGang Gwaay is a highlight that should not be missed.

As you paddle south, be very careful of the wave action caused by the shallows off Benjamin Point and the current and wind interaction entering Houston Stewart Channel. Camping is a little tough between Skincuttle Inlet and Kunghit Island, but there are a number of possible sites in and around the channel. For those interested in some luxury, consider making arrangements to spend a few nights in Rose Harbour.

Rose Harbour Rose Harbour is a beautiful little community located on the north shore of Kunghit Island, the last remaining vestige of privately held land in Gwaii Haanas. The site was originally purchased by G.A. Huff of Alberni for a syndicate of businessmen from Vancouver and Victoria in 1910; the Queen Charlotte Whaling Company began operations that summer. By late fall, Rose Harbour had already put through 80 whales and employed 150 men. Over time, the station's annual catch went from 300 whales to 150, and operations were eventually shut down in 1941.

Rose Harbour is now owned by 14 shareholders but only three families live here. The harbour is relatively busy during the summer and has a number of facilities that might interest paddlers, including a guest house, kayak rentals, boat tours and organic meal services. Visitors are welcome to explore the old boilers and digesters of the whaling station, but call ahead if you plan on staying in or using any of the facilities. Please respect the homes and property of the shareholders.

∧ *SG̲ang Gwaay 'llnaggay (Ninstints)*, GRANT THOMPSON/TOFINO EXPEDITIONS

SG̲ang Gwaay (Anthony Island) Perched at the southern tip of Moresby Island, and exposed to the full force of the Pacific Ocean, lies the secluded island of SG̲ang Gwaay—which in Haida means Wailing Island—and the magical village of SG̲ang Gwaay 'llnagaay (formerly Ninstints). Although the Kunghit Haida have moved away, they are still very much connected to this village, and their legacy continues as the totems watch over the village in silence, slowly succumbing to the climate of the Pacific northwest coast.

Due to the popularity of the site, please ensure that you radio ahead to arrange access with the Watchmen. You may have to wait elsewhere until enough people have left the island to make room for more. The result will be a better experience for all once you get to SG̲ang Gwaay.

Visitors to SG̲ang Gwaay should enter the village site from the back end of the island, at the protected bay to the north. In case of weather, it is possible to use the south end but the walk over is less enjoyable. In any event, the experience from the back of the island is one of discovery—beaching the kayaks, walking through the quiet forest and coming out upon the village site. Please don't approach via the front of the village. This results in crowding and interference with the solitary experience most visitors are looking for at SGang Gwaay 'llnagaay. And please: no camping in the village site.

ADDITIONAL ROUTES

For the more adventurous, the Haida Gwaii/Queen Charlotte Islands offer stunning paddling on the west coast of both Moresby and Graham Islands, but the shore is typically steep and rocky, with pounding surf. For huge stretches landing may be impossible or, at best, very difficult, and exploring this region should be attempted only by experienced paddlers and even then, only with extreme caution. For more information, contact the BCMTA. If you are looking for less intense alternatives, try kayaking from a mothership base camp or some of the following areas:

- Skidegate Inlet is an extensive area that can be explored for a couple of hours, a day or several days. There are islands to visit, fascinating geology and the company of oystercatchers, pigeon guillemots, herons, harlequin ducks, bald eagles, loons and other water birds. The adventurous, and experienced, can opt for several day trips out through Skidegate Narrows for a taste of the islands' west coast.
- Rennel Sound, accessible by logging road, offers the west coast in a relatively sheltered setting.
- North Beach on Graham Island is for paddlers who like fun in the surf.
- Masset Inlet is where the waters of Dixon Entrance penetrate right to the heart of Graham Island.
- Mayer Lake is probably the most accessible of the islands' larger lakes.

Wherever you choose to go, Haida Gwaii offers you the experience of healthy ecosystems, Haida culture, a unique island way of life and a strong connection to an inspiring place. Island people are trying to develop a tourism industry that respects these elements of their heritage. Enjoy the unique aspects of the islands but please leave them as you found them.

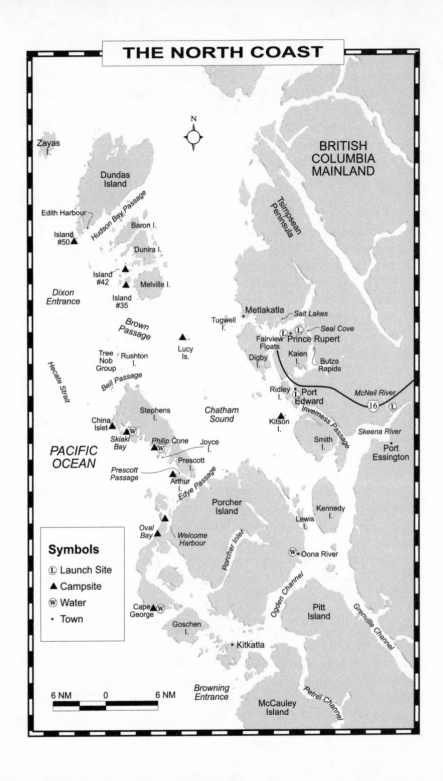

THE NORTH COAST

N

Zayas I.

Dundas Island

BRITISH COLUMBIA MAINLAND

Edith Harbour

Baron I.

Island #50 ▲

Hudson Bay Passage

Tsimpsean Peninsula

Dunira I.

Island #42 ▲

Melville I.

Island #35

Dixon Entrance

Brown Passage

Tugwell I.

Metlakatla

Salt Lakes

Lucy Is. ▲

Fairview Floats Ⓛ Ⓛ

Seal Cove

Ⓛ Prince Rupert

Tree Nob Group

Rushton I.

Digby I.

Kaien I.

Butze Rapids

Bell Passage

Hecate Strait

Stephens I.

Chatham Sound

Ridley I.

Ⓛ Port Edward

McNeil River

16

Ⓛ

China Islet ▲

Ⓦ

Kitson I.

Inverness Passage

Skeena River

Skiakl Bay

Philip Cone ▲

Ⓦ

Joyce I.

Smith I.

Port Essington

PACIFIC OCEAN

Prescott Passage

Prescott I.

Arthur I. ▲

Edye Passage

Porcher Island

Kennedy I.

Lewis I.

Oval Bay ▲

Welcome Harbour

Porcher Inlet

Ⓦ Oona River

Symbols

Ⓛ Launch Site

▲ Campsite

Ⓦ Water

• Town

Cape George ▲ Ⓦ

Goschen I.

Ogden Channel

Pitt Island

Grenville Channel

• Kitkatla

Browning Entrance

Petrel Channel

McCauley Island

6 NM   0   6 NM

19

The North Coast

Charles Justice

The extreme north end of British Columbia's Inside Passage comprises the islands that border Chatham Sound on their east and Hecate Strait and Dixon Entrance on their west. Located only 32 km (20 mi.) south of the Alaskan border at their northernmost point, these islands are largely uninhabited and pristine. Their western coastlines are beautiful, rugged and irregular, affording shelter in small bays as well as the occasional sandy beaches. Although exposed and not for the faint of heart, islands such as Porcher, Stephens and Dundas provide some of the best paddling B.C. has to offer.

BACKGROUND

The nearest access point for all these trips is Prince Rupert, a deep-water port located near the mouth of the Skeena River with a population of 15,000. Prince Rupert was created in the early decades of this century as the Pacific terminus of the now defunct Grand Trunk Pacific Railway. The railroad's founder, Charles Hays, died aboard the *Titanic*.

There are three permanent Tsimshian villages in the area. Kitkatla is the southernmost, situated in a protected area close to the south end of Porcher Island. Port Simpson is the oldest European settlement in the area; it started out as a Hudson's Bay Company trading post in 1834 and is now an Indian Reserve. Metlakatla, at the outer limits of Prince Rupert Harbour, was started in 1862 as a utopian native community by the lay Anglican minister William Duncan. It once had the largest church north of San Francisco but that has since burnt down. In 1887, due to a dispute with the Anglican hierarchy, Duncan and half the population moved to Alaska and established a second Metlakatla just outside Ketchikan.

The Tsimshian are currently involved in a major land claim that could affect any or all of the islands situated off Prince Rupert. As always, we ask that you treat any cultural sites you come across with the utmost respect.

GETTING THERE

Please see the Getting There section of chapter 18 for information about reaching Prince Rupert, the gateway to paddling routes of the North Coast.

Once in Prince Rupert, you will likely launch either from the Fairview floats, located about 15 minutes from the town centre, or from the Port Edward boat launch. If you do not feel like paddling Chatham Sound's exposed crossing, a boat charter company can take you from Prince Rupert to the starting point of your choice. Prices usually begin at about $200, depending on the number of people.

WEATHER AND HAZARDS

Northwesterlies are the prevailing winds in the region from July to September. Southeasterlies are common for the remainder of the year though they also occur during the summer. Gusty winds are found in Prince Rupert Harbour during southeast gales produced by airflow over the local mountains. Strong northeasterlies, which can occur in fair weather, can lead to a build up of seas in north Chatham Sound.

Prince Rupert is an active port, and there is considerable boat traffic in and around the area. Of particular concern are Alaskan tugs towing barges at 18 knots, ocean liners and the Alaskan and B.C.

ferries. Because of this traffic, crossing Chatham Sound in the fog is not advised.

Close to the mouth of the Skeena you will encounter the effects of the river and the tides, which can create difficult seas particularly when there is an ebbing tide and a westerly or northwesterly wind. Numerous commercial fishers work the mouth of the Skeena so beware of boats and nets. As always, watch for enraged sea lions.

During gales, seas can be quite hazardous on the west coast of the outer islands; fortunately a number of bays and smaller islands afford shelter.

SPECIAL CONSIDERATIONS

When paddling on the North Coast, you are in Tsimshian territory. *Tsimshian* means "going into the river of mists" and refers to the mighty Skeena River. Seven Tsimshian communities currently occupy the lower portions of the Skeena and much of the coast on either side of the river mouth. Tsimshian history is well documented in the middens that abound in this part of the coast as well as in the Tsimshian science of the past, the *adawx*, or oral record of events. Please respect this history and the Tsimshian territories in your travels by following the guidelines on cultural impacts outlined in chapter 1. As with any other First Nations traditional territory, seek permission to visit the area as part of your trip planning process. See Useful Contacts at the back of the book or contact the BCMTA for more information.

NORTH COAST TRIPS (42–44)

The North Coast is an enormous area with unlimited paddling potential. If you have at least 5 days, heading almost due west from Prince Rupert to explore Stephens Island and the Tree Nob Group provides spectacular views and puts you on the edge of Hecate Strait. With a bit more time, it is worthwhile to head south and explore Porcher Island or to venture to the northern extremes of the B.C. border and the waters surrounding Dundas Island. Recommended times are based on fair weather, and it is best to leave a buffer of a few days. If the following trips are beyond your skill level, consult Additional Routes at the end of the chapter for a few beginner and intermediate trips in the sheltered bays and inlets surrounding Prince Rupert.

Because some of the sites overlap on these trips, they have been arranged from south to north, not from shortest to longest.

Please note that Porcher, Stephens, the Tree Nobs, Dunira and Dundas Islands have small Indian Reserves and the occasional unoccupied fisher's cabin. Please respect the owner's privacy. Camping on reserves or occupying cabins should not be done without permission.

TRIP 42   Porcher Island

SKILL: Intermediate to advanced

TIME: 3–7 days

HAZARDS: Winds and currents in Edye Passage, boat traffic

ACCESS: Port Edward boat launch

CHARTS: 3717 · Approaches to Skeena River · 1:25,000
3761 · Kitkatla Inlet · 1:36,500
3773 · Grenville Channel, Baker Inlet to Ogden Channel · 1:36,500
3956 · Malacca Passage to Bell Passage · 1:40,000
3957 · Approaches to Prince Rupert Harbour · 1:40,000
3958 · Prince Rupert Harbour · 1:20,000
3927 · Bonilla Island to Edye Passage · 1:77,800

TIDE BOOK: Vol. 7

Porcher Island and its close environs boast four small communities. On its north coast are Humpback Bay and Hunts Inlet. On the south coast, on an island all to itself, lies the First Nations community of Kitkatla. Finally, on the east coast of Porcher is the teeming metropolis of Oona River.

To reach the northern tip of Porcher Island, it is best to depart from the Port Edward boat launch, paddle to Kitson Island Provincial Marine Park and then cross the southern end of Chatham Sound. From here you can continue to Edye Pass, Welcome Harbour and Oval Bay on the west coast of Porcher, past Fan Point and on to Cape George at the southern tip of the island. At this point, you can either double back or circumnavigate Porcher Island, visiting the communities of Kitkatla and Oona River as you go. If you are camping near Kitkatla please get Band permission first. Call (250) 848-2214.

∧ *Oona River,* NEIL GREGORY-EAVES

LAUNCHING

To reach the Port Edward boat launch from Prince Rupert, take Highway 16 across the bridge from Kaien Island to the mainland and take the first right. Follow the signs to Port Edward, then continue down the road for just under a mile to the big fish plant. Look for a sharp right turn just before the plant and take that road down to the boat launch. You can park your vehicle in the big lot across from the plant for free.

SITES

Kitson Island Provincial Marine Park This little island is less than an hour's paddle from the Port Edward boat launch. There is a nice sand beach at its eastern end, behind which there is room for about 6 tents.

Beach camping is possible though space is limited. Although close to Port Edward, the beach affords complete privacy because, apart from other paddlers, any boat traffic passes at a distance. The view to the south of Porcher Island is beautiful. Unfortunately, there is no fresh water. Take note of the shoal to the north of the island, which can create some steep waves when the wind is blowing.

Welcome Harbour Across Chatham Sound, you will likely be able to see the profile of Porcher Island. Head for its northern tip and work your way along its northwestern shore. The west coast of Porcher Island forms a long, narrow, bifurcating peninsula. Welcome Harbour, a popular sailboat anchorage, is nestled in the east side of the northern end of the peninsula. It is a picturesque lagoon with a maze of protected islets. The Forest Service and the Prince Rupert Sailing Club maintain a small site at the beach with a picnic table and outhouse, and there is room in the woods for several tents. A short trail connects the two sides of the peninsula. There is no fresh water.

Oval Bay This is a beautiful 6-km (3.7-mi.) gently curving sand beach on the west coast of Porcher Island. There are a few small creeks along the beach except during extended dry spells, and good beach camping on virtually the entire stretch. You may have to camp in the woods during an extreme high tide; otherwise the beach is plenty wide. It is exposed to Hecate Strait, however, and has surf with any strong wind except an easterly. Some protection is afforded by the extensive kelp beds along the coast.

Cape George There is a sandy bay with rock outcroppings just east of Cape George at the extreme south end of Porcher Island. Exposed to the south, the site has ample room above the high tide level for tents, as well as a small creek with questionable water. A shipwreck is in the bay.

Porcher Island (East Side) If you are circumnavigating Porcher Island, be forewarned that camping on the east side is quite tough and finding sites should not be left for the end of the day. The community of Oona River is very friendly, with a government wharf and pay phone and the choice of two B&Bs (see Useful Contacts). A little farther north, just outside the harbour, a few of the islands have gravel beaches and some room for tents.

TRIP 43 Stephens Island and the Tree Nobs

SKILL:	Intermediate to advanced
TIME:	3–7 days
HAZARDS:	Winds, currents and boat traffic
ACCESS:	Port Edward boat launch
CHARTS:	3717 · Approaches to Skeena River · 1:25,000
	3956 · Malacca Passage to Bell Passage · 1:40,000
	3957 · Approaches to Prince Rupert Harbour ·
	1:40,000
	3958 · Prince Rupert Harbour · 1:20,000
	3927 · Bonilla Island to Edye Passage · 1:77,800
TIDE BOOK:	Vol. 7

This trip takes you from the Port Edward boat launch across Chatham Sound to the north end of Porcher Island. From Porcher, cross to Prescott and Arthur Islands well before you enter Edye Passage—this will help you avoid a strong tidal current and the nasty williwaws that sweep down the mountains of Porcher. You can then follow the shoreline to the northwest tip of Stephens Island or to the Tree Nob Group and back. It is possible to accomplish this trip in as little as 4 days though a week is recommended; the Chatham Sound crossing is quite exposed and dependent on favourable weather.

LAUNCHING

For directions on how to reach the Port Edward boat launch, see the Porcher Island trip (above).

SITES

Kitson Island Provincial Marine Park If you plan to visit Kitson Island, see the Porcher Island trip. If you have experience in exposed crossings, you can avoid Kitson Island and head directly from the Port Edward boat launch to Porcher Island. The crossing usually takes 2–4 hours.

Arthur Island Arthur Island forms the north side of Edye Passage. There is a small beach on the east end of the island facing Prescott

Passage, but the best camping spot is farther up the passage on the northwest tip of Arthur. This is a well-protected sand beach with a beautiful view of Prescott Island. Beach camping is not practical but there are level spaces behind the fringe of trees. There is no fresh water.

Philip Cone Paddling northwest brings you to Stephens Island. Just west of Philip Cone is a narrow inlet that mostly dries at high tide. Good water can be obtained at the creek at the head of this inlet, and good camping can be had at a tiny beach just west of the inlet, virtually around the corner. There is thick salal at the edge of the beach but behind are lots of fairly level tent spaces. Be warned: The west coast of Stephens Island is exposed to Hecate Strait and, when the swells are running, confused seas around the headlands can cause havoc.

Skiakl Bay Skiakl Bay is a lagoon on the south side of Stephens Island. It can be divided into two parts: the wide mouth of the bay, which is exposed to waves from Hecate Strait, and the head of the bay, which is much more protected. About five creeks flow into the bay. The more placid part of Skiakl Bay is best explored at high tide, as is the case with all lagoons. Cloudy days, when the mists are partially obscuring the forested hills, are a magical experience.

Near the mouth of Skiakl Bay, at the north end of Skiakl Island, is a small oval island joined to Skiakl by a white sand beach. The sand gives way easily, and even at low tide you sink at least a foot while walking here. The beach is well protected from wind and waves and is mostly sand with a few barnacle-covered rocks. Behind the beach is a small area thick with moss and with enough space for several tents. There is no fresh water at the site, but water is available from numerous creeks at the head of Skiakl Bay.

China Islet With its spectacular view of the Tree Nobs, China Islet offers a superb campsite in fair weather. However, it is exposed to north and south winds. China Islet sticks out into Hecate Strait more than any other part of the Stephens Island complex. It is very rugged and forms a contrast to nearby Philip Island. The sand beach that joins these two islands is flat and exposed to the south. About 1.2 m (4 ft.) above the beach is a small, level wildflower meadow with plenty of room for tents. Avoid damaging the vegetation and tie down your tents well.

Tree Nob Group A photogenic spread of small islands off the north end of Stephens Island, the Tree Nobs form a kind of boundary between Chatham Sound and the north end of Hecate Strait. These charming little islands give the illusion of being tropical. There are so many of them, they afford some protection from Hecate Strait. Unfortunately, there are not many good campsites here. The best one is on a white sand beach adjoining Rushton Island. Rushton Island is an Indian Reserve, so you must receive permission to camp from the Metlakatla Indian Council.

Getting to the Tree Nobs is easiest from the north end of Stephens Island, though you need to watch the strong current between Chatham Sound and Hecate Strait.

TRIP 44 Dundas and Melville Islands
SKILL: Advanced
TIME: 3–10 days
HAZARDS: Winds, currents and boat traffic
ACCESS: Fairview floats
CHARTS: 3957 · Approaches to Prince Rupert Harbour · 1:40,000
3958 · Prince Rupert Harbour · 1:20,000
3959 · Hudson Bay Passage · 1:40,000
3960 · Approaches to Portland Inlet · 1:40,000
TIDE BOOK: Vol. 7

LAUNCHING
To reach the Fairview floats in Prince Rupert, drive west along Highway 16 as though you were heading to the B.C. and Alaskan ferry docks. As you approach the terminals, keep in the left lane and head for the Coast Guard trailer and the fish plant. Between those two buildings is the government wharf. If you are unloading a lot of gear, be sure not to get in the way of the commercial traffic. Free parking can be found along the road or at the ferry terminal.

Launch from the Fairview floats, cross the harbour and continue through Venn Passage past Metlakatla over to Tugwell Island. From Tugwell, head to the Lucy Islands. Be wary of the extensive rocky shoal that juts out from Tugwell's south end.

∧ *Outer coast, Porcher Island,* PETER MCGEE

From the Fairview floats to Tugwell Island typically takes 3–4 hours in these relatively protected waters. The crossing from Tugwell to the Lucy Islands puts you in the middle of Chatham Sound and takes about 2–3 hours. This crossing can be dangerous even in fair weather. Strong outflows blow down Portland Canal into the north end of Chatham Sound and can build up steep, heavy seas around the Lucy Islands, especially during an ebb tide.

SITES

Lucy Islands The Lucy Islands are halfway between Tugwell and Melville Islands in the middle of Chatham Sound. The largest island is narrow with a white sand beach at one end and an automated light-house at the other; a boardwalk connects the two ends. The campsite is just off the beach on the west side of the largest island. It has an outhouse, which is a rarity in these parts. The island is frequented by powerboats during the summer. Nevertheless, the Lucy Islands are an excellent stopping-off point for kayakers paddling to or from Melville Island. There is usually no fresh water on the island during the summer months.

From here you will cross Chatham Sound to Melville Island. This should be done with caution; the passage takes about 2 hours, weather permitting.

Melville Island and Dunira Island Lagoon The west side of Melville and Dunira Islands forms a complex maze of small islands and spacious lagoons that is wonderful for exploring in kayaks. Because of the variety of seacoasts all in one place, this area has become a popular spot for kayak charters and groups. A number of these islands have suitable camping spots, both for large and small groups, and fresh water is available from creeks on both islands.

Island #42 (chart 3959) offers a superb campsite that is often frequented by powerboaters in the summer. There is a rock fireplace and beaten trails as well as cleared space for a number of tents. The beach is white sand, shell and gravel and very protected. Water can be found from various creeks on Melville Island.

Island #35 (chart 3959) offers a well-protected, flat sand beach that is accessible at any tide. A couple of places behind the beach are suitable for tents, though there are lots of deadfalls and thick devil's club. There is a small stagnant creek to the south that can be reached by walking or paddling along the shore.

From these islands you will cross Hudson Bay Passage and head to Edith Harbour on Dundas Island, preferably within a few hours of high tide slack.

Dundas Island Although the west coast of Dundas is exposed to the swells of Dixon Entrance, Edith Harbour, a tidal narrows at the southwestern tip of Dundas, is a peaceful sanctuary. It is so protected by topography that even if there were a gale out in Dixon Entrance, you would never know it. The harbour has several reversing rapids, fascinating rock formations and a beautiful painted cliff—a wonderful place to kayak.

Just south of Edith Harbour on the west side of Dundas is Island #50 (chart 3959). A small beach with rock outcroppings connects this island to Dundas. The beach is well protected, with lots of room for tents behind it.

From here you can double back and head north along the spectacular west coast of Dundas, continuing as far as the island's north coast, just east of the White Islets. The east coast of Dundas is not recommended paddling: it is monotonous and affords no shelter. Dundas Island is best visited in the spring or fall when the mosquitoes are not so ferocious.

ADDITIONAL ROUTES

Prince Rupert is surrounded by beautiful islands, channels and inlets that are accessible to a wide range of kayaking abilities. Prince Rupert Harbour, Tuck Inlet, Venn Passage, Kloiya Bay and Dodge Cove are all suitable trips for beginner paddlers, as are the trips to the Salt Lakes and Butze Rapids described below. In contrast, the trip to Port Essington requires intermediate level skills.

Salt Lakes Most people who have lived in Prince Rupert for more than a few years have heard of the area locally known as Salt Lakes, the old local swimming hole for Ruperites. Formerly connected to the ocean, it was dammed to keep it warmer than the ocean. The float, changing house and boardwalk have all deteriorated but the lakes are still worth a visit. To get here, depart from Fairview floats (see above) and paddle straight across to the north side of Prince Rupert Harbour. Have a chart handy so you know which of those inlets leads to the Salt Lakes. You are looking for Russel Arm and will know you've reached it when you see a group of funky shacks lining both sides. A footpath to Salt Lakes can be reached from the end of Russel Arm to the right of the rapids. The rapids are navigable from high to midtide, except for the passage to the very last lake, which requires a 6.7-m (22-ft.) tide.

Seal Cove to Butze Rapids One of the most pleasant, protected and picturesque paddles in the region is along Fern Passage from Seal Cove to Butze Rapids. The rapids, at full force, are impossible to miss, so it is easy to keep your distance while you admire this raw force of nature. At high water slack, however, they are no more than flat water with ripples. To get there, leave from the Seal Cove floats, which are located at the north end of Prince Rupert. There is a place to launch kayaks right alongside the on-ramp to the floats. Keep well clear of any float planes landing or taking off. Bring charts and a tide table. It is best to leave towards the end of a flooding tide so the current will be with you as you round the Coast Guard base to your right. Strong currents at the narrow parts of Fern Passage can sometimes prevent upstream passage. Note the strong eddy current just east of the Coast Guard base. With mountains all around, this is a spectacular paddle not unlike being in a fiord. Butze Rapids is located just beyond the new sawmill.

Near Prince Rupert For those with a bit more experience, Ridley Island to the Kinahan Islands, Ridley Island to Digby Island and circumnavigating Digby are all good possibilities. Avoid these routes in strong southerlies, however, as both wind and water can really kick up. It will take at least 6 hours to circumnavigate Digby so it is best reserved for strong, fit paddlers. Port Edward to Osland is also a great paddle as long as you do it with the tides. Inverness Passage is almost always windy and choppy, and an inexperienced kayaker can easily be tipped—be careful.

Port Essington and Ecstall River Port Essington is a ghost town located on the nearly uninhabited south side of the Skeena River, at the mouth of the Ecstall. It was originally a stopping-off point for native people on the way up and down the Skeena. In the 1870s, Robert Cunningham put up a store and way station. In its heyday at the turn of the century, Port Essington had a hotel, two canneries and a multinational population. It died in the 1960s after a series of fires levelled most of the town. Nearby Ecstall is a very picturesque tidal river with steep sides and magnificent waterfalls.

To get to Port Essington from Prince Rupert, head east on Highway 16 (the Yellowhead). After passing Rainbow Summit, the highway descends. At the bottom of the long hill, the highway turns to the left and crosses McNeil River, a sluggish tidal river that flows into the Skeena. The bank is steep, but it is possible to launch here just before or at high water. It takes about 10 minutes to reach the Skeena. Once there, head straight across to Port Essington. The crossing should take 1–2 hours but may be longer depending on the current.

Crossing the Skeena River is not for beginners. Very strong outflow and inflow winds can whip up big standing waves. The best time to cross is at high water slack. Low water slack is not a good time unless you enjoy slogging through the mud and dragging your kayak over sandbars. Overcast days are preferable as the wind is usually calm.

After arriving at Port Essington, be prepared for a lot of bush-whacking—a machete would be handy. There are houses, a church and a schoolhouse buried in the bush, and good beachcombing for old bottles at low tide. Be sure to visit the mayor of Port Essington, which presently has a population of one. Len Croteau also runs the Port Essington Museum.

Heading south If you decide to go south of Prince Rupert down Grenville Channel, you will find camping spots at Stuart Bight and Nabannah Bay. If you go down Petrel Channel, there is some camping near the creek on the south side of the large elbow bend. For more information, check with the BCMTA.

Heading north Crossing the border to Alaska requires that you pass through U.S. Customs. (If possible, call the Ketchikan office before you go: tel.: 907-225-2291.) Once in Alaska, there is a lifetime of paddling opportunities, including the wild experience of paddling in glacial ice. One of the highlights of the area is the fishing town of Petersburg. Located on Mitkof Island near the mouth of the Stikine River, the LeConte Glacier and the humpback feeding grounds of Frederick Sound, Petersburg is a playground of natural delights.

If you are looking for campsites directly north of the border, try Tongass Island in Nakat Bay or the lighthouse at Tree Point in Revillagigedo Channel.

This guidebook now ends, perched on the Alaskan border. Beyond is a region where the landscape begins to overwhelm humans and the drama of the North takes over. One day, the marine trail that passes through Washington and B.C. will be joined to Alaska and beyond. That, however, is for another time and another book.

Useful Contacts

EMERGENCIES

U.S. Coast Guard, tel. 1-800-982-8813 or 911.

Group Portland, tel. (503) 240-9311.

SAFETY INFORMATION

Boat Washington, Webpage: www.boatwashington.org.

Oregon State Marine Board, P.O. Box 14145, 435 S. Commercial St., NE #400, Salem, OR 97309–5065. Tel. (503) 378-8587. Webpage: www.marinebd.osmb.state.or.us.

WEATHER & MARINE RADIO

National Oceanic and Atmospheric Administration (NOAA) National Weather Forecast Service Office and Marine Forecast Center, tel. (503) 261-9246. Webpage: www.noaa.gov.

MARINE CHARTS,
TIDE TABLES, MAPS & BOOKS

Alder Creek Kayak & Canoe, 250 NE Tomahawk Island Dr., Portland, OR 97217. Tel. (503) 285-0464. Webpage: www.aldercreek.com.

NOAA Distribution Branch, N/CG33, National Ocean Service, Riverdale, MD 20737–1199. Tel. (301) 436-6990, fax (301) 436-6829. Webpage: mapindex.nos.noaa.gov/. Phone or fax for a catalogue of nautical charts.

West Marine, 1176 N. Hayden Meadows Dr., Portland, OR 97217. Tel. (503) 289-9822.

GETTING THERE

Bus

Greyhound Lines, P.O. Box 660689, MS 490, Dallas, TX 75266–0689. Toll-free 1-800-231-2222. Webpage: www.greyhound.com.

Railway

Amtrak, toll-free 1-800-872-7245. Webpage: www.amtrak.com.

PARKS & TOURISM

Oregon State Parks, 1115 Commercial St. NE, Salem, OR 97301. Tel. (503) 378-6308. Webpage: www.prd.state.or.us.

Oregon Tourism Commission, 775 Summer St. NE, Salem OR 97301–1282. Tel. (503) 986-0000, fax (503) 986-0001. Webpage: www.traveloregon.com.

Vancouver-Clark Parks & Recreation, tel. (360) 619-1111. Webpage: www.ci.vancouver.wa.us/ parks-recreation.

Washington State Parks and Recreation Commission, 7150 Clearwater Lane, P.O. Box 42650, Olympia, WA 98504–2650. Tel. (360) 902-8844. Webpage: www.parks.wa.gov.

Washington State Tourism, tel. (360) 725-5052. Webpage:www.tourism.wa.gov.

NATIVE AMERICAN CONTACTS

Columbia River Inter-Tribal Fish Commission, 729 NE Oregon St., Suite 200, Portland, OR 97232. Tel. (503) 238-0667. Webpage: www.critfc.org.

EQUIPMENT RENTALS/TOURS

Alder Creek Kayak & Canoe, 250 NE Tomahawk Island Dr., Portland, OR 97217. Tel. (503) 285-0464. Webpage: www.aldercreek.com.

Ebb and Flow Paddlesports, 0604 SW Nebraska, Portland, OR 97201. Tel. (503) 245-1756. Webpage: www.ebbnflow.citysearch.com.

Lake River Kayak & Sporting Goods, 214 Pioneer, Ridgefield, WA 98642. Tel. (360) 887-2389.

Northwest Discoveries, P.O. Box 23171, Tigard, OR 97281. Tel. (503) 624-4829. Webpage: www.nwdiscoveries.com.

Pacific Wave, 21 Highway 101, Warrenton, OR 97145. Toll-free 1-888-223-9794.

Portland River Company, 0315 SW Montgomery, Suite 330, Portland, OR 97201. Tel. (503) 229-0551. Webpage: www.portlandrivercompany.com.

Scappoose Bay Kayaking, 57420 Old Portland Rd., Warren, OR 97053. Tel. (503) 397-2161. Webpage: www.scappoosebaykayaking.com.

Skamokawa Paddle Center, P.O. Box 212, 1391 West State Rd. 4, Skamokawa, WA 98647. Toll-free 1-888-920-2777.

KAYAKING & OUTDOOR ASSOCIATIONS

Lower Columbia Canoe Club, 17005 NW Meadowgrass Dr., Beaverton, OR 97006.

Oregon Ocean Paddling Society, P.O. Box 69641, Portland, OR 97239.

PDX Sea Kayaker, Webpage: seakayaker@yahoogroups.com.

Scappoose Bay Paddling Association, c/o Scappoose Bay Kayaking, 57420 Old Portland Rd., Warren, OR 97053. Tel. (503) 397-2161.

Southwest Washington Canoe Club, tel. (360) 274-6930.

Washington Kayak Club, c/o Mark Freeland, 5150 SW 326th Place, Federal Way, WA 98023. Tel. (hotline) (206) 433-1983. Webpage: www.washingtonkayakclub.org.

Washington Water Trails Association, 4649 Sunnyside Ave. N., Room 305, Seattle WA 98103–6900. Tel. (206) 545-9161, fax (206) 547-0350. Webpage: www.wwta.org.

PUGET SOUND (WASHINGTON STATE)

EMERGENCIES

U.S. Coast Guard, tel. (360) 734-1692 (Bellingham), tel. (425) 252-5281 (Everett), tel. (360) 452-2342 or

(360) 457-2226 or (360) 457-2200 (Port Angeles). To contact the Coast Guard on a cellular phone, tel. CG.

WEATHER & MARINE RADIO
National Oceanic and Atmospheric Administration (NOAA) National Weather Forecast Service Office, Seattle, tel. (206) 526-6087; Olympia NOAA broadcast: VHF WX3 (162.475 MHZ); Seattle NOAA broadcast: VHF WX1 (162.55 MHZ). Webpage: www.wrh.noaa.gov/seattle/.

MARINE CHARTS & TIDE TABLES
Captain's Navigation Supplies, Inc., 2500 16th Ave. W., Seattle, WA 98119. Toll-free 1-800-448-2278, tel. (206) 283-7242, fax (206) 261-4921. Webpage: www.captainsnautical.com.

GETTING THERE

Ferries
Black Ball Transport, 101 E. Railroad Ave., Port Angeles, WA 98362. Tel. (250) 386-2202 (Victoria), fax (250) 386-220; tel. (360) 457-4491 (Port Angeles), fax (360) 457-4493. Vehicle ferry between Port Angeles and Victoria. Webpage: www.cohoferry.com.

Clipper Navigation, Inc., 2701 Alaskan Way, Pier 69, Seattle, WA 98121. For reservations, tel. (250) 382-8100 (Victoria) or (206) 448-5000 (Seattle) or toll-free outside Seattle and Victoria 1-800-888-2535, fax (206) 443-2583. Webpage: www.victoriaclipper.com. Service between Victoria and Seattle: *Victoria Clipper* (passengers only) and *Princess Marguerite* (car ferry).

Washington State Ferries, 801 Alaskan Way, Seattle, WA 98104–1487. Tel. (206) 464-6400 (Seattle) or (250) 381-1551 (Victoria) or (250) 656-1531 (Sidney) or toll-free within Washington 1-800-843-3779. Webpage: www.wsdot.wa.gov/ferries/. Vehicle ferry from Anacortes to Sidney, B.C.; other routes available within Puget Sound.

Air
Baxter Aviation Ltd., 52 Anchor Way, Seaplane Terminal, Box 1110, Nanaimo, B.C. V9R 6E7. Toll-free 1-800-661-5599, tel. (250) 754-1066, fax (250) 754-1075. Webpage: www.baxterair.com. Destinations include San Juan Islands and Seattle.

Kenmore Air, Box 82064, Kenmore, WA 98028–0064. Toll-free 1-800-543-9595, tel. (425) 486-1257, fax (425) 485-4774. Webpage: www.kenmoreair_com/. Serving Seattle, Victoria and San Juan Islands by float plane. Adventure packages for kayaking and grizzly bear viewing in B.C. also available.

Bus
Greyhound Bus Lines, toll-free 1-800-231-2222. Webpage: www.greyhound.com.

Webpage for bus services in Washington State: www.wsdot.wa.gov/choices/bus.cfm.

PARKS & TOURISM
Washington Water Trails Association, 4649 Sunnyside Ave. N., Room 305, Seattle, WA 98103–6900. Tel. (206) 545-9161, fax (206) 547-0350. Webpage: www.wwta.org.

Washington State Parks and Recreation Commission, Box 42650, Olympia, WA 98504–2650. Toll-free (information center) 1-888-CAMPOUT. Webpage: www.parks.wa.gov.

NATIVE AMERICAN CONTACTS
Governor's Office of Indian Affairs, tel. (360) 753-2411.

EQUIPMENT RENTALS/TOURS
Aquasports, 7907–159th Place NE, Redmond, WA 98052. Tel. (425) 869-7067. Webpage: www.aquasports.com.

Backpackers Supply, 5206 S. Tacoma Way, Tacoma, WA 98409. Tel. (253) 472-4402, fax (253) 475-6575. Webpage: www.marmotmountain.com. Tours in the San Juan Islands and rentals.

BEWET (Boeing Employees Whitewater & Touring Club), Webpage: http://avsp.org/bewet/.

Blue Moon Explorations, Box 2568, Bellingham, WA 98227. Tel./fax (360) 856-5622. Tours in the San Juan Islands and rentals.

Cascade Canoe and Kayak Centers, P.O. Box 4173, Renton, WA 98957–4173. Tel. (425) 430-0111.

Elakah Expeditions, Box 4092-B, Bellingham, WA 98227. Toll-free 1-800-434-7270, tel. (360) 734-7270. Tours in the San Juan Islands.

Gig Harbor Kayak Center, 8809 N. Harborview Dr., Gig Harbor, WA 98335. Tel. (253) 851-7987. Webpage: www.clearlight.com/kayak/.

Northwest Outdoor Center, 2100 Westlake Ave. N., Seattle, WA 98109. Tel. (206) 281-9694, fax (206) 282-0690. Webpage: www.nwoc.com. Tours in the San Juan Islands and rentals.

Olympic Outdoor Center, 18971 Front St., Poulsbo, WA 98370. Tel. (360) 697-6095, fax (360) 697-1102. Webpage: www.kayakproshop.com. Tours in the San Juan Islands and rentals.

Olympic Raft and Kayak, 123 Lake Aldwell Rd., Port Angeles, WA 98363. Toll-free 1-888-452-1443, tel. (360) 452-1443, fax (360) 452-5268. Webpage: www.raftandkayak.com.

Outdoor Odysseys, 12003 23rd Ave. NE, Seattle, WA 98125. Toll-free 1-800-647-4621, tel./fax (206) 361-0717. Webpage: www.outdoorodysseys.com. Tours in the San Juan Islands.

Pacific Water Sports, 11011 Tukwila Intl. Blvd., Tukwila, WA 98168. Tel. (206) 246-9385. Webpage: www.pwskayaks.com.

Shearwater Adventure, P.O. Box 787, Eastsound, WA 98245. Tel. (360) 376-4699, fax (360) 376-2005. Webpage: www.shearwaterkayaks.com. Tours and classes in the San Juan Islands.

Vashon Island Kayak, P.O. Box 2957, Vashon, WA 98070. Tel. (206) 463-9257. Webpage: www.pugetsoundkayak.com. Rentals.

GENERAL CONTACTS (BRITISH COLUMBIA)

EMERGENCIES
Canadian Coast Guard, Victoria Rescue Centre, toll-free 1-800-567-5111 or cellular 311 B.C. Tel/Cantel. The Victoria Rescue Centre coordinates emergency responses for the entire B.C. coast. Webpage: www.pacific.ccg-gcc.gc.ca.

The Pacific regional webpage includes marine weather forecasts and information on marine communication and search and rescue.
Poison Control Centre, toll-free 1-800-567-8911.
Police/RCMP, tel. 911.
RCMP Coastal Watch, toll-free 1-800-855-6655.

WEATHER & MARINE RADIO

Environment Canada, Manager, Commercial Services, 120–1200 W. 73rd Ave., Vancouver, B.C. v6P 6H9. Tel. (604) 664-9080, fax (604) 664-9081. Webpage:www.weatheroffice.ec.gc.ca For purchase of *Marine Weather Hazards Manual* and other products.
Environment Canada Weather, tel. (604) 664-9010. Free recorded marine forecasts for Howe Sound, Strait of Georgia, Haro Strait and Juan de Fuca Strait.
VHF Weather Radio: WX1 (162.55 MHz), WX2 (162.40 MHz), WX3 (162.475 MHz) and 21B (161.65 MHz).
Weather One-on-One, tel. 1-900-565-5555. Talk directly to a weather forecaster for $1.95/minute, 2-minute minimum. Using a cellular phone, dial 0-955-656-5555. Credit card needed.

MARINE CHARTS, TIDE TABLES, MAPS & BOOKS

Canadian Hydrographic Service, Chart Sales and Distribution, Institute of Ocean Sciences, 9860 West Saanich Rd., Sidney, B.C. v8L 4B2. Tel. (250) 363-6358, fax (250) 363-6841. Webpage: www.chs-shc.dfo-mpo.gc.ca/pub/en.

Coastal Waters Recreation, Suite 547, 185–911 Yates St., Victoria, B.C. v8v 4Y9. Tel./fax (250) 383-5555. Webpage: www.coastalwatersrec.com. Recreation kayaking maps of Nootka Sound, Kyuquot Sound, Esperanza Inlet and Clayoquot Sound. Others available in the future.
Crown Publications Inc., 521 Fort St., Victoria, B.C. v8w 1E7. Tel. (250) 386-4636, fax (250) 386-0221. Webpage: www.crownpub.bc.ca. Specializes in government publications, nautical charts, topographical maps, marine books, natural history books and First Nations culture books.
Ecomarine, 1668 Duranleau St., Vancouver, B.C. v6H 3S4. Tel. (604) 689-7575, fax (604) 689-5926. Webpage: www.ecomarine.com. Kayaking books, laminated nautical charts, etc.
International Travel Maps & Books, 539 W. Pender St., Vancouver, B.C. v6B 1V5. Tel. (604) 687-3320. Second location at 530 W. Broadway, tel. (604) 879-3621. Extensive selection of books and nautical charts.
Nanaimo Maps and Charts, 8 Church St., Nanaimo, B.C. v9R 5H4. Toll-free 1-800-665-2513, tel. (250) 754-2513, fax 1-800-553-2313. One of the largest selections of Canadian and American nautical charts, from the West Coast to the Arctic.

GETTING THERE

Ferries
B.C. Ferries Corporation. Head Office: 1112 Fort St., Victoria, B.C. v8v 4V2. Tel. (250) 386-3431, fax (250) 381-5452. For 24-hour pre-recorded schedule information on major routes, tel.

(250) 381-5335 (in Victoria or outside
B.C.) or toll-free 1-888-223-3779
(within B.C.). Webpage:
www.bcferries.com. Includes all
schedules, fare information, reservations, etc. For automated (quicker)
vehicle reservations from the Lower
Mainland to Nanaimo, Duke Point or
Swartz Bay (fee for service), toll-free
1-888-724-5223 (within B.C.),
(604) 444-2890 (outside B.C.).

Air

Baxter Aviation Ltd., 52 Anchor Way,
Seaplane Terminal, Box 1110,
Nanaimo, B.C. v9r 6e7. Toll-free
1-800-661-5599, tel. (250) 754-1066,
fax (250) 754-1075. Destinations in-
clude the Gulf Islands, Nanaimo,
Victoria, Bamfield, Tofino,
Ucluelet, Alert Bay, Campbell River,
Comox/Courtenay, Gold River, Port
Alberni, Pender Harbour, Powell
River, Sechelt, Tahsis and Vancouver.

Coval Air, Mailing address: Box 1451,
Campbell River, B.C. v9w 5c7.
Street address: 3050 Spit Rd. Tel.
(250) 287-8371, fax (250) 287-8366.
Float plane charters and scheduled
flights, including Campbell River,
Cortes, Rivers Inlet, Vancouver and
numerous coastal destinations.

Harbour Air, 4760 Inglis Dr.,
Richmond, B.C. v7b 1w4. Toll-free
1-800-665-0212, tel./fax (604)-274-1277
(Vancouver), tel. (250) 385-2203 (Victoria), fax (250) 385-2234. Webpage:
www.harbour-air.com/. Scheduled
flights, charters and sightseeing by
float plane; serving Victoria, Vancouver, the Gulf Islands, Nanaimo, Pender Harbour, Masset, Prince Rupert
and Sandspit.

Kenmore Air, Box 82064, Kenmore, WA
98028-0064. Toll-free 1-800-543-9595,
tel. (425) 486-1257, fax (425) 485-4774.
Webpage: www.kenmoreair.com/.
Serving Seattle, Victoria and San
Juan Islands by float plane. Adventure
packages for kayaking and grizzly bear
viewing in B.C. are also available.

Pacific Coastal Airline, 117–4440 Cowley
Cres., Richmond, B.C. v7b 1b8.
Toll-free 1-800-663-2872, tel.
(604) 273-6864. Serving Bella Bella,
Powell River, Rivers Inlet, Port Hardy
and Vancouver.

Pacific Spirit Air, 3rd floor, Bellevue
Centre, 235–15th St., West Vancouver,
B.C. v7t 2x1. Toll-free tel./fax
1-800-665-2359. Scheduled flights and
charters throughout coastal B.C.

Sound Flight, Inc., Box 812, Renton,
WA 98057. Toll-free 1-800-825-0722,
tel. (425) 255-6500. Scheduled flights
(floats and wheels) from Seattle.
Destinations include Barkley Sound,
Ucluelet, Tofino, Johnstone Strait,
the Gulf Islands, the San Juan Islands,
Desolation Sound and the Discovery
Islands.

Vancouver Island Air, Box 727, Campbell River, B.C. v9w 6j3. Tel.
(250) 287-2433, fax (250) 286-3269.
Scheduled flights on wheels and
floats, serving Vancouver Island and
mainland destinations.

West Coast Air, Box 48197, Bentall
Centre, Vancouver, B.C. v7x 1n8.
Toll-free 1-800-347-2222, fax
(604) 688-7042. Scheduled flights
between Vancouver and Victoria,
and charter services to the Gulf
Islands by float plane.

Bus

Greyhound Canada, 850 16th St. SW, Calgary, AB P3B 3V8. Toll-free in Canada 1-800-661-8747, tel. (403) 260-0877. Webpage: www.greyhound.ca/. Servicing mainland British Columbia, including Prince Rupert.

Island Coach Lines (Gray Line of Victoria), 700 Douglas St., Victoria, B.C. V8W 2B3. Toll-free 1-800-318-0818 (within B.C.), tel. (250) 385-4411, fax (250) 388-9461. Webpage: www.victoriatours.com/. Servicing Vancouver Island.

Pacific Coach Lines, 1150 Station St., Vancouver, B.C. V6A 4C7. Tel. (604) 662-8074, fax (604) 681-1515, tel. (250) 385-4411 (Victoria). Webpage: www.pacificcoach.com. Servicing Victoria to Vancouver, and connecting to Vancouver International Airport.

Railway

VIA Rail Canada, 1150 Station St., Vancouver, B.C. V6A 4C7. Toll-free 1-888-842-7245. Webpage: www.viarail.ca/. Servicing Vancouver, Prince Rupert and points in between.

PARKS

B.C. Parks, Ministry of Water, Land and Air Protection, 800 Johnson St., 2nd floor, Victoria, B.C. V8V 1X4. Tel. (250) 387-5002, fax (250) 387-5757. Webpage: http://wlap.www.gov.bc.ca/bc.parks/. To make reservations for provincial parks, toll-free 1-800-689-9025, tel. (604) 689-9025 (March 15–Sept. 15).

Parks Canada Pacific Region, 300–300 W. Georgia St., Vancouver, B.C. V6B 6C6. Tel. (604) 666-0176, fax (604) 666-3508. Webpage: www.parkscanada.pch.gc.ca/. For information and reservations in national parks.

TOURISM & ACCOMMODATION

B.C. Adventure Network, Webpage: www.bcadventure.com/. A comprehensive Web site on tourist services, accommodation and transportation in B.C. An excellent source for vacation planning.

Hostelling International Canada, B.C. Region, 402–134 Abbott St., Vancouver, B.C. V6B 2K4. Toll-free 1-800-661-0020, tel. (604) 684-7111.

Tourism B.C., 812 Wharf St., Victoria, B.C. V8W 1T3. Toll-free 1-800-663-6000, tel. (604) 663-6000, fax (604) 801-5710 (Vancouver). Webpage: www.tourism.bc.ca. Tourism B.C. makes reservations for hotels, motels and B&Bs and distributes tourism guides, free of charge, including *B.C. Accommodations, B.C. Bed & Breakfast Directory* and *Outdoor & Adventure Guide.*

KAYAKING & OUTDOOR ASSOCIATIONS

B.C. Marine Trail Association, Webpage: www.bcmarinetrail.com.

Outdoor Recreation Council, 334–1367 W. Broadway Ave., Vancouver, B.C. V6H 4A9. Tel. (604) 737-3058, fax (604) 737-3666. Webpage: www.orcbc.ca. Advocacy body for outdoor recreational interests, with over 40 affiliates.

Pacific International Kayaking Association, 2415 Aladdin Cres., Abbotsford, B.C. V2S 5K7. PIKA organizes an annual sea kayaking symposium at Thetis Island, where paddlers can build their paddling skills.

Sea Kayak Association of B.C., Box 751, Stn. A, Vancouver, B.C. V6C 2N6.

WaveLength magazine, 2735 North Road, Gabriola Island, B.C. VOR 1X7. Tel. (250) 247-8858. Webpage: www.wavelengthmagazine.com.

FIRST NATIONS

First Nations Summit, tel. (604) 990-9939. Webpage: www.fns.bc.ca.

Union of B.C. Indian Chiefs, tel. (604) 684 0231. Webpage: www.ubcic.bc.ca.

OTHER CONTACTS

Department of Fisheries and Oceans, Pacific Region, tel. (604) 666-0384. Webpage: www.dfo-mpo.gc.ca

Enquiry B.C., tel. (604) 387-6121 (Victoria), tel. (604) 660-2421 (Vancouver), toll-free 1-800-663-7867 (elsewhere in B.C.). Provides any provincial government phone or fax number and connects you free of charge.

GULF ISLANDS

EMERGENCIES

Saltspring Island RCMP, tel. 911 or (250) 537-5555.

Gabriola Island RCMP, tel. 911 or (250) 247-8333.

WEATHER & MARINE RADIO

Comox Weather Services, tel. (250) 339-8044.

Environment Canada: Marine weather recording for Victoria, tel. (250) 363-6717.

VHF Weather Radio: channel 21B (161.65 MHZ).

Weather Radio Canada, Victoria, 1260 KHZ AM band.

GETTING THERE

See GENERAL CONTACTS (B.C.) for information about B.C. Ferries and air carriers.

Water Taxis

Gulf Island Water Taxi Ltd., 181 Old Divide Rd., Saltspring Island, B.C. V8K 2G7. Tel. (250) 537-2510, fax (250) 537-9202. Servicing the Gulf Islands from Gabriola to Saturna.

PARKS AND TOURISM

B.C. Forest Service, South Island District, 4885 Cherry Creek Rd., Port Alberni, B.C. V9Y 8E9. Tel. (250) 731-3000.

BC Parks, Goldstream Office, Ministry of Water, Land and Air Protection, 2930 Trans-Canada Highway, R.R. 6, Victoria, B.C. V9B 5T9. Tel. (250) 391-2300, fax (250) 478-9211. Webpage: http://wlap.www.gov.bc.ca/bc.parks/. To make reservations for provincial parks, toll-free 1-800-689-9025, tel. (604) 689-9025 (March 15–Sept. 15).

Canada Customs, Bedwell Harbour on Pender Island. All foreign vessels and individuals entering the country must check in. Toll-free 1-888-226-7277 (to contact Customs upon arrival).

Gabriola Travel Infocentre, 575 North Road, Box 249, Gabriola Island, B.C. VOR 1X0. Toll-free 1-888-284-9332.

Parks Canada, Coastal BC Field Unit, 2nd Floor, 711 Broughton St., Victoria, B.C. v8w 1e2. Toll-free 1-800-748-7275.

Nanaimo Travel Infocentre, toll-free 1-800-663-7337.

Qualicum Travel Infocentre, tel. (250) 752-9532.

Saltspring Island Travel Infocentre, 121 Lower Ganges Rd., Saltspring Island, B.C. v8k 2t1. Tel. (250) 537-5252 or (250) 537-4223, fax (250) 537-4276. Webpage: www.saltspringtoday.com.

FIRST NATIONS

Lyackson First Nation, 9137 Chemainus Rd., Chemainus, B.C. vor 1k5. Tel. (250) 246-5019, fax (250) 246-5059. Traditional territory includes Valdes Island.

Penelakut Indian Band, Box 360, Chemainus, B.C. vor 1k0. Tel. (250) 246-2321, fax (250) 246-2725. For permission to camp at Tent Island 1r.

Qualicum Indian Band, 5850 River Rd., Qualicum Beach, B.C. v9k 1z5. Tel. (250) 757-9337, fax (250) 757-9898. Operates a commercial campground (summer only) accessible by kayak.

Snuneymuxw Band (Nanaimo), 668 Center St., Nanaimo, B.C. v9r 4z4. Tel. (250) 740-2300.

Tsawout Indian Band, Box 121, Saanichton, B.C. v8m 2c3. Tel. (250) 652-9101, fax (250) 652-9114. For permission to camp on Saturna Island 1r.

EQUIPMENT RENTALS/TOURS

Alberni Outpost, 3200 North Island Hwy, Country Club Centre, Nanaimo, B.C. v9t 1w1. Tel. 1-866-760-0011. Webpage: www.albernioutpost.com. Tours, lessons, rentals.

Andale Kayaking, Saltspring Island, B.C. v8k 1b2. Tel. (250) 537-0700. Webpage:http://saltspring.gulfislands.com/allanmather. Rentals, lessons, tours.

Blue Vista Resort, 563 Arbutus Dr., Mayne Island, B.C. von 2j0. Tel. 1-877-535-2424. Webpage: www.bluevistaresort.com. Rentals, lessons, tours.

Casa Blanca By the Sea, 1707 El Verano Dr., Gabriola Island, B.C. vor 1x0. Tel. (250) 247-9824. b&b, rentals, tours.

Coastal Connections, 1027 Roslyn Rd., Victoria, B.C. v8s 4r4. Toll-free 1-800-840-4453 (North America), tel. (250) 480-9560, fax (250) 598-7043. Guided kayaking, hiking or sailing tours in the Gulf Islands.

Comox Valley Kayaks Ltd., 2020 Cliffe Ave., Courtenay, B.C. v9n 2l3. Toll-free 1-888-545-5595, tel. (250) 334-2628. Webpage: www.comoxvalleykayaks.com. Rentals and tours on Vancouver Island.

Ecosummer Expeditions, Box 1765, Clearwater, B.C. v0e 1n0. Toll-free 1-800-465-8884, fax (604) 669-3244. Webpage: www.ecosummer.com. Guided tours.

Gabriola Cycle and Kayak Ltd., 910 Clarendon Rd., S-1, C-23, Gabriola Island, B.C. vor 1x0. Tel. (250) 247-8277. Webpage: www.gck.ca. Tours, rentals, lessons.

Gulf Island Kayaking, S-24, C-34, Galiano Island, B.C. von 1p0. Tel./fax: (250) 539-4224. Webpage: www.seakayak.ca. Tours and rentals.

Hornby Ocean Kayaks, Box 1-11, Hornby Island, B.C. vor 1z0. Tel./fax (250) 335-2726. Tours, rentals and lessons.

Island Escapades, Fulford-Ganges Rd., Saltspring Island, B.C. V8K 2T9. Toll-free 1-888-529-2567, tel. (250) 537-2571. Webpage: www.islandescapades.com. Tours, lessons, rentals, sales.

Island Outdoor Centre, 610 Oyster Bay Rd., Ladysmith, B.C. V9G 1A5. Tel. (250) 245-7887. Webpage: www.islandoutdoorcentre.com. Rentals, tours, sales.

Jim's Kayaking, Gabriola Island, B.C. Mailing address: 387 Lyngail Place, Nanaimo, B.C. VOR 1X1. Tel. (250) 247-8335 or (250) 751-5887. Webpage: www.jimskayaking.com. Tours, rentals, lessons.

Kayak Pender Island, 2319 Mackinnon Rd., Pender Island, B.C. VON 2M1. Tel. (250) 629-6939. Webpage: www.kayakpenderisland.com. Tours, lessons, rentals.

Mayne Island Kayak & Canoe Rentals Inc., C-54, Miners Bay, Mayne Island, B.C. VON 2J0. Tel./fax (250) 539-5599. Webpage: www.maynekayak.com.

Mouat Point Kayaks, 1615 Storm Cres., R.R. 2, Pender Island, B.C. VON 2M2. Tel. (250) 629-6767.

Ocean River Sports, 1437 Store St., Victoria, B.C. V8W 3J6. Tel. (250) 381-4233, fax (250) 361-3536. Webpage: www.oceanriver.com/. Tours, lessons and kayaking supplies. Rentals in downtown Victoria and Sidney.

Saltspring Kayaking Ltd., 2935 Fulford-Ganges Rd., Saltspring Island, B.C. VOS 1CO. Tel. (250) 653-4222. Rentals and tours.

Seadog Kayaking, Box 45, R.R. 1, Nanoose Bay, B.C. VOR 2RO. Tel./fax (250) 468-5778. Webpage: www.nanaimo.ark.com/~seadog/. Tours, lessons and rentals, including Jedediah Island and Ballenas/Winchelsea Islands.

Sea Otter Kayaking, 1186 North End Rd., Saltspring Island, B.C. V8K 1M1. Tel. (250) 537-5678.

Strathcona Outfitters, 2–6683 Mary Ellen Dr., Nanaimo, B.C. V9V 1T7. Tel. (250) 390-0400.

Tree Island Kayaking Co., 3025 Comox Rd., Courtenay, B.C. V9N 3P7. Tel. (250) 339-0580. Lessons, tours and rentals.

Vancouver Island Canoe & Kayak Centre, 575 Pembroke St., Victoria, B.C. V8T 1H3. Toll free 1-877-921-9365, tel. (250) 361-9365, fax (250) 361-9375. Webpage: www.canoeandkayak-centre.com. Rentals, lessons, tours, repairs and sales.

Wilderness Kayaking Co., 1130 Bazett Rd., Duncan, B.C. V9L 5S8. Tel./fax (250) 746-0151. Tours, rentals and lessons.

Wildheart Adventures, 2774 Barnes Rd., Nanaimo, B.C. V9R 5K2. Tel. (250) 722-3683, fax (250) 722-2175. Tours throughout the Gulf Islands and Vancouver Island.

IN AND AROUND VANCOUVER

EMERGENCIES
Tel. 911.

WEATHER & MARINE RADIO
Canadian Coast Guard Weather Report, tel. (604) 666-3655. Continuous marine recording.

Vancouver Coast Guard Radio,
tel. (604) 775-8920. Webpage:
www.pacific.ccg-gcc.gc.ca. For
weather information or to file a float
plan.
VHF **Weather Radio:** channel WX3
(162.475 MHZ).

GETTING THERE
See GENERAL CONTACTS (B.C.) for
information about B.C. Ferries and
air carriers.

PARKS & TOURISM
B.C. Forest Service, Vancouver Region,
2100 Labieux Rd., Nanaimo, B.C.
V9T 6E9. Tel. (250) 751-7001, fax
(250) 751-7190. Webpage:
www.for.gov.bc.ca.
BC Parks, Lower Mainland Parks District, 1610 Mt. Seymour Rd., North
Vancouver, B.C. V7G 1L3. Tel. (604)
924-2200, fax (604) 924-2244. Webpage: www.elp.gov.bc.ca.
Greater Vancouver Regional Parks,
4330 Kingsway, Burnaby, B.C. V5H
4G8. Tel. (604) 432-6355, fax (604)
432-6296. Webpage: www.gvrd.bc.ca.
Travel Infocentre, 200 Burrard St.,
Vancouver, B.C. V6C 3L6. Tel.
(604) 683-2000, fax (604) 282-6839.

FIRST NATIONS
Musqueam Nation, 6735 Salish Dr.,
Vancouver, B.C. V6N 4C4.
Tel. (604) 263-3261, fax (604) 263-4212.
Semiahmoo First Nation, 16049 Beach
Rd., Surrey, B.C. V3S 9R6. Tel. (604)
536-3101, fax (604) 536-6116. Webpage: www.semiahmoofirstnation.org.
Squamish Nation, 320 Seymour Blvd.,
North Vancouver, B.C. V7L 2J3,
tel. (604) 980-4553, fax (604) 980-
4523. Webpage: www.squamish.net.

Tsleil-Waututh First Nation,
3075 Takaya Dr., North Vancouver,
B.C. V7H 2V6. Tel. (604) 929-3454,
fax (604) 929-4714.

EQUIPMENT RENTALS/TOURS
Adventure Fitness, cell (604) 715-7174.
Seasonally located. Sales and rentals.
BC Dive and Kayak Adventures,
1695 W. 4th Ave., Vancouver, B.C.
V6J 1L9. Tel. (604) 732-1344,
fax (604) 732-1373. Webpage:
www.bcdive.com. Retail.
Deep Cove Canoe & Kayak Centre,
Mailing address: 2007 Rockcliff Rd.,
North Vancouver, B.C. V7G 1X3.
Street address: 2156 Banbury Rd.,
North Vancouver. Tel. (604) 929-
2268, fax (604)924-2049. Webpage:
www.deepcovekayak.com. Rentals,
tours and lessons; open spring
through fall.
Ecomarine Ocean Kayak Centre,
1668 Duranleau St., Vancouver,
B.C. V6H 3S4. Tel. (604) 689-7575
(store), tel. (604) 689-7520 (school),
fax (604) 689-5926. Webpage:
www.ecomarine.com. Extensive
retail selection, including
laminated charts, books, kayaking
gear, signal devices, etc. Tours,
rentals and lessons.
Natural West Coast Adventures,
1308 Everall St., White Rock, B.C.
V4B 3S6. Tel./fax (604) 535-7985.
Webpage: www.bckayaks.com.
Instruction, tours and rentals.
Ocean West Expeditions Ltd., Toll-free
1-800-660-0051, tel. (604) 688-5770.
Webpage: www.ocean-west.com.
Rentals (English Bay beach) and
lessons. Tours in Gulf Islands, Johnstone Strait and Desolation Sound.

Western Canoeing & Kayaking, Box 115, 1717 Salton Rd., Abbotsford, B.C. v2s 4n8. Tel. (604) 853-9320, fax (604) 852-6933. Webpage: www.westerncanoekayak.com. Rentals and sales.

HOWE SOUND

EMERGENCIES
Squamish RCMP, tel. 911 or (604) 898-9611.

WEATHER & MARINE RADIO
Canadian Coast Guard Weather Report. Tel. (604) 666-3655. Continuous marine recording.
Vancouver Coast Guard Radio, tel. (604) 775-8920. For weather information or to file a float plan.
VHF Weather Radio: channel WX3 (162.475 MHZ).

GETTING THERE
See GENERAL CONTACTS (B.C.) for information about B.C. Ferries and air carriers.

Water Taxis
Cormorant Marine Water Taxi, R.R. 1, A-4, Bowen Island, B.C. von 1g0. Cell (604) 250-2630, tel. (604) 947-2243, fax 947-9615.
Gambier Island Water Taxi, R.R. 3, Gibsons, B.C. von 1v0. Cell (604) 740-1133, tel. (604) 886-8321. Will also tow kayaks.
Squamish Tug, Box 1099, Squamish, B.C. vom 3g0. Tel. (604) 898-3733 (24 hrs), fax (604) 898-9177.

PARKS & TOURISM
B.C. Forest Service, Squamish District, 42000 Loggers Lane, Squamish, B.C. von 3g0. Tel. (604) 898-2100, fax

(604) 898-2191. Webpage: www.for.gov.bc.ca/dsq.
BC Parks, Garibaldi/Sunshine Coast District (Ministry of Water, Land and Air Protection, Lower Mailand Region, Environmental Stewarship Office), Box 220, Brackendale, B.C. von 1h0. Tel. (604) 898-3678, fax (604) 898-4171. Webpage: http://wlap.www.gov.bc.ca/bc.parks/. To make reservations for provincial parks, toll-free 1-800-689-9025, tel. (604) 689-9025 (March 15–Sept. 15).
Squamish/Howe Sound Visitor Information Centre, 37950 Cleveland Ave., Box 1009, Squamish, B.C. von 3g0. Tel. (604) 892-9244, fax (604) 892-2034. Webpage: www.squamishchamber.com.

FIRST NATIONS
Squamish Nation, 320 Seymour Blvd., North Vancouver, B.C. v7l 2j3. Tel. (604) 980-4553, fax (604) 980-4523. Webpage: www.squamish.net.

EQUIPMENT RENTALS/TOURS
Bowen Island Sea Kayaking, Box 87, Bowen Island, B.C. von 1g0. Tel. (604) 947-9266, toll-free 1-800-60-KAYAK, fax (604) 947-9717. Tours, instruction and rentals.
See also GULF ISLANDS and IN AND AROUND VANCOUVER.

SUNSHINE COAST

EMERGENCIES
Tel. 911.
Sunshine Coast RCMP, tel. (604) 885-2266.

WEATHER & MARINE RADIO

Canadian Coast Guard Weather Report, Vancouver. Tel. (604) 666-3655. Continuous marine recording.

Vancouver Coast Guard Radio, tel. (604) 775-8920. For weather information or to file a float plan.

VHF **Weather Radio:** channel 21B (161.65 MHZ).

GETTING THERE

See GENERAL CONTACTS (B.C.) for information about B.C. Ferries and air carriers.

Water Taxis

Egmont Water Taxi, R.R. 1, S-9, C-1, Garden Bay, B.C. VON 1S0. Tel./fax (604) 883-2092. Serving Desolation Sound and the Sunshine Coast.

PARKS & TOURISM

B.C. Forest Service, Sunshine Coast District, 7077 Duncan St., Powell River, B.C. V8A 1W1. Tel. (604) 485-0700, fax (604) 485-0799. Webpage: www.for.gov.bc.ca/dsc.

B.C. Parks, Garibaldi/Sunshine Coast District (Ministry of Water, Land and Air Protection, Lower Mainland Region, Environmental Stewardship Office), Box 220, Brackendale, B.C. VON 1H0. Tel. (604) 898-3678, fax (604) 898-4171. Webpage: http://wlap.www.gov.bc.ca/bc.parks/. To make reservations for provincial parks, toll-free 1-800-689-9025, tel. (604) 689-9025 (March 15–Sept. 15).

Gibsons Travel Infocentre, Box 1190, 900 Gibsons Way, Gibsons, B.C. VON 1V0. Tel. (604) 886-2325, fax (604) 886-2379. Webpage: www.gibsonschamber.com.

Sechelt Travel Infocentre, Box 360, Trail Bay Centre, Sechelt, B.C. VON 3A0. Tel. (604) 885-0662, fax (604) 885-0691.

FIRST NATIONS

Sechelt Indian Band, Box 740, Sechelt, B.C. VON 3A0. Tel. (604) 885-2273, fax (604) 885-3490.

EQUIPMENT RENTALS/TOURS

Halfmoon Bay Sea Kayaks, 7787 Lohn Rd., Halfmoon Bay, B.C. VOM 1Y0. Tel. (604) 885-2948. Webpage: www.halfmoonseakayaks.com. Sales, lessons, rentals and tours.

Pedals & Paddles, Box 2601, Tillicum Bay Marina, Sechelt, B.C. VON 3A0. Toll-free 1-866-885-6440, tel. (604) 885-6440, fax (604) 885-3064. Webpage: www.pedalspaddles.com. Rentals, lessons and trip planning.

Seadog Kayaking, 3521 Dolphin Dr., Nanoose Bay, B.C. V9P 9JP. Toll-free 1-866-468-5778, tel. (250) 468-5778. Webpage: www.seadog.bc.ca. Tours, lessons and rentals, including Jedediah Island and Ballenas/Winchelsea Islands in the Nanaimo area.

Sunshine Kayaking, Box 35, Gibsons, B.C. VON 1V0. Tel. (604) 886-9760. Webpage: www.sunshinekayaking.com. Day tours, instruction and rentals.

Tzoonie Outdoor Adventures Ltd., Box 157, Sechelt, B.C. VON 3A0. Tel. (604) 885-9802, fax (604) 885-9826. Webpage: www.tzoonie.com. Operates Tzoonie Wilderness Camp.

DESOLATION SOUND

EMERGENCIES

Powell River RCMP, tel. 911 or (604) 485-3400.

WEATHER & MARINE RADIO

Environment Canada,
tel. (250) 339-0748. Continuous
weather recording, Johnstone Strait
to Nanaimo.

North Island Marine Report, Campbell
River, tel. (250) 286-3575.

Comox Coast Guard Radio,
tel. (250) 339-3613. For weather
information or to file a float plan.

VHF Weather Radio: channel WX1
(162.550 MHZ).

GETTING THERE

See GENERAL CONTACTS (B.C.) for
information about B.C. Ferries and
other air carriers.

Air

Island West/Rush Air, Box 728, Campbell River, B.C. V9W 6J3. Tel. (250)
287-7555, fax (250) 287-7760. Webpage: www.islandwestair.com. Can
provide drop-off service to remote
areas; 2 hard-shelled boats maximum
per trip.

Water Taxis

Discovery Launch Water Taxi,
Box 164, Campbell River, B.C.
V9W 5A7. Tel. (250) 287-7577,
fax (250) 923-7700.

Lund Water Taxi, Box 196, Lund, B.C.
VON 2G0. Tel. (604) 483-9749. Service from Lund to Cortes Island.

Sutil Charters, Box 82, Heriot Bay,
Quadra Island, B.C. V0P 1H0.
Tel. (250) 285-3689. Webpage:
www.sutilcharters.com.

PARKS & TOURISM

**B.C. Forest Service, Sunshine Coast
District,** 7077 Duncan St., Powell
River, B.C. V8A 1W1. Tel. (604)
485-0700, fax (604) 485-0799.

**BC Parks, Ministry of Water, Land and
Air Protection, Lower Mainland
Region, Environmental Stewardship Office,** Box 220, Brackendale,
B.C. VON 1H0. Tel. (604) 898-3678,
fax (604) 898-4171. Webpage:
http://wlap.www.gov.bc.ca/bc.parks/.
To make reservations for provincial
parks, toll-free 1-800-689-9025, tel.
(604) 689-9025 (March 15–Sept. 15).

Powell River Travel Infocentre,
4690 Marine Ave., Powell River,
B.C. V8A 2L1. Tel. (604) 485-4701,
fax (604) 485-2822.

FIRST NATIONS

Homalco Indian Band, 1218 Bute Cres.,
Campbell River, B.C. V9H 1G5.
Tel. (250) 923-4979, fax (250) 923-
4987. Discovery Islands, Desolation
Sound and Bute Inlet.

Klahoose Indian Band, Box 9, Squirrel
Cove, Cortes Island, B.C. V0P 1K0.
Tel. (250) 935-6536, fax (250) 935-
6997.

Sliammon Native Council, R.R. 2,
Sliammon Rd., Powell River, B.C.
V8A 4Z3. Tel. (604) 483-9646,
fax (604) 483-9769

EQUIPMENT RENTALS/TOURS

Coast Mountain Expeditions, Box 25,
Surge Narrows, B.C. V0P 1W0.
Tel. (250) 285-2823. Webpage:
www.coastmountainexpeditions.com.
Multi-day expeditions, lodge, instruc-
tion.

Misty Isles Adventures, Manson's Landing, Cortes Island, B.C. V0P 1K0.
Tel. (250) 935-6756. Webpage:
www.island.net/~mistyis/. Tours and
rentals.

Powell River Sea Kayaks, C63, R.R. 2, Malaspina Rd., Powell River, B.C. v8a 4z3. Toll-free 1-866-617-4444, tel. (604) 483-2160, fax (604) 483-2388. Webpage: www.bcseakayak.com. Rentals. Closed in winter.

Wolfson Creek Canoe Rentals, 9537 Nassichuk Rd., Powell River, B.C. v8a 5c1. Tel. (604) 487-1699, fax (604) 487-4445. Webpage: www.canoeingbc.com. Lessons and guiding.

DISCOVERY ISLANDS

EMERGENCIES

Campbell River RCMP, tel. 911 or (250) 286-6221.

Quadra Island RCMP, tel. 911 or (250) 285-3631.

WEATHER & MARINE RADIO

Comox Coast Guard Radio, tel. (250) 339-3613. For weather information or to file a float plan.

Environment Canada, tel. (250) 339-0748. Continuous weather recording, Johnstone Strait to Nanaimo.

North Island Marine Report, Campbell River, tel. (250) 286-3575.

VHF Weather Radio: channels wx1 (162.550 MHz) and 21B (161.65 MHz).

GETTING THERE

See GENERAL CONTACTS (B.C.) or information about B.C. Ferries and air carriers. For water taxis, see DESOLATION SOUND.

PARKS & TOURISM

B.C. Forest Service, Campbell River District, 370 S. Dogwood St., Campbell River, B.C. v9w 6y7. Tel. (250) 286-9300, fax (250) 286-9490.

BC Parks, Rathtrevor Office, Ministry of Water, Land and Air Protection, Box 1479, Parksville, B.C. v9p 2h4. Tel. (250) 954-4600, fax (250) 248-8584. Webpage: http://wlap.www.gov.bc.ca/bc.parks/. To make reservations for provincial parks, toll-free 1-800-689-9025, tel. (604) 689-9025 (March 15–Sept. 15).

Campbell River Visitor Infocentre, 1235 Shoppers Row, Box 400, Campbell River, B.C. v9w 5b6. Tel. (250) 287-4636, fax (250) 286-6490.

FIRST NATIONS

Cape Mudge Indian Band, Box 220, Quathiaski Cove, B.C. v0p 1n0. Tel. (250) 285-3316, fax (250) 285-2400. Quadra Island and area. Cape Mudge Museum and Cultural Centre, tel. (250) 285-3733.

Homalco Indian Band, 1218 Bute Cres., Campbell River, B.C. v9h 5g1. Tel. (250) 923-4979, fax (250) 923-4987. Discovery Islands, Desolation Sound and Bute Inlet.

Klahoose Indian Band, Box 9, Squirrel Cove, Cortes Island, B.C. v0p 1k0. Tel. (250) 935-6536, fax (250) 935-6997. Cortes Island and area.

Kwakiutl District Council, 1400A Drake Rd., Campbell River, B.C. v9w 7k6. Tel. (250) 286-9766, fax (250) 949-9677. Council of nine bands on northeast Vancouver Island, from Comox to Port Hardy.

EQUIPMENT RENTALS/TOURS

Coast Mountain Expeditions, Box 25, Surge Narrows, B.C. v0p 1w0. Tel. (250) 285-2823. Webpage: www.coastmountainexpeditions.com. Multi-day expeditions, lodge, instruction.

Comox Valley Kayaks Ltd.,
2020 Cliffe Ave., Courtenay, B.C.
V9N 2L3. Toll-free 1-888-545-5595,
tel. (250) 334-2628. Webpage:
www.comoxvalleykayaks.com. Sales,
lessons, tours and rentals.

Discovery Islands Lodge, Box 570, Heriot
Bay, Quadra Island, B.C. V0P 1H0.
Tel. (250) 285-2823. Webpage:
www.discovery-islands-lodge.com.
Tours, accomodations and rentals.

Strathcona Outfitters, 134–1416 Island
Hwy., Campbell River, B.C. V9W
8C9. Tel. (250) 287-4453, fax (250)
287-7354. Retail sales and rental of
camping and kayaking gear.

Strathcona Park Lodge, Box 2160,
Campbell River, B.C. V9W 5C9.
Tel. (250) 286-3122, fax (250) 286-6010.
Webpage: www.strathcona.bc.ca.
Wilderness courses and outdoor
adventures.

JOHNSTONE STRAIT

EMERGENCIES
Port McNeill RCMP, tel. 911
or (250) 956-4441.
Alert Bay RCMP,
tel. 911 or (250) 974-5544.

WEATHER & MARINE RADIO
Comox Coast Guard Radio,
tel. (250) 339-3613. For weather
information or to file a float plan.
Environment Canada. Continuous
weather recording, tel. (250) 974-
5305, northeast Vancouver Island;
(250) 339-0748, Johnstone Strait to
Nanaimo.
North Island Marine Weather Office,
Port Hardy, tel. (250) 949-7148.
VHF Weather Radio: channel 21B
(161.65 MHZ).

Weather Radio Canada, Port Hardy,
130.7 MHZ.

GETTING THERE
See GENERAL CONTACTS (B.C.) for
information about B.C. Ferries and
other air carriers.

Air
Pacific Eagle, Box 1487, Port McNeill,
B.C. V0N 2R0. Tel. (250) 956-3339.
Float plane service — up to 2 hard-
shelled kayaks per trip.

Water Taxis
Adventure Center, 8635 Granville St.,
Port Hardy, B.C. V0N 2P0. Toll-
free 1-866-902-2232. Webpage:
www.adventurecenter.ca.
Rainbow Express Water Taxi, Box 97,
Port McNeill, B.C. V0N 2R0.
Tel. (250) 956-2999.
Viking West Charters, Box 113, Port
McNeill, B.C. V0N 2R0. Toll-free
1-877-956-3431, tel. (250) 956-3431.
Webpage: www.vikwest@island.net.

PARKS & TOURISM
**B.C. Forest Service, North Island Dis-
trict,** Box 7000, Port McNeill, B.C.
V0N 2R0. Tel. (250) 956-5000, fax
(250) 956-5005.
**BC Parks, Rathtrevor Office, Ministry
of Water, Land and Air Protection,**
Box 1479, Parksville, B.C. V9P 2H4.
Tel. (250) 954-4600,
fax (250) 248-8584. Cape Scott Zone,
tel. (250) 949-2800. Webpage:
http://wlap.www.gov.bc.ca/bc.parks/.
To make reservations for provincial
parks, toll-free 1-800-689-9025, tel.
(604) 689-9025 (March 15–Sept. 15).
Port McNeill Travel Infocentre,
Box 129, Port McNeill, B.C.
V0N 2R0. Tel. (250) 956-3131.

FIRST NATIONS

Kwakiutl District Council, 1400A Drake Rd., Campbell River, B.C. V9W 7K6. Tel. (250) 286-9766. Council of nine bands on northeast Vancouver Island, from Comox to Port Hardy.

Mamaleleqala Que'Qwa'Sot'Enox Band, 1400 Weiwaikum Rd., Campbell River, B.C. V9W 5W8. Tel. (250) 287-2955, fax (250) 287-4655. For permission to visit Village Island IR and Compton Island IR.

Musgamagw Tsawataineuk Tribal Council, Box 90, Alert Bay, B.C. VON 1AO. Tel. (250) 974-5516, fax (250) 974-5466. A council of bands in the Alert Bay area, including the Tlowitsis-Mumtagila Band.

U'mista Cultural Centre, Box 253, Alert Bay, B.C. VON 1AO. Tel. (250) 974-5403, fax (250) 974-5499. An excellent museum dedicated to First Nations culture.

EQUIPMENT RENTALS/TOURS

Adventure Center, 8635 Granville St., Port Hardy, B.C. VON 2PO. Toll-free 1-866-902-2232. Webpage: www.adventurecenter.ca. Kayak rentals, guided kayak trips, retail outfitting sales and rentals, water taxi for Central Coast, Queen Charlotte Strait and Johnstone Strait/Broughton Archipelago.

Alder Bay Resort, Box 1090, Port McNeill, B.C. VON 2RO. Tel. (250) 956-4117, fax (250) 956-2552. Boat launching, camping and pay parking.

Discovery Expeditions, 2755 Departure Bay Rd., Nanaimo, B.C. V9S 3W9. Tel./fax (250) 758-2488. Tours.

Ecosummer Expeditions, R.R. 1, Box 1765, Clearwater, B.C. VOE 1NO. Toll-free 1-800-465-8884. Webpage: www.ecosummer.com. Guided tours.

Gabriola Cycle and Kayak Ltd., 910 Clarendon Rd., S-1, C-23, Gabriola Island, B.C. VOR 1XO. Tel. (250) 247-8277. Webpage: www.gck.ca. Tours.

North Island Kayak Rentals. Mailing address: Box 291, Port Hardy, B.C. VON 2PO. Street address: 8635 Granville St., with 2 shops in the Telegraph Cove Marina and Resort, toll-free 1-877-949-7707, tel./fax (250) 949-7707. Webpage: www.kayakbc.ca. Rentals in Alder Bay, Port Hardy and Quatsino, and kayak tours.

Northern Lights Expeditions Ltd. Toll-free 1-800-754-7402. Port McNeill: tel. (250) 956-2080 (summer only); Bellingham: tel. (360) 734-6334, fax (360) 734-6150. Webpage: www.seakayaking.com. Guided kayak tours.

Ocean West Expeditions Ltd., 40450 Cheakamus Place, Garibaldi Highlands, B.C. VON 1TO. Tel. (604) 898-4979, fax (604) 898-4980. Webpage: www.ocean-west.com. Tours in the Gulf Islands, Johnstone Strait and Desolation Sound.

Odyssey Kayaking, 9590 Scott St., Port Hardy, B.C. VON 2PO. Tel./fax (250) 902-0565. Rentals, instruction and tours.

Pacific Rim Paddling Company, Box 1840, Victoria, B.C. V8W 2Y3. Tel. (250) 384-6103, fax (250) 361-2686. Webpage: www.pacificrimpaddling.com. Guided tours.

Telegraph Cove Kayak Co., Box 291, Port Hardy, B.C. VON 2PO. Toll-free 1-877-949-7707. Webpage: www.kayakbc.ca. Operates 2 shops next to the boat ramps in Telegraph Cove.

Telegraph Cove Resorts, Box 1, Telegraph Cove, B.C. VON 3J0. Toll-free 1-800-200-4665, tel. (250) 928-3131, fax (250) 928-3105. Webpage: www.telegraphcoveresort.com. Boat launching, car parking, camping, cafe and fishing charters.

Telegraph Cove Marine and RV Resort. Toll-free 1-877-835-2683. Email: tcv@island.net. Launching, parking, RV camping and accommodation as well as facilities.

Tofino Expeditions Ltd., Box 15280, Seattle, WA 98115–0280. Toll-free 1-800-677-0877, tel. (206) 517-5244, fax (206) 517-5203. Webpage: www.tofino.com. Guided tours throughout B.C., including Johnstone Strait.

Wildheart Adventures, 2774 Barnes Rd., Nanaimo, B.C. V9R 5K2. Tel. (250) 722-3683, fax (250) 722-2175. Webpage: www.island.net/~wheart. Tours throughout the Gulf Islands and Vancouver Island.

QUEEN CHARLOTTE STRAIT

EMERGENCIES

Port Hardy RCMP, tel. 911 or (250) 949-6335.

WEATHER & MARINE RADIO

Environment Canada. Continuous weather recording, tel. (250) 974-5305, northeast Vancouver Island.

North Island Marine Weather Office, Port Hardy, tel. (250) 949-7148.

VHF Weather Radio: channel 21B (161.65 MHZ).

GETTING THERE

See GENERAL CONTACTS (B.C.) for information about B.C. Ferries and other air carriers.

Air

Pacific Coastal Airlines, 117–4440 Crowley Cres., Richmond, B.C. V7B 1B8. Toll-free 1-800-663-2872, tel (604) 273-8666, fax (604) 273-6864. Or Box 2186, Port Hardy, B.C. VON 2P0. Tel. (250) 949-6477. Webpage: www.pacific-coastal.com. Scheduled and chartered air service.

Bus

North Island Transportation, Box 1074, Port Hardy, B.C. VON 2P0. Tel. (250) 949-6300, fax (250) 949-6388. Passenger transportation from B.C. Ferries terminal and Port Hardy Airport into Port Hardy.

Water Taxis

Adventure Center, 8635 Granville St., Port Hardy, B.C. VON 2P0. Toll-free 1-866-902-2232. Webpage: www.adventurecenter.ca.

Catala Charter, 6170 Hardy Bay Rd., Port Hardy, B.C. VON 2P0. Toll-free 1-800-515-5511, tel. (250) 949-7560.

Sea Legend Charter Ltd., 4990 Beaver Harbour Rd., Port Hardy, B.C. VON 2P0. Toll-free 1-800-246-0093, tel. (250) 949-6541.

Viking West Charters, Box 113, Port McNeill, B.C. VON 2R0. Toll-free 1-877-956-3431, tel. (250) 956-3431. Webpage: www.vikwest@island.net.

PARKS & TOURISM

B.C. Forest Service, North Island District, Box 7000, Port McNeill, B.C. VON 2R0. Tel. (250) 956-5000, fax (250) 956-5005.

BC Parks, Cape Scott Zone, Bag 11000, 8785 Gray St., Port Hardy, B.C. VON 2P0. Tel. (250) 949-2800, fax (250) 949-6346.

BC Parks, Rathtrevor Office, Ministry
of Water, Land and Air Protection,
Box 1479, Parksville, B.C. v9p 2h4.
Tel. (250) 954-4600,
fax (250) 248-8584. Webpage:
http://wlap.www.gov.bc.ca/bc.parks/.
To make reservations for provincial
parks, toll-free 1-800-689-9025, tel.
(604) 689-9025 (March 15–Sept. 15).
Port Hardy Travel Infocentre, Box 249,
Port Hardy, B.C. von 2p0. Tel.
(250) 949-7622, fax (250) 949-6653.

FIRST NATIONS
Gwa'sala-Nak'waxda'wx Nation,
154 Tsulquate Reserve, Port Hardy,
B.C. von 2p0. Tel. (250) 949-8424.
Kwakiutl District Band Office,
99 Tsakis Way, Port Hardy, B.C.
von 2p0. Tel. (250) 949-9442.

EQUIPMENT RENTALS/TOURS
Adventure Center, 8635 Granville St.,
Port Hardy, B.C. von 2p0. Toll-free
1-866-902-2232. Webpage: www.ad-
venturecenter.ca. Kayak rentals,
guided kayak trips, retail outfitting
sales and rentals, water taxi for Central Coast, Queen Charlotte Strait
and Johnstone Strait/Broughton
Archipelago.
North Island Kayak Rentals. Mailing
address: Box 291, Port Hardy, B.C.
von 2p0. Street address: 8635
Granville St., with 2 shops in the
Telegraph Cove Marina and Resort.
Toll-free 1-877-949-7707, tel./fax (250)
949-7707. Webpage: www.kayakbc.ca.
Rentals in Alder Bay, Port Hardy and
Quatsino, and kayak tours.
Odyssey Kayaking, 9590 Scott St., Port
Hardy, B.C. von 2p0. Tel./fax
(250) 902-0565. Rentals, instruction
and tours.

Telegraph Cove Kayak Co., Box 291,
Port Hardy, B.C. von 2p0. Toll-
free 1-877-949-7707. Webpage:
www.kayakbc.ca. Operates 2 shops
next to the boat ramps in Telegraph
Cove.

BARKLEY SOUND

EMERGENCIES
Tofino rcmp, tel. 911 or (250) 725-3242.
Ucluelet rcmp, tel. 911 or
(250) 726-7773.

WEATHER & MARINE RADIO
Tofino Coast Guard Radio, tel. (250)
726-7312. For weather information
and to file a float plan.
Vancouver Island (west coast) Marine
Weather Forecast, tel. (250) 726-3415.
vhf Weather Radio: channel 21B
(161.65 mhz).

GETTING THERE
See GENERAL CONTACTS (B.C.) for
information about B.C. Ferries and
other air carriers.

Bus
West Coast Trail Express, 3954 Bow Rd.,
Victoria, B.C. v8n 3b1. Toll-free
1-888-999-2288, tel. (250) 477-8700.
Between Victoria and Bamfield.

Water Taxis
Alberni Marine Transport, Box 188, Port
Alberni, B.C. v9y 7m7. Toll-free
1-800-663-7192 (April–September),
tel. (250) 723-8313, fax (250) 723-8314.
For travel on the mv *Lady Rose* and
mv *Frances Barkley*; also kayak
rentals and Sechart Lodge.

Subtidal Adventures, Box 78, Ucluelet,
B.C. VOR 3A0. Tel. (250) 726-7336.
Transportation to the Broken Group
from Ucluelet.

PARKS & TOURISM

Alberni Valley Visitor Information,
R.R. 2, S-215, C-10, Port Alberni, B.C.
V9Y 7L6. Tel. (250) 724-6535,
fax (250) 724-6560.

B.C. Forest Service, Port Alberni
District, 4885 Cherry Creek Rd.,
Port Alberni, B.C. V9Y 8E9.
Tel. (250) 731-3000.

BC Parks, Rathtrevor Office,
Ministry of Water, Land and Air
Protection, Box 1479, Parksville,
B.C. V9P 2H4. Tel. (250) 954-4600,
fax (250) 248-8584. Webpage:
http://wlap.www.gov.bc.ca/bc.parks/.
To make reservations for provincial
parks, toll-free 1-800-689-9025, tel.
(604) 689-9025 (March 15–Sept. 15).

Parks Canada, Pacific Rim National
Park Reserve, Box 280, Ucluelet,
B.C. VOR 3A0. Tel. (250) 726-7721,
fax (250) 726-4720.

Ucluelet Visitor Information, Box 428,
Ucluelet, B.C. VOR 3A0. Tel. (250)
726-4641, fax (250) 726-4611.

FIRST NATIONS

Huu-ay-aht First Nation, Box 70,
Bamfield, B.C. VOR 1B0. Tel. (250)
728-3414, fax (250) 728-1222.

Nuu-chah-nulth Tribal Council,
Box 1383, Port Alberni, B.C.
V9Y 7M2. Tel. (250) 724-5757,
fax (250) 723-0463.

EQUIPMENT RENTALS/TOURS

Alberni Marine Transport. See Water
Taxis (above).

Majestic Ocean Kayaking, Box 287,
Ucluelet, B.C. VOR 3A0. Toll-free
1-800-889-7644. Guided tours.

Pacific Rim Paddling Company,
Box 1840, Victoria, B.C. V8W 2Y3.
Tel. (250) 384-6103,
fax (250) 361-2686. Webpage:
www.pacificrimpaddling.com.
Guided tours.

Pristine Adventures, Box 795, Ucluelet,
B.C. VOR 3A0. Tel. (250) 726-4477.
Guided canoe tours, bear watching,
bird-watching and fly-fishing.

Wilderness Kayaking Co., 1130 Bazett
Rd., Duncan, B.C. V9L 5S8.
Tel./fax (250) 746-0151. Tours, rentals
and lessons.

Wildheart Adventures, 2774 Barnes Rd.,
Nanaimo, B.C. V9R 5K2. Tel. (250)
722-3683, fax (250) 722-2175. Webpage:
www.island.net/~wheart. Tours.

CLAYOQUOT SOUND

EMERGENCIES

Tofino RCMP, tel. 911 or (250) 725-3242.

WEATHER & MARINE RADIO

Tofino Coast Guard Radio,
tel. (250) 726-7312. To file a float plan.

Vancouver Island (west coast) Marine
Weather Forecast. Tel. (250) 726-3415.

VHF Weather Radio: channels WX1
(162.55 MHZ), WX3 (162.475 MHZ) or
21B (161.65 MHZ).

Weather Radio Canada, Tofino,
1260 KHZ AM.

GETTING THERE

See GENERAL CONTACTS (B.C.) for
information about B.C. Ferries and
other air carriers.

Air

Atleo River Air, Box 896, Tofino, B.C. VOR 2Z0. Toll-free 1-866-662-8536, tel. (250) 725-2205, fax (250) 725-3118. Webpage: www.atleoair.ca. Serving Clayoquot, Nootka and Kyuquot Sounds.

North Vancouver Air, 311–5260 Airport Rd. S., Richmond, B.C. V7B 1B4. Toll-free 1-800-228-6608, tel. (604) 278-1608, fax (604) 278-2608. Scheduled destinations include Ucluelet, Tofino, Port Alberni, Victoria and Vancouver.

Tofino Air, Box 99, Tofino, B.C. VOR 2Z0. Tel. (250) 725-4454, fax (250) 725-4421. Webpage: www.tofinoair.ca. Float plane charters for sightseeing and drop-off.

Bus

Tofino Bus, 564 Campbell St., Tofino, B.C. VOR 2Z0. Toll-free 1-866-986-3466, tel. (250) 725-2871. Webpage: www.tofinobus.com. Locally based bus service that picks up and drops off at the Nanaimo ferry terminal, as well as in downtown Victoria. Carries kayaks.

Water Taxis

Ahousaht Pride (sea bus to Ahousat). VHF channel 68A. Contact Ahousat Band office for information, tel. (250) 670-9563.

Matlahaw Water Taxi, VHF channel 66A. Toll-free 1-888-781-9977, tel. (250) 670-1110. Webpage: www.tourismhotsprings.com. Transport of people and kayaks to Hot Springs Cove.

Vargas Island Inn, Box 267, Tofino, B.C. VOR 2Z0. Tel. (250) 725-3309. Water taxi service. Also an excellent kayak-friendly hostel in the middle of the Clayoquot Sound wilderness.

PARKS & TOURISM

B.C. Forest Service, Port Alberni District, 4885 Cherry Creek Rd., Port Alberni, B.C. V9Y 8E9. Tel. (250) 731-3000.

BC Parks, Rathtrevor Office, Ministry of Water, Land and Air Protection, Box 1479, Parksville, B.C. V9P 2H4. Tel. (250) 954-4600, fax (250) 248-8584. Webpage: http://wlap.www.gov.bc.ca/bc.parks/. To make reservations for provincial parks, toll-free 1-800-689-9025, tel. (604) 689-9025 (March 15–Sept. 15).

Parks Canada, Pacific Rim National Park Reserve, Box 280, Ucluelet, B.C. VOR 3A0. Tel. (250) 726-7721, fax (250) 726-4720.

Tofino Visitor Infocentre, Box 249, 1426 Pacific Rim Hwy. Tofino, VOR 2Z0. Tel. (250) 725-3414, fax (250) 725-3296.

FIRST NATIONS

Ahousaht Band Office, General Delivery, Ahousat, B.C. VOR 1A0. Tel. (250) 670-9563, fax (250) 670-9531.

Hesquiaht Band Office, Box 2000, Tofino, B.C. VOR 2Z0. Tel. (250) 670-1100.

Hot Springs Lodge. Toll-free 1-866-670-1106. Webpage: www.tourismhotsprings.com.

Nuu-chah-nulth Tribal Council, Box 1383, Port Alberni, B.C. V9Y 7M2. Tel. (250) 724-5757, fax (250) 723-0463.

Tla-ook Cultural Adventures,
Box 899, Tofino, B.C. VOR 2Z0.
Tel. (250) 725-2656. Experience paddling in a real traditional dug-out canoe with local Nuu-chah-nulth guides.

Tla-o-qui-aht First Nation, Box 18, Tofino, B.C. VOR 2Z0, tel. (250) 725-3233, fax (250) 725-4233.

Walk the Wild Side, Box 150, Ahousat, B.C. VOR 1A0. Toll-free 1-888-670-9586, fax (250) 670-9696. First Nations tourism resource centre; water taxis, accommodations and hiking guides.

EQUIPMENT RENTALS/TOURS

Majestic Ocean Kayaking, Box 287, Ucluelet, B.C. VOR 3A0. Toll-free 1-800-889-7644. Webpage: www.oceankayaking.com. Guided tours.

Paddle West Kayaking, Box 764, 305 Campbell St., Tofino, B.C. VOR 2Z0. Tel. (250) 725-4253. Guided day tours.

Rainforest Kayak Adventures, Box 511, Tofino, B.C. VOR 2Z0. Toll-free 1-877-422-wild (9453). Tel./fax (250) 725-3117. Webpage: www.rainforestkayak.com. Surf and guide training courses, camping and lodge-based overnight tours.

Remote Passages, Box 624, Tofino, B.C. VOR 2Z0. Toll-free 1-800-666-9833, tel. (250) 725-3330, fax (250) 725-3360. Webpage: www.remotepassages.com. Guided tours.

Tofino Sea Kayaking Company/ Paddler's Inn. Mailing address: Box 620, Tofino, B.C. VOR 2Z0. Street address: 320 Main St. Toll-free 1-800-863-4664, tel. (250) 725-4222, fax (250) 725-2070. Webpage: www.tofino-kayaking.com. Lessons,

B&B, tours, rentals and kayaking gear sales. Also a great little bookstore.

NOOTKA SOUND

EMERGENCIES
Gold River RCMP, tel. 911 or (250) 283-2227.

WEATHER & MARINE RADIO
Tofino Coast Guard Radio, tel. (250) 726-7312. For weather information and to file a float plan.

Vancouver Island (west coast) Marine Weather Forecast, tel. (250) 726-3415.

VHF **Weather Radio:** channel WX2 (162.40 MHZ).

GETTING THERE
See GENERAL CONTACTS (B.C.) for information about B.C. Ferries and other air carriers.

Air
Air Nootka, 800 Mill Rd., Box 19, Gold River, B.C. VOP 1G0. Tel. (250) 283-2255. Scheduled stops in Nootka and Kyuquot Sounds.

Atleo River Air, P.O. Box 896, Tofino, BC, VOR 2Z0. Toll-free 1-866-662-8536, tel. (250) 725-2205, fax (250) 725-3118. Webpage: www.atleoair.com. Serving Clayoquot, Nootka and Kyuquot Sounds.

Water Taxis
Maxi's Water Taxi, Government Wharf, Gold River, B.C. VOP 1G0. Tel. (250) 283-2282, fax (250) 283-7718.

Nootka Sound Service, P.O. Box 57, Gold River, B.C. VOP 1G0. Tel. (250) 283-2515, fax (250) 283-7582.

Webpage: www.mvuchuck.com. Transportation aboard the MV *Uchuck III*.

PARKS & TOURISM

B.C. Forest Service, Campbell River District, 370 S. Dogwood St., Campbell River, B.C. V9W 6Y7. Tel. (250) 286-9300, fax (250) 286-9490.

BC Parks, Rathtrevor Office, Ministry of Water, Land and Air Protection, Box 1479, Parksville, B.C. V9P 2H4. Tel. (250) 954-4600, fax (250) 248-8584. Webpage: http://wlap.www.gov.bc.ca/bc.parks/. To make reservations for provincial parks, toll-free 1-800-689-9025, tel. (604) 689-9025 (March 15–Sept. 15).

Gold River Travel Infocentre, Box 610, Gold River, B.C. V0P 1G0. Tel. (250) 283-2418, fax (250) 283-7500. Open May 15 to September 25. Tel. (250) 283-2202 during the off-season.

Mowachaht/Muchalaht First Nations (formerly Ahaninaquus Tourist Centre), 100 Owatin Rd., Tsaxana Reserve, Gold River, B.C. V0P 1G0. Tel. (250) 283-2015, fax (250) 283-2335.

FIRST NATIONS

Mowachaht/Muchalaht Band, Box 459, Gold River, B.C. V0P 1G0. Tel. (250) 283-2015.

EQUIPMENT RENTALS/TOURS

Nootka Sound Kayaking Adventures Ltd., Merville, B.C. V0R 2M0. Toll-free 1-800-661-9393, tel. (250) 337-5292.

Tuta Marina and Campgrounds, Box 765, Gold River, B.C. V0P 1G0. Tel. (250) 283-7550. Launching and parking.

Wilderness Kayaking Co., 1130 Bazett Rd., Duncan, B.C. V9L 5S8. Tel./fax (250) 746-0151. Tours, rentals and lessons.

Wildheart Adventures, 2774 Barnes Rd., Nanaimo, B.C. V9R 5K2. Tel. (250) 722-3683, fax (250) 722-2175. Webpage: www.island.net/~wheart. Guided tours.

KYUQUOT SOUND

EMERGENCIES

Tahsis RCMP, tel. 911 or (250) 934-6363 (inquiries are routed to Kyuquot detachment).

WEATHER & MARINE RADIO
See NOOTKA SOUND.

GETTING THERE
See GENERAL CONTACTS (B.C.) for information about B.C. Ferries and other air carriers.

Air

Air Nootka, 777 Mill Rd., Box 19, Gold River, B.C. V0P 1G0. Tel. (250) 283-2555. Webpage: www.airnootka.com. Scheduled stops in Nootka and Kyuquot Sounds.

Atleo River Air, Box 896, Tofino, B.C. V0R 2Z0. Toll-free 1-866-662-8536, tel. (250) 725-2205, fax (250) 725-3118. Webpage: www.atleoair.com. Serving Clayoquot, Nootka and Kyuquot Sounds.

West Coast Helicopter Ltd., P.O. Box 1030, 1011 Airport Rd., Port McNeill Municipal Airport, Port McNeill, B.C. V0N 2R0. Toll-free 1-800-966-9229, tel. (250) 956-2244. Webpage: www.island.net/~wcheli.

Water Taxis

Kyuquot Tours and Water Taxi, General Delivery, Kyuquot, B.C. VOP 1J0. Tel. (250) 332-5301. Webpage: www.kyuquotwatertaxi.com.

Nootka Sound Service, P.O. Box 57, Gold River, B.C. VOP 1G0. Tel. (250) 283-2515, fax (250) 283-7582. Webpage: www.mvuchuck.com. Transportation aboard the MV *Uchuck III.*

Qwath (Hilda Hansen) Water Taxi, General Delivery, Kyuquot, B.C. VOP 1J0. Tel. (250) 332-5232.

Slam Bang Lodge, General Delivery, Kyuquot, B.C. VOP 1J0. Tel. (250) 332-5313.

PARKS & TOURISM

B.C. Forest Service, Campbell River District, 370 S. Dogwood St., Campbell River, B.C. V9W 6Y7. Tel. (250) 286-9300, fax (250) 286-9490.

BC Parks, Cape Scott Zone, Bag 11000, 8785 Gray St., Port Hardy, B.C. VON 2P0. Tel. (250) 949-2800, fax (250) 949-6346. Before you go to Kyuquot, please get an area brochure from this office.

BC Parks, Rathtrevor Office, Ministry of Water, Land and Air Protection, Box 1479, Parksville, B.C. V9P 2H4. Tel. (250) 954-4600, fax (250) 248-8584. Webpage: http://wlap.www.gov.bc.ca/bc.parks/. To make reservations for provincial parks, toll-free 1-800-689-9025, tel. (604) 689-9025 (March 15–Sept. 15).

Kyuquot Environment and Economic Protection Society, tel. (250) 332-5287.

The Old Co-op B&B and Miss Charlie's Restaurant, Kyuquot, B.C. VOP 1J0. Tel. (250) 332-5293.

FIRST NATIONS

Che: k' tles7et'h' and Ka:' yu: 'kt'h' First Nations, General Delivery, Kyuquot, B.C. VOP 1J0. Tel. (250) 332-5259, fax (250) 332-5210. You are asked to stop at the band office before heading into Kyuquot Sound.

EQUIPMENT RENTALS/TOURS

Slam Bang Lodge. See Water Taxis (above).

West Coast Expeditions, Box 3733, Courtenay, B.C. V9N 7P1. Toll-free 1-800-665-3040, tel. (250) 338-9789. Webpage: www.island.net/~nature. Guided kayak tours and water taxi service.

Wilderness Kayaking Co., 1130 Bazett Rd., Duncan, B.C. V9L 5S8. Tel./fax (250) 746-0151. Tours, rentals and lessons.

QUATSINO SOUND

EMERGENCIES

Port Hardy RCMP, tel. 911 or (250) 949-6335.

WEATHER & MARINE RADIO

See NOOTKA SOUND.

VHF Weather Radio: channel 21B (161.65 MHZ).

GETTING THERE

See GENERAL CONTACTS (B.C.) for information about B.C. Ferries and other air carriers.

Air

Pacific Coastal Airlines, 117–4440 Cowley Cres., Richmond, B.C. V7B 1B8. Toll-free 1-800-663-2872, tel. (604) 273-8666, fax (604) 273-6864. Or Box

2186, Port Hardy, B.C. VON 2PO.
Tel. (250) 949-6477. Webpage:
www.pacific-coastal.com.

Bus

North Island Transportation, Box 1074,
Port Hardy, B.C. VON 2PO. Tel. (250)
949-6300, fax (250) 949-6388. Passenger transportation from B.C. Ferries
terminal and Port Hardy Airport into
Port Hardy.

Water Taxis

D.H. Timber Towing and Salvage,
Box 69, Coal Harbour, B.C.
VON 1KO. Tel. (250) 949-6358,
fax (250) 949-9886.

PARKS & TOURISM

**B.C. Forest Service, North Island Dis-
trict,** Box 7000, Port McNeill, B.C.
VON 2RO. Tel. (250) 956-5000, fax
(250) 956-5005.

BC Parks, Cape Scott Zone, Bag 11000,
8785 Gray St., Port Hardy, B.C. VON
2PO. Tel. (250) 949-2800, fax (250)
949-6346.

**BC Parks, Rathtrevor Office, Ministry
of Water, Land and Air Protection,**
Box 1479, Parksville, B.C.
V9P 2H4. Tel. (250) 954-4600,
fax (250) 248-8584. Webpage:
http://wlap.www.gov.bc.ca/bc.parks/.
To make reservations for provincial
parks, toll-free 1-800-689-9025, tel.
(604) 689-9025 (March 15–Sept. 15).

Port Hardy Travel Infocentre, Box 249,
Port Hardy, B.C. VON 2PO. Tel.
(250) 949-7622, fax (250) 949-6653.

FIRST NATIONS

Quatsino Band Council, Box 100,
Coal Harbour, B.C. VON 1KO. Tel.
(250) 949-6245, fax (250) 949-6249.

EQUIPMENT RENTALS/TOURS

North Island Kayak Rentals, Mailing
address: Box 291, Port Hardy, B.C.
VON 2PO. Street address: 8635
Granville St., with 2 shops in the
Telegraph Cove Marina and Resort,
toll-free 1-877-949-7707, tel./fax (250)
949-7707. Webpage: www.kayakbc.ca.
Rentals in Alder Bay, Port Hardy and
Quatsino, and kayak tours.

Odyssey Kayaking, 9590 Scott St.,
Port Hardy, B.C. VON 2PO. Tel./fax
(250) 902-0565. Rentals, instruction
and tours.

CENTRAL COAST

EMERGENCIES

Bella Bella RCMP, tel. 911
or (250) 957-2388.

WEATHER & MARINE RADIO

Environment Canada, tel. (250) 974-
5305. Continuous weather recording.

Prince Rupert Coast Guard, tel. (250)
627-3081 or 627-3074. For weather
information or to file a float plan.

VHF Weather Radio: channels WX1
(162.55 MHZ), WX2 (162.40 MHZ) or
WX3 (162.475 MHZ).

GETTING THERE

See GENERAL CONTACTS (B.C.) for
information about B.C. Ferries and
other air carriers.

Air

Pacific Coastal Airlines, 117–4440 Cowley Cres., Richmond, B.C. V7B 1B8.
Toll-free 1-800-663-2872, tel. (604)
273-8666, fax (604) 273-6864. Or Box
2186, Port Hardy, B.C. VON 2PO. Tel.
(250) 949-6477. Webpage:
www.pacific-coastal.com.

Bus

Gold Pan City Stage Lines, 1471 Quesnel-Hixon Rd., Quesnel, B.C. V2J 5Z3. Toll-free 1-888-992-6168. Bookings can be made with Tweedsmuir Travel in Bella Coola, tel. (250) 799-5638. Bus service between Williams Lake and Bella Coola; stops include Anahim Lake and Nimpo Lake.

North Island Transportation, Box 1074, Port Hardy, B.C. V0N 2P0. Tel. (250) 949-6300, fax (250) 949-6388. Passenger transportation from B.C. Ferries terminal and Port Hardy Airport into Port Hardy.

Water Taxis

Adventure Center, 8635 Granville St., Port Hardy, B.C. V0N 2P0. Toll-free 1-866-902-2232. Webpage: www.adventurecenter.ca. Kayak rentals, guided kayak trips, retail outfitting sales and rentals, water taxi for Central Coast, Queen Charlotte Strait and Johnstone Strait/Broughton Archipelago.

Campbell Island Charters, Box 781, Waglisla, B.C. V0T 1Z0. Tel. (250) 957-2319, fax (250) 957-2710. Fishing and sightseeing charters.

Catala Charter, 6170 Hardy Bay Rd., Port Hardy, B.C. V0N 2P0. Toll-free 1-800-515-5511, tel. (250) 949-7560.

Sea Legend Charter Ltd., 4990 Beaver Harbour Rd., Port Hardy, B.C. V0N 2P0. Toll-free 1-800-246-0093, tel. (250) 949-6541.

PARKS & TOURISM

B.C. Forest Service, Mid Coast District, Box 190, Hagensborg, B.C. V0T 1H0. Tel. (250) 982-2000, fax (250) 982-2090.

BC Parks, Bella Coola Zone Office, Ministry of Water, Land and Air Protection, Box 907, Bella Coola, B.C. V0T 1C0. Tel. (250) 982-2701, fax (250) 799-5568.

BC Parks, Cariboo District Office, Ministry of Water, Land and Air Protection, 281 North 1st Ave., Williams Lake, B.C. V2G 1Y7. Tel. (250) 398-4530, fax (250) 398-4686. Webpage: http://wlap.www.gov.bc.ca/bc.parks/. To make reservations for provincial parks, toll-free 1-800-689-9025, tel. (604) 689-9025 (March 15–Sept. 15).

Port Hardy Travel Infocentre, Box 249, Port Hardy, B.C. V0N 2P0. Tel. (250) 949-7622, fax (250) 949-6653.

FIRST NATIONS

Heiltsuk Nation, Box 880, Waglisla, B.C. V0T 1Z0. Tel. (250) 957-2381, fax (250) 957-2544. Contact the Heiltsuk Cultural Centre at tel. (250) 957-2626, fax (250) 957-2780.

Kitasoo Indian Band, General Delivery, Klemtu, B.C. V0T 1L0. Tel. (250) 839-1255, fax (250) 839-1256.

Klemtu Tourism, General Delivery, Klemtu, B.C. V0T 1L0. Toll-free 1-877-644-2346, tel. (250) 839-2346. Webpage: www.klemtutourism.com.

EQUIPMENT RENTALS/TOURS

Adventure Center, 8635 Granville St., Port Hardy, B.C. V0N 2P0. Toll-free 1-866-902-2232. Webpage: www.adventurecenter.ca. Kayak rentals, guided kayak trips, retail outfitting sales and rentals, water taxi for Central Coast, Queen Charlotte Strait and Johnstone Strait/Broughton Archipelago.

Gistala Adventures, Box 78, Bella Bella, B.C. VOT 1BO. Tel./fax (250) 957-2652.

North Island Kayak Rentals. Mailing address: Box 291, Port Hardy, B.C. VON 2PO. Street address: 8635 Granville St., with 2 shops in the Telegraph Cove Marina and Resort, toll-free 1-877-949-7707, tel./fax (250) 949-7707. Rentals in Alder Bay, Port Hardy and Quatsino, and kayak tours.

Odyssey Kayaking, 9590 Scott St., Port Hardy, B.C. VON 2PO. Tel./fax (250) 902-0565. Rentals in Port Hardy.

Tofino Expeditions Ltd., Box 15280, Seattle, WA 98115–0280. Tel. (206) 517-5244, fax (206) 517-5203. Webpage: www.tofino.com. Guided tours throughout B.C., including Cape Caution beaches.

HAIDA GWAII/ QUEEN CHARLOTTE ISLANDS

EMERGENCIES
Masset and Port Clements RCMP, tel. 911 or (250) 626-3991.
Queen Charlotte Islands (QCC) RCMP, tel. 911 or (250) 559-4421.

WEATHER & MARINE RADIO
See CENTRAL COAST.
VHF Weather Radio: channels WX1 (162.55 MHZ), WX2 (162.40 MHZ), WX3 (162.475 MHZ) or 21B (161.65 MHZ).

GETTING THERE
See GENERAL CONTACTS (B.C.) for information about B.C. Ferries and other air carriers.

Air
South Moresby Air, Box 969, Queen Charlotte City, B.C. VOT 1SO. Toll-

free 1-888-551-4222, tel. (250) 559-4222. Float plane charters; will carry hard-shell kayaks.

Water Taxis/Ferry
Alaska Marine Highway (Alaskan Ferries), Box 25535, Juneau, AK 99802–5535. Toll-free 1-800-642-0066 (for reservations), 1-800-665-6414 (in Canada), tel. (250) 627-1744 (Prince Rupert), fax (907) 277-4829 (Juneau). Webpage: www.alaska.gov/ferry/. Destinations include Bellingham, WA, Prince Rupert and Juneau. Please call to confirm ports of call.

Moresby Explorers, Box 109, Sandspit, B.C. VOT 1TO. Toll-free 1-800-806-7633, tel. (250) 637-2215. Webpage: www.moresbyexplorers.com.

Queen Charlotte Adventures, Box 196, Queen Charlotte City, B.C. VOT 1SO. Toll-free 1-800-668-4288, tel. (250) 559-8990.

PARKS & TOURISM
B.C. Forest Service, Queen Charlotte Islands District, Box 39, Queen Charlotte City, B.C. VOT 1SO. Tel. (250) 559-6200, fax (250) 559-8324.

BC Parks, Queen Charlotte Island Zone Office, Ministry of Water, Land and Air Protection, Box 19, Tlell, B.C. VOT 1YO. Tel. (250) 557-4390, fax (250) 557-4629. Webpage: http://wlap.www.gov.bc.ca/bc.parks/. To make reservations for provincial parks, toll-free 1-800-689-9025, tel. (604) 689-9025 (March 15–Sept. 15).

Parks Canada, Gwaii Haanas National Park Reserve and Haida Heritage Site, Box 37, Queen Charlotte City, B.C. VOT 1SO. Tel. (250) 559-8818, fax (250) 559-8366. Webpage: www.parkscanada.gc.ca/gwaiihaanas.

Queen Charlotte Visitor Centre,
Box 819, Queen Charlotte City,
B.C. VOT 1SO. Tel. (250) 559-8316,
fax (250) 559-8952. In Sandspit, call
(250) 637-5362. Webpage:
www.qcinfo.com. Open May 1 to
Labour Day (first Monday in Sept.).
Teal Jones Logging, Box 470, Sandspit,
B.C. VOT 1TO. Tel. (250) 637-5323.

FIRST NATIONS

Council of the Haida Nation, Box 589,
Masset, B.C. VOT 1MO. Tel.
(250) 626-5252, fax (250) 626-3493.
Haida Gwaii Watchmen, VHF
channel 6. Tel. (250) 559-8225.
Skidegate Indian Band, Box 1301, Skide-
gate, Haida Gwaii, B.C. VOT 1S1.
Tel. (250) 559-4496, fax (250) 559-8247.

EQUIPMENT RENTALS/TOURS

Check www.parkscanada.gc.ca/gwaii-
haanas for updates of licenced
operators.
Anvil Cove Charters, Box 454,
Queen Charlotte, B.C. VOT 1SO.
Tel. (250) 559-8207. Webpage:
www.qcislands.net/anvilcove.
Mothership tours.
Archipelago Ventures Ltd., Box 999,
Queen Charlotte, B.C. VOT 1SO.
Toll-free 1-888-559-8317,
tel. (250) 559-8317. Webpage:
www.island.net/~archipel.
Mothership tours.
Butterfly Tours, 305–5855 Cowrie St.,
Sechelt, B.C. VON 3A3.
Tel. (604) 740-7018. Webpage:
www.butterflytours.bc.ca. Guided
tours.
Ecosummer Expeditions, R.R. 1, Box
1765, Clearwater, B.C. VOE 1NO.
Toll-free 1-800-465-8884,
fax (604) 669-3244. Webpage:
www.ecosummer.com. Guided tours.

Gabriola Cycle and Kayak, 910 Clarendon Rd., Gabriola, B.C. VOR 1X1.
Tel. (250) 247-8277. Webpage:
www.gck.com.
**Gwaii Haanas Guest House and
Kayaks,** Box 578, Queen
Charlotte City, B.C. VOT 1SO.
Tel. (250) 559-8638,
autotel, (250) 624-8707. Webpage:
www.gwaiihaanas.com. Guest house
and meals at Rose Harbour; kayak
rentals and customized group trips.
Moresby Explorers, Box 109, Sandspit,
B.C. VOT 1TO. Toll-free 1-800-806-
7633, tel. (250) 637-2215. Webpage:
www.moresbyexploreres.com. Kayak
rentals and transportation.
Ocean Sound Kayaking Company,
17 East 23rd Ave., Vancouver, B.C.
V5V 1W8. Toll-free 1-888-736-0377,
tel. (604) 736-0377. Webpage:
www.oceansound.net. Guided tours.
Queen Charlotte Adventures, Box 196,
Queen Charlotte City, B.C. VOT
1SO. Tel. (250) 559-8990, toll-free
1-800-668-4288. Guided tours, kayak
rentals and transportation.
Rose Harbour Guest House, Box 437,
Queen Charlotte City, B.C. VOT
1SO. Tel. (250) 559-2326. Webpage:
www.roseharbour.com. Local guide
in Rose Harbour.
Tofino Expeditions Ltd., Box 15280,
Seattle, WA 98115–0280.
Tel. (206) 517-5244, fax (206) 517-5203.
Webpage: www.tofino.com. Guided
tours throughout B.C., including
the Haida Gwaii/Queen Charlotte
Islands.
**Whitney & Smith Legendary Expedi-
tions,** Box 8576, Canmore, AB T1W
2V3. Tel. (403) 678-3052. Webpage:
www.legendary.ca. Guided tours.

NORTH COAST

EMERGENCIES
Port Simpson RCMP, tel. 911
or (250) 625 3400.
Prince Rupert RCMP, tel. 911
or (250) 627-0700.

WEATHER & MARINE RADIO
See CENTRAL COAST.
VHF Weather Radio: channels WX1
(162.55 MHZ), WX2 (162.40 MHZ), WX3
(162.475 MHZ) or 21B (161.65 MHZ).

GETTING THERE
See GENERAL CONTACTS (B.C.) for
information about B.C. Ferries, bus,
train and air carriers.

Water Taxi/Ferry
Alaska Marine Highway. See HAIDA
GWAII/QUEEN CHARLOTTE
ISLANDS.
**Prince Rupert Water Taxi/Metlakatla
Ferry Service,** Box 224, Prince
Rupert, B.C. v8J 3P4. Tel. (250)
624-3337 or (250) 628-3201. Charters.

PARKS & TOURISM
**B.C. Forest Service, North Coast Dis-
trict,** 125 Market Pl., Prince Rupert,
B.C. v8J 1B9. Tel. (250) 624-7460,
fax (250) 624-7479.
**BC Parks, Skeena District, Ministry of
Water, Land and Air Protection,**
Bag 5000, Smithers, B.C.
v0J 2N0. Tel. (250) 847-7320,
fax (240) 847-7659. Webpage:
http://wlap.www.gov.bc.ca/bc.parks/.
To make reservations for provincial
parks, toll-free 1-800-689-9025, tel.
(604) 689-9025 (March 15–Sept. 15).

Oona River B&Bs: Brad Procher,
tel. (250) 628-3136, or Jan Leman,
tel. (250) 628-3241.
Tourist Bureau, 100–215 Cow Bay Rd.,
Prince Rupert, B.C. v8J 1A2. Tel.
(250) 624-5637, fax (250) 627-8009.

FIRST NATIONS
Kitkatla Indian Band, Box 149, Kitkatla,
B.C. v0V 1C0. Tel. (250) 848-2214,
fax (250) 848-2238.
Metlakatla Indian Band, Box 459,
Prince Rupert, B.C. v8J 3R2. Tel.
(250) 628-3234, fax (250) 628-9205.

EQUIPMENT RENTALS/TOURS
Lutz Budde, General Delivery,
Oona River, B.C. v0N 1E0.
Tel. (250) 628-3214, email:
oonariv@citytel.net.

Equipment Checklist

ESSENTIALS

- kayak with secure buoyancy fore and aft, and decklines and webbing to assist with self-rescues
- paddle
- spare paddle
- properly fitted spray skirt
- properly fitted lifejacket with a whistle and rescue knife
- pump or bailer that floats
- paddle float
- compass, charts, tide tables (current tables, if appropriate) and chart case
- flares (for day and night use)
- repair kit
- weather radio or VHF in a waterproof case
- extra batteries
- rescue sling
- tow line
- first aid kit
- matches or a lighter, and fire starter
- knife
- waterproof flashlight
- waterproof strobe
- water bottle
- water purification system or tablets
- sunglasses with retainer straps (for eyeglasses too)
- sunscreen
- sponge
- waterproof watch
- reflective tape for paddles, kayak, PFD, paddling jacket

ADDITIONAL GEAR

- wet suit or dry suit (advised)
- helmet (for surf landings)
- paddling jacket
- cockpit cover
- rain gear and extra clothing in waterproof bags (avoid cottons if possible — always be prepared for cold water immersion)
- tent, sleeping bag and sleeping pad in waterproof bags
- tarp
- stove, fuel and other cooking utensils
- personal items including toiletries
- fishing gear and licence
- ropes and containers to bear-proof camp (including bear spray)

About the Contributors

Jamie Boulding first experienced boating in Nootka Sound as a child in the 1960s and has been coming back ever since. He is the owner of Strathcona Park Lodge and the Canadian Outdoor Leadership Training School (COLTS), through which he is able to introduce hundreds of people to paddling every year. Jamie operates the lodge and the school with the belief that training people to travel safely and experience wilderness by themselves is healthier for both people and the land.

Frank Brown is a member of the Heiltsuk Nation and a tourism operator in Bella Bella. Active in the resurgence of canoe building and paddling, Frank helped make history organizing the voyage of a traditional canoe from Bella Bella to Expo 86 in Vancouver. Frank has a degree in outdoor recreation from Capilano College.

Michele Deakin has worked for Parks Canada since 1985. She started in Ontario and moved westward until she reached Haida Gwaii in 1991. She has paddled Gwaii Haanas for pleasure and for business and believes strongly that the rawness and power of the area must be protected for future generations. Gwaii Haanas contributions to this book were based on information developed over the years by many staff. Thanks also to Meredith Reeve, Pauline Scott and the Archipelago Management Board for their assistance.

Bodhi and Dorothy Drope have been paddling in British Columbia for 15 years. They make their home on the Sunshine Coast and know that area most intimately. In 1991, they established Sunshine Kayaking in Gibsons, offering kayak classes, day tours, extended tours and rentals. The luscious natural environment of coastal B.C. gives inspiration for the painting, drawing, fabric work and writing that occupies them during the off-season.

Debbie Erickson draws her knowledge and experience from over 25 years of exploring the waters surrounding northern Vancouver Island and the Central Coast. She grew up in the Broughton Archipelago and the remote mainland inlets that are still only accessible by boat or float plane. She took over North Island Kayak in 1997 and has expanded the business into Telegraph Cove as well as opening the Adventure Center in Port Hardy in 2000. Since then, she has been thoroughly enjoying introducing paddlers to some of the B.C. coast's best areas.

Bonny Glambeck has lived and kayaked in Tofino since 1988 and is active in the movement to save Clayoquot Sound. She is an expedition kayaker, a certified full guide, and has been guiding and teaching professionally since 1995. Her special passion is sharing paddling skills with other women, so they can enjoy wilderness travel as much as she does. She owns and operates Rainforest Kayak Adventures with Dan Lewis.

Edwin Hubert is a marine biologist and kayak guide who operated Seabird Kayaking out of Bamfield in the late 1990s. He has a strong historical interest in the coastal town and authored a self-guided historical walking tour of the Bamfield boardwalk on behalf of the Bamfield Preservation and Development Society.

Fran Hunt-Jinnouchi and Marc Jinnouchi owned and operated North Island Kayak Rentals until 1997. Fran is Kwakwa̱ka'wakw First Nation and has a great love for her ancestral home of Quatsino Sound. Both Fran and Marc are active in their community.

Darryl Jensen is a graphic designer who has worked with the B.C. Marine Trail Association on various projects, including the maps to this guidebook. Since leaving the coast for Calgary via Yellowknife, Darryl has all but exchanged his paddles for rock shoes and crampons. He misses terribly the smell of salt water but finds some solace in the mountains. He can be found at www.djensen.ca

Liz Johnston is the owner-operator of Tyee Resort in Bamfield on Vancouver Island. She has lived on the West Coast all her life, never too far from the ocean, on boats, islands, float homes and in small villages. She has been kayaking for more than 20 years, has travelled all over the world on expeditions and now offers accommodation, fishing, hiking and kayak tours at her resort. She is also actively involved with the Loyal Bamfield Kayak Club and is a member of the Auxilliary Coast Guard.

Charles Justice is a nurse, president of the Prince Rupert Kayak Club and
northern coordinator for the B.C. Marine Trail Association. He has kayaked
extensively throughout the North Coast and occasionally teaches sea kayaking.
The last we heard from Charles, he was writing and giving talks on eco-Earth
spirituality.

Ralph Keller has been exploring Desolation Sound and the Coast Mountains
since he and his wife, Lannie, settled on Read Island 23 years ago. Ralph is
knowledgeable in homestead and alternative energy technologies and is an
active environmentalist with a keen interest in forest biology. As the owners of
Coast Mountain Expeditions, Ralph and Lannie take great pleasure in sharing
their remote island lifestyle and the natural beauty of their home at the edge of
the mountains.

Dan Lewis started sea kayaking in 1978 and has been teaching kayaking professionally since 1980. He was a founder of the Ecomarine Coastal Kayaking
School in 1984, designing courses and teaching there until 1991. His 1990 circumnavigation of Vancouver Island led him to become a strong advocate for
wildland protection. He lives and paddles year-round in Tofino, where he
owns and operates Rainforest Kayak Adventures with Bonny Glambeck. He is
a regular columnist for *WaveLength* paddling magazine.

Evan Loveless works as a tourism consultant and is the tourism advisor to the
Kitasoo/Xaixais First Nation. He has had the opportunity to explore much of
the Central Coast, especially the region near Klemtu. Evan started paddling
boats and spending time in the wilderness when he was a teenager. He grew
up in a boating family and spent lots of time on the water, so sea kayaking became second nature to him. Evan has worked as a professional guide for more
than 10 years, leading trips in Canada and abroad. When not working at Bryn-
mor Consulting in Victoria, Evan spends time paddling and adventuring with
his wife, Sue, and son, Zach.

Peter McGee has been paddling for over 15 years and has guided in B.C.,
Alaska and Mexico. In 1993, following a trip that covered much of the B.C.
coast, he founded the B.C. Marine Trail Association as a means of preserving
and caring for areas that are critical to the paddling community. Pete was executive director of the association until 1997.

Bill McIntyre has been chief naturalist at Pacific Rim National Park Reserve
for 15 years and currently works there as an outreach and environmental education coordinator. He has also worked and volunteered in research, sailing

and coastal expeditions and tours in Alaska, the Queen Charlottes, the Gulf Islands and Vancouver Island. Bill makes his home in Ucluelet, on the edge of Barkley Sound—an area he has travelled extensively since 1973.

Donna Matrazzo is one of the founders of the Oregon Ocean Paddling Society and has been guiding sea kayak trips around Portland for two decades. Her adventures in folding and inflatable kayaks include trips to Fiji, Alaska and Belize. She is a freelance writer of nature and environmental films, and has a passion for sharing her love and knowledge of the outdoors through compelling stories.

John Nelson has worked over the years with B.C. Wild, the Steelhead Society of B.C. and the Sierra Club of B.C. on numerous conservation issues. In the fall of 1996 his passion for paddling brought him in contact with the B.C. Marine Trail Association, and he served as executive director from 1997 to 1999.

Allen Palmer, an outdoors enthusiast, was first introduced to the paddling wonders of Puget Sound over 10 years ago and has been exploring its nooks and crannies ever since. Allen has been involved in the Washington Water Trails Association since the early 1990s and served on its board until 1996.

Tessa van Scheik has been kayaking for many years, both river and ocean; she also competed as a runner in the Olympics for her mother country, South Africa. Although she is involved in many outdoor sports, including windsurfing, her passion is kayaking. Tessa worked as a kayak guide for North Island Kayak Rentals for three years before returning to South Africa.

Cindy Scherrer's favourite pastime is travelling and camping by boat, especially along the Columbia River. She is the president of the Columbia River Outrigger Canoe Club and co-owner of Alder Creek Kayak & Canoe. In her 20 years of paddling, she has explored rivers around the country in both flatwater and whitewater kayaks and canoes.

Steve Scherrer has been paddling since he was 10 years old. He's the founder and co-owner of Alder Creek Kayak & Canoe and heads the company's guiding and instruction departments. Among the adventure trips he has led are journeys to Costa Rica, Baja and the Pacific Northwest and regular forays down the Columbia River. Steve is an American Canoe Association instructor trainer educator in both coastal and whitewater kayaking.

Reed Waite is executive director of the non-profit membership organization the Washington Water Trails Association (WWTA) and he is a lifelong water lover. Reed worked in park jobs and in food-related industries in the profit and non-profit arenas before joining WWTA. He learned to sail on Lake Chargoggagoggmanchauggauggagoggchaubunagungamaugg in Massachusetts, has canoed on Belize's Makal River and has kayaked off the North Island of New Zealand. He claims to have no favourite place on the Cascadia Marine Trail and is happy boating on all Washington State waters.

Catrin Webb is a Capilano College outdoor recreation graduate who is both a canoe and kayak instructor and guide. During the summer she is the assistant manager at Deep Cove Canoe and Kayak Centre, a full-service kayak rental operation located on Indian Arm that also offers instruction and tours. When the weather turns cold, Catrin heads to the mountains, where she works at the North Shore Outdoor School.

Alan Wilson is managing editor of *WaveLength* magazine and coordinator of the Annual Ocean Kayak Festival. He was born on the West Coast and has lived in the Gulf Islands for many years, writing, publishing and paddling. For the latest happenings in the paddling community, be sure to check out www.wavelengthmagazine.com.

Rupert Wong is a professional biologist who works primarily in the Kyuquot area. He works with First Nations, local industry and governments to restore watershed habitat, and he volunteers as warden for the Checleset Bay Ecological Reserve. Rupert is the owner of West Coast Expeditions, an educational nature tour company. He was 11 years old when he first visited Kyuquot.

Howard Zatwarnitski is the owner and operator of Natural West Coast Adventures, a kayak tour, instruction and rental operation based out of White Rock with a sub-office in Victoria. Natural West Adventures has been offering kayak instruction and paddling excursions since 1993. The company launched Natural West Coast Adventure Gear, its own line of paddling safety equipment, in 2000. The paddling gear is manufactured in Victoria by Wanda McCannell (Howard's sister).

Sources

BOOKS

Campbell, Ken. *A Kayaker's Guide to the Mid Puget Sound.* Tacoma: Salmon Bay Press, 2002.

—— *A Kayaker's Guide to the South Sound.* Tacoma: Salmon Bay Press, 2002.

—— *Shades of Grey.* Tacoma: Salmon Bay Press, 2002.

Chappell, John. *Cruising beyond Desolation Sound: Channels and Anchorages from the Yuculta Rapids to Cape Caution.* Surrey: Naikoon Marine, 1987.

Coull, Cheryl. *A Traveller's Guide to Aboriginal B.C.* Vancouver: Whitecap Books, 1996.

Dalzell, Kathleen E. *The Queen Charlotte Islands—Places and Names.* Vol. 2. Prince Rupert: Cove Press, 1973.

Dowd, John. *Sea Kayaking: A Manual for Long-Distance Touring.* 5th ed. Vancouver: Greystone Books/Douglas & McIntyre, 2004.

Drope, Bodhi, and Dorothy Drope. *Paddling the Sunshine Coast.* Madeira Park, B.C.: Harbour Publishing, 1997.

Duff, Wilson, and Michael Kew. *Ninstints.* Victoria: Report of the Provincial Museum, 1957.

Gardner, Julia E. *Pressure Group Politics and the Campaign to Protect South Moresby Island.* Vancouver: UBC Press, 1990.

Hendrickson, Robert. *The Ocean Almanac.* Toronto: Doubleday, 1984.

Ince, John, and Hedi Kottner. *Sea Kayaking Canada's West Coast.* Vancouver: Raxas Books, 1982.

Macdonald, Bruce. *Vancouver: A Visual History.* Vancouver: Talonbooks, 1992.

MacDonald, George F. *Haida Monumental Art: Villages of the Queen Charlotte Islands.* Vancouver: UBC Press, 1983.

MacFarlane, J.M., et al. *Official Guide to Pacific Rim National Park Reserve.* Calgary: Blackbird Naturgraphics, 1996.

Maine Island Trail Association. *The Maine Island Trail Guidebook.* Portland, ME: MITA, 1996.

May, Elizabeth. *Paradise Won: The Struggle for South Moresby.* Toronto: McClelland & Stewart, 1990.

National Outdoor Leadership School. *Leave No Trace: Temperate Coastal Zones.* Lander, WY: NOLS, 1996.

Pengelly, Marianne, and Eldon Oja. *Marine Weather Hazards Manual: A Guide to Local Forecasts and Conditions.* 2d ed. Ottawa: Environment Canada, 1990.

Renner, Jeff. *Northwest Marine Weather: From the Columbia River to Cape Scott.* Seattle: The Mountaineers, 1993.

Rogers, Joel. *The Hidden Coast: Kayak Exploration from Alaska to Mexico.* Anchorage: Alaska Northwest Books, 1991.

—— *The Hidden Path through Puget Sound.* Seattle: Sasquatch Books, 1998.

Snowden, Mary Ann. *Island Paddling: A Paddler's Guide to the Gulf Islands and Barkley Sound.* Victoria: Orca Books, 1997.

Walbran, John T. *British Columbia Coast Names.* Vancouver: Douglas & McIntyre, 1991.

Washington Water Trails Asociation. *Cascadia Marine Trail Guidebook: Ten Year Anniversary Edition.* Seattle: WWTA, 2003.

—— *A Guide to the Cascadia Marine Trail System.* Port Orchard, WA: Pack and Paddle Publishing, 1994.

Wilson, Ian R., et al. *Cultural Heritage Background Study.* Victoria: Clayoquot Sound Sustainable Development Strategy, 1991.

Wolferstan, Bill. *Cruising Guide to British Columbia.* Vol. 2, *Desolation Sound and the Discovery Islands.* Vancouver: Whitecap Books, 1987.

OTHER

BC Parks. "The Legend of Princess Louisa Inlet." Victoria: Queens Printer, 1992.

Ecomarine Ocean Kayaking Centre. "Cultural Impacts." Vancouver: Ecomarine, 1997.

Energy, Mines and Resources Canada. "The Geology of Howe Sound." Vancouver: EMR Canada.

Leave No Trace. "Leave No Trace Sea Kayaking Skills and Ethics." 2003.

Ministry of Forests. "A Safety Guide to Bears in the Wild." Victoria: MOF, 1997.

Ministry of Small Business, Tourism and Culture. "Middens." Victoria: MSBTC, 1997.

Outdoor Recreation Council. "Back Country Sanitation: Protecting Yourself against Water-Borne Disease." Vancouver: ORC, 1996.

—— "A Wilderness Code of Ethics." Vancouver: ORC, 1996.

Schroeder, Bob. "Routes to Jedediah Island." *WaveLength*, August–September 1995.

Index

Italicized numbers indicate maps